KARUNASIRI MUTHUMALA

MATARA AND ITS HINTERLAND

A GEOGRAPHICAL ANALYSIS OF A MEDIUM SIZE TOWN IN SOUTH-WESTERN SRI LANKA

BEITRÄGE ZUR SÜDASIENFORSCHUNG
SÜDASIEN-INSTITUT
UNIVERSITÄT HEIDELBERG

BAND 186

FRANZ STEINER VERLAG
STUTTGART
1999

MATARA AND ITS HINTERLAND

A GEOGRAPHICAL ANALYSIS OF A MEDIUM SIZE TOWN IN SOUTH-WESTERN SRI LANKA

von

Karunasiri Muthumala

FRANZ STEINER VERLAG
STUTTGART
1999

Die Deutsche Bibliothek – CIP-Einheitsaufnahme

Muthumala, Karunasiri:
Matara and its hinterland : a geographical analysis of a medium size town in south-western Sri Lanka / by Karunasiri Muthumala. – Stuttgart : Steiner, 1999
(Beiträge zur Südasienforschung ; Bd. 186)
Zugl.: Heidelberg, Univ., Diss., 1996
ISBN 3-515-07658-1

D 16

Herstellung: Strauss Offsetdruck GmbH, 69509 Mörlenbach,
Printed in Germany

This book is dedicated to my loving mother and to the memory of my loving father, whose principles and way of life have been worthy of emulation. Their prudent guidance has sustained me in a struggle against ignorance and prejudice.

Contents

List of Maps Page

List of Diagrams

List Of Tables

List of Charts

List Of Photographs

Acknowledgement

This book presents a shortend version of my doctoral dissertation which was stimulated by the advice of Professor Dr. U. Schweinfurth.

My sense of gratitude goes first to Professor Dr. U. Schweinfurth who inspired me to write this dissertation under his guidance. His patient guidance of my work and his helpful advice and criticism always served as an eye opener.

I owe sincere thanks to Professor Dr. Werner Fricke for his guidance as well as for his valuable suggestions in the preparation of this dissertation.

I am very grateful for all the help that I received during my field work. The names of those individuals that rendered help are too numerous to mention. The great help extended by Professor Kanthi Rathnayaka (Dept. of Geography at University of Ruhuna), My cousin Raju de Silva and sister-in-law Chandramali Muthumala who helped me to aquire the important data should not be forgotten. In particular, I appreciate the co-operation extended by my cousin Benet de Silva and his family for providing me with accommodation during my field work.

I wish to express my sincere thanks to Mr. Jeffry Barov, Mr. C.H.A. Baumrich, Mr. C. Anderson, Mr. Jim Gall, Mr. Timothy Moore, Mr. Bob Kohl, Miss Ann Ainsworth, Miss Cheryl Momen, Mr. & Mrs. Johnson, Mr. & Mrs. Lynn Courtland Hall, Mr. Richard Tabor, and Mr. Steve Peele who edited parts of my dissertation.

My gratitude goes to Mr. Barry Baumrich, Mr. Rick Gibson, David Powell, Miss Cindy Lettner, and Mr. Nick Olguin for typing parts of this dissertation.

I wish to offer my thanks to Mr. William Banchard, Dr. Markus Faas and Mr.Billy Joyce who lent me the nescessary computer equipment which was invaluable to this book.

My thanks also goes to Mr. George Riley, Ms. Ilga Gröschel and Miss Lilli Hofstätter who helped in typing my book.

I wish to express my gratitude to Mr. John R. Ridlen and Miss H. Nischk for their contribution of Diagrams and Graphics.

Professor Dr. U. Schweinfurth, Mr. Bryan Hartsell, Mr. Bernd Zimmermann , Mr. and Mrs. Roy and Janet Flanders deserve appreciation and thanks for their careful scrutiny of the manuscript.

I wish to express my gratitude to Mrs. Brunhilde Lenz who allowed me to have time off, whenever I needed it, to attain the seminars during my work at the Officer's club.

I owe sincere thanks to Mr. Jim Wagner, Mrs. Gabriele Vries, Mrs. and Mr. Mc Naught and Mr. Hans Underwood for their unstinted co-operation in printing this dissertation.

I place on record my sincere thanks to Dr. D.Schmidt - Vogt who dealt with the labours of publishing this book.

My special thanks go to Mr. Philip A. Snell, Mrs. Susan Monahan and Mr. Robert B. Willard, Dr. Patrick Amarasingha and Dr. Markus Faas, who helped me in preparing this dissertation from beginning to end. I am deeply grateful to them for the many sacrifices made on my account.

Finally, I am most indebt to Professor Dr. U. Schweinfurth and my friend Lakshman Kumarasingha from which I recieved both moral support and continious encouragement. I express my heart felt thanks to them. Without their support this book would have never been completed.

Foreword

The emergence of urban settlements in the world is said to have taken place in the seventh millennium B.C. which reflects that the custom of living in towns had become standard at the beginning of the historical period. However, the rapid expansion of urban settlements was the result of the industrial revolution dating back to the early 19th century.

Urban development, and its association with various new inventions and practices, is regarded as a cultural advance by some scholars in the capitalistic world. However, some writers (specially sociologers) regarded this as the downfall of the human society.

Nevertheless, towns perform the dual functions of service centres and as centres of diffusion of information and innovation. They play a vital role in the habitat, economy and life of the people.

The study of urban settlements inquiring into their history, typology, classification and service areas is an important aspect of urban geographic researches. The towns in the developing world in general, and south Asia in particular, have intrigued both Oriental and Occidental scholars and planners. However, in contrast to traditional Indian towns, the towns of Sri Lanka have received very little attention by either group of scholars. The literature on urban studies in Sri Lanka as compared to the physical and geographical studies is relatively scarce and is still in an infancy stage.

The earliest contribution to the historical development of urban settlement in Sri Lanka was done by Cave in 1900. Since then only a few studies (Perera 1960; Ratnayaka 1983; Jones 1970; Silva 1979; Seneviratne 1979) have been performed on this subject.

The hitherto written articles and dissertations on urban settlements, except a few (Badulla; Dicke, 1987, Galle; Wellmer,1989, Nuwara-Eliya; Bührlein,1991), are relatively old and mostly confined to the larger urban settlements such as Colombo (Panditaratna 1960,1961; Hulugalla 1965), Jaffna (Jaysingham 1958), Galle (Peiris 1959) and Kandy (Panditaratna 1967, Seneviratna 1983). The most investigated urban settlement in Sri Lanka is Colombo, the commercial metropolis of the Island. Much has been written about the growth, commercial activities and its service areas by numerous scholars (Panditaratna 1964, 1965; Dahrmasena 1973; Rankine 1955; and Gunawardana 1980) .

The small and medium size towns, which play a vital role as either suburban commercial centres or as important sub-regional centres, have been given little attention by the writers. These centres, in the urban perspective, have become significant as service centres to the rural hinterland and as market towns for the rural producers. In addition, these centres absorb the surplus rural labour and prevent the large scale migration to the larger towns.

The few works which have been written on this subject are: "The service centres in southern Sri Lanka", (Gunawardana 1964); "A conventional study of Ambalantota", (Gunawardana 1974); Nuwara- Eliya, (Silva 1978, Schweinfurth 1982, Bührlein 1991); Hambantota and Mannar, (Johnson / Scrivenor 1981, in People and Economy); Tissamaharama (Babara Hariss, 1977, in Rural- Urban Transactions); and "Small and Medium size Towns in Sri Lanka", (Mendis 1982), Badulla (Dicke 1987). Whereas Wellmer's Galle 1989 is, basically, a geomedical analysis.

In the 1970's, the establishment of the Urban Development Authority and the Urban Development Department of Towns and Country Planning at the University of Moratuwa was a direct result of the growing problems in the urban settlements, i.e., land utilization conflicts and housing problems. These two institutions have done many surveys and published some reports on this subject, including the town of Matara ("Structure Plan Matara 1981", "Preliminary Report of Matara 1981", "Final Report of Matara 1982", "Peiris / Doidge 1976, 1977, 1978"; "Balakrishan 1982"; "Fernando 1984"). Sri Lanka's Centre for Development Studies, Marga Institute, has done surveys and has published reports (1976,1978) on the housing problems (shanty-towns) in the major towns.

It is noteworthy to mention the great contribution which is extended by the department of geography, South Asian Institute in the University of Heidelberg under the guidance of Prof. Dr. U. Schweinfurth. The relatively neglected medium size towns such as Badulla (Dicke 1987) and Nuwara-Eliya (Bührlein 1991) were brought into focus under his guidance. This dissertation is a realization of his inspirations. This dissertation, "Matara and its Hinterland", is a detailed account of the least studied urban settlements in Sri Lanka. This work is an expansion of an M.A. thesis to a Ph.D. dissertation. In this dissertation, the whole Matara district is regarded as an integral part of Matara town, as this town is tightly connected to the whole district by administration ("Gebundene Zentralität"). The relatively few commercial and social services among the smaller urban centres, and the high concentration of these services in Matara lead to the high level of communication between these two entities ("Ungebundene Zentralität").

This dissertation is divided into two parts. The first part deals with Matara town. It investigates the physical features, history, population characteristics, living conditions, economy, social services and land utilization of the town. The second part "Centrality", investigates the commercial hegemony of Matara town, its area of influence and the hierarchical order of urban settlements in the Matara District.

The contents in this dissertation are original except where indicated by references. This work is based on seven types of information:

1) Published data available from the census and other publications
2) Unpublished data obtained from officials and other sources
3) Interview surveys and observations made in the field
4) A questionnaire survey, 1989
5) Interpretation of Aerial Photographs of Matara town

6) Interpretation of Topographic Map of Matara district, 1974, scale 1:63,360 (one inch to one mile)
7) Land use Map of Matara and Hambantota district, 1983, scale 1 : 100,000.

Several problems were encountered in preparing this dissertation. One problem was that data of the desired degree of detail was not available and had to be obtained from unpublished materials, field work and sample surveys. Another problem was that the political unrest in Sri Lanka since 1983 made it extremely difficult to obtain the information and data from authorities. For instance, during an interview survey with a shop owner in Akuressa in January 1990 I was taken into custody by the police. I was not allowed to take any photos during my survey. Because of this only a few photos of some shopping centres are presented in this work.

The delay in presenting this work is mainly attributed to the following facts:

1) The problems I faced in doing such a comprehensive study in a language other than my own.
2) The political unrest in Sri Lanka which caused difficulties in obtaining information and data.

This dissertation is meant to be a contribution towards the hitherto little investigated small and medium size towns of Sri Lanka. It is hoped that this work may stimulate interest in this topic and deepen the knowledge in the urban geographical field in Sri Lanka.

CHAPTER 1

1. Matara Town

1.1. Location, Area and Physical Features and Regional Linkages of the Town

Matara is the capital of its district and has held the urban council status since 1946. According to the size of the population it comes under the medium size towns category. It had a population of 39,162 in 1981. The growth rate of Matara between 1971-1981 with 0.69% not only lies below the growth rate of the other smaller towns in the district such as Akuressa (0.7%) and Weligama (0.84%) but also lies below the growth rate of the national urban population (1.2%).

The town of Matara is located at the mouth of the Nilwala river in the coastal zone of its district which lies about 160 km south of Colombo. Matara is situated between 5.9° and 5.7° north latitude and between 80.32° and 80.34° east longitude (Map 1). Sri Lanka comes nearest to the equator at Dondara in the Matara district.

The area of the town of Matara, according to the 1981 statistics is about 8.29 sq. kilometres. The town is divided into 11 wards (Map 2). The topography is generally flat with parts below sea level and the eastern extreme along the coast is characterised by a small hillock with an elevation of about 30 meters (Photo 1). The rest of the town has an elevation of about 3 meters at its maximum. The areas such as Piladuwa, which lie below sea level, are subjected to flooding and stagnation of water.

The town has a `Ria Coast' which is exposed to the Monsoon winds. The coastal areas of the town, particularly the Polhena beach, is subjected to heavy erosion during the monsoon period. Though erosion around the coast would have taken place throughout geological time, the rate of erosion seems to have increased alarmingly in recent times. The islets off Matara town, such as Parey Duwa and Galgodiyama Duwa, would have been an integral part of the mainland in the recent past (Map 1, Photos 2&3). The removal of sand and coral reef from the beach for commercial purposes has aggravated the sea erosion. The result is the reduction of the land area of the town year by year[1].

The river which flows in a general north-south direction through the district has its source in the Rakwana hills. It takes a westward flow on the edge of the town, almost parallel to the coast, before entering the sea. While passing through, it divides the town into two parts, the southern part being about one-third of its northern counter-part.

There is geological evidence to suggest that the Matara area would have once been an extensive lagoon which was later subjected to silting and upheaval.[2]

---

1 Preu, C., 1989.

2 Deraniyagala, P.E.P., 1958.

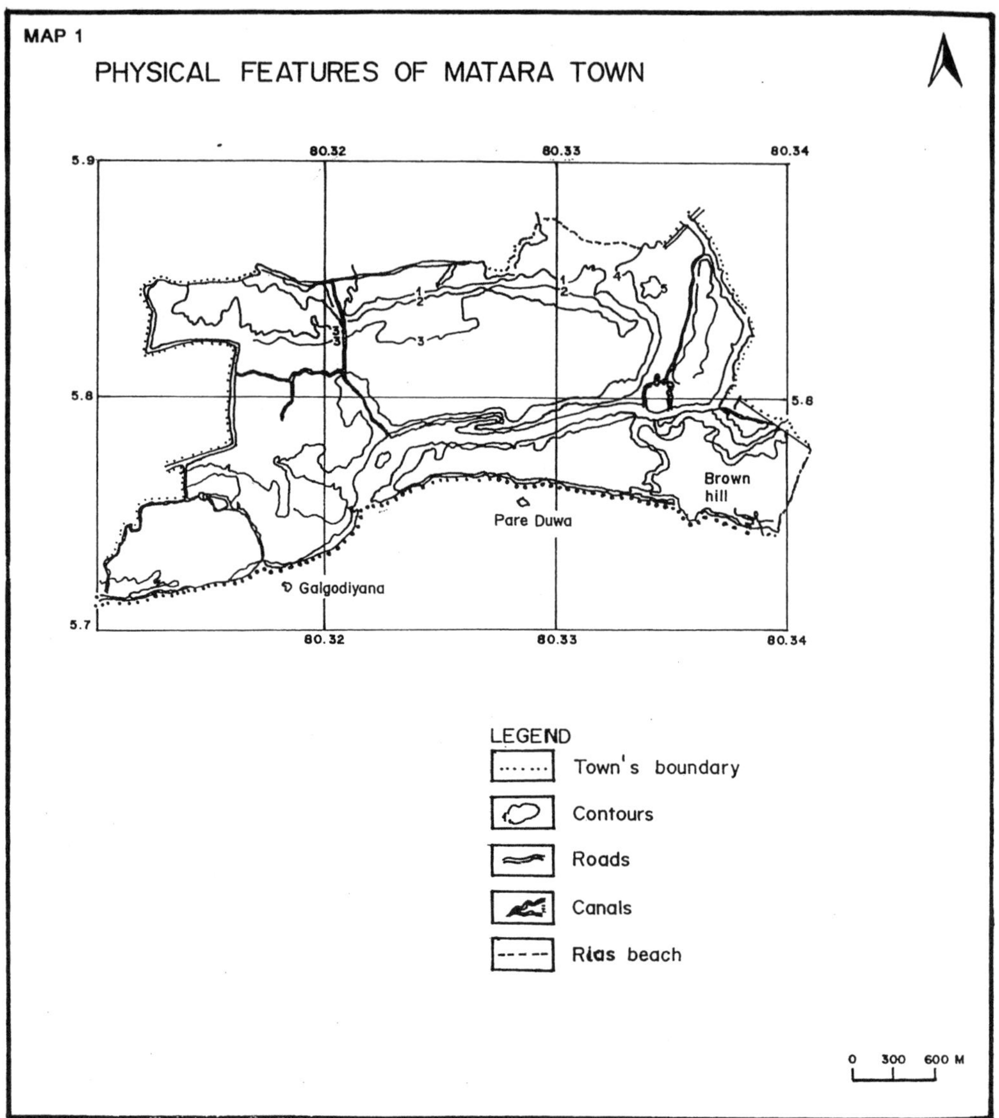
MAP 1
PHYSICAL FEATURES OF MATARA TOWN
80.32
80.33
80.34
5.9
5.8
5.7
Brown hill
Pare Duwa
Galgodiyana
LEGEND
Town's boundary
Contours
Roads
Canals
Rias beach
0 300 600 M

MAP - 02

Wards of Matara Town - 1984

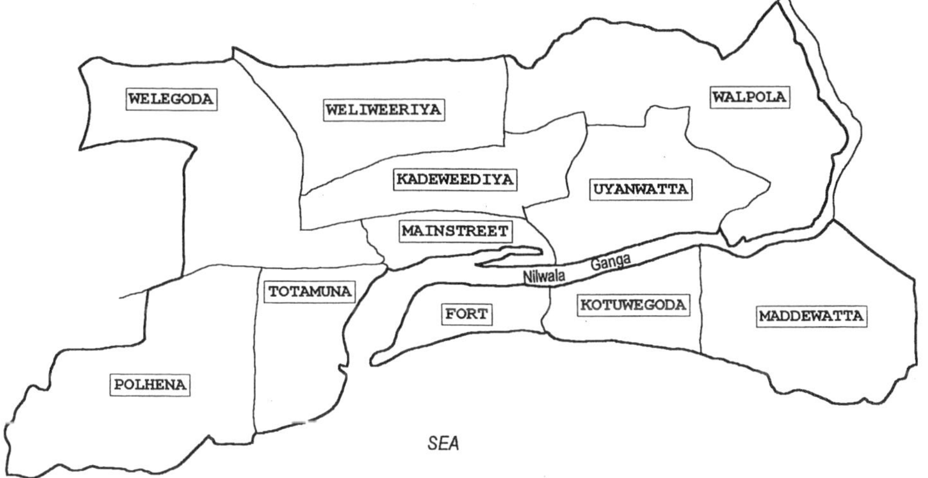

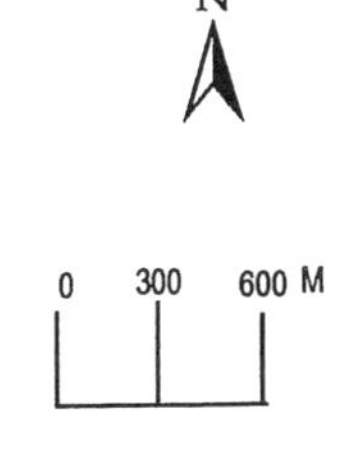

1.1.1. Climate and Soil

The climate of the town is the coastal area climate of the district. High temperatures prevail (26.5°C) with an absence of diurnal extremes and humidity as high as 80% almost throughout the year. The urban area of Matara receives an average rainfall of about 2285 mm.

The soil of this area mainly consists of red and yellow Podzolic soil, Alluvial and Ragosol.

1.2. Regional Linkages

Matara town is connected by the coastal highway with larger urban centres such as Galle and Colombo in the west and with some service centres (shop centres) such as Dickwella, Tangalle, Ambalantota in the east and further with the urban centre Hambantota (Map 3).

In the north, it is connected with the town Akuressa in the central zone and to the service centre Deniyaya in the extreme north of the district. It is further connected beyond to the northern region of the district and into the Galle district. Towards the north-east, it is connected with the service centres such as Hakmana, Urubokka, Beralapanetara and into the south-western parts of Hambantota district. Two other routes, the Naimane and the Kekunadura roads connect the north-eastern regions with the Matara town. Matara town is the southern terminus of the Ruhuna Railway line connecting it through Galle to Colombo (Map 3). The port function, which Matara had in the early days of its history, does not exist today. The export products of the Matara district are shipped through Galle harbour.

1.3. History and Evolution of the Structure of Matara Town.

Today, Matara is a medium size town according to population size and the prime city of the Matara district. It lies on the Colombo-Hambantota coastal highway 160 km south of Colombo. Matara was a port town prior to the arrival of the Portuguese. As there is no archaeological evidence to study the pre-colonial history of Matara town, other disciplines such as written evidence, linguistic investigations and particularly oral traditions have to be used to reconstruct the history.

It is said to have been known as "Mahatota", the big port in ancient times. But the available historical evidence does not prove it to have been a large port. To some historians this settlement might have been known as "Mahatota" just because of the ferry at the Nilwala river which ferried the people from one side to the other. To prove this they present names of some settlements which lie at the mouth of some rivers such as Kalutara, Bentota and Gintota.[3] Historical evidence involving the growth of Matara

---

3 Kamburupitiye Wanarathna Himi, 1950., pp. 2 - 8. Statistical Book, Matara, 1983, pp. 1 - 5.
Final Report- Matara, Urban Development Authority, 1981, p. 13.

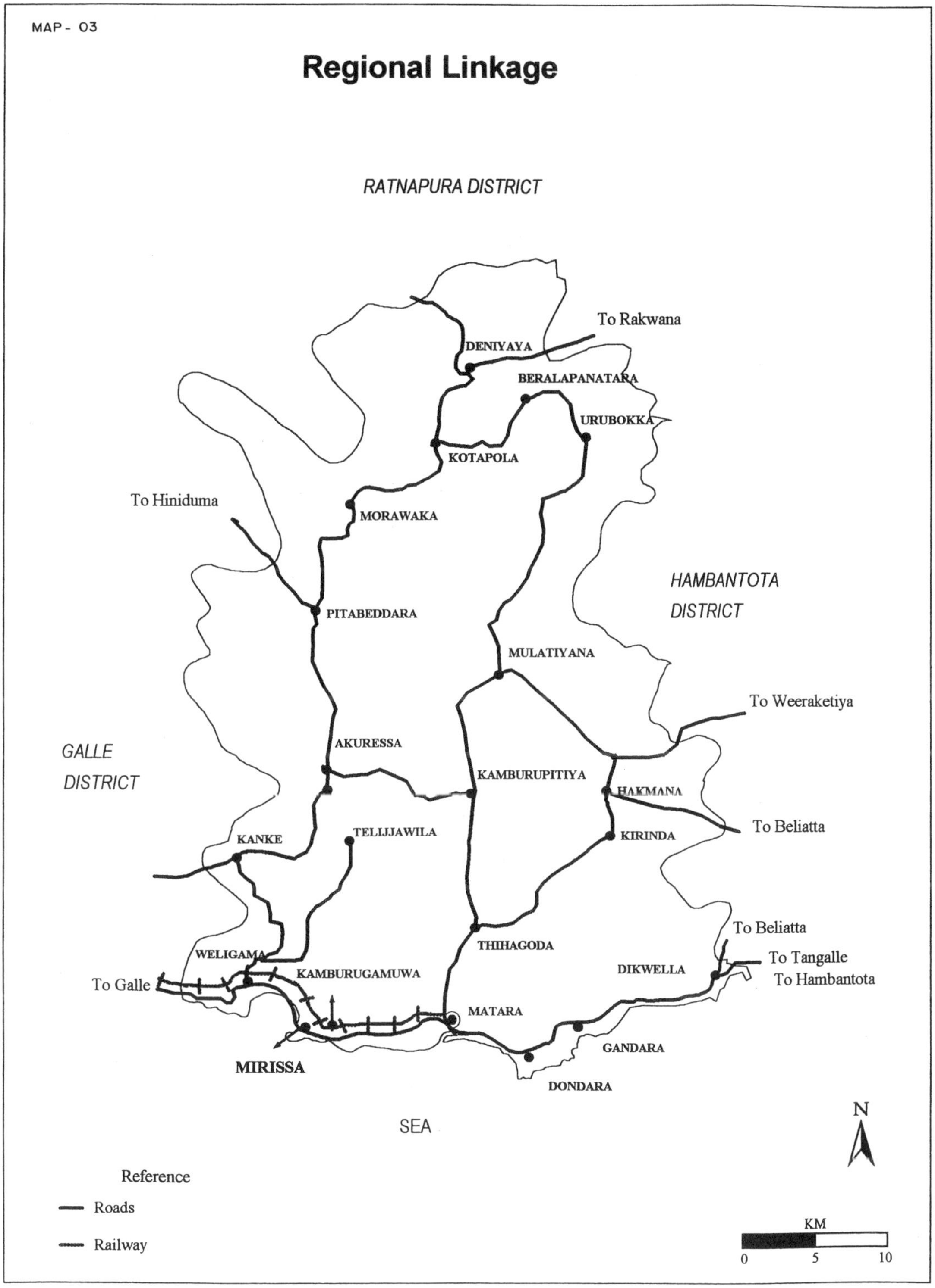

MAP - 03

Regional Linkage

RATNAPURA DISTRICT
To Rakwana
DENIYAYA
BERALAPANATARA
URUBOKKA
KOTAPOLA
To Hiniduma
MORAWAKA
HAMBANTOTA DISTRICT
PITABEDDARA
MULATIYANA
To Weeraketiya
GALLE DISTRICT
AKURESSA
KAMBURUPITIYA
HAKMANA
To Beliatta
KIRINDA
KANKE
TELIJJAWILA
To Beliatta
THIHAGODA
To Tangalle
To Hambantota
WELIGAMA
DIKWELLA
To Galle
KAMBURUGAMUWA
MATARA
GANDARA
MIRISSA
DONDARA
SEA
N

Reference
Roads
Railway

KM
0 5 10

indicates it was a small port which served Dondara, the most renowned pilgrimage centre during this period[4].

Some historians assume "Totamuna"[5], the village which lies at the Estuary of Nilwala river, to be the ancient port of Matara. To prove this they forward the village name "Totamuna" which means the port. This is the only existing port today which gives shelter to small fishing boats around Matara town (Photo 4).

The town was known by various names at different times. It was called Mahatira (the settlement of the great bank river) prior to the colonial period, while the Portuguese called it Matvre and the British called it Matura.[6]

The growth and evolution of the structure of the Matara town can be divided into three major periods:

1) Pre-Colonial Period
2) Colonial Period
3) Post Colonial Period

1.3.1. Pre-Colonial Period

Matara seems to be a settlement of ancient origin. A starting point for the development of this settlement is closely connected with the political organization. On the basis of historical evidence this settlement was founded by the Naga before the beginning of the Christian era (the exact period is not known)[7]. According to some historians, the surrounding village names, which hold the morpheme Na such as Naimana, Nadugala, Naimbala, Naotunna and Nakande are good examples to this tribal relationship. This settlement was supposed to be a place of residence of the King Kumaradasa as early as 415[8]. According to the letter of Bronze "Panakaduwa", the great Vijabahu had spent his childhood in Matara.[9] The only evidence to support the antiquity of the site is a group of place names such as Gabada Weediya (street of stores), Maligawatta, and Uyanwatta (the garden of the palace). At the advent of the Portuguese era in Sri Lanka, Matara was the administrative centre of the Matara Province. Matara gained increasing popularity since it started to serve as a port as well as a by-pass town to the pilgrimage centre Dondara which lies about 12 km east of Matara. The Ambalams (rest houses) which are identified in the old Dutch Map of Matara might have been built prior to the arrival of the foreign powers.

This gives clues to the fact that this place had been visited by many people. As discussed earlier, the southern ports of Sri Lanka such as Galle and Matara became more important during the fourth century due to the change in the trade pattern. The growth of this settlement as a commercial centre is mainly attributed to the trade activities of the

---

4 Raven-Hart, R., 1964, p.164.
5 Today, Totamuna is one of the ward of Matara Urban Council.
6 Kamburupitiye Wanarathna Himi, 1950.
7 Ibid, p. 8.
8 Ibid, p. 8.
9 Ibid, p. 2.

Moors. Although the Sinhalese might have taken part in the trade, it probably would not have lasted long. At the time of the Portuguese invasions the external as well as internal trade was in the hands of the Moors. Matara was regarded to be a prosperous harbour town with wealthy merchants.

In addition to cinnamon, the export of elephants might have played an important role in the pre-colonial economy of Matara. The pre-colonial literature work of Parevi Sandeshiya describes the elephant stalls in Matara during this period. Wild elephants were found abundantly around Matara.

The trading pattern of the island of Ceylon (Sri Lanka) with the outside world had been dominated by the commercial links which had been developed with the neighbouring coasts of Malabar and Coramandal.[10] It can be presumed with little doubt that some of the people were engaged in the service sector of trade such as providing the materials for the provisioning of ships, coir ropes, coconut oil, food stuffs and providing the manpower resources for activities pertaining to trade .

The shop centre of ancient Matara might have been situated along the ancient route Mantota Dondara near Totamune (Map 4). This was the only route which connected Matara to other ancient important centres of the island. The shape of the shop centre was linear.

The ancient buildings were built of wood and mud. They have since disintegrated.

1.3.2. Portuguese Period (1505-1658)

During the Portuguese period Matara became an administrative centre as well as a collection centre for spices.

> "There also resided at "Matvre" the Dissawa[11] of that district with one company of infantry a Franciscan Monk as Chaplain and three or four thousand Lascarians and their officers. His jurisdiction extended as far as the frontiers of Uva and Baticalow and along the seashore up to Colombo".[12]

According to Valentyn, Matara was fortified by the Portuguese with the permission of King Dharmapala of Kotte as early as 1550.[13] To the historian Ribeyro, there was no evidence involving fortification in Matara at this time, but the Portuguese might have put up a camp to give shelter to the soldiers who were stationed in Matara during this period .[14]

The main trade items, such as cinnamon and arecanut (wild grown), were brought from the surrounding areas for shipping through the port of Matara as in the pre-colonial

---

10 Samaraweera, V., 1972.
11 An Administrator during the Dutch period.
12 Pieris, P.E., 1909, p. 132.
13 Brohier, R.L., 1970, p. 47.
14 Pieris, P.E., 1909, p. 132.

Map - 4

Location of Ancient Shop Centre - Matara
Pre - Colonial Period

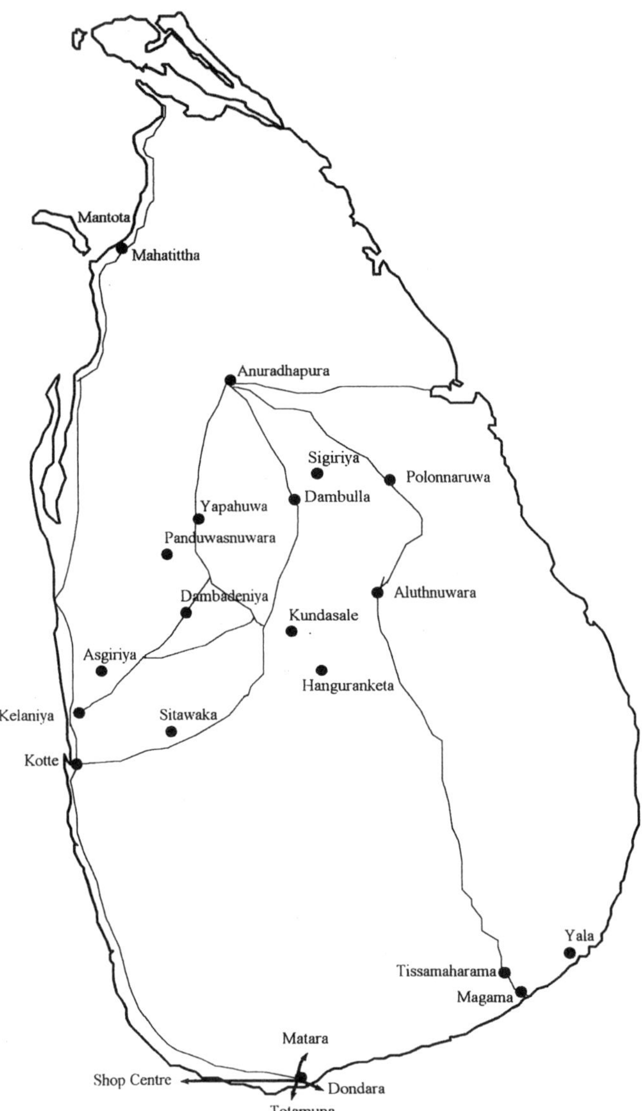

Chief Ruined Cities and the Ancient Roads indicated in the Mahawansa. Sitawaka is near the modern Avissawella. Compare with modern routes and towns.

Quelle :- Cook, E.K. , Ceylon (its Geography and its people), Macmillan and Company, ltd., London, 1953

days. Incessant warfare[15] between the Portuguese and the Sinhalese and the discriminatory measures taken against the Moors by the Portuguese did not leave much room for development of trade in this centre.

> "The oppression by the Portuguese was worse than that of the Dutch, because it involved religion as well as administration and trade. Their aim was to win the island for the Catholic Church..."[16]

There was no extension of roads which might have facilitated export of items to the Port of Matara during this period (Map 5).

The structure and the shape of this trade centre did not experience any changes and remained much the same as in the pre-colonial period.

1.3.3. The Dutch Period (1659-1796)

During the Dutch era, Matara gained more popularity as a collection centre for agricultural products while it became one of the most important ports which exported cinnamon.

The administrative functions which Matara used to exercise over the whole southern province during the pre-colonial and in the Portuguese period was lost to Galle. It became a part of the Galle commendary, but one of the "Dissawa" (administrator) still lived in Matara.

Cinnamon and elephants became the major components of the Dutch economy. These two items were found in and around Matara in abundance[17].

The trade was mainly accomplished by Moors and the Dutch, even though they later discriminated against the Moors. The existing rest-house which was built during the Dutch regime, supported the theory that Matara was visited by tourists as well as traders.

The inefficiency of the Dutch settlers in business, the discriminatory measure against the Moors and the landlessness in the south-western part of the island might have led to influx of Sinhalese into trade in this centre.

The market centre continued to stay in the same place in Totamuna along the main road, Mannar - Dondara. The shape and the structure of Matara experienced a change during this period. The very first road network came into existence: Matara - Akuressa, Matara - Aparakka, Matara - Hakmana roads and the canal network, which connected Matara to its hinterland. These networks were developed to transport agricultural products (Map 6). The ancient main road, Mannar - Dondara via Matara, was evidently reconstructed by the Dutch"[18]

---

15 Akuressa war in 1643.

16 Cook, E.K., 1931, p. 36.

17 De Siva , S.F., 1954, p.119, Percival , R., 1975, p. 101.

18 Mendis, G.C., 1957, p. 58.

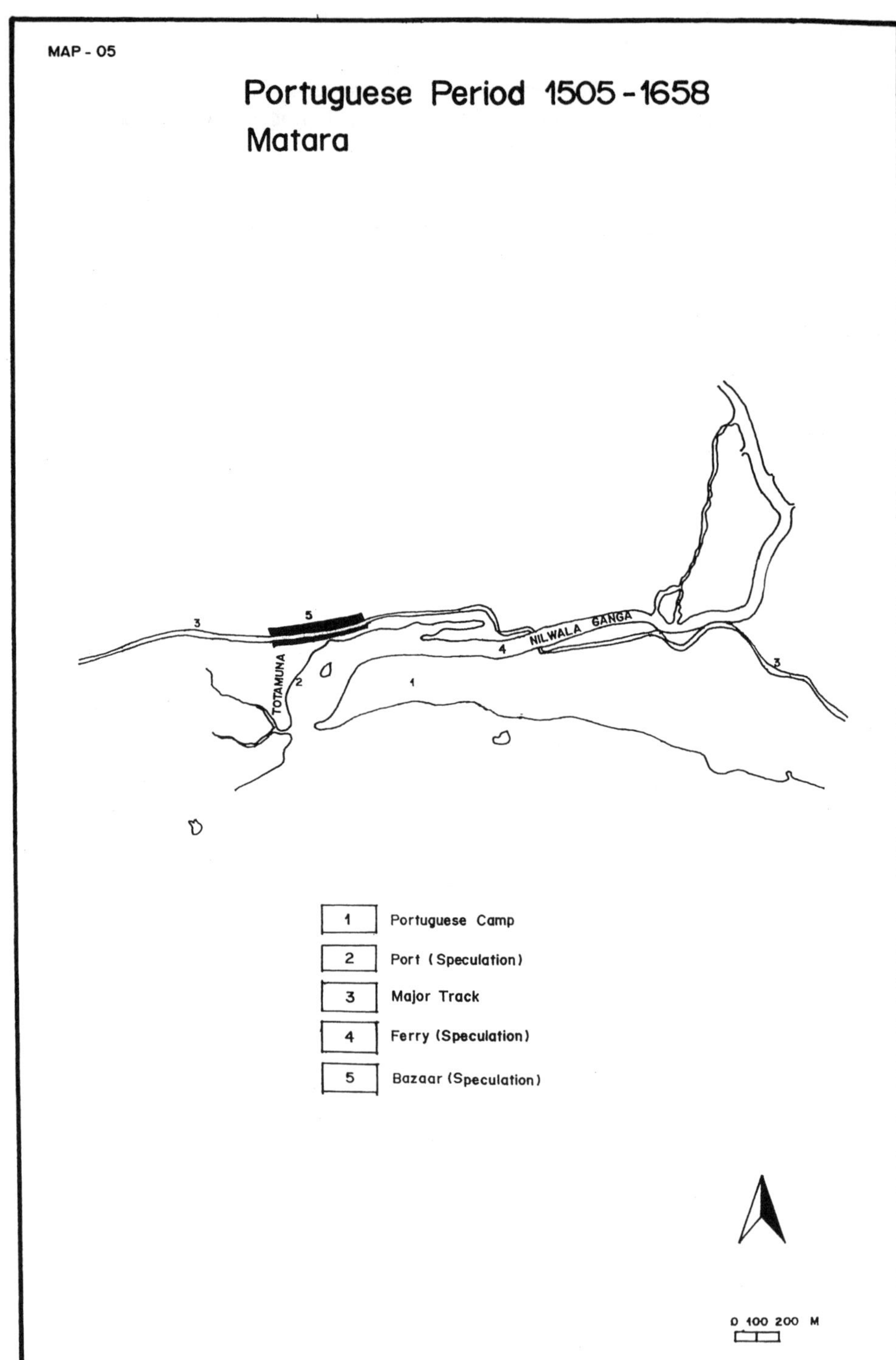
MAP - 05
Portuguese Period 1505-1658
Matara
5
3
NILWALA GANGA
4
TOTAMUNA
2
1
3
1 Portuguese Camp
2 Port (Speculation)
3 Major Track
4 Ferry (Speculation)
5 Bazaar (Speculation)
0 100 200 M

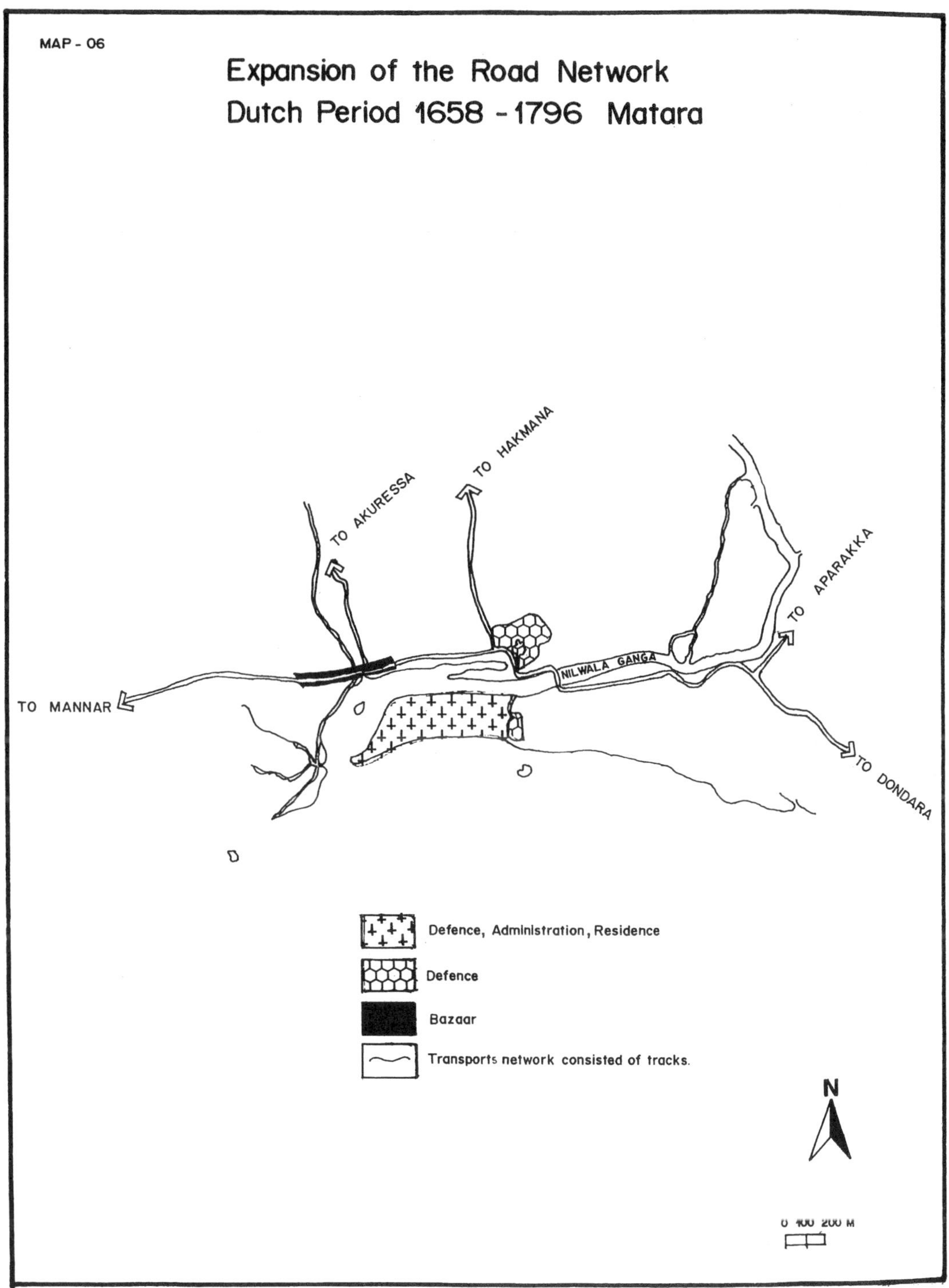
MAP - 06
Expansion of the Road Network
Dutch Period 1658 - 1796 Matara
TO HAKMANA
TO AKURESSA
TO APARAKKA
TO MANNAR
NILWALA GANGA
TO DONDARA
Defence, Administration, Residence
Defence
Bazaar
Transports network consisted of tracks.
N
0 400 200 M

The canal system served not only for transportation and sewage but also prevented flooding of the town and neighbouring rice fields. A wooden bridge was built over the river to supplement the existing ferry boat service[19]

The Dutch settlements were constructed for defence. The south bank of the river was fortified by a wall up to the mouth. The Star Fort on the northern bank of the river was built by the Dutch in 1762 to guard the river crossing[20] (Map 7 & Photo 5). The wall ramparts, narrow gateways and watch towers in every corner of the wall are evidence to prove that the Dutch were concerned with defence.

The central institutions such as administration, hospitals and churches which gave rise to urban settlements were established in the Fort of Matara during this period.

Racial discrimination against the natives can be seen for the first time in the history of the colonial powers in this era. The colonial masters built their houses on the western side of the fort where the colonists found natural scenic beauty and good atmospheric conditions prevailing, while the quarters of the natives were located on the eastern side of the fort where the elephant wallow and stables were located (Map 8).

The Dutch limestone "Street houses" with large verandas and roofed with tiles stood in stark contrast to the native temporary houses[21], built of tree trunks or wigs plastered with mud and thatched with straw or plaited (woven) coconut leaves. This contrast was a new phenomenon in the urban landscape. Dutch houses built over 200 years ago, still in existence, are the oldest permanent houses in Matara (Photos 6 & 7).

The above facts prove that Matara grew economically as well as structurally in this era.

1.3.4. The British Period (1815-1948)

Instead of cinnamon and elephants, coffee, tea and rubber became the major components of the British economy. The favourable agro-climatic conditions, relief and soil conditions led to the emergence of a plantation economy in the Matara district. To achieve their goals, the British introduced the primary capital intensive infrastructure services. Roads, schools, churches and public and administrative units were established after the western style.

The first planned road network, which still exists today, was the work of the British. The existing pathway and tracks connecting the hinterland to service centre Matara had been developed.

> "Strictly speaking there are no roads in Ceylon. Carts and wheeled carriages can only be used in th neighbourhood of the large European settlements which are still situated on the sea coast".[22]

---

19 Ref. Muthmala, K., 1984.

20 Ibid.

21 Knox, 1961.

22 Cordiner, J.A.M., 1807, p. 107.

Map - 07

The Star Fort of Matara-Dutch Period.

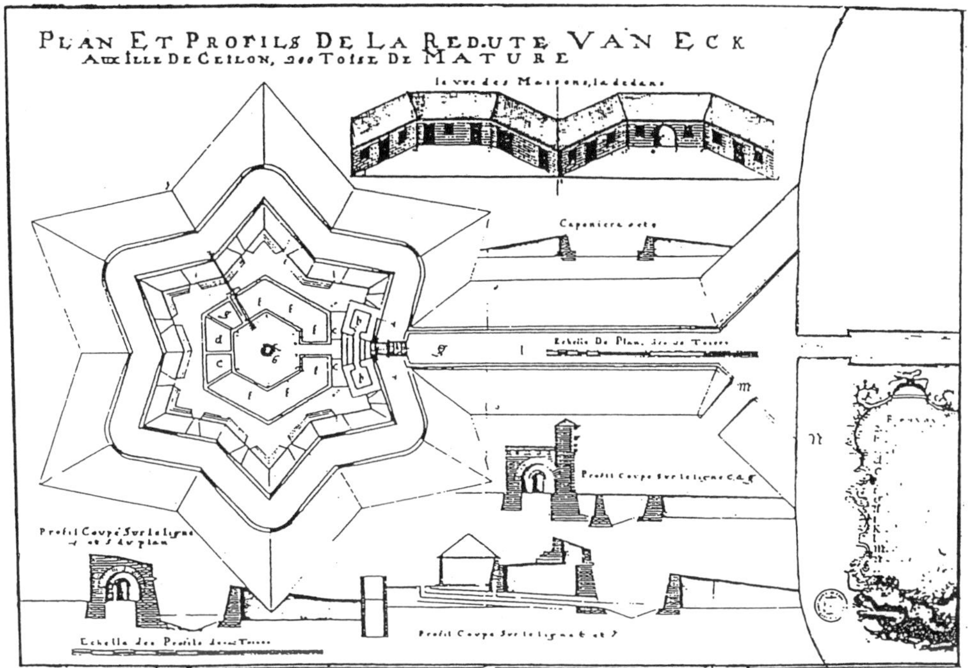

Source: Rijksmuseum (Rijksarchief (Algemeen)) Amsterdam

Map 8: Ground - Plan of the Fort of Matara - Dutch Period

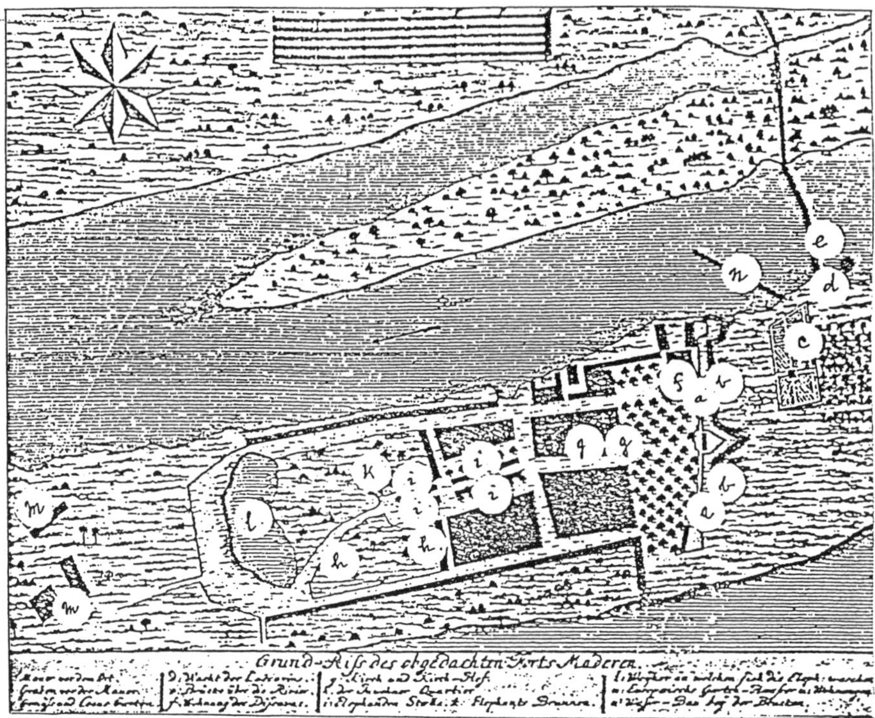

72 Ground-Plan of the aforesaid Fort of Maderen.

a. WALL IN FRONT OF THE PLACE.
b. DITCH BEFORE THE WALL.
c. VEGETABLE AND COCONUT-GARDEN.
d. GUARD-HOUSE OF THE LASCARS.
e. BRIDGE OVER THE RIVER.
f. RESIDENCE OF THE DISSAVA.
g. CHURCH AND CHURCHYARD.
h. QUARTERS OF THE INHABITANTS.
i. ELEPHANT STABLES.
k. ELEPHANT WELL.
l. TANK IN WHICH THE ELEPHANTS BATHE.
m. EUROPEAN GARDENS, HOUSES AND DWELLINGS.
n. GROYNE NEAR THE BRIDGE.

Quelle: Heydt's Ceylon, Wilhermsdorff. Translated by R. Ravenhart, published by Ceylon Information Department, printed by Ceylon Government Press Colombo 1952, Fig. 72

In expanding the road network the British connected all the other important commercial and administration centres of the island to Matara. In 1895 the first rail road from Colombo to Matara was opened. Expansion and development of the land transport system led to the decline of Matara's popularity as a port. Since then, the agricultural products from Matara and adjoining districts were sent either to Colombo or Galle by train for export. Matara continued to play its role as a collection centre for agricultural products while it lost its role as a port. Matara was vested with new functions such as distribution centre for imported and local products to its district as well as to other adjoining districts. Matara became the administrative centre for the whole Matara district. Since then Matara began providing goods and services increasingly to an area and population other than itself. The basic elements of the central place theory of Christaller became more visible in this shop centre than in the pre-British era.

Matara was granted "local board" status in 1871. The local board had an area of 704 hectares. The population of this local board increased from 1,522 in 1881 to 22,908 in 1946.

The trade in Matara, like in all the other commercial centres of the island, was dominated and controlled by either the Moors or the British. This led to the occurrence of the first serious riots between Moors and Sinhalese in 1915 in many commercial centres, including Matara and Galle.

The building morphology of the town had experienced a considerable change during this period. The elephants stables and elephant wells had vanished in the Fort. Public and administrative buildings were constructed on those sites. The Dutch built market which is located in the vicinity of the shop centre and the railway station use by the British to collect agricultural products and to distribute imported products. The British interchanged imported foods and clothes with locally cultivated crops. This market which still exists today is preserved as a colonial landmark (Photo 8).

In the early British period the commercial centre was located at the same place (in Totamuna) as in the pre-colonial and pre-British period. The growth of the transportation system led to the movement of the commercial centre from Nupe to Kottuwegoda which is the nodal point of Matara town. A grid pattern road network had come into existence in the core area of the town (Map 9).

To some extent, different functional zones in the town had come into existence during this era. The fort became the administration centre while Kotuwegoda became the commercial centre of the town. The British residential area was confined to the Brownhill area in the ward of Maddawatta, while the residential area of the local population (employees) was confined to the commercial area of the town.

In addition to the Dutch street house, a new type of dwelling (Bungalow) was introduced by the British. These were built of Cabook stone and the roofs were made of red tiles. These had deep verandas supported by rows of large white pillars. The verandas generally occupied as much space as the rest of the house. These dwellings

MAP - 09

British Period (1796 - 1956) - Matara

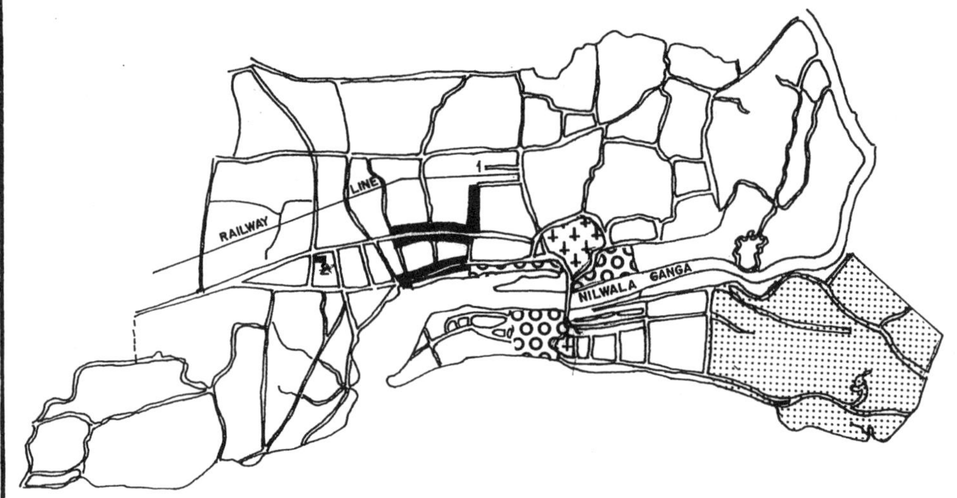

Administration

Green Area

Commercial Zone

Residential Area of European

1, 2 Railway & Bus Station

Residential Areas of Natives

0 100 200 M

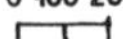

were surrounded by large gardens with flowering trees (photo 9). Originally these were occupied by the British but gradually also by Sinhalese.

Matara, the shop centre which boasts of a history prior to the advent of the European, became an urban settlement and grew as the most important commercial and administrative centre of the Matara district during the British period.

1.3.5. Post Independence Period (Since 1948)

In 1955 Matara was granted the urban council status which it still holds[23]. Although the local authorities have jurisdiction only over a strictly delimited area, their establishment tends to attract economic activities and new residents. In most areas of local authorities, central government institutions are also present. The influence exercised by the central government institutions are usually of greater importance than by the local units. All the main commercial and public administrative units which were established in Matara U.C. have controlling power over the minor units in the district as well as in some of the other adjoining districts. This led to Matara becoming the capital city of the Matara district.

In addition to its historical role as administrative and distribution centre, Matara undertook the new role as the major commercial centre for the whole as well as for the adjoining Hambantota district. The infiltration of Sinhalese into trade was stronger and faster in this era than ever before. This was influenced by social and economic conditions of the society. Sinhalese took part in all kinds of commercial activities while Moors confined their trade to business specialities such as jewellery, gems, cloth and hardware.[24] The Muslim dominance in trade was broken in the late seventies. According to one of my surveys in 1985, 62% of the total commercial shops of the town were owned by Sinhalese while only 38% were owned by Muslims.

Except in area and a few minor changes, the shape and structure of the Matara town did not experience a substantial change in the post independence era. It remained almost the same from 1948-1990. The area of the town, however has increased from 704.6 hectare to 807.6 hectare in 1971 with the annexation of "Isdeentown" (Map 10).[25] Matara urban council was divided in 1957 into eleven wards for the following reasons:[26]

1) Inequitable distribution of votes and population.
2) A remedy for the enmity between Muslims and Sinhalese in Ward 2 Kotuwegoda.
3) For better and more efficiency in urban council administration.

---

23 Government Gazette, No. 10, July 1955.

24 According to my survey in 1984, 98% of the total hardware shops, 87.6% of the total textile shops and 48% of the total jewellery shops in the core area of the Matara town were owned by the Muslims.

25 Isdeen town is a sub-service centre of Matara town which lies north-west part of the town.

26 A letter to the commissioner of local government from the urban council office of Matara, 28th of Nov. 1957.

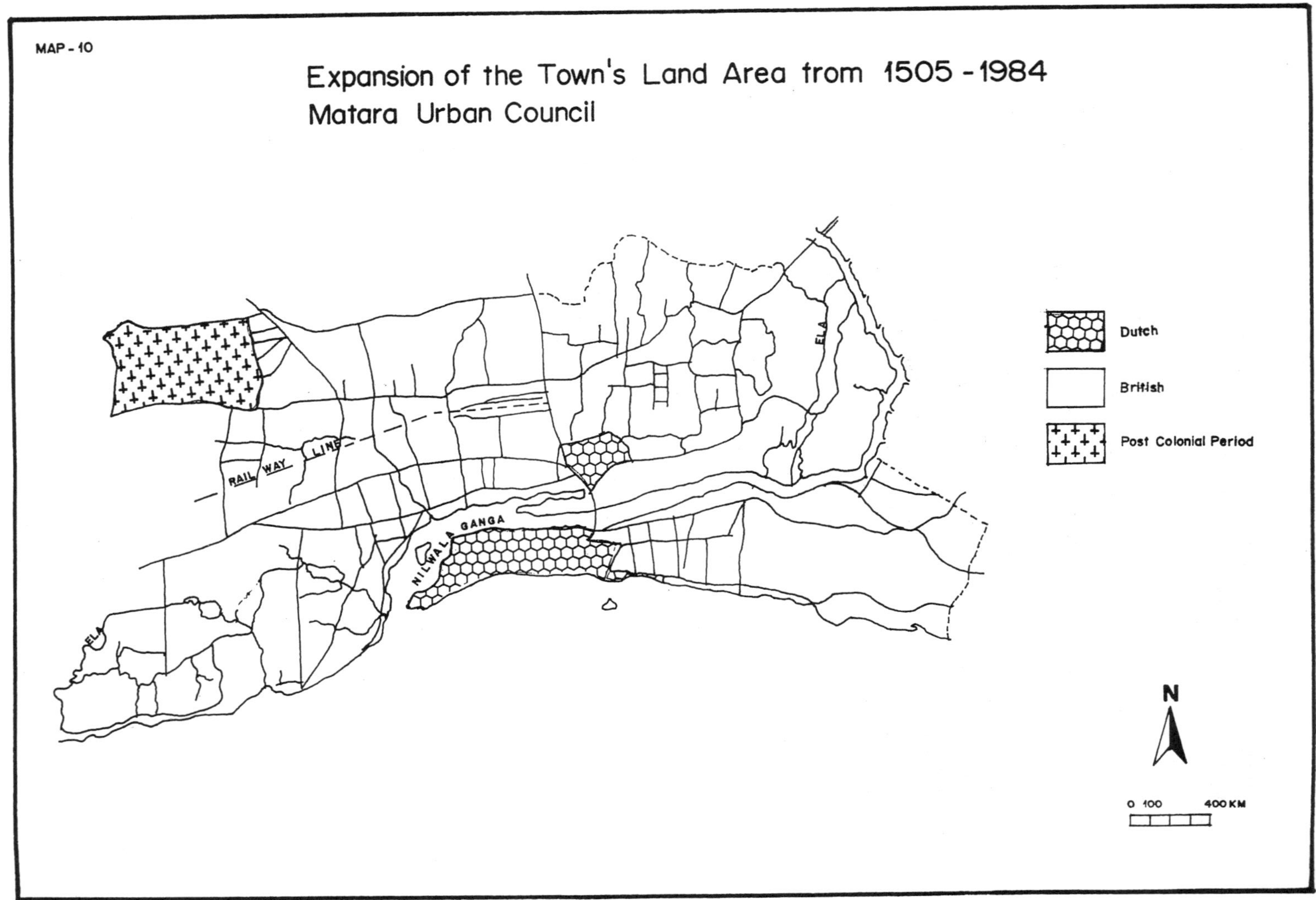
MAP - 10
Expansion of the Town's Land Area from 1505 - 1984
Matara Urban Council
Dutch
British
Post Colonial Period
N
0 100 400 KM
NILWALA GANGA
RAILWAY LINE
ELA
ELA

There had been no change in the main transportation network. The British built main roads continue in use virtually unchanged until today although there has been heavy growth in traffic during the post-independence era especially after 1970's.

Some British names of the roads have been replaced by Sinhala names. The Broadway Road and Main Street was renamed as Dharmapala Mawatha and Kumaratunga Mawatha. The British built iron bridge was replaced by a new bridge.
The larger western style commercial buildings which have more than two storeys, were constructed in this era. They comprise 1.5% of the total commercial buildings in the town today (Photo 10).[27]

The larger commercial buildings in the urban landscape of Matara give a more urban look to the town and they display their commercial hegemony over the other urban centres of the district. The commercial units grew in linear form along the major roads such as Kumarathunga Mawatha (Main Street),Dharmapala Mawatha (Broadway Road), Hakmana Road, Akuressa Road, Old Tangalle and New Tangalla Road. Priority was no longer given to establish administration units in the fort. The administrative and public units which were established in the post-independence era, lie scattered throughout the town.

The residential areas are distributed all over the town. In addition to "Dutch Street" house types and the British Bungalows a new Sinhalese house type called "Walawwa" had come into existence in the urban landscape of Matara (Photo 11). Later in this century, modern European style houses were built in the urban landscape of Matara by affluent Sri Lankans (Photo 12). These possess some architectural elements of the street houses and bungalow but preserve certain characteristics of Sinhala architecture as well.

The population of the Matara urban council increased from 22,908 in 1946 to 39,162 in 1981.

Although the government of Sri Lanka has taken steps to decentralise services since 1980, Matara continues its role as the administrative centre for the Matara district and major collection and distribution centre for agricultural products for Matara district as well as for adjoining districts.

---

27 Survey 1985.

CHAPTER 2

2. The Population and the Living Conditions of Matara Town

This chapter deals with the population and economy of Matara town as these two aspects are the basis for the existence of the town.

A reciprocal relationship exists between the population and the economy of a town. The population of a town affects its economic development through its size and composition as well as its rate of growth. The size of the population affects and determines the labour force as well as the town's per capita income. In turn, per capita income determines the size of the market for finished goods and the town's savings.

2.1. Population Growth

As discussed earlier in Chapter 1, Matara is the largest urban centre of the district. According to the census, Matara U.C. has 39,162 inhabitants. This is 55% of the total urban population of the district. The population of the town between 1881 and 1981 shows a continuous increase (Table 1 & Diag. 1). It increased from 7,522 persons in 1881 to 39,162 persons in 1981. The highest increase ever experienced by the town in one decade was 37% between 1891 and 1900. The urban population doubled during this period. The growth rate has been declining steadily over the past three inter-censal periods (1953-63 and 1971-1981 - Diag.2). This is in keeping with the trend of the gradual decline in birth-rates, an almost steady death-rate and the migration of the town's inhabitants to areas or centres of economic opportunity, particularly to Colombo and the Middle East countries (Tables 1 and 2).

Table 1
Population Growth - Matara U.C.

YEAR	POPULATION
1881	7,522
1891	8,602
1900	11,848
1911	13,851
1921	16,893
1946	22,908
1953	27,641
1963	32,284
1971	36,544
1981	39,162

Source: Population Census of 1871 - 1981

Diag.1: Population Growth, Matara, 1881 - 1981

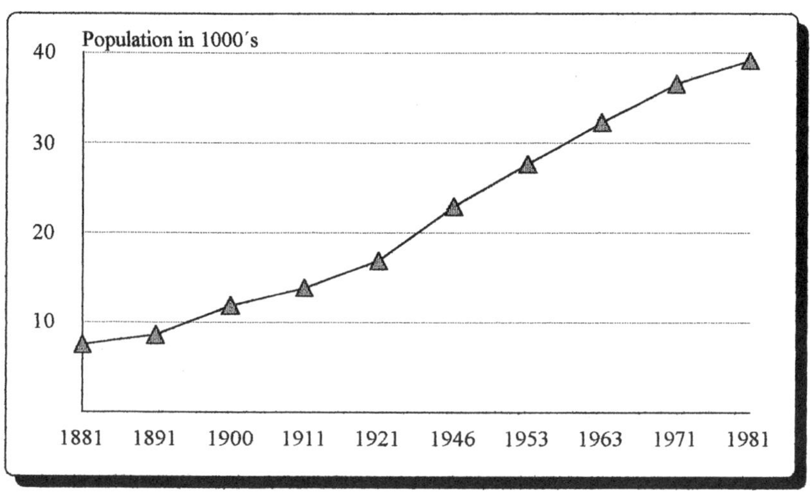

Diag.2: Population Increase Rate, Matara, 1891 - 1981

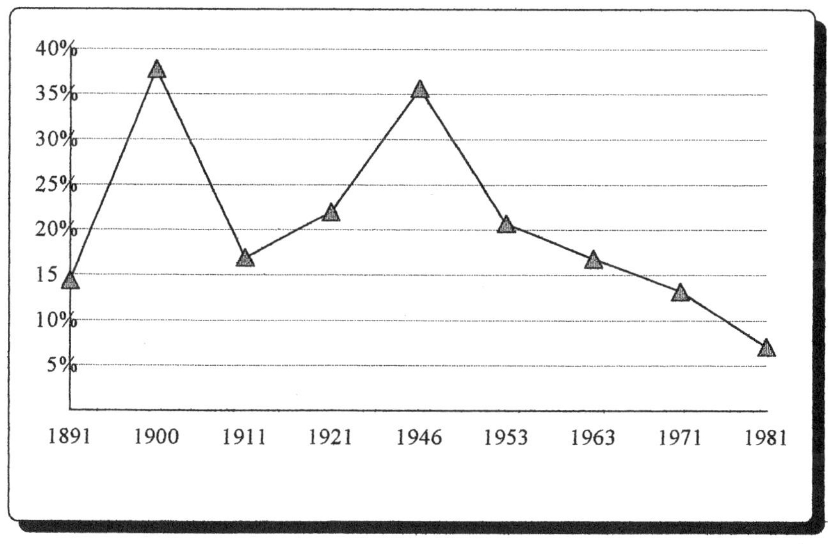

Table 2
Birth Rate and Death Rates
Matara District
1969 - 1978

	1969	1970	1971	1972	1973	1974	1975	1976	1977	1978
Death Rate	6.7	6.5	7.1	7.0	7.2	8.1	8.5	7.5	6.8	6.4
Birth Rate	31.0	28.2	31.7	29.8	29.8	28.6	27.9	27.2	26.0	26.0

Source: "Bulletin of Vital Statistics - 1978", Colombo, in: Structure Plan, Matara, Katubedda 1980/81

The sex ratio, which has declined by 7.10% over the decade, indicates the out-migration of the male component of the population and the high infant mortality rate (see tables 3 and 4).

Table 3
The Sex Ratio / Matara Town
Matara district, 1979
1946 - 1971 - 1981

	1946	1971	1981
male	11,436	18,648	19,287
female	11,472	17,906	19,875
total	22,908	35,554	39,162
sex ratio	99.68	104.14	97.04

Source: Census of Population 1946, 1971, 1981

Table 4
Infant Mortality Rates,
by sex (for 1000 infants)
Matara district 1979

type of mortality	Male	Female
Neo-Natal	26.2	22.6
Post Natal	12.4	10.1
Total	38.6	32.7

Source: Poshana Handa (The Sound of Nutrition) Matara district 1985.

Population data for the component below and above 18 years of age shows an increase in population above 18 years of age from 54.7% in 1971 to 60.&% in 1981 (Table 5). This indicates a cycle of in-migration of working population from the hinterland or from other centres into the town, which does not compensate for the out-migration. The Ruhuna University Project and the development's inputs could be mainly attributed to the in-migration into the town.

Table 5
The Population below and over 18 years
Matara town 1971-1981

	1971	1981	Change during the decade %
Percentage of Population Below 18 Years	45.30	38.27	(-)7.03
Percentage of Population Above 18 Years	54.70	61,73	7.03

Source: Matara, final report: Urban Development Authority, 1982, (Table 6).

2.1.1. Population Composition, Age and Sex Structure

Matara urban council area is mainly inhabited by young population groups. The age structure of the Matara U.C. area indicates that the majority (almost 64%) of the inhabitants are under 30 years of age (Table 6).

The pyramid for Matara U.C. in 1971 indicates a typical expanding type of population with high birth rates and rapidly decreasing death rates (Diagram 3).

Table 6
Population by Five Year Age Group
Matara U.C. - 1971.

Age Group	Number	%	Males	%	Females	%
< 1	850	2.3	439	2.4	411	2.3
1-4	3067	8.4	1511	8.1	1556	8.7 .
5-9	4069	11.1	2021	10.8	2048	11.4
10-14	4442	12.2	2239	12.0	2203	12.3
15-19	4137	11.3	2103	11.3	2034	11.4
20-24	3807	10.4	2068	11.1	1739	9.7
25-29	2981	8.2	1525	8.2	1456	8.1
30-34	2171	5.9	1075	5.8	1096	6.1
35-39	2222	6.1	1126	6.0	1096	6.1
40-44	1885	5.2	992	5.3	893	5.0
45-49	1485	4.1	787	4.2	698	3.9
50-54	1341	3.7	694	3.7	647	3,6
55-59	1150	3.1	592	3.2	558	3.1
60-64	988	2.7	522	2.8	466	2.6
65-69	757	2.1	367	2.0	390	2.2
70-74	554	1.5	286	1.5	268	1.5
75-79	318	0.9	148	0.8	170	0.9
80-84	197	0.5	97	0.5	100	0.6
85 & over	133	0.4	56	0.3	77	0.4
Total	36554	100.0	18648	100.0	17906	100.0

Source: Census of Population, Vol. 7, Part 7, Matara District, 1974.

Diag.3: Population by Sex and Age(%), Matara, 1971

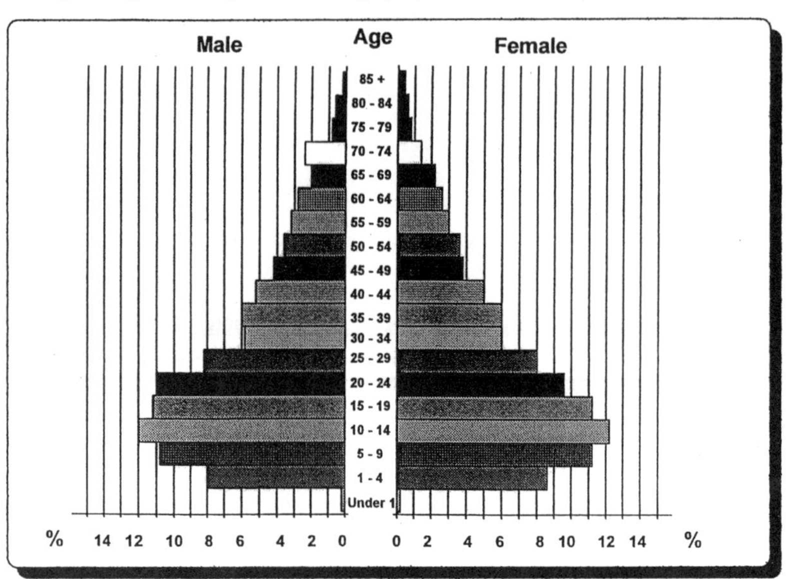

Table 7.
The population under 15 years of age and over 65 years
Urban Settlements of Matara district 1971 - 1981

Total Urban	Percent	Under 15 Years	Percent	Over 65 Years	Percent
1971 36554	100	23,382	38.7	3,832	6.3
1981 71,151	100	22,871	32.1	4,679	6.6

Source: These data are based upon the exploitation of 1971 and 1981 Census of Population.

An examination of the age structure shows that the age structure became slightly higher between the period of 1971 and 1981. The percentage of children under 15 years declined from 38.7% in 1971 to 32.1% in 1981 and the percentage of people over 65 years of age increased from 6.3% to 6.6% during the same period[1] (Table 7).

---

1 Population by five year age groups are not given in population of 1981. Therefore, the population by five year intervals of all the urban settlements are used here to compare the structural change between the five year intervals during the period 1971 to 1981. As Matara town accounts for almost 55% of the urban population of the district, it is reasonable to assume that the age structure of Matara U.C. will more or less reflect the urban sector of the district. This data is based upon the exploitation of 1971 and 1981 census of population.

2.1.2. Ethnic Composition

According to the population census of 1981, the Matara urban council population consists of five major ethnic groups: Sinhalese, Tamil, Moors, Burghers and Malay (Table 8 & Diag 4). The Tamils are further divided into two basic groups according to their origin. The predominating ethnic group of the town is Sinhalese, which comprises 89% of the total population, which is less than the district's percentage (94.6%) but higher than the Sri Lankan percentage (86.6%). The Moors, with a percentage of 9.3% of the town's population is much higher than the district(2.6%) and the Sri Lankan percentage (7.1%). They can be identified as the major ethnic group among the minority groups.

Indian and Sri Lankan Tamils represent 0.9% of the total population of the town. This is far below the district (2.7%)and Sri Lankan percentage (18.6%). The majority of the Tamils are government officials and professionals such as lawyers and doctors.

An examination of population increase among the ethnic groups between 1946 and 1981 indicates that the Sinhalese and the Moor populations have been increasing while the other ethnic groups have been decreasing (Table 8).

The decline of the Tamil population could be attributed to the ethnic conflict (violence) on the island since 1983 while the decline of the Burgher population could be attributed to the de-westernization of the island since 1956.

Table 8
Ethnic Composition % Matara U.C. 1946, 1981
Percentage increase and decrease Matara district and Sri Lanka 1981

Ethnic Groups	1946 %	1981 %	Increase/ decrease % 1981	Matara district % 1981	Sri * Lanka
1 Sinhalese	87.0	89.0	(+) 2.0	94.6	73.98
2 Sri Lankan Tamil	1.3	0.7	(-) 0.6	0.6	12.60
3 Indian Tamil	1.0	0.2	(-) 0.8	2.1	5.56
4 Moors	9.2	9.3	(+) 0.1	2.6	1.12
5 Burghers	1.0	0.3	(-) 0.7	0.04	0.26
6 Malays	0.025	0.024	(-) 0.01	0.01	0.29
7 Others	0.3	0.3	---	0.04	0.20

Source : Census of Population and Housing, Sri Lanka, 1981 Preliminary release No. 1
* Statistical pocket book, Sri Lanka 1984 Census of population 1946
* Statistical Handbook, Matara district 1983

2.1.3. Religion

The religion is closely associated with ethnicity. Buddhism, the main religion of the Sinhalese ethnic group in the island, is the predominant religion in the Matara urban council area. According to the census of 1981, the Buddhists comprise 87.8% of the total

Diag.4: Ethnic Composition, 1981

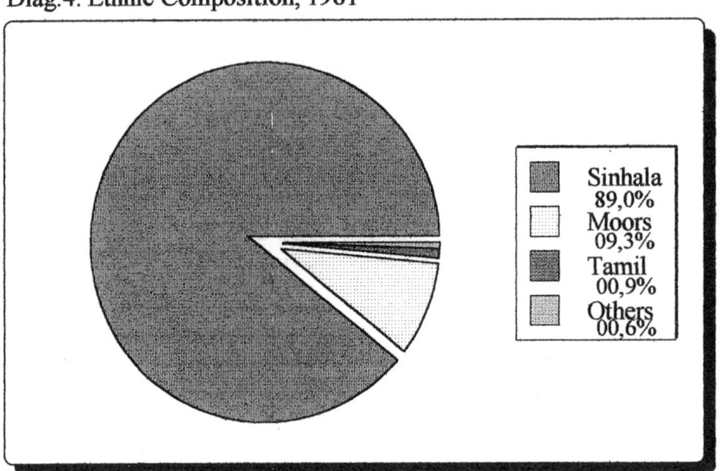

population of the town which is less than the district percentage but higher than the Sri Lankan percentage (Table 9 & Diag. 5). The Muslims, mostly Moors, represent only 9.7% of the total town's population, but this is higher than the district percentage and the Sri Lankan percentage (Table 9). The Hindus, mostly Tamils, are a very small segment of Matara's population although the district and the Sri Lankan percentages are high. The Catholic population represent only 1.6%, which is higher than the district's percentage but lower than the island's percentage.

This data indicates the non-reception of foreign influence by the Matara inhabitants even after 443 years of being subjected to foreign rule.[2]

---

[2] Historians give adequate credit to the Kandyans for their various resistance to foreign rule. But they have failed to assess the cost of this non-reception of foreign influence and the importance of the compromise position arrived at by the southerners whereby Buddhist and Sinhalese cultural values were upheld while at the same time the best of what the foreigners had to give was imbibed and put to good use. (Chandraprema, C.A. Ruhuna, 1989.)

Table 9
Religious Composition %
Matara U.C. 1946, 1981

Religious groups	1946 %	1981 %	increase decrease	districts %	Sri Lankan* %
1 Buddhists	84.0	87.8	(+) 3.8	94.55	69.3
2 Hindus	1.5	0.8	(-) 0.7	2.38	15.5
3 Muslims	9.6	9.7	(+) 0.1	2.62	7.6
4 Roman Catholics & other Christians	4.7	1.6	(-) 3.1	0.42	7.5
5 other groups	0.2	0.1	(-) 0.1	0.03	0.1
Total	100	100	---	100	100

Source: Census of Population and Housing, Sri Lanka 1981, preliminary release no. 1.
Census of Population 1946 Statistical Handbook, Matara district 1983
*Statistical pocketbook, Sri Lanka, 1984

Diag.5: Religious Composition, Matara, 1981

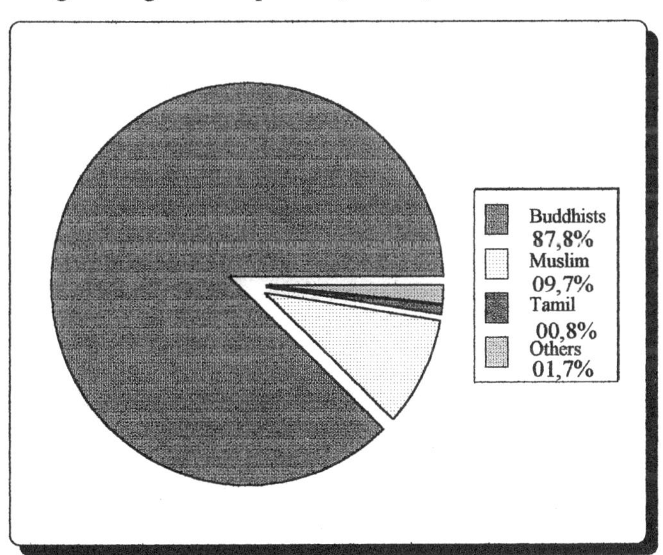

2.1.4. Population Distribution by Ward, Growth and Density

As per 1981 population census, the total area and the population of the town are 808.6 hectares and 39,162 persons respectively. The density of the town was only 48.47% persons per hectare. The low density of the population in town was attributed to the large amount of land under plantation (coconut), the dense vegetation and the bodies of water. There was an increase of 3.23 persons per hectare over the decade (Table 10).

An examination of the population distribution among the wards of the town shows Welegoda has the highest number of residents with 5,058 (12.9% of the total town's population) followed by Kadeweediya and Uyanwatta with 4,290 (10.9%) and 4,179 (10.6%) respectively . The lowest number of residents is found in the ward of Fort with 1,634 (4.1%) followed by Mainstreet with 2,326 (5.9%).

The largest extension of land areas are found in the wards which are located at the periphery of the town, while the smallest extension of land areas are found in the wards which are located in the town centre. The largest ward, in terms of the land area, is Walpola with 138.3 ha. which accounts for 17.12% of the total land area of the town followed by Polhena with 107.6 ha. (13.3%), while the ward Fort has the lowest extension of land area with 29.2% ha. (3.6%) followed by Mainstreet with 39.6 ha. (4.9%).

A comparative analysis of the persons per housing unit shows that Kotuwegoda and Mainstreet, which belong to the commercial core area of the town, have the highest number of persons per housing unit with 8.62 and 8.28 respectively (lies much higher above the average value of 5.6). These two wards belong to the "Multiracial Residential" area of the town. The figures for Fort (7.5), Kadeweediya (7.4), and Weliweeriya (6.59) lie little above the average value. Fort and Weliweeriya are wards adjoining to commercial core areas while Kadeweediya belongs to the commercial core area and "Multiracial Residential Area" of the town. Figures for the other wards are lower than the average figures and are located in the peripheral areas of the town. These wards are predominantly populated by Sinhalese.

An examination of the wardwise population growth and the densities shows a different picture due to the different resources, background and physical development of each area. The higher population densities are found in the wards which lie in the commercial core and its adjoining wards, while the low densities are found in the peripheral areas where physical constraints exist (Map 11).

MAP - 11

Population Density - Matara Town, 1981

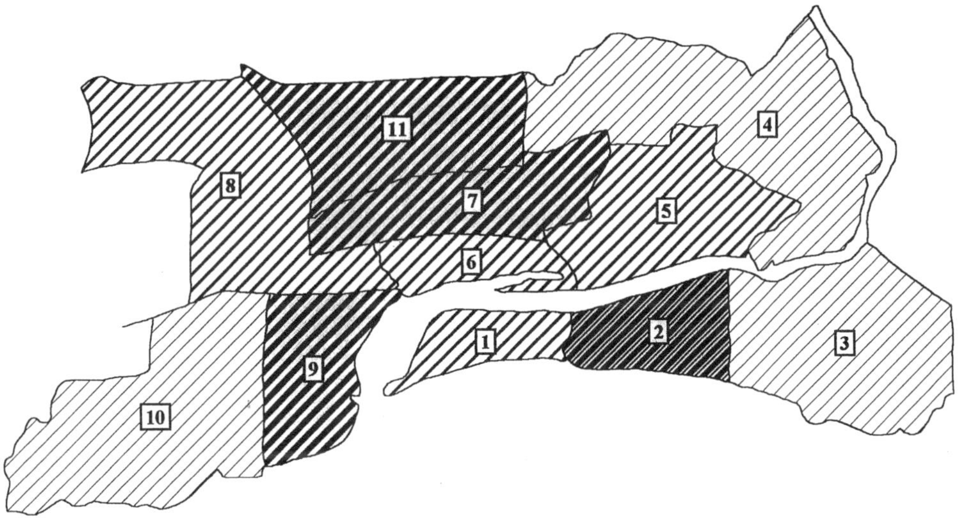

Legend

Person per Hectares

 Over 90

 60 to 90

 30 to 60

 Under 30

0 300 600 M

Note :- 1-11 Wards

Table 10
Matara town - Wardwise Growth of Population and Densities
1971- 1981

Name Ward	area ha.	population 1971	population 1981	percentage growth	density persons/ha. 1971	density persons/ha. 1981	Change in the density persons/ha.
1 Fort	29.2	2179	1634	(-)25.0	74.5	55.95	18.6
2 Kotuwegoda	42.6	3580	3973	10.90	83.8	93.15	9.3
3 Maddewatta	92.5	2082	2427	16.50	22.5	26.20	3.7
4 Walpola	138.3	3616	3919	8.30	26.1	28.30	2.2
5 Uyanwatta	79.3	3888	4176	7.00	49.0	52.60	3.6
6 Mainstreet	39.6	2239	2326	3.80	56.4	58.70	2.3
7 Kadeweediya	50.1	3858	4290	11.10	76.9	85.50	8.6
8 Welegoda	99.2	4817	5179	7.80	48.6	52.40	3.8
9 Totamuna	50.1	2928	3082	5.20	58.4	61.50	3.1
10 Polhena	107.4	2856	3080	7.80	26.5	28.60	2.1
11 Weliweriya	79.3	4511	5058	12.10	56.9	63.80	6.9
Total	808.6	36554	39162	7.13	45.2	48.40	3.2

Source: U.D.A. Final report, Matara, 1982 (Table 10)

Kotuwegoda (commercial core area) is ranked first in the density groups with 93.15 persons per hectare, followed by Kadeeweediya (commercial core area), Weliweriya (a ward adjoining a commercial core area), Totamuna (a ward adjoining a commercial core area and the ancient Bazaar centre), Mainstreet (commercial centre), Fort (administration centre from colonial period to post colonial period and a ward adjoining a commercial core area), Uyanwatta and Welegoda (wards adjoining a commercial core area) with 85.50 persons per hectare, 63.80 persons per hectare, 61.50 persons per hectare, 58.70 per hectare, 55.95 persons per hectare, 52.60 persons per hectare and 52.40 persons per hectare respectively.

Low densities are found in Polhena, Walpola, and Meddewatta with 28.60 persons per hectare, 28.30 persons per hectare, 26.20 persons per hectare respectively. The low densities in Polhena and Walpola are mainly attributed to the bad physical conditions in these two wards. Large areas of land in these two wards are low lying and susceptible to flooding. The lowest density in Maddewatta was mainly attributed to the bungalows with large plot areas.

A comparative analysis of the population growth and the change in density is given in Table 10. Maddewatta (Ward 3) the residential area of the colonial masters in the British era, experienced the highest population growth with 16.50% (change in density is only 3.7%) followed by Weliweriya with 12.10% (change in density 6.9%) over the decade. Even though there is a poor road network in this ward, the favourable environmental conditions, the moderate land value (ranges between 2000 Rupees to 4000 Rupees per perch), social facilities and the other amenities at convenient distance would have attracted the people into this ward.

Although Weliweriya is considered to be a residential area, it includes almost 11.2% of the total commercial units of the town (Map 12).[3] The two important interior roads of the district, Hakmana and Akuressa, as well as the other important roads of the towns, such as Rahula and Tudawa road, pass through this ward. This led to the emergence of some commercial units along these roads. Moderate land values (1000 Rupees to 4000 Rupees per perch) social facilities at convenient distance and better environmental conditions attracted the inhabitants to this ward (Map 13).

Kotuwegoda and Kadeweediya, which have the highest population densities, experienced high population growth after Maddewatta and Weliweriya over the decade by 10.90% (change in density 9.3 persons/ha.) and 11.10% (change in density 8.6 persons /ha.). Although these two wards belong to the commercial core area of the town, the area under commercial land use in comparison to Mainstreet is very low. Only 10.5% and 10.9% of the total area of these two wards are occupied by commercial units while the majority of the area is under residential land use.[4] Although the high land values which lie between 4000 rupees to 10,000 rupees per perch (low compared to Mainstreet), still existing absorption capacity, moderate environmental conditions, social facilities and other amenities at convenient distance were the main reasons which led to the high population growth and densities in these two wards.

Population and density of the commercial centre of the town, the Mainstreet, have increased by 3.80% only and 2.3 people per hectare. The major area of this ward (43%) is occupied by commercial units while only 10.3% is under residential use. Since this ward is the commercial centre, there is a concurrence between population increases and the commercial institutional activities (concurrence between residential and commercial land use). Thus the commercial land use is slowly edging out the residential land use. In addition to the high land values which range between 4000 rupees to 10,000 rupees per perch, the exhausted absorption capacity and bad environmental conditions have attributed to the low percentage in population growth in this ward.

The remaining wards of the town have the percentage population growth and density over the decade varying between 5.20% and 8.30%, and 2.1 persons by hectare and 3.8 persons per hectare. Although the land values are low (between 1000 - 4000 rupees) the slow growth of these wards has been mainly attributed to either less developed road network (Walpola, Polhena, Welegoda, Totamuna), bad physical conditions (major areas of Polhena and Walpola are low lying, while some parts of the Uyanwatta and Totamuna are also low lying and prone to flooding), bad environmental conditions (Polhena is considered to be the health hazardous area of the town. Poor sanitary conditions and the stagnation of water led to an increase of infectious diseases such as malaria, leprosy, dysentery and filariasis in the ward), or to inconvenient distances to social facilities and other amenities.

Fort (Ward 1), the administrative centre since the Portuguese period, is the only ward which experienced a decline of population over the decade. The population and density declined by about 28% and 18 people per hectare during the period between

---

3 Final Report (U.D.A.), Matara, 1981.

4 Structure Plan, Matara, 1980 / 81.

MAP - 12

Percentage Distribution of Commercial Units in Total Building Units Among The Wards - Matara Town, 1981

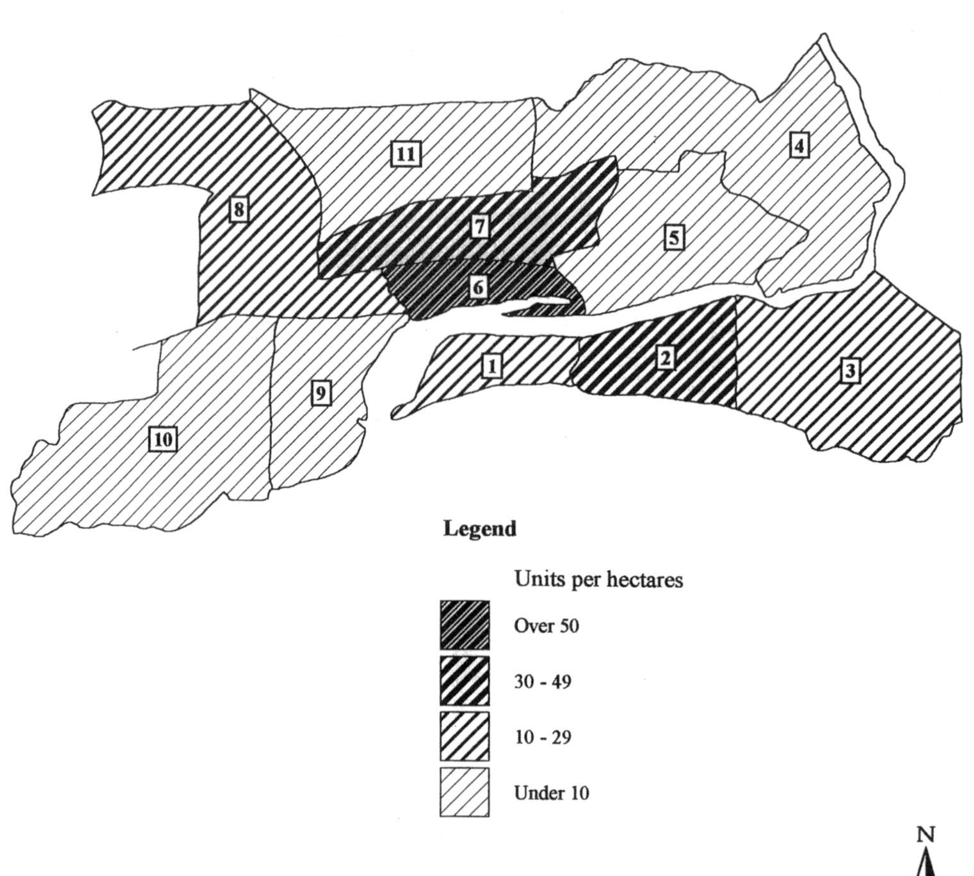

Note:- 1-11 Wards

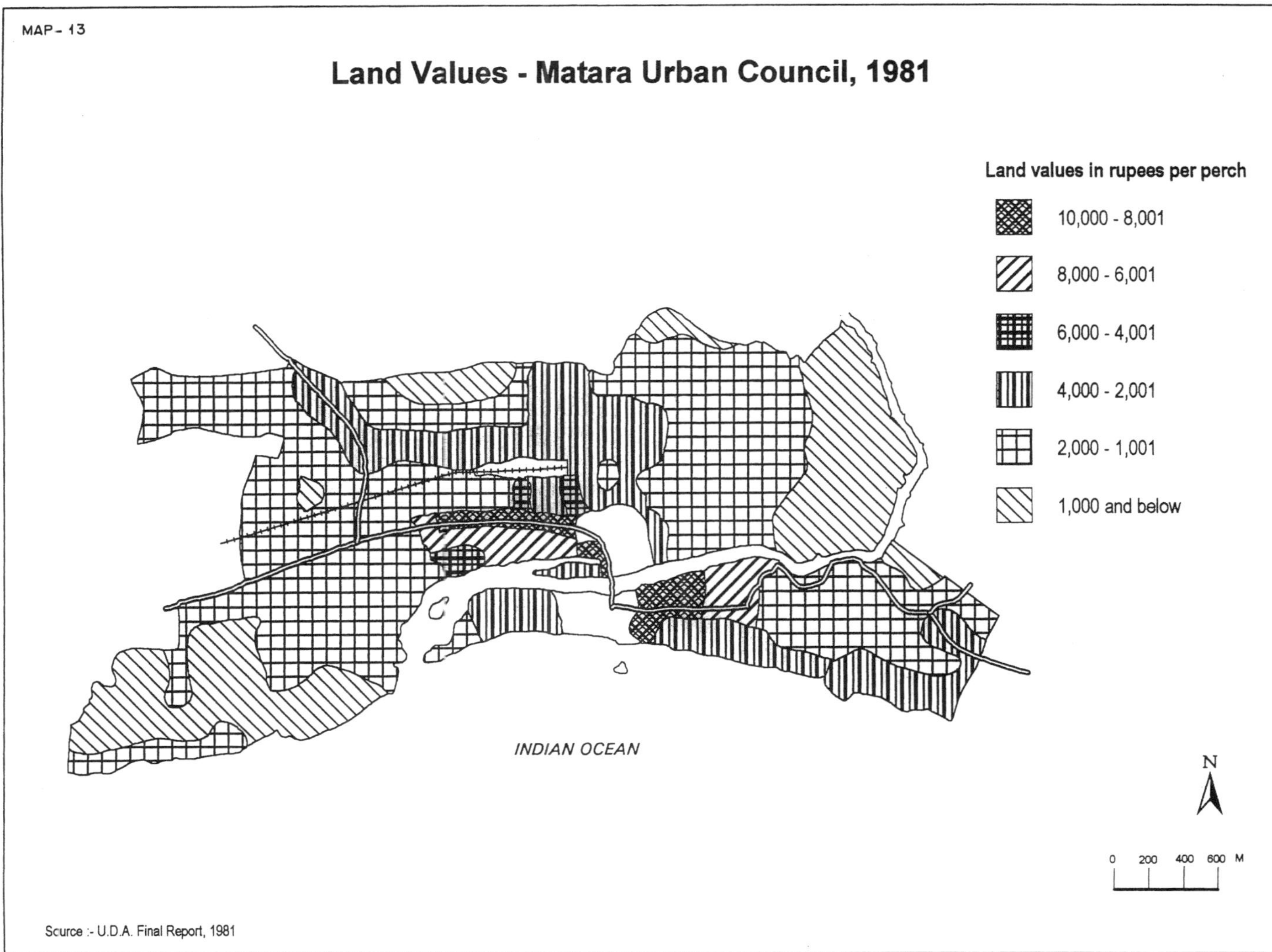
MAP - 13
Land Values - Matara Urban Council, 1981
Land values in rupees per perch
10,000 - 8,001
8,000 - 6,001
6,000 - 4,001
4,000 - 2,001
2,000 - 1,001
1,000 and below
INDIAN OCEAN
N
0 200 400 600 M
Scurce :- U.D.A. Final Report, 1981

1971-1981. Although land values are high in this ward lying between 1000- 4000 rupees, the apparent reason for this decline in population is that the conservation laws enforced by the archaeological department prohibit alterations, repairs, and construction of new buildings in the Fort. Therefore, there is no replenishment of the existing housing stock. Hence the affected population is moving out. In addition, due to the (generally) higher level of education among the residents of this ward, there is a tendency to migrate to larger towns, mainly to Colombo, for better job opportunities.

2.1.5. Population Distribution among the Wards of Matara U.C. by Major Ethnic Groups.

An examination of the distribution of major ethnic groups, indicates that the Sinhalese are predominant in 10 wards out of 11. High concentrations of Sinhalese are found outside of the commercial core area while the minorities are concentrated in the commercial core area.

Totamuna (Ward 9), has the highest concentration of the Sinhala ethnic group with 100%,followed by Polhena (No. 10), Walpola (No. 4) Uyanwatte (No. 5). Welegoda (No. 8) Weliweeriya (No. 11) and Fort with 99%, 98%, 97%, 93% and 84% respectively. The lowest concentration of Sinhalese is found in the Mainstreet (No. 6) with 42% of the total ward's population (Map 14).

The largest minority ethnic group, Muslims, are concentrated in Mainstreet (Ward 6) with 52% of the total ward's population. A high percentage of Muslims also live in Kotuwegoda (Ward 2) and Kadeeweediya (Ward 7) with 32% and 20%. A small percentage of Muslims live in Fort (Ward 1) and Weliweeriya (Ward 11) with 0% and 12%.

The Tamils represent only 0.9% of the total population of the Matara U.C. The majority of these Tamils live in Mainstreet (Ward 6) with 3% of the total ward's population.

After examining the population distribution by ethnic groups, the residential area of Matara U.C. can be divided into the following two major groups:

1) "Sinhalese Residential Areas," where the Sinhalese ethnic group is predominant and also has a low percentage of other ethnic groups (Ward 1, 4, 5, 8, 9, 10, and 11). These areas lie outside of the commercial core area.

2) "Multiracial Residential Areas," where either ethnic group Moors or Sinhalese are predominant but also have some concentration of other ethnic groups such as Tamils and Malays (Ward 2, 6, and 7). These areas lie in the commercial core area (Map 15).

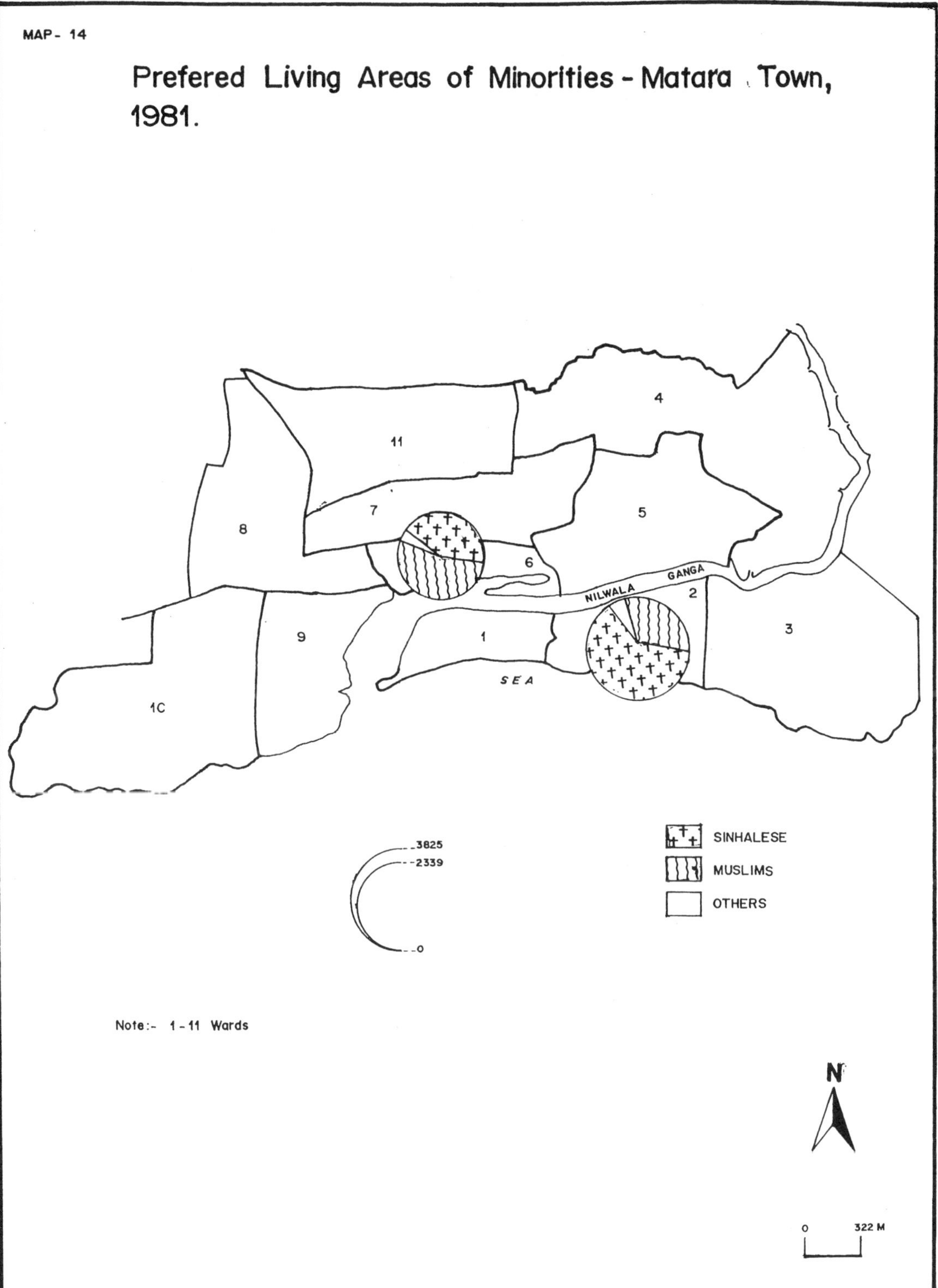
MAP- 14
Prefered Living Areas of Minorities - Matara Town, 1981.
11
4
7
5
8
6
NILWALA GANGA
2
9
1
3
SEA
1C
3825
2339
0
SINHALESE
MUSLIMS
OTHERS
Note:- 1-11 Wards
N
0
322 M

MAP - 15

Residential Areas by Ethnic Groups, 1981.

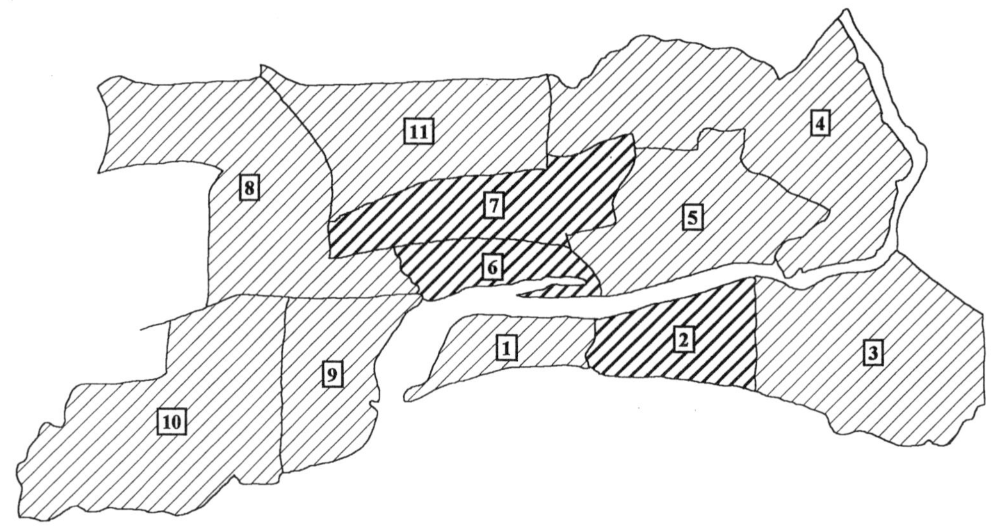

Legend

Multi racial residential areas

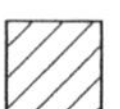

Sinhala residential areas

0 300 600 M

Source :- Population Census - 1981

Note :-- 1-11 Wards

2.2. Living Conditions

High population growth (4.2% per year) and the slow growth rate of housing units (3.4% per year) between 1881-1971 led to large household sizes. It decreased by 14.2% between 1971 and 1981 due to the increased high rate of housing units and the slow growth rate of population. However, the household size of the urban sector lies above the rural sector's household size of 5.3%[5] (Map 16,compare with the table 11.).

2.2.1. Building Density

High building densities are found in the commercial core area of the town (Table 11). Kotuwegoda (Ward 2) has the highest density followed by Mainstreet (Ward 6) and Kadeweediya (Ward 7) respectively (Map 17). A high percentage of these buildings consist of commercial units (about 70% of the commercial units of the town lie in these three wards). The majority of the inhabitants belong to the middle income groups while a substantial portion of low income groups also live here. Two housing schemes for low income groups are located here.

Table 11
Distribution of Population, Households, Land Area, Non-Residential Building Units and the Building and Housing Density.

Name of ward	Popula-tion	Housing units	Living quarters	Non-housing units	Total building units in each ward	Average House-hold size	Land area	Number building units per hec.	No. house units per hec.	%. of Com. Units in Total Building
1 Fort	1,634	217	5	89	311	7.52	29.2	10.6	7.43	28.62
2 Kotuwegoda	3,973	461	30	389	880	8.62	42.7	20.61	10.8	44.2
3 Maddewatta	2,427	354	4	55	413	6.86	92.5	4.46	3.82	13.32
4 Walpola	3,919	621	18	50	689	6.31	138.3	4.98	4.5	7.26
5 Uyanwatte	4,176	689	7	22	718	6.06	79.3	9.05	8.69	3.06
6 Mainstreet	2,326	281	30	366	677	8.28	39.6	17.1	7.1	54.06
7Kadeweediya	4,290	579	13	283	875	7.4	50.1	17.47	11.56	32.34
8 Welegoda	5,179	884	24	126	1,034	5.86	99.2	10.42	8.91	12.19
9 Totamuna	3,082	520	14	6	540	5.92	50.1	10.78	10.38	1.1
10 Polhena	3,080	568	11	228	607	5.42	107.6	5.64	5.28	4.61
11Weliweriya	5,058	765	6	82	853	6.61	79.3	10.76	9.65	9.61
Total	39162	5939	162	1496	7597	6.59	807.9	9.4	7.35	19.69

Source: U.D.A. Final report, 1981, p 38, Structure plan - Matara town, volume 1,2, 1980/81, Census of Statistics 1981

[5] Census of Population and Housing, Matara District. 1981.

MAP - 16

Residents per Housing Unit
Matara Town, 1981

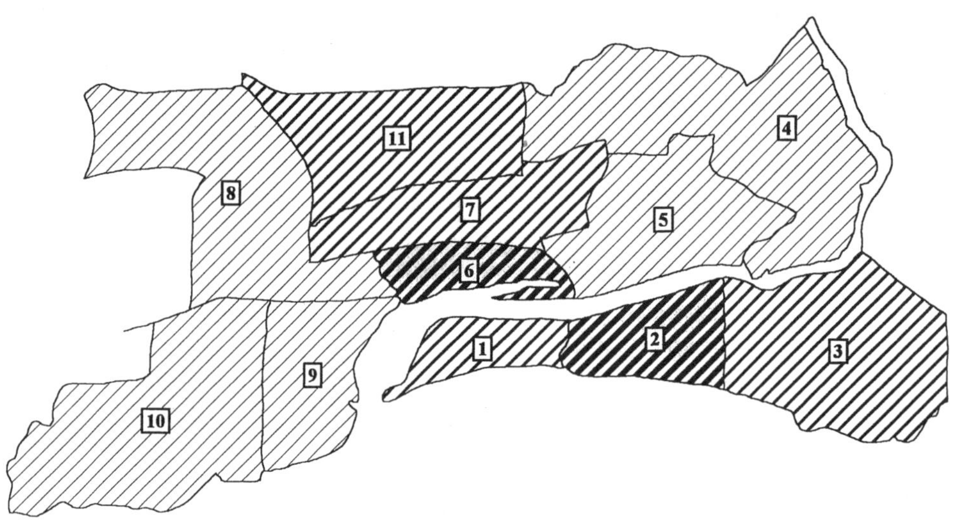

Legend

 Much higher above average value

 Average & little above average value

 Lower than average value

Note :- 1-11 Wards

MAP - 17

Building Density per Hectares by Wards
Matara Urban Council - 1981

11
8
7
5
4
6
1
2
3
9
10

Legend

Building per Hectares

Over 20

15 - 19.9

10 - 14.9

05 - 09.9

Less 4.9

N

0 300 600 M

Note :- 1 - 11 Wards

There are four adjoining wards to the commercial core area which have higher densities than the average density of the town:

1. Totamuna (Ward 9), which lies on the western side of the commercial core area is one of the preferred residential areas of the middle and low income groups. One housing scheme for low income groups is found here. The percentage of the commercial units of the total building units is very low.

2. Weliweeriya (Ward 11), which lies on the northern part of the commercial core area, is one of the preferred residential areas of the middle income groups, although there are low income groups that live here as well. One housing scheme for low income groups is found here. The percentage of the commercial units in the total building units is low.

3. Welegoda (Ward 8), which adjoins to the commercial core area on the western side, is a residential area for high and middle income groups with some low income groups. One housing scheme for low income groups is found here. Although it has a low percentage of commercial units in the total building units of the ward, about 8% of the commercial units of the Matara town lies in this ward.

4. Fort (Ward 1), the administrative centre of the town lies on the western side of Kotuwegoda. This is the residential area of the high and middle income groups, but also has some low income groups. One housing scheme for low income groups is found here. It has a high percentage of non-residential units in the total building units. The majority of these units are used for administrative purposes.

   Uyanwatta, Maddawatte, Polhena and Walpola have less building densities than the average density for the town.

Uyanwatta, which is a ward adjoining the commercial core area on the north side, is inhabited by high, middle as well as low income groups. The high and middle income groups have their dwellings along the Uyanwatta Circular road and Esplanade road while the low income groups have their dwellings where problems of accessibility, drainage, sanitation and flooding exist. One housing scheme for low income groups is found here. The percentage of commercial units in the total building units of the ward is very low.

Meddawatta (Ward 3) is the residential area of the high income groups, but also has low income groups where physical constraints exist. This ward adjoins to the commercial area on the eastern side. The low building density in this ward is the result of bungalows with large plots of land and large coconut plantations. The percentage for the commercial units, in the total building units of the ward, is substantial. All these commercial units lie at the boundary of the commercial core area.

Polhena (Ward 10) and Walpola (Ward 4) are fringing areas of the town which have severe physical constraints as discussed earlier. These two wards are mostly inhabited by low income groups with a small portion of middle income groups. One housing scheme for low income groups is found in Polhena and a housing scheme for low income groups in Walpola has been proposed. The percentage of commercial units in the total building units is very low.

2.2.2. Housing Types, Nature of Construction and Building Materials

A survey in 1981, "Matara Development Plan" identified six housing types in the urban landscape of Matara. The differentiation of houses in this survey is solely based on their shape (look) and their location.[6]

As this survey takes into account very little about the layout, basic services and amenities, it is hard to affirm the housing quality of the dwellings, but sufficient to highlight their character to some degree. The six housing types which are identified by the survey are:

A) Farmhouses
B) "Palpath" (Huts, Jerry built residences)
C) Cluster houses
D) Bungalows
E) Row houses
F) Government schemes

2.2.2.1. Farmhouses

These are permanent types of dwellings and are generally found in the peripheral areas of the town where low residential densities are located. They are characterised by large plots having, in addition to the house, a plantation of coconut and sometimes fruit trees although the economic dependence on plantation produce may or may not be a characteristic of the owner of the house. This type of house is found in Brown's Hill area and along Tangalle road in Meddawatta (Ward 3) and in the western parts of Polhena (Ward 10). The demand for housing in the future could lead to subdivision and sale of these lands.

2.2.2.2. Palpath (Jerry built residences)

These are structurally of a temporary nature being constructed out of mud, wood and thatch (Photo 13). They are found in some areas of the following wards: Weragampitiya in Walpola (Ward 4), Kadeweediya (Ward 7), Totamuna (Ward 9), Fort (Ward 1), Polhena (Ward 10), where there are physical constraints. They are generally lacking basic services such as water supply, electricity, as well as easy accessibility. These dwellings are inhabited by low income groups such as unskilled labourers, the fishing community and field hands .

---

6 Development plan, Matara U.C., 1981, p.40.

2.2.2.3. Cluster Houses

These are houses clustered or grouped together and mostly located in places of poor accessibility. These houses are either permanent or semi-permanent in structure. No definite plot boundaries are noticeable, and a group of such houses is usually served by a single pathway meandering from one doorstep to another. Concentrations of these houses are found in Polhena (Ward 10), Walpola (Ward 4), western parts of Meddawatta (Ward 3), Totamuna (Ward 9), and along the railway lines in Kadeweediya (Ward 7). Predominantly cluster houses are inhabited by the lower income segments of the population.

2.2.2.4. Bungalows

These houses, which came into existence in the urban landscape of Matara during the British period, are permanent structures and have distinct plot demarcations with open spaces on at least three sides. These houses are found in areas where good environmental conditions and accessibility exist. This house type generally occupies land with high land values. They are inhabited by middle and high income groups. A concentration of these houses is found in Issadeen town in Welegoda (Ward 8), along old Tangalle road, Pallimulla road in Kotuwegoda (Ward 2), a few isolated areas in Mainstreet (Ward 6), Kadeweediya (Ward 7), the eastern parts of Meddewatta (Ward 3), in the major portion of Uyanwatta (Ward 5) and Fort (Ward 1). The "Walawwas" houses, built in an indigenous architectural style, also fall in this category.

2.2.2.5. Row houses

These houses are permanent in structure and came into existence during the Dutch period (Dutch street house). They are mostly found in commercial areas where high population densities exist. Concentration of these houses are found along Kumarathunga Mawatha (early Mainstreet) and in Mainstreet (Ward 6) along old Tangalle road in Kotuwegoda (Ward 2) and Fort (Ward 1). Such houses share their side walls with neighbouring houses and may or may not have front open spaces. Some of these have commercial establishments in the front with the residences in the back, and others have a commercial establishment on the ground floor with the residence above.[7] These houses are occupied by mostly middle and higher income groups.

2.2.2.6. Government Housing Schemes

The N.H.D.A. (National Housing Development Authority), the Matara Urban Council and the Urban Development Authority play an important role in the housing projects in the Matara U.C. area.

Although deficits in the middle income housing groups are evident, the utmost priority is given to the low income housing units. These schemes are dependent of

---

7 Most of the time these housing units are categorized as commercial units in the housing census without taking their residence function into consideration.

assistance from the local government. For facilities to be provided and for costs of site development and construction for low income housing, the standards adopted by the National Housing Development Authority and the Urban Development Authority have been generally followed. For the low income housing schemes undertaken in the public sector, about 12 hectares of land shall be developed in Meddawatta (Ward 3), Polhena (Ward 10) and Walpola (Ward 4). Matara U.C. area has seven low income housing schemes which are located in Walpola (Ward 4), Kaddeweediya (Ward 7), Polhena (Ward 10), Mainstreet (Ward 6), Fort (Ward 1) and Kotuwegoda (Ward 2). Two middle income housing units are also found in Kotuwegoda (Ward 2) and in Walpola (Ward 4)[8] .

According to "Structure plan - Matara 1980/81", Matara Urban Council and N.H.D.A. have built 50 and 28 housing units respectively, giving permanent shelter to 95 fishing families out of 260. The fisheries department has given (under a financial assistance program) 1,800 rupees to each fishing family to build a permanent house for themselves, but as this money was not sufficient, only 7 houses were completed.[9]

These housing schemes are located in Polhena, Fort, and Walpola. They are very small housing units and are permanent in structure. The shape and layout of these units is very simple and repetitive. The dwellings are square and have four rooms. A certain degree of basic services such as roads, water supply and electricity are provided (Photo 14).

The layout of the middle income housing units is basically the same as the low income housing units. They are twice as big as the low income housing units and square in shape. These housing units have a veranda on the front side. Basic services such as water, electricity and roads are provided.

A resettlement project has been proposed to resettle about 110 families belonging to the low income group presently occupying crown lands in Kaddeweediya (Ward 7). Under this project, land shall be developed in the Walpola (Ward 4). This is a service-cum-self-help housing scheme, whereby each family will be provided with a serviced plot of 50 square meters on which they will be able to build their own dwellings.

According to U.D.A.'s "environmental improvement scheme", the shanty settlements of 72 families in Totamuna (Ward 10) and in Fort (Ward 1) are to be provided with basic amenities such as water, toilets and garbage bins.

2.3. Housing Deficit

The 1981 census definition of a housing unit includes the existing houses and living quarters of permanent, semi-permanent and temporary structural conditions. Matara's total population based on 1981 census is 39,162 persons. The total housing units are 5,939. The average household size is 6 persons per housing unit. According to this data, it is apparent that there is no severe housing deficit, as the entire population of the town is housed in some sort of living quarters.

8 Structure plan - Matara town, 1980 / 81.

9 Ibid.

But when data on the building materials, sanitary accommodations and age, which determines the condition of the housing units, is taken into consideration, it is apparent that there is a great deficit in the housing stock in qualitative terms. The deficit in the existing house stock is of two kinds - housing units which have deteriorated due to ageing and are in need of major repairs, and the temporary type of structures which lack basic amenities and are in poor environmental condition.

Detailed data on urban housing units for Matara U.C. cannot be found in the 1981 housing census, thus compelling the author to use the 1971 housing census for this purpose. The data on the nature and type of construction of the building material used, sanitary accommodations and the age according to the housing census 1971 has been presented below.

Table 12
Matara town - Housing units by nature of construction, 1971

Category	Number	Percentage
Permanent	3.743	71,8
Semi-permanent	821	15.7
Temporary	652	12.5
Total	5.216	100

Source: Department of Census and Statistics, Housing Census, 1971

Table 13
Housing units by material of construction & sanitary accommodation, Matara town, 1971.

Housing units	Wall					Roof				
Total	Brick	Mud	Wood	Cad-jan	Other	Tile	Asbas-tos	Metal-sheet	Cad-jan	Others
5216	3887	653	39	543	94	3181	630	188	1193	19
100%	74.5	12.5	0.7	10.4	1.8	61.1	12.1	3.6	22.9	0.4

Sanitary Accommodation

Housing units (Total)	Have Latrine facilities	No Latrine facilities	Have Water supply	No Water supply	Have elec-tricity	No elec-tricity.
5216	3739	1477	1216	4000	2258	2958
100%	74.9	25.1	23.3	76.7	43.3	56.7

Source: Housing Census 1971, Vol. 2, Part 3, Galle, Matara and Hambantota district.

Table 14
Matara Town - Housing Units by period of construction, 1971

Period	Number	Percentage (%)
Before 1920	949	18.2
1921 - 1945	908	17.4
1946 - 1960	1413	27.1
1961 - 1965	834	16.0
1966 - 1971	1015	19.5
Years Unspecified	97	1.8
Total	5216	100.0

Source: Housing Census, 1971.

It is evident from the data in the above table that 28% of the existing housing stock in the town is of a semi-permanent or temporary nature, constructed out of material which deteriorates within a short time and cannot withstand the natural forces such as wind, rain, etc (Diag.6). These houses, which are owned by low income groups, are concentrated along the coastal belt of the town especially in Polhena (Ward 10) and Fort (Ward 1), in the commercial core area especially along old Tangalle road (Ward 2, Kotuwegoda), along Mainstreet alias Kumarathunga Mawatha at Station road (Ward 6 Mainstreet), along Broadway road alias Anagarika Dharmapala Mawatha close to Nupe market. Concentrations of these houses are also found in the peripheral area of Walpola(Ward 4) along the Uyanwatta Circular road. The data also shows that over 35% of the units were built prior to 1945 (i.e., they are at least 46 years old),with 18% out of this total being over 70 years old. A large number of these houses are in very poor condition and in need of major repairs. The majority of the street houses in Fort (Ward 1) and Mainstreet (Ward 6), which were built during the colonial period or right after the post independence period, are in a poor state of maintenance. Some are in ruin conditions although these houses are still inhabited.

The backlog housing units in the town amounts to 1,950 units[10]. It should be noted here that the great demand for commercial space in the commercial core has led to the rise in land values which resulted in many old residential buildings being converted into commercial units with haphazard alterations and renovations. This will deteriorate the urban form and image leading the two functions of "living" and "working" to exist in one room and will worsen the living conditions of the urban households. Data on this phenomenon is not found in the housing census of Sri Lanka. The majority of these housing units are found in Fort (Ward 1), Mainstreet (Ward 6), Kadeweediya (Ward 7) and Kotuwegoda (Ward 2).

The major portion of the housing units in town lack basic amenities and utilities, resulting in health and environmental hazards. As the above table shows, 25% of the housing units have no latrine facilities while 77% and 56% have no water service and no electricity (Diag. 6). The occupants of this segment belong to the vulnerable sections of the society and need immediate attention.

---

10 Final Report (U.D.A.), 1981.

Although the census of statistics categorises urban council areas (U.C.) as well as developed areas with basic amenities and utilities, the majority of the housing units in these areas are deprived of these services.

Diag.6: Housing Units by Nature of Construction and Sanitary Accommodation,1971

Nature of Construction

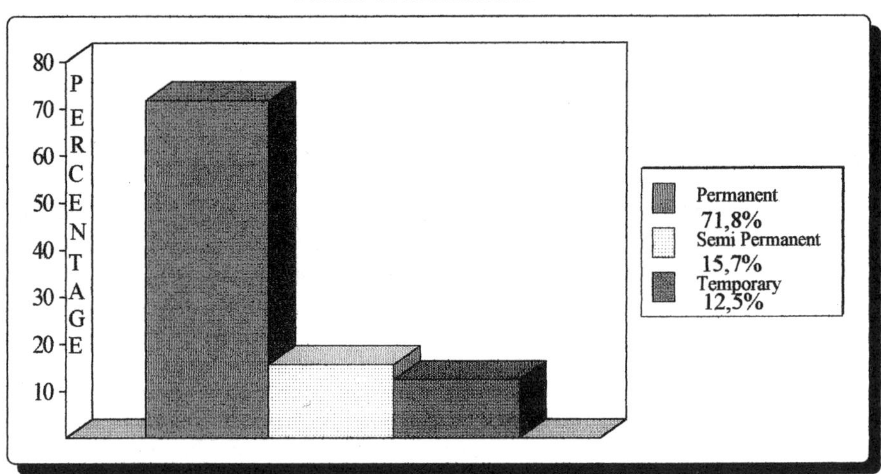

Latrine Facilities

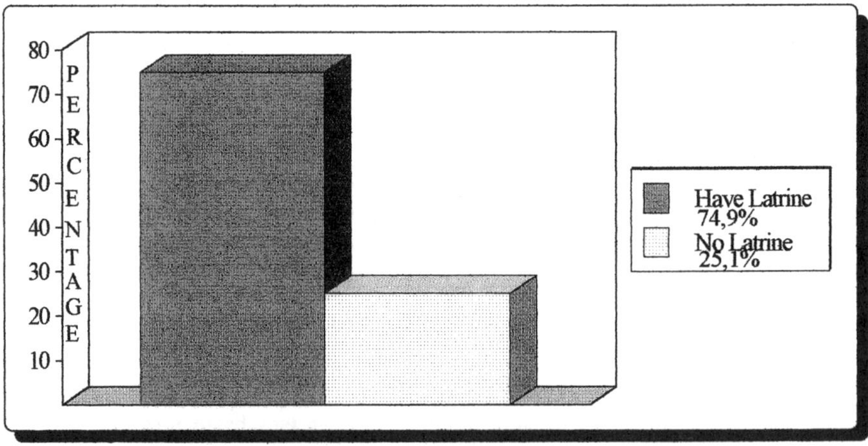

Water Supply

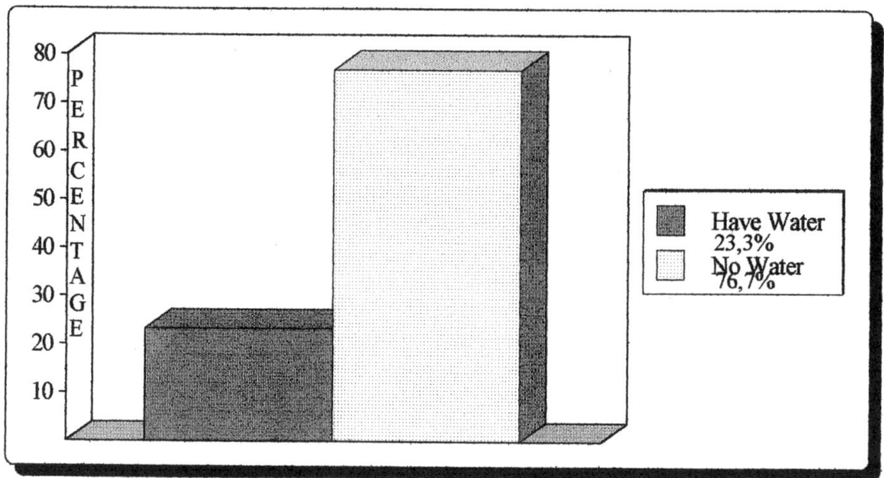

Electricity Supply

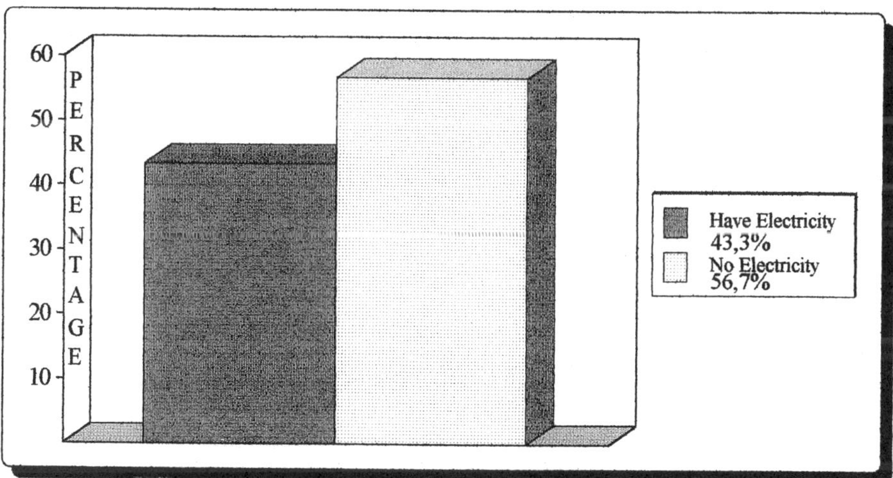

CHAPTER 3

3. The Economy of Matara Town

The economic activities of the Matara town consist of primary and modern sector activities. Fishing is the most important activity in the primary sector. Administration and trade activities are the most important activities in the modern sector. Due to the role of the town as headquarters of the district, all the major administrative functions are located here. The town serves as a major collective and trading centre for the agro-products of the hinterland, which extends beyond the district boundaries into the western part of the Hambantota district. In addition, it serves as a major service centre for the whole Matara district as well as for the adjoining Hambantota district. These services include the sectors of health, education, trade, commerce and transportation.

3.1. The Employment Structure of Matara

A comparative analysis of the population growth, potential work force, employed population and dependants between 1881 and 1981 (100 years) show that, with the expansion of the population, the potential work force grew by 4.1% per year while the employed population decreased from 55% to 24%. The dependency rate remained almost at the same level (Table 15). The main attribute to the poverty of the households in town is the high dependency load of the population in relation to the productive segment of the population (Diag. 7). The majority of these dependants consists of under 15 year age group while the elderly group over 59 years old is very low in this category. According to the 1871, 1971 and 1981 census, the population under 15 years represented 35%, 34% and 30.8% respectively. The over 59 years age groups were only 8.0% in 1971 and 9.4% in 1981.

Table 15
Distribution of Work force (Age Group 15 - 59 and over) and employed population by sex 1871, 1971, 1981., Matara U.C.

	1881			1971			1981		
	Total	Male	Female	Total	Male	Female	Total	Male	Female
Population	7522	3846	3676	36554	18648	17906	38843	19080	19763
Percentage %	100	51.1	48.9	100	51.1	48.9	100	49.1	50.8
Potential work force	4507	2152	2355	21179	10962	10217	23210	16630	11580
%	59.9	47.7	52.3	57.9	29.9	27.9	59.75	29.92	29.82
Employed Population	4129	1896	2233	9817	7972	1845	9257	7018	2239
%	54.9	25.1	29.6	26.8	21.8	5.0	23.83	18.06	5.76
Dependants	3015	1694	1321	15385	7686	7699	15633	7806	7827
%	40.0	22.5	17.5	42.0	21.0	21.0	40.24	20.09	0.15

Source: These calculations are based on Census of Statistics 1871, 1971 and 1981.

Diag.7: Employed and Dependents of the Total Population, Matara, 1981

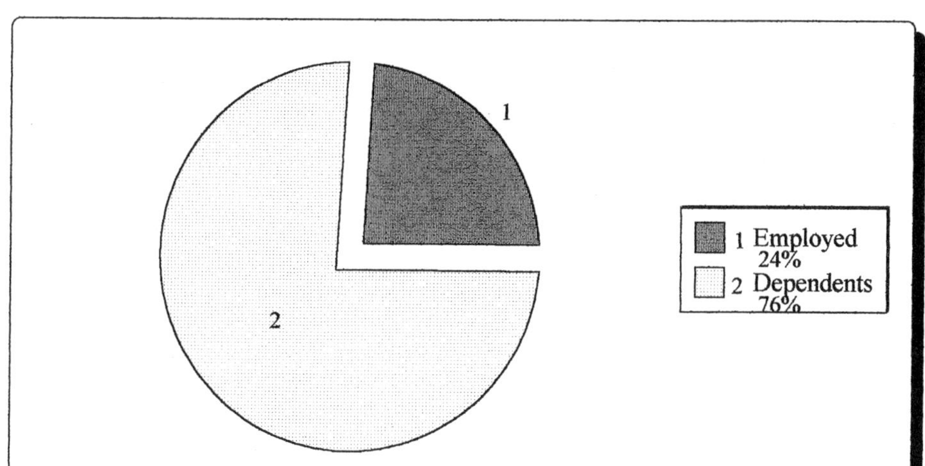

The economically non-active population (dependants) who belong to the potential work force are mostly female. As per 1981 census, the total female population between 15 and 59 years of age in the urban settlements of the Matara district was 22,812. Out of this total, 12,861 females (56%) have been engaged in domestic work whereas only 1% of the total male population in this age group has been engaged in domestic work. Employment among females decreased from 29.81 % in 1881 to 5.76% in 1981. The high percentage of working population and the high percentage of employed female population in 1881 can be mainly attributed to house maids, who constituted 32% of the total working population and 72% of the total female working population. Female participation in other professions was very low. However, this situation has been changing since. In the 1981 census, the total employed female population in the urban settlements of Matara District was 3,277. Out of this total only 1,100 (34%) were employed as housemaids while only 2% of the total male working population were engaged in this line of work. This data indicates that domestic employment is still mostly performed by females although numbers are decreasing.

Another interesting feature in the employment structure, is the large presence of females in professional, technical and related activities despite the contrast between female and male employed population. In 1981 there were 2,765 employees in this category in the urban settlements of Matara district. Almost 56% of these occupations were held by females. High concentration of females are found specially in teaching (65% of the employed teachers in the urban settlements of the Matara district were females).

According to the 1981 census, the total potential work force was 59.75% of the total population of the town. The male workforce and female workforce were 29.9% and 29.8% respectively. Against this available work force only 23.83% of the total population was employed. The percentage of the employed males and females of the total population was 18.06 and 5.76. The decline of employed population between 1881 and 1981 indicates the structural weakness of the urban economy of Matara.

Matara is not in the position to create more employment opportunities for the increasing workforce. The precarious economic situation of the town can also be evaluated by the following table.

Table 16
Employed Population of Matara U.C. by Age and Sex, 1981.

Age Groups	No. of Total	Employed Population Male	%	Female	%
10 - 14	92	37	0.5	55	0.6
15 - 29	2567	1881	20.3	686	7.4
30 - 59	5945	4522	48.8	1423	15.2
60 - 74	580	510	5.5	70	0.8
75 Over	73	68	0.7	5	---
Total	9257	7018	75.8	2239	24.2

Source: Statistical Branch, Matara U.C., 1981. (Unpublished Data)

Seven percent of the working population of the town belong to the dependent groups. Due to the poverty of Matara households, children under 15 years and adults over 59 years are forced to work to supplement the family income.

The other striking feature of the economy of the Matara town is, in addition to the high female unemployment rate, the high unemployment rate among educated groups. 1971 census statistics depict 23.80% out of 15,375 total unemployed population had six passed subjects in G.C.E. O/L (General Certificate Examination Ordinary Level).[1] 28.01% had grade 8 and up to G.C.E. O/L with 5 subjects (Table 17). The significant feature of the unemployed educated population is the very high female unemployment rate (72%) in comparison to male unemployment rate (28%) despite the fact that females are generally more qualified than the males.

[1] The minimum qualification to obtain a clerical job in public or private sector is to have 6 passed subjects with Arithmetic in G.C.E.(O/L)

Table 17
Unemployment distribution by level of education and sex, Matara U.C. 1981.

Total Unemployment		%	G.C.E. (A.L) with 3 subjects	% ----	G.C.E. (O.L.) with 6 subjects	% ---
Male	7686	----	144	0.93	873	5.67
Female	7689	----	353	2.30	2291	14.90
Total	15375	100.0	497	3.23	3164	20.57

	Grade 8 passed	%
Male	1387	9.02
Female	2920	18.99
Total	4307	18.01

Source: Census of Statistics 1971.
Structure Plan, Matara Town, Vol. 2., 1980/81.

The main reason for the unemployment of those who have obtained secondary education is caused today not so much by the total absence of jobs, but because of the lack of jobs that people want to do. The job preference of this category aspired to seek jobs (white collar) which not only involved a higher social status but also provided a regular and stable income.

The division of employed population into agriculture and non-agricultural activities shows that the agricultural sector activities in Matara in contrast to some Sri Lanka district headquarter towns like Badulla[2] (the population in 1981 was 32,954 and working population under agricultural sector was 25%) or North Ghanan's district headquarter towns like Thamala and Yendi[3] (the population in these two towns in 1960 were 58,183 and 16,096 respectively and the working population under agricultural sector were 17.5% and 65% respectively) is extremely low. (Table 18 & Diag.8)

---

2 Dicke. S., 1987, p. 105.
3 Mahn, C., 1980, p. 47.

Table 18
Percentage distribution of employed population by agriculture and non-agriculture, Matara U.C., 1871, 1971, 1981.

Employed population by sex (% of the Total Population)		Employed population (Total Percentage)	Agriculture	Non-Agriculture
			1871	
Total	54.89	100.00	11.63	88.37
Male	25.21	46.90	11.40	61.29
Female	29.68	54.10	0.23	27.08
			1971	
Total	26.86	100.00	4.50	95.50
Male	21.81	81.20	4.40	76.80
Female	05.05	18.80	0.10	18.70
			1981	
Total	23.83	100.00	3.40	96.60
Male	18.88	79.24	3.30	72.57
Female	4.95	20.76	0.20	24.03

Source: These calculations are based on Population Census of 1881, 1971, 1981.

The percentage of female agricultural workers in the town is lower than the male agricultural workers. This could be attributed to the misinterpretation of data in the census of statistics. The majority of the female workers over 15 years are categorised as non-productive housemaids, although they are engaged, in addition to their housework, in agricultural and trade sectors.[4]

As the table `occupational structure of the employed population' shows, the majority of the employers in the urban sector of the Matara district, between 1971 and 1981, had their working place in the tertiary sector which comprises 1, 2, 3, 4 and 5 occupational groups (Diag. 9). Although the total employment decreased by 1.7% between 1971 and 1981, the tertiary sector employment grew from 54% in 1971 to 63% in 1981 in the urban sector of Matara district. All the occupational groups in this sector, except the fourth (sale workers decreased by 131 persons), experienced a minor increase. The increase of 1,301 new jobs in this sector compared to the high unemployment rate (45 %), is just a drop of water on a hot stone in the urban sector of Matara district.

4 There are some women sellers who sell agricultural products and fish at daily and periodic markets in Matara town.

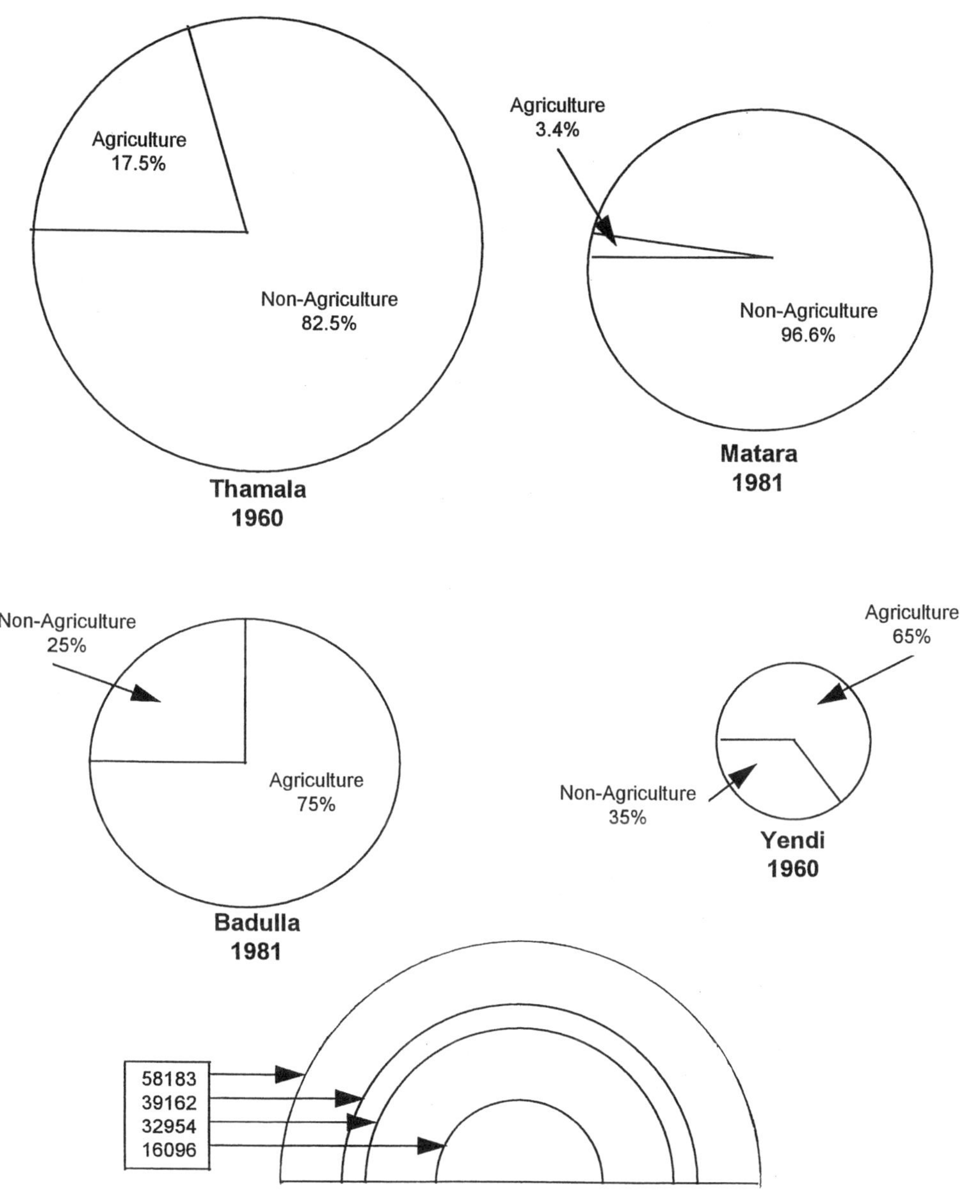

Diag.8:

Distribution of employed population by agriculture and non-agricultue, Matara, Badulla (1981); Thamala, Yendi (1960).

Table 19
Employed Population of the Urban Sector of Matara District by Occupation, Sex and Status in 1971, 1981 and Employed Population of Matara U.C. by Occupation in 1981.

Occupational groups(*1	1971	Male	Female	1981	Male	Female
Professional, Technical & related Workers	1965	996	969	2765	1224	1541
%	12.2	6.2	6.0	17.5	7.7	9.8
Administration & Managerial Workers	118	104	14	260	244	16
%	0.7	0.6	0.1	1.6	1.5	0.1
Clerical Workers	1151	1370	181	1828	1392	436
%	9.6	8.5	1.1	11.6	8.8	2.8
Sales Workers	3104	2945	159	2973	2797	176
%	19.3	18.3	1.0	18.8	17.7	1.1
Service Workers	1887	1144	743	2100	1447	653
%	11.7	7.1	4.6	13.3	9.2	4.1
Production related Workers, Transport equipment Opera - tors	4992	4363	629	3928	3599	329
%	31.0	27.1	3.9	24.8	22.7	2.1
Agricultural, Animal husbandry, Forestry Workers & Fishermen	1744	1644	80	1570	1519	51
%	10.8	10.3	0.5	9.9	9.6	0.3
Workers not classified by occupation	726	617	109	391	316	75
%	4.5	3.8	0.7	2.5	2.0	0.5
Total	16087	13203	2884	15815	12538	3277
%	100.0	82.0	18.0	100.0	79.2	20.8

Occupational Groups	STATUS		Matara U.C.	% of District's Total
	Semi-Govt. Employee	Govt. Employee		
1.	2380	385	1620	58.58
%	86.1	13.9	17.5	-----

(contd. in the following page)

2.	116	144	153	58.54
%	44.6	55.4	1.7	-----
3.	1572	256	1070	58.33
%	86.0	14.0	11.6	-----
4.	187	2786	1740	58.52
%	6.3	93.7	18.8	-----
5.	662	1438	1230	58.57
%	31.5	68.5	13.2	-----
6.	1190	2738	2298	58.50
%	30.3	69.7	24.8	-----
7.	75	1497	918	58.47
%	4.6	95.4	9.9	-----
8.	158	236	228	58.31
%	39.6	60.0	2.5	-----
Total	6335	9480	9257	58.51
%	40.0	60.0	100.0	-----

Source: Population Census, Matara District, Vol. 1, Part 7.,1971.
Population Census, Matara District, Vol. 1, Part V11, 1981.
Statistical Branch, Matara U.C., 1981.

Remarks: Occupation refers to the type of work performed by the person irrespective of the industry concerned or his place of work.

Diag.9: Occupational Structure, Employed Population, Urban Sector, Matara - District, 1981

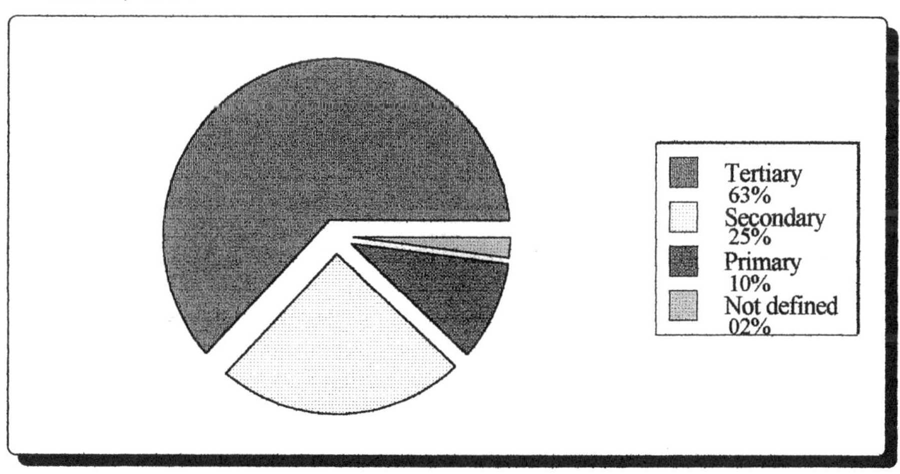

The secondary sector consisting of the occupational groups production related workers and transport equipment workers takes the second place in this category. The secondary sector decreased from 31% in 1971 to 24.8% in 1981, by 6.2%.

Although primary sector (No. 7 in the Table) employees decreased by 0.1% during this decade, the number of fishermen who play a major role in the urban economy of Matara district (in Weligama Urban council, Matara Urban Council and Dondara Council) increased from 899 in 1971 to 1,017 persons in 1981. This increase was mainly contributed by the migration of Singhala fisherman to Matara district from Trincomalee due to communal riots.

An examination of the employment status (Table 19) indicates, although the percentage of private sector employees is higher than public sector employees, government and semi-government institutions play a major role in creating job opportunities to the urban labour force of Matara District. Almost 40% of the urban employees in the Matara District in 1981 were employed by these institutions. Creation of new jobs in government and semi-government sectors was mostly done not due to necessity but to keep promises which had been made to the public during the parliamentary elections. These contributions are mostly administered by party supporters of the government. Mostly recruited are family members, relatives and party supporters.

The occupational structure of the Matara U.C. reflects the similar features of the Matara district's urban sector as Matara U.C. possess 55% of the total urban population and 58% of the total employed urban population of the district. According to 1981 population census Matara U.C. area had 9,257 employees (58% of the total employment in the Matara district urban sector). In each of these occupational groups it comprised more than 58% of the urban sector employees of the district. The tertiary sector is the major employer offering 62.8% of the total employment of the Matara U.C.. The secondary sector activities consists of 24.8% of the town's total employment. The primary sector constitutes only 9.9% of the town's total employed population.

The division of employed population into industries indicates the kind of establishment in which their occupations are performed. Detailed data for Matara U.C. in this regard is available neither in the census of 1971 and 1981 nor in statistical branch of Matara U.C. Therefore the author was compelled to use the urban sector statistics of Matara district for this purpose. It will be reasonable to assume that the occupational structure of the districts urban sector seems to reflect the occupational characteristics of the Matara town without any distortion, since the majority of the district's urban employees (58%) have their working place in the Matara U.C. area. The table "Employed Population by Industry" depicts the occupational structure of the urban sector in which the largest segment (36.1%) is categorised in community, social and personal services. The major fields of activity in this category is public administration (27%), education (37%) and health (10%). The high employment percentage in this sector is mainly attributed to the town's hegemony as the major service centre to its district as well as to the adjoining districts (specifically to Hambantota district; Table 20 & Diag. 10).

Table 20
Employed Population by Industry, Urban Sector,
Matara District, 1971 & 1981.

Industry	1971 (Total)	%	1981 (Total)	%
1. Agriculture, Hunting, Forestry & Fishing	1835	11.4	1578	9.9
2. Mining & Quarrying	14	0.1	15	0.1
3. Manufacturing	1460	9.1	1239	7.8
4. Electricity, Gas & Water	75	0.5	110	0.7
5. Construction	591	3.7	552	3.5
6. Whole Sale, Retail Trade, Restaurants & Hotels	3487	21.7	3882	24.6
7. Transport, Storage & Communication	1328	8.3	1210	7.7
8. Finance, Insurance, Real State & Business Services	148	0.9	421	2.7
9. Community, Social & Personal Services	5266	32.7	5716	36.1
10. Activities not adequately defined	1883	11.6	1092	6.9
All Industries (Total)	16087	100.0	15815	100.0

Source: Census of Population, Matara District, vol. 1 - Part 7, 1974.
Census of Population & Housing, Matara District, Vol. 1., Part. V111, 1981.

Remarks: Industry refers to the branch of economic activity in which a person is employed or in other words, to the kind of establishment or place of work in which his occupation performed.

Diag.10: Employed Population by Industry, Urban Sector, Matara District, 1981

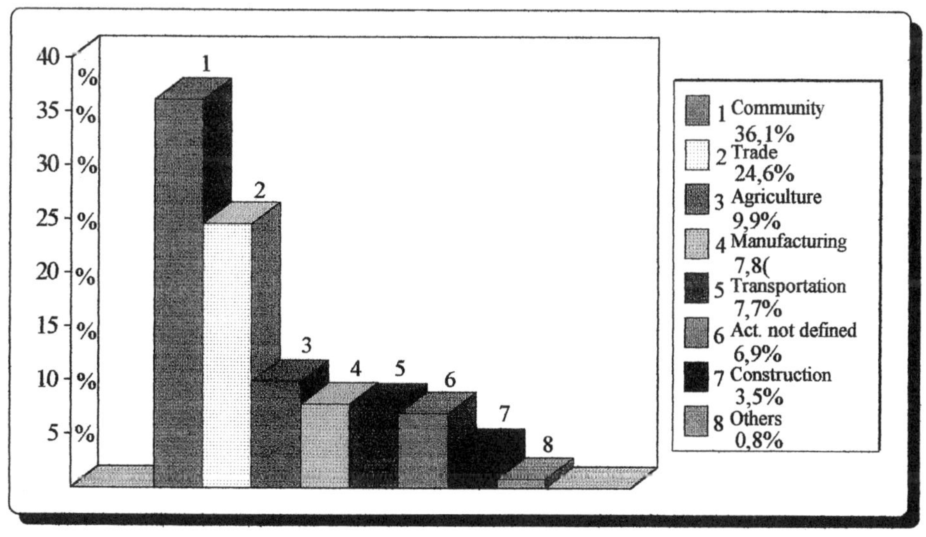

Retail and wholesale trade (24.6%) are second in this category. The next major group is agriculture, forestry and hunting and fishing (9.9%), which for this coastal town obviously represents employment in fishing activities. Closely following are manufacturing (7.8%) and transportation, storage and communications (8.4%). Manufacturing mainly consists of coir products, furniture, textile, spinning and weaving, cloth painting and varied products of rice and coconut mills. The major industries in the town include coconut oil mills, paddy hulling (de-husking) mills, power looms, and a number of servicing workshops. There are a few Batik textile painting establishments, and furniture making units also found in the Matara urban area.

An examination of the growth of employment by industries over the decade shows that the two major industry sectors in the community, social personal service (No. 9) and wholesale/retail trade restaurants hotels (No. 6) had experienced a minor increase of 3.4% and 1.9% respectively.

Job opportunities in the next three major sectors of hunting, agriculture, forestry and fishing (No. 1), manufacturing (No. 3), and transport[5], storage and communication (No. 7) decreased by 1.5%, 1.3%, 0.9 % respectively. Minor sectors like electricity, gas and water (No. 4), construction (No. 5), mining and quarrying (No. 2) show a stagnation trend while the sectors finance, insurance, real estate and business[6] services (No. 8) increased by 1.8%.

After discussing the employment by industry and occupations, it is important to portray here the employment rate by wards in Matara U.C. to find the structural weakness in the economy of the town in different locations. The workforce by wards (15 years to 59 years) for 1971, employed population by wards 1971, 1981 growth of job opportunities over the decade, commercial units by wards for 1981 and agriculture workers by wards 1971 and 1981 are reflected in the Table 21.

---

5 According to 1981 Census, about 125 vehicle drivers lost their jobs over the decade.

6 The most important activities in this sector are Monetary, insurance and other business services.

Table 21
Employed Population by Ward
Matara U.C., 1971 - 1981.

Ward No.	Population 1971	Population 1981	Population increase/ decrease over decade	Work Force (15 years & 59 years) 1971	Work Force 1981	Employed Population 1971	Employed Population 1981
1.	2179	1992	+ 187	1621	----	1147	503
2.	3580	3833	+ 253	2216	----	1070	1109
3.	2082	2388	+ 306	1189	----	518	892
4.	3616	3766	+ 150	2008	----	822	852
5.	3888	4782	+ 895	2246	----	903	1092
6.	2239	2183	- 56	1369	----	666	671
7.	3858	4129	+ 271	2195	----	1053	1077
8.	4817	5011	+ 194	2664	----	1207	1200
9.	2928	2991	+ 63	1576	----	599	541
10.	2856	2956	+ 100	1542	----	637	522
11.	4511	4812	+ 301	2553	----	1195	1097
Total	36554	38843	+2289	21179	----	9817	9257

Ward No.	% of total Work Force (Employed Population) 1971	1981	Increase/ decrease over the decade	Commercial units	Agriculture 1971	Agriculture 1981	Increase/ decrease over the decade
1.	70.75	----	- 644	15	181	47	- 134
2.	48.28	----	+ 39	369	16	27	+ 11
3.	43.56	----	+ 75	13	1	21	+ 20
4.	40.93	----	+ 30	39	37	20	- 17
5.	40.20	----	+ 189	26	63	69	+ 6
6.	48.64	----	+ 5	258	7	6	- 1
7.	47.97	----	+ 24	192	4	9	+ 5
8.	45.30	----	- 7	40	29	31	+ 2
9.	38.00	----	- 58	8	72	61	- 11
10.	41.30	----	- 115	21	6	9	+ 3
11.	46.80	----	- 98	106	26	15	- 15
Total	46.35	----	- 560	1037	442	315	- 169

Source: Census of Population 1971 & unpublished data of 1981.

Remarks: The Work Force by Wards is not given for 1981. Therefore the author was compelled to use the unpublished population data of 1981 for this purpose. The number of inhabitants in these two sources do not tally with each other. There is a differnce of 319 people.

Wards.

1. Fort	2. Kotuwegoda	
3. Meddawatta	4. Walpola	
5. Uyanwatta	6. Main Street	
7. Kadeweediya	8. Welegoda	
9. Totamuna	10. Polhena	11. Weliweriya.

The workforce and the employed population by wards in 1971[7] indicate Fort, the administrative centre and the residential area of the higher social groups which grew since colonial era, has the highest employment rate (70%) among the wards although it has only 1.46% of the total commercial units of the town. The majority of these employees are engaged in white collar jobs. An examination of the employments between 1971 and 1981 shows a decline of employment by 644. The agricultural workers decreased by 134 over the decade. This could be attributed to the out-migration of employees to other centres, especially to Colombo for better employment opportunities. This ward is experiencing a decline of population since 1971 due to the conservation laws as discussed earlier.

The employment rate of the commercial core area (comprised of Kotuwegoda (No. 2) Mainstreet (No. 6) and Kadeewediya (No. 7) in which the majority of the Muslims (88%) and the other minorities live), lies slightly above the average employment rate of the town, although it possesses almost 79% of its total commercial units (Map 18). The number of employees increased only by 98 over the decade. The agricultural workers in this area, except Kotuwegoda (No. 2) is very low and insignificant. The given data indicates the structural weakness of the economy of the commercial core area.

Weliweriya (No. 11) which is a ward adjoining to the commercial core area, also has an employment rate slightly above the average values. The two important roads Matara-Hakmana and Matara-Akuressa, which pass through this ward, generated commercial units. 10.2% of the total commercial units of the town lie in this ward. The total number of employees decreased by 98 over the decade. The agricultural workers decreased by 15.

The remaining wards (No. 3, 4, 5, 8, 9, 10 and 11) have lower employment rates than the average rate. These wards are solely residential areas and have very few commercial units. Some lie in the peripheral areas of the town (No. 10, No. 4) with severe physical constraints and the others (No. 9, 3, 5) lie close to the commercial core area but with physical constraints and poor accessibility. These wards, except Maddewatta (No. 3), are densely inhabited by low and middle class groups. The wards No. 3, 4, 5, 8 and 9 have a substantial amount of agricultural workers. There was a decline of employees in the wards, No. 10, 9, 8 while wards No. 3, 4. 5 experienced a slight increase over the decade.

---

7 Absence of detailed data in 1981 Census compelled the author to use the 1971 Census for this purpose. It can be assumed that these data are still applicable to the current situation as there were no substantial structural changes over the decade.

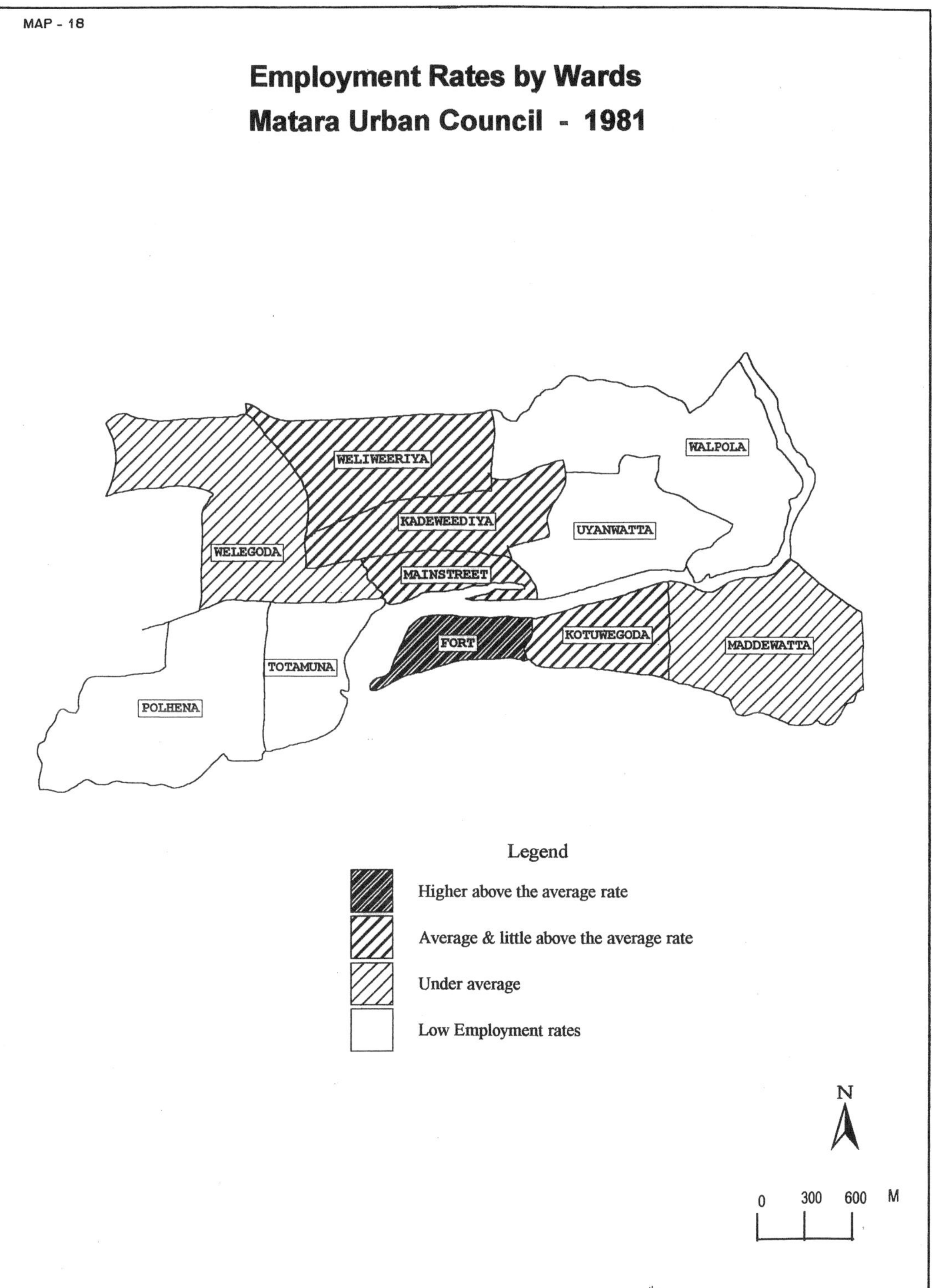
MAP - 18
Employment Rates by Wards
Matara Urban Council - 1981
WALPOLA
WELIWEERIYA
KADEWEEDIYA
UYANWATTA
WELEGODA
MAINSTREET
FORT
KOTUWEGODA
MADDEWATTA
TOTAMUNA
POLHENA
Legend
Higher above the average rate
Average & little above the average rate
Under average
Low Employment rates
N
0 300 600 M

3.2. Primary Sector

The primary sector activities of the town consist of agriculture and fishery.

3.2.1. Agriculture

Although since the colonial period the agricultural land area of the town had been reduced substantially, high utilisation of urban land area still remains a predominant feature of the urban landscape of Matara Town. This shows the unbroken traditional agricultural roots up to the present time. The agricultural sector land use holds the second major place in the land use of the town with 24.05%. This is one of the major factors which reflects the dominance of rural characteristics in the town. As an employer it plays a minor role in the economy of the town. In 1981, only 3.4% of the total employed population of the town worked in the agricultural sector.[8] The agricultural sector of the town can be regarded as commercial as well as subsistence.

The cultivated land area can be further divided into three major categories(Table 22).

Table 22
Agricultural Land Use - Matara U.C. 1981
Total Land Area of Matara Town is 808.64 hectares

Crop	Land Area	Percent
Paddy	12.23	6.29
Coconut	162.22	83.42
Other crops (includes home gardens)	20.00	10.29
Total	194.45	100.00

These agricultural activities are spread mainly over the eastern, north-eastern and western parts of the town, namely Polhena, Maddawatta, Katuwegoda, Piladuwa and Welegoda. Polhena and Meddawatta have a wide range of coconut land (Map 19). These are smallholdings which do not exceed more than 3 acres(1.21 ha). The surplus production is mostly sold to the coconut collectors (middle men) who in their turn sell these coconuts to coconut sellers at the weekly and daily markets of the town or export them to the hinterland of Matara District.

Paddy cultivation is confined to Piladuwa area (Map 19). A large portion of this land lies along the Nilwala river and is susceptible to floods. Due to frequent floods most of these paddy lands become unusable. The size of these fields is very small and does not exceed one hectare. This is a subsistence activity of the urban farmers. The physical constraint areas, which account for 90.12 hectares[9] of the total land area of the town, could be utilised for paddy cultivation after the completion of the Nilwala river flood project. This could increase the employment, production and the income of the households.

---

8 Population Census, 1981.

9 Structure Plan, Matara Town, 1980 / 81.

MAP - 19

Agricultural Land area of Matara Town, 1984

Legend

- Coconut
- Other Utilization
- Vegetable
- Flood Prone Areas
- Marshy Lands
- Paddy

Note :- Flood prone areas are used for Paddy and vegetable cultivation during the off Monsoon period.

Source :- Structure Plan - Matara Town 1980/81
Matara Town - Urban Development Authority, 1981.
Planing office, Matara U.C., 1984
Own observation 1984.

Market gardening is carried on in a small scale in the Piladuwa area along the Nilwala basin. According to oral information by the planning officer at Kachcheri, the average size of the plots is between 10-20 perches (250-450 q.m). The cultivation methods are very traditional. Chemical fertilisers and pesticides are rarely used. This market gardening is done not only by full-time farmers but mostly by people who are engaged in other sector activities. This is a free time activity for them which brings supplementary income for the households[10]. The major vegetable varieties are beans, tomatoes, cucumber, eggplant, fingernails (Occapi) and vegetable leaves . The main fruits are papayas, mangoes and bananas. The surplus vegetable and fruit production in this area is sold at the weekly and daily markets of the town. Intensification of these vegetable plots, better fertilisation, watering and manuring, could create more jobs and increase the production and income of the households. Home gardens and other crop lands constitute 10.22% of the total land area of the town and play a vital role in providing food to the households. These are therefore vital and functional units for different socio-economic households. The cultivators of these home gardens are mostly women. Fertiliser used in these gardens is household garbage. The production is low and mostly consumed by the households. Reorientation of the crops, that is change in the choice of crops such as vegetable instead of many trees, to adjust to the needs of the households as well as to market conditions is needed. Improvement and intensification of home gardens, that is better seed and planting material, better fertilisation, manuring and watering, can substantially contribute to the solution of nutrition, employment and financial problems of the town.

3.2.2. Fisheries

Although only 2.02% of the total population of the Matara district is engaged in the fisheries sector, the production is substantial, especially when compared with the total island production. This district's fishery contribution to the national production had increased from 2.6% in 1980 to 4.6 % in 1984 .[11]

Unlike in the north and east of Sri Lanka (Jaffna, Batticaloa, Muttur), the Matara district has no fisherwomen. According to the 1981 census fishery was a male dominated industry. The reason for this was probably cultural. In the north and east this industry is mostly performed by non-Buddhists (Hindu, Catholics & Muslims). The percentage of those joining the fishing industry from the Roman Catholic group is higher than that of the Sinhala Buddhist group on the island .[12]

In Matara District marine fishing is predominantly performed by Sinhala Buddhist fishermen. The influence of the church has made fisher folk, in some areas of the island, followers of Catholic traditions. Catholic fishermen in Beruwela, Alutgama, Payagala, Maggona, Moratuwa and Negombo (southwest coast) rear poultry and pigs etc., to make additional income. This feature is absent in Matara district where

10 This information is derived from a conversation with the Planning Officer at Matara Kachcheri, 1987.

11 Netrakavesna, M., 1985, P.13.

12 Compare with Fernando, S. 1984, pp. 110 -162, Wickramasingha, M., 1964.,pp. 52 - 55, Ven'ble Dharmakirti, Sri- Mirissa Indaratana, 1980.

Buddhists are predominant. Due to the fact that the Matara district is predominantly a Buddhist area, 50 to 70% of its production will be consumed in this region.[13]

The marketing system of fish in Sri Lanka operates through a set of intermediaries performing all the way from producer to the final consumer. The commercial units of the fish marketing system can be placed under three categories: fish assemblers, fish wholesalers, and fish retailers[14].

Thirty to fifty percent of the district's fish production is sent to Colombo and Kandy and the rest is sold in the local markets and in the hinterland markets such as Ratnapura, Balangoda, Badulla, Udawalawe, Embilipitiya and Bandarawela.

In general, facilities serving the fishing industry are limited. In particular, there is lack of repair facilities while difficulties are also experienced in obtaining spare parts and replacement fishing gear. There are only two ice plants in the district which produce only 50% of the total requirement of the district. Only two boat yards are in operation in the district[15].

The district's marine fishery is handicapped by a number of other continuing problems. The inadequacy of sheltered harbour facilities is a major handicap, the only fishing harbour being at Mirissa. In centres such as Kottegoda, Weligama, Kapparatota and Matara, the anchorages are exposed and boats left vulnerable to storm damage. The presence of underwater rock and coral reefs at some fishing centres is a hazard that fishing vessels have to face. Serious damages and substantial financial losses occur as a result of collision with these rocks and coral reefs. Some fish landing centres are handicapped by bad accessibility. Some roads are not motorable.

Fishery industry plays a very important role in the primary sector of the town. The fishermen population in Matara town has increased from 177 persons in 1881 to 749 persons in 1987.[16] This was only 3.8% of the total fishermen population of the district and 1.9% of the total population of the Matara Town in 1987. This increase, as discussed earlier, was attributed to the migration of fishermen from northern and eastern parts of Sri Lanka due to political unrest. The following table indicates the family distribution and the number of fishermen in the Matara U.C. area.

---

13 Netrakavesna, M., 1985.

14 Glässer, T., Fischerei und Fischereiwirtschaft im nordlichen Ceylon., Beitr. Südasien forsch, 1983, 1984

15 Ibid.

16 Population Census 1881 & Dept. of Fisheries 1987.

Table 23.
Distribution of the Fishing Population in Matara U.C. Area 1987

Location	Families	Fishermen	percent (%)
Polhena	20	105	14
Totamuna	83	397	53
Ginigasmulla	41	247	33
Total	144	749	100

Source: Fisheries Dept. Matara, 1987.

The highest concentration of fishing families is found in Polhena with 83 followed by Ginigasmulla with 41. Fishing is solely performed by men while women take part in connected secondary activities such as drying and conservation ,for example the production of Maldive fish, salted fish and Jadi.

The town's contribution to the district's fish production is very low. According to the Fisheries Department, Matara U.C. area caught only 1.6% (150 metric tons) of the district's total catch (9,369 metric tons) in 1987.[17] The low prodution figures were caused mainly due to the application of the traditional methods. According to the census of department of fisheries, Only 3.1% of the district's modern fishing vessels were used in Matara U.C. area (Photo 15 & 16).

The marketing of fish in Matara U.C. area is mainly done by the Muddalali (Middlemen) and the majority of the fishermen are indebted to them. In 1987, there were three Mudalalis who controlled the marketing of fish in Matara town. A high percentage of this production is sold at their stalls in the weekly and daily markets of the town[18].

3.3. Industry

The direction of industrial activities in Sri Lanka has been greatly affected by the political ideology of the particular government in power.

The goal of industrialization after the independence of Sri Lanka until 1977 was the establishment of import substitute industries and the creation of more employment in this sector. Local raw material and labour intensive techniques were given priority to achieve this goal. The public sector industry was considered as the main instrument for industrialization.

In 1977 the open economy was introduced. The main objective of this phase was the creation of employment through industrial exports. Unlike in the previous phase, greater reliance was placed on the private sector to promote industrial development.

---

17 Dept. of Fisheries, Matara, 1987.

18 Ref.Glässer,1983 for northern Sri Lanka.

The term "manufacturing" cannot be taken to mean all that it connotes in industrialized countries. Factories in the sense of using machines, power, organised labour and high capital are generally absent here.

Cottage industries such as coir, mat weaving, broom making and basket weaving are done either by hand-operated machines or by hand using very limited primitive tools. The majority of the district's industries utilize simple and indigenous machinery and equipment while some tea factories, oil mills and rice mills use imported and mostly old machinery.[19]

Almost all the manufacturing industries in the Matara district are agro-based which mainly use local raw material such as tea, coconut, rubber, cinnamon, citronella and paddy.

The contribution of these industries to the development of the Matara district in terms of income and employment generating capacity, is very low. In 1981 only 8.8%, 12,877 persons of the total working population of the district found jobs in the manufacturing sector.[20] According to the classification of industries, the number of employees indicated that 93.22% of the industries had lower than 5 employees.[21]

The development of the large/small scale and cottage industries are of vital importance in the generation of income and employment. This could help to promote the economic growth of the regional economy and reduce the unemployment rate in a district with high population densities and high rates of unemployment.

If the distribution pattern of the industries is taken into consideration, a higher concentration of manufacturing industries in the Matara district is located in rural areas than in the urban areas. Only 25.3% of the district's total industries are located within urban limits. The distribution of the large and small scale and cottage industries shows that only 10.6% and 24.0% of these industries are located within the urban boundaries of the district[22].

The distribution pattern of industries among the urban centres of the district indicates that 56% of the large/small scale industries and 78% of the cottage industries are located in Matara town. This proves its hegemony as a commercial centre over the other commercial centres in the district[23](Map 20).

Tea and rubber factories are completely absent in Matara Town as the surrounding areas of Matara have no such cultivation. Akuressa (situated in the central zone) is the only urban centre in the district which has five tea and three rubber factories. This is due to the fact that this town is surrounded by tea and rubber growing areas.

---

19 State sector factories utilise more sophisticated imported or locally fabricated machines while private sector mostly use old machines.

20 Population Census 1981.

21 Hossein, N., 1985.

22 Village Survey, Dept. of Census of statistics, 1979.

23 Ibid.

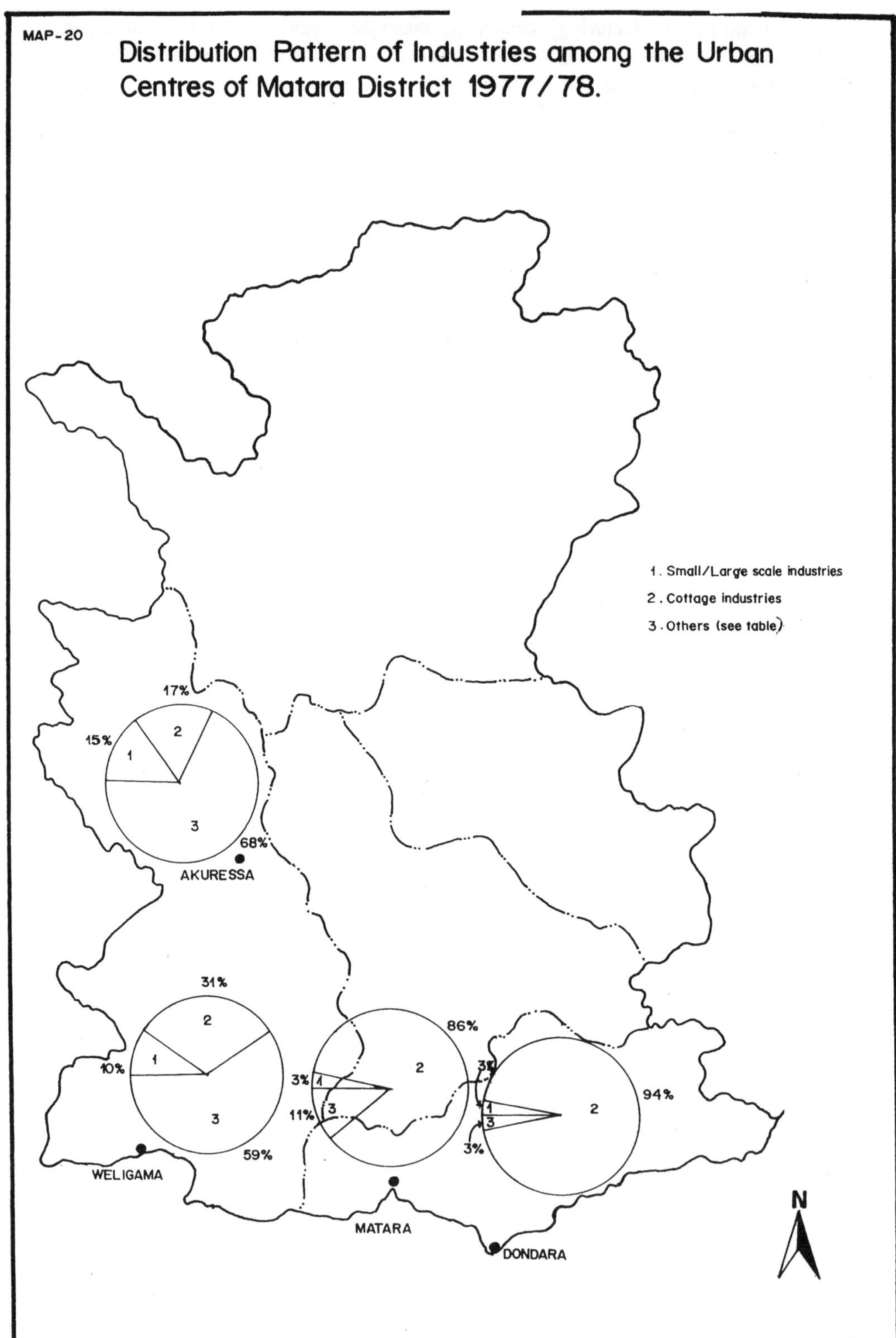
MAP-20
Distribution Pattern of Industries among the Urban Centres of Matara District 1977/78.
1. Small/Large scale industries
2. Cottage industries
3. Others (see table)
17%
15%
1
2
3
68%
AKURESSA
31%
10%
59%
WELIGAMA
86%
3%
11%
MATARA
94%
3%
DONDARA
N
0 2 4 6 KM

Matara has the highest number of rice (6) and coconut (5) mills[24]. Among the cottage industries, coir plays a major role followed by carpentry. Almost 50% of the coir industry units of this district and 15% of the district's carpentry units are located within the boundary of the Matara U.C.

A comparison of the registered industrial establishments in the Matara U.C. area between 1975 and 1986 reveals a substantial increase in the number of establishments. This proves the impact of the open economic policy on the growth of the industries in the Matara town (Table 24).

Table 24
The growth of registered industrial establishments
by type between 1975 and 1986 - Matara U.C.

Type of Industry	Number of Establishments		increase	
	1975	1986	numerical	%
Service Industry	79	196	117	14.8
Metal related manufacturing	11	37	26	23.6
Textile	-	6	6	-
Food and Beverage	41	55	14	3.4
Carpentry	15	22	7	3.6
Leather	-	08	8	-
Total	146	324	178	12.1

Source: License Register 1975/1986, Matara U.C.
* Some cottage industry units in the town are not registered.
* The majority of the service industries constitute repair centres and garages.

This increase was mainly attributed to the growth of the service and metal related industries. The rapid expansion of the transport sector led to the spring up of garages and other repair units in every corner of the urban landscape in the country. The total number of road vehicales registered with the register of motor vehicales amounted to 365,275 at the end of 1986 revealing an increase of 15% as against 318,301 in 1985[25].

The industrial sector plays a minor role in the economy as well as in the urban landscape of Matara town. According to the 1981 census, only 20% of the total working population engaged in the industrial sector. The industries occupied only 0.98% (8.01 hectare) of the total landscape of the town. The total consumption of electricity by the industries was only 8.3% of the town's total consumption.

The division of industries on the basis of capital shows that the cottage industries are large in number (89%) followed by small scale industries (10.56%).

---

24 village survey, 1979.

25 Review of the Economy, 1986.

Table 25
Scale of Industry - Matara U.C. 1980

Scale of Industries	No.of.Units	Percentage(%)
Large - Scale Industries	2	0.15
Small - Scale Industries	138	10.56
Cottage Industries	1167	89.29
Total	1307	100.00

According to Table 27, the majority (51%) of the industries fall into the category "basic metal and machinery" followed by "agro-based industries" with 15%.

The agro-based Harischandra and Odris de Silva companies could be identified as the largest companies in town. These two establishments occupy almost 26% of the total land area within the industrial sector and consume 50% of the total electricity consumption by industry. In terms of employment these two establishments absorb 39% of the total working population who are engaged in the industrial sector of the town.[26]

The main product of Oderis De Silva is coconut oil while the Harischandra company produces various kinds of food products and soap. In 1986 the Harischandra company bought 67,988,036 rupees worth of raw materials for its production. From this total, 99% of the raw materials went to the production of foodstuffs.[27]

Among the large and small scale industries, manufacturing and processing play a dominant role followed by the service industry (Table 26).

Table 26
Type of Industries (Large/Small scale), Matara U.C., 1981.

Type	No.of Establishments	Percentage (%)
Manufacturing & Processing	66	47.00
Assembling & Fitting	12	9.00
Servicing	62	44.00
Total	140	100.00

Source: I.D.B. (Industrial Development Board and Ministry of Industrial and Statistic Affairs), in: Structure Plan - Matara Town, Vol. 1.

The type of industry can also be classified by the type of product they produce (Table 27 & Diag. 11).

26 Structure Plan - Matara Town, Vol. 1 & 2 , 1980/81 Preliminary Report 1980, Urban Development Authority 1980. Final Report 1981, Urban Development Authority 1981.

27 Annual Audit Report 1986., Harischandra Mills Limited, Matara. I am very much indebted to my sister-in-law Chandramali who helped me to get these data.

Table 27
Industries by type of products, Matara U.C. 1981.

Industry	No.of.Units	Percentage (%)
1. Basic Metal & Machinery	71	51.0
2. Agro-based	20	15.0
3. Food,Beverages & Cereals	9	6.0
4. Chemicals	9	6.0
5. Garments	7	5.0
6. Weaving & Textile	4	3.0
7. Electrical Goods	4	3.0
8. Leather & Rubber	4	3.0
9. Wood & Paper	4	3.0
10. Others	4	3.0
11. Plastic Goods	2	1.0
12. Animal Goods	2	1.0
Total	140	100.0

Source: Structure Plan - Matara Town, Vol. 1, 1980 / 81.

Diag. 11: Industries by Type of Products, Matara, 1981

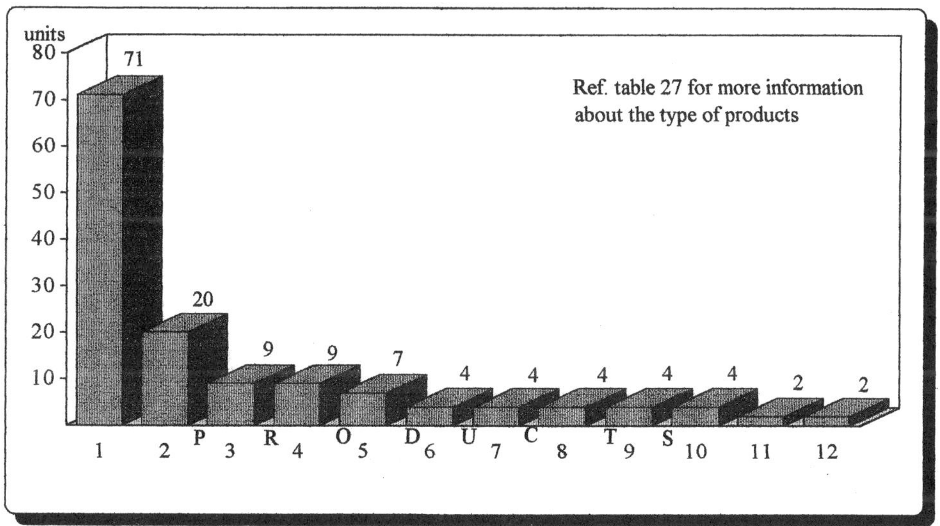

High percentage of the family owned industries in Matara town are cottage based and of very small scale. The capital investments for these are often very low. These industries are equipped with mostly primitive technology which results in poor quality of the product. Therefore the products are not competitive with their counterparts and are sold on the rural markets.

The economic behaviour of these family entrepreneurs is mostly traditional and 'rentencapitalistic'. This prevents high investments and slows development. In such a situation the process of innovation which starts from the towns and spreads into the rural areas cannot be realised.

In addition to these facts it should also be mentioned here that the employment generating capacity of these industries is very low. The labour force in the largest industrial establishment of Matara, Harischandra Mills, has decreased by 3 employees during the period 1980 - 1987.

When cottage industries are classified, 81% of housing units account for coir industries and the second largest share (11%) belong to carpentry (Table 28). By no means are all of the 1,167 housing units involved in the cottage industry operating on a full-time basis. Many serve to provide a supplementary source of income over and above the return from fishing or farming.

Table 28
Type of Cottage Industries - Matara U.C., 1977 / 78.

Industry	No. of Housing Units	Percentage (%)
Coir	940	81.0
Carpentry(Furniture)	131	11.0
Tailoring & Needle Work (Cloths)	32	3.0
Metal Work	29	2.0
Textiles	19	2.0
Tags	12	1.0
Bricks & Tile Work	4	---
Total	1167	100.0

Source: Basic Village Statistics 1978, In: Structure Plan - Matara town, 1980/81

3.3.1. Coir Yarn Industry[28]

The coir yarn industry should be given special attention here as it plays an important role in the economic activities of the fishing community in town.

This industry is based on the coconut husk which is used as a source of fibre, fuel and soil & moisture conservation.An estimated 24% of the Matara district's husk production goes into the fibre production, while the rest is used as a source of fuel and moisture conservation[29]

---

28 Production of coconut fibre products.

29 Montipa, M., 1985, p. 31.

Fifty percent of the Matara district's housing units, which are engaged in the coir yarn industry, lie within the boundaries of the Matara town. The fishing industry in the town is still highly seasonal in nature due to the inadequate use of mechanised vessels (less use of mechanised modern vessels). Coir yarn industry is an additional source of income for those who are unemployed and who do not have work during the off season. This gives employment opportunities for the economically active female population in the town who are unemployed, underemployed or seasonally unemployed.

The fibre industry of Matara town is exclusively confined to the coastal areas namely Polhena and Totamuna. These areas have a high concentration of coconut cultivation and natural brackish water pits for fermentation of the husks which are indispensable for this industry[30].

The four types of intermediaries involved in this industry are coconut landowners,husk traders, pit owners, and labourers. The land owners sell their crop to husk or nut traders. The husk traders sell the husk to the pit owners who are mostly the fibre producers. The price of the fibre is determined by the large pit owners.

The extraction of fibre is mostly achieved by the women labourers in the fishing community . Their wages per day range between 7 and 15 rupees. Meanwhile, the women who make the coir ropes get about 10 rupees (1981). This amount is equivalent to 25 pfennig to 50 pfennig in German mark. The white fibre is purchased by the yarn spinners who in turn produce a variety of coir goods. One of the major coir products in the town is coir yarn ropes. The coir ropes are still manufactured by traditional methods (Photo 17).

Promotion of this industry could provide more job opportunities to the large non-working female labour force in town.

3.3.2. Locational Distribution Pattern of the Industries - Wardwise Distribution.

The locational distribution of the industries has taken place in a scattered way. Due to a lack of planning they have sprung up like mushrooms all over the town. A high concentration of industrial establishments are found in the commercial core area which consists of the ward Kadeweediya with 25% of the total establishments, Mainstreet with 16% and Kotuwegoda with 16% (Table 29).

---

30 Samarawickrema, 1982, Schweinfurth, U., 1983, 1984

Table 29
Distribution Pattern of Industries, Matara U.C., 1978.

Ward	No. of Industries	Percentage (%)
1. Fort	4	4
2. Kotuwegoda	23	16
3. Maddewatta	14	10
4. Walpola	2	1
5. Uyanwatta	9	6
6. Main Street	23	16
7. Kadeweediya	34	25
8. Welegoda	10	7
9. Totamuna	4	3
10. Polhena	6	4
11. Weliweriya	11	8
Total	140	100%

Source: Structure Plan - Matara Town 1980 / 81.

3.3.3 Industrial Employment

Though agro-based industries are only 20 in number, they offer more jobs to the towns inhabitants than the other industries (Table 30 & Diag.12).

Table 30
Employment in Industries (Large / Small Scale),
Matara U.C., 1977 / 78.

Type of Industry	No. of Employees	Percentage (%)
Agro-based	636	33
Food, Beverages, Cereals	525	27
Basic Metal & Machinery	425	22
Leather & Rubber	68	4
Other	62	3
Chemicals	51	3
Wood & Paper	41	2
Garments	41	2
Weaving & Textile	31	2
Animal Food	21	1
Electrical Goods	9	--
Plastic Goods	8	--
Total	1918	100%

Source: Structure plan - Matara 1980/81

Diag.12: Employment in Industries, Large/Small Scale, 1981

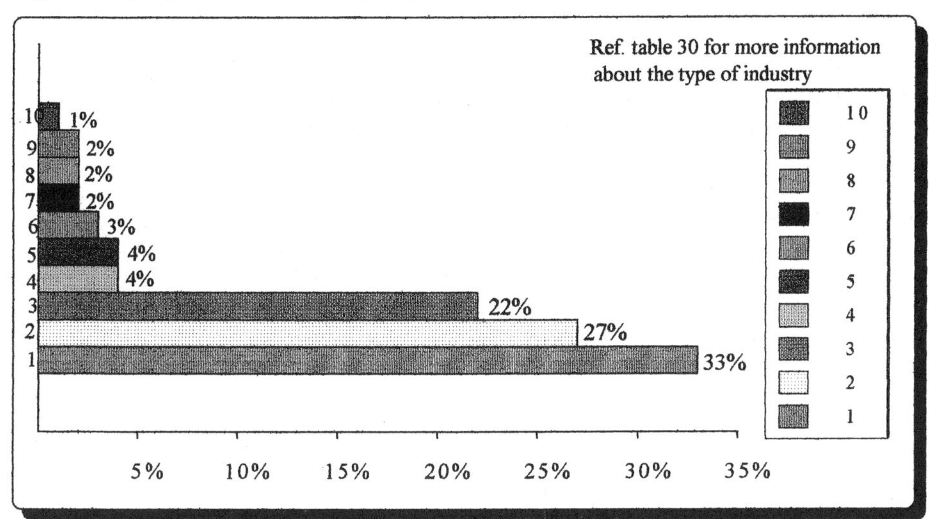

They employ 33% or 636 persons of the total industry. Two hundred and seventy employees out of this total work in the rice mills. The second highest employers in the town are food, beverage and cereal sector industries. This sector offers employment to 27% or 525 people of the total industrial population. Out of this total 445 people work in the large scale industrial establishment Harischandra Mills. The third highest industrial employer, basic metal and machinery, absorbs only 22% of the total industrial working population.

Although 1,167 housing units in town are engaged in cottage industries, the data depicting how many people work in this industry is not available.

3.3.4. Industrial Pollution

The number of industries (140 establishments) in town is very small and they occupy an equally small portion (0.9%) of the town's land area. The pollution caused by them can not be identified as a major problem for the town. However, a few industries, like Harischandra and Odiris Silva mills in the ward Kadeeweediya (No. 7), power looms at Issadeen town in the ward Welegoda (No. 8) and the Husk pits at Polhena area in the ward Polhena (No. 10), pollute these areas by means of water, air and noise. Diseases such as filaria[31], malaria and dysentery have spread over these areas.

---

31 Schweinfurth, U., 1984, 1983.

3.4. The Commercial and the Service Sector

Matara, the small port and shop centre, prior to the Colonial period became an important administrative centre and a commercial centre for spices and elephant trade during the Portuguese and Dutch periods. During the British and the post-colonial period it became the major administration centre for its district and the major commercial centre for Matara district, as well as the neighbouring Hambantota district ,due to its linkage with major urban centres and the rural areas in this region.

Matara can be identified as the major commercial centre in terms of the number of commercial establishments among the other urban centres of the district (Table 31). It offers a larger variety of items to the buyers in this region than the other centres. The commercial area of the Matara U.C., in contrast to the other centres, is characterized by its large expansion and the structural differentiation (Map 21).

Table 31

The number of commercial establishments in Urban centres of Matara district, 1986, and the percentage; the population in each urban centre in 1981, and the percentage; the shop density and the area under commercial activities in the urban areas 1981.

Centre	1981 Area ha	% of Total urban land area	No. of Shops	1986 %	Population	1981 %	Shop density
Matara (U.C.)	33.94	4.21	1698	60.0	39162	55.0	0.043
Weligama (U.C.)			466	17.0	17872	24.0	0.026
Akuressa (T.C)			588	21.0	6885	10.0	0.085
Dondara (T.C.)			52	02.0	7628	11.0	0.006
Total			2804	100.0	71547	100.0	0.039

Source : *(1 U.D.A. Final Report, 1981.
*(2| Register of Commercial establishments, 1981, Matara U.C.
*(3| Preliminary Report, Census of population, 1981.

*

The land use data for other centres except Matara are not available.
The area under commercial activities in the other urban centres is very small. The shops are found only along the major roads. In Weligama the majority of shops are found along the Colombo - Matara highway. In Akuressa, the majority of shops are found along the Deniyaya - Matara main road. The shops in Dondara are found along the Matara - Hambantoto highway.

According to the above table, Matara has the highest number of commercial establishments with 60% of the districts total. The commercial units in Matara town grew by 60% between 1981 and 1986 (the number of units increased from 1,037 to 1,698 units, Table 31). However, its frequency in terms of the towns population is lower

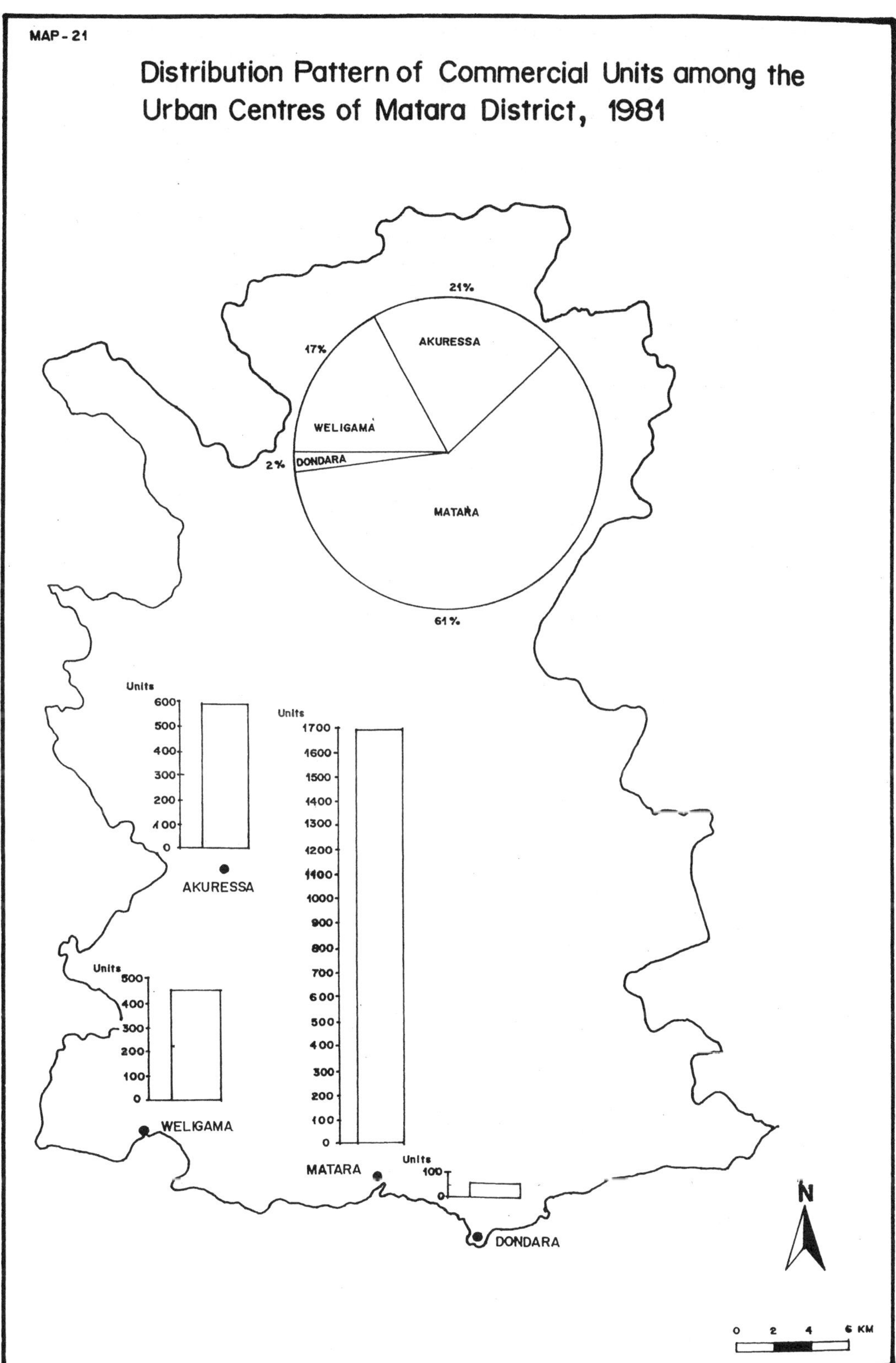
MAP - 21
Distribution Pattern of Commercial Units among the Urban Centres of Matara District, 1981
21%
AKURESSA
17%
WELIGAMA
2%
DONDARA
MATARA
61%
Units
600
500
400
300
200
100
0
AKURESSA
Units
1700
1600
1500
1400
1300
1200
1100
1000
900
800
700
600
500
400
300
200
100
0
MATARA
Units
500
400
300
200
100
0
WELIGAMA
Units
100
0
DONDARA
N
0 2 4 6 KM

(0.43) than that of Akuressa. Akuressa has the highest density of shops (0.85) among the urban centres in the district, although it has only 10% of the districts urban population. The other striking feature in these statistics is the reverse relationship between the number of inhabitants and the commercial shops in some centres. Generally the number of shops in a centre would increase with the increase of the population. However, this tendency cannot be identified in the urban centres of Weligama and Dondara.

Weligama is a higher order urban centre (U.C.) than Akuressa (T.C.) with 24% of the districts total urban population, yet it has only 17% of the districts total urban shops, which is less than the number of shops in Akuressa (21%). Akuressa is a lower order urban centre with only 10% of the district's total urban population. Although Dondara, the lower urban centre (T.C.) has more inhabitants (11% of the districts total urban population) than Akuressa (T.C.), it has only 2% of the districts urban shops.

The high frequency of commercial units in Akuressa is due to its favourable location. This town is situated further away from Matara town (32 Km) than Weligama (12 Km) and Dondara (6 Km). This is the only urban centre for the whole central and northern zone in which the main cash crops (Tea & Rubber) and minor cash crops (Cinnamon & Citronella)are grown. The growth of the other two urban centres is hampered by the close proximity to the district capital Matara. (This will be discussed later in Chapter 6).

The commercial and service sector plays a major role in the town as an employer offering 63.6% of the total employment and occupying only 4.06% of the total town area. Based on the nature of shops in Matara town, generally 9 types are recognised numbering 1,698 units altogether (Table 32 & Diag. 13).
Specialized markets in any form are not found in the town.

Diag. 13: Type of Commercial Units, Matara, 1981

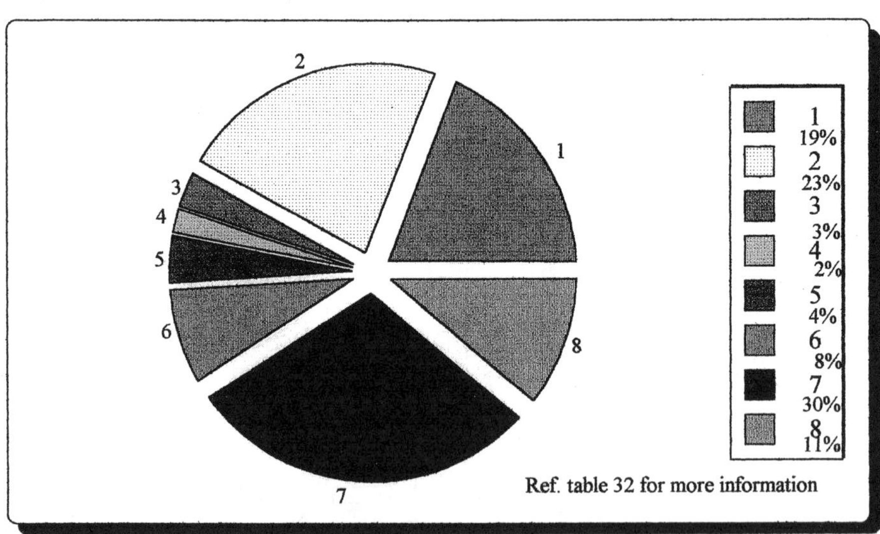

Table 32
The Type of Commercial Units, Matara U.C.
1981 / 1986

Type of Units	No. of Units 1981	No. of Units 1986	Percentage -----	Remarks
1. Primary Consumer Goods Short term need (food)	-	318	19.0	* The two daily and the weekly markets are included.
2. Secondary - Consumer goods, midterm and long term needs.	-	382	23.0	
3. House Hold Goods	-	55	03.0	
4. Construction Related Goods	-	40	02.0	
5. Vehicle Related Goods	-	71	04.0	
6. Manufacturing Service cum sale related units	-	140	08.0	
7. Service cum Sale related units	-	507	30.0	
9. Warehouses	-	180	11.0	
8. Others	-	05	-	
TOTAL	1037*	1698	100%	

Source: This classification is based on the Register Book of the Commercial Establishments, Matara U.C. 1986

* The data for the commercial units in 1981 was found in the Structure Plan, Matara town 1980 / 81. As the categorization of these units into groups in this plan was not clear, the author was compelled to take only the total number of units for this purpose.

* The full details of the categorization is given in the following table.

Table 33
Total Registered Commercial Establishment by Type, Matara U.C., 1986.

A. Primary Consumer Goods Related Shops.	No.	Total.
1. Beverages	11	
2. Liquor (Foreign & Local)	6	
3. Sweetmeat	21	
4. Vegetable & Fruit	44	
5. Daily & Weekly Markets	3	
6. Other Primary Goods Related Shops	233	318
B. Secondary Consumer Goods Related Shops:		
1. Textile	66	
2. Footwear	26	
3. Books	16	
4. Gems	2	
5. Drugs(Local & Foreign)	14	
6. Jewellery	49	382
7. Misellaneous	209	

(contd. in the following page)

B.1.		
Household Goods		
1. Furniture	19	
2. Electrical Goods	18	
3. Chinaware	15	
4. Florist	3	55
B.2.		
Construction Goods		
1. Hardware	36	
2. Others	4	40
B.3.		
Transportation Related Goods		
1. Motor Spare Parts	40	
2. Motorbicycle	7	
3. Bicycle	6	
4. Cars & Property Sales	13	
5. Petrol Stations	5	71
B.4.		
Manufacturing & Manufacturing cum Sale		
1. Batik (Textile)	1	
2. Footwear	8	
3. Textile Garments	5	
4. Metal Work	50	
5. Carpentry(Furniture,Casket & Timber)	12	
6. Cane Goods	7	
7. Rice Mills & Other Mills	22	
8. Soap Production	2	
9. Coconut & Copra	4	
10. Coir Yarn	2	
11. Bakery	20	
12. Ice Cream	3	
13. Ice	1	
14. Other Food (Papadam & Others)	3	140
B.5.		
Service Cum Sale		
1. Cars, Trucks, & Motorbicycle repair & sale	121	
2. Tailoring	32	
3. Audio Rentals	6	
4. Photo Studios & Record Bars	15	
5. Printing Shops	14	
6. Laundry & Saloon	55	
7. Hotels	8	
8. Restaurants	45	
9. Tea Shops	130	
10. Bicycle Repair	38	
11. Clock Repair	6	
12. Radio Repair	17	
13. Other Rentals	5	
14. Others	15	507

(contd. in the following page)

B.6.

Warehouses		
1. Beverages	3	
2. Timber	11	
3. Fire Wood	5	
4. Kerosene Oil	4	
5. Diesel	4	
6. Cinnamon Oil	3	
7. Citronella Oil	1	
8. Cement	11	
9. Paints & Varnish	41	
10. Animal Food	3	
11. Tobacco	15	
12. Empty Bottles	2	
13. Gunny Bags	9	
14. Old Hardware	9	
15. Spirits	4	
16. Coir Yarn Ropes	5	
17. Tyres & Tubes	8	
18. Food	16	
19. Copra	1	
20. Coconut Oil	2	
21. Tea	5	
22. Honey (Coconut & Kitul)	1	
23. Grains	6	
24. Other Oil	5	
25. Salted Fish	3	
26. Rubber	6	
27. Cigarette	3	
C. Others	5	
		185
Total		1698

Source: Tax Register - Commercial Establishments, Matara U.C., 1986

Of all the commercial units, a dominant number are service related. The shops in this category such as tailors, hair cutting salons, restaurants and tea shops, are to be found in groups in the commercial core area. Meanwhile, the repair work shops, which need more space, are found in the outer zone of the core area where the land prices and the rents are low. The "informal sector"[32] activities, such as cobblers sitting by the road sides, are not included in the table. This is a common picture in the urban landscape of the Third World . This sector should also be included as part of this category since this is an important element in the urban economy. The informal sector activities are a good example of the precarious economic situation in urban areas. There were, in all, 96 such service establishments found in the commercial core area in 1987. Tea shops and restaurants in the town render not only a service but also sell food items. Therefore they can be regarded as service cum sale units.

---

32 Ref. Escher, A., 1985.

Of all commodity shops, the secondary consumer (mid-term needs) goods related shops dominate with 382 units, and are to be found in groups in the commercial core area.

The primary consumer goods related shops for short term needs take the third place with 318 units and are to be found not only in the commercial core area but also scattered in the residential areas. High concentrations of these shops are found in the core area. There are also mobile shops of edibles (informal sector) like ice cream sellers, fruit sellers, and fish sellers who roam about in the various parts of the town. They spend the whole day with their goods on cycles, trolleys, carts, or human carriers, using Pingo, or carrying on the head. Apart from the aforesaid commercial activities in this category, the two daily markets and the weekly or periodic market are of great importance in the economic and commercial life of the town. The weekly market at Kotuwegoda and the daily market at Pallimulla are held in the town centre (core area) while the daily market at Hunukotuwa on the Batuta Road, is situated at the boundary of the commercial core area. Their functions and their structures will be discussed later in this chapter.

Manufacturing and service cum sale units number 140. These units practice three functions in one place. For instance, some Artisans, such as goldsmiths, ironsmiths, and shoemakers, use their residential quarters as workshops not only to manufacture and sell products, but also to repair them . The commercial units of goldsmiths and shoemakers are found in the commercial core area while the ironsmith units reside in the outer zone.

Domestic need shops such as furniture and electrical appliances as well as construction goods and vehicle shops can be found in the commercial core area. The warehouses are mainly found in areas around the railway station. This area has been chosen by large scale regional distributors, especially the government controlled ones such as C.W.E. (Ceylon Wholesale Establishment), Petroleum Corporation (petro products), Timber Corporation (timber products), and Building Materials Corporation. This warehousing centre is used for storage and distribution of consumer goods for the region.

In the past the town has grown in a haphazard manner along main roads such as Mainstreet (Kumarathunga Mawatha), Broadway Road (Dahrmapala Mawatha), Hakmana Road, Old Tangalle Road, and Pallimulla Road (new Tangalle Road). This haphazard growth has resulted in conflicting land uses and conditions of general congestion in the central area and a low level of development in the rest of the town. The concentration of commercial, institutional, industrial activities and transportation nodes in the central area has contributed to this situation, resulting in the formation of spatial gaps in the distribution of services and facilities. About half of the total land area in the town remains underdeveloped due to the existing spatial gaps in the network. The low population densities in the major parts of the town are due to the physical constraints and to the poor distribution of services. For example, the location of the Kotuwegoda weekly market in the town core area is a major traffic generating activity in the town centre. The existing location of the market across the Nilwala river bridge necessitates three-fourths of the town's population to cross the bridge in order to use the market for their daily needs.

An examination of the distribution pattern of commercial units among the wards of the town shows that Kotuwegoda has the highest number of units with 31%, followed by Mainstreet and Kadeweediya with 25% and 19% respectively[33].

3.4.1. The Daily Markets and the Weekly Market(Periodic Market or Pola)

There are two daily markets and one weekly market (Pola or periodic market) in the town, which cater to the daily needs of the town and the population of the surrounding areas. As mentioned earlier, the daily market at Pallimulla lies in the commercial core area while the daily market at Hunukotuwa lies at the boundary of the commercial core area (Photo 18 & 19). The periodic market (Pola) is situated near the bridge on the right bank of the river in the commercial core area (Photo 20). These three markets are not run by private dealers but by the Matara urban council. They are considered to be money-making operations. The major function of these three markets is collection of agricultural products, specially purchase of agricultural products and the distribution of these products to the local and surrounding areas. These three markets have been of great importance to the economic and commercial life of the town. The two daily markets were established 100 years ago when the British ruled over the country. Meanwhile, the weekly market is a relatively new establishment which came into effect in the 1970's.

The periodic market (Pola), which is held on two days (Wednesday and Sunday) per week only, is the most important commercial establishment among the aforementioned three markets (Table 34). Seventy-four percent of the total market sellers in Oct. 1987 had sold their goods in the periodic market (Pola), while 54% of the total revenue (tax) was collected from this market.

Table 34
The Amount of Collected Tax and the Number of Sellers in the three markets of the Matara town in Oct. 1987.

Market	Sellers	%	Collected Tax		%
Hunukotuwa Daily Market (Batuta)	30-45	11%	3227	Rupees	15%
Kotuwegoada Daily Market	48-62	15%	6408	"	31%
Pola (Periodic Market)	215-310	74%	11210.25	"	54%
TOTAL	293-417	100%	20845.25	"	100%

Source: Daily tax record, Kotuwegoda daily market and Hunukotuwa daily market,Matara U.C., 1987.
Taxbook, Peoples weekly market (Pola), 1987, Matara U.C.
Receipt book, Peoples weekly market, 1987 Matara U.C.

---

33 Structure Plan - Matara Town, 1980 / 81

Diag.14: Sellers versus Collected Tax, two Daily Markets and Periodic Market, Matara, 1987

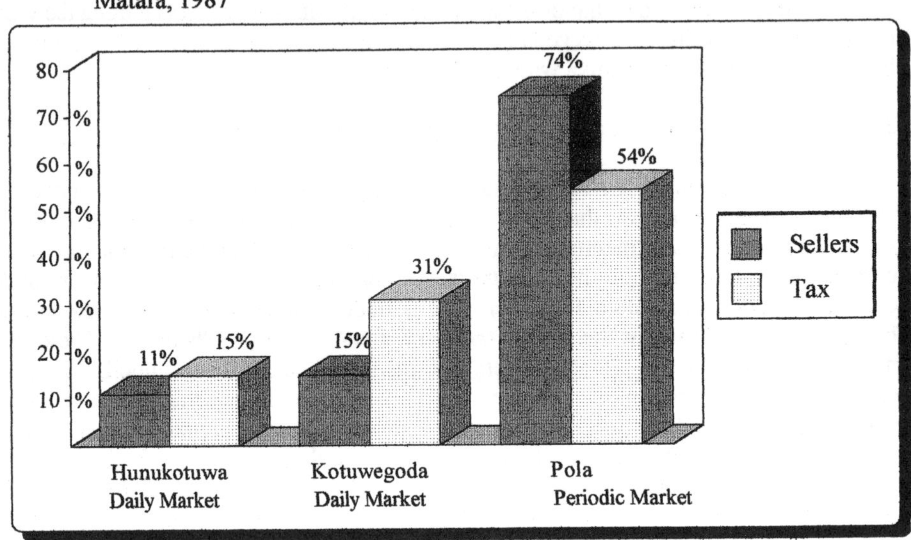

3.4.1.1. The Two Daily Markets

The two markets of British colonial origin had been important to the commercial life of the town prior to the introduction of the weekly market (Pola). Although they have lost the major role as commercial institutions to the weekly market, they still play a significant role in the urban economy. Among these two markets, Kotuwegoda daily market plays a more important role than the Hunukotuwa daily market as proven by the number of sellers who have visited these two markets and the amount of tax collected from them (33 and Diag.14). The number of sellers and the collected tax (15% and 31%) of the Kotuwegoda market lie above the Hunukotuwa market (only 11% and 15%), and can be attributed to its favourable location. The market itself is situated in the heart of the commercial core area and is visited by buyers from every part of town. Hunukotuwa market, on the other hand, lies in the outer zone of the commercial core area and is mostly visited by buyers who live in the western part of the town. Both of these markets are permanent in structure but their condition today is extremely poor due to lack of maintenance. Some temporary fish stalls (simply assembled wooden stalls) can also be found outside of these markets.

Both of these markets deal primarily with vegetables while a small portion of the sellers deal in betel leaf, arecanut, dry fish, dry chillies, rice, and spices for cooking. Ninety percent[34] of the vegetables sold in these two markets are low country vegetables

[34] I have visited the Hunukotuwa (Batuta) daily market on 15.1.87 and counted 35 sellers. Out of this total, only 4 sellers dealt with highland vegetables. In Kotuwegoda market there were 52 sellers on 18.1.87. Out of this total only 5 sellers had highland vegetables.

grown in Umland and Hinterland of Matara. Only 10% of the offered vegetables are identified as highland vegetables. The area where these vegetables come from will be discussed in the Chapter 6. The overwhelming majority of sellers in both markets are men, with almost 85%. Although both of these markets perform retail and wholesale trade, only a very small portion of the trade is involved with wholesale trade. Therefore, these markets can be identified as retail consumer markets. The following diagram shows the layout of the Kotuwegoda Market (Diag. 15).

3.4.1.2. Periodic Market (Pola)

Until some years ago periodic markets in third world countries had been studied mainly by Ethnographers and Anthropologists (e.g. Thurnwald, Frölich). In recent times (early seventies), this theme has attracted geographers such as Hodder, Smith, Bohle, H. and Gormsen, E. as a phenomenon which constitutes an important element in the economic life of an area. Since the introduction of "Central Place Theory" by Christaller and Losch there is a great deal of interest in the study of markets as central places (Christaller 1933, 1966 - Losch 1944, 1954). In some regions these markets are the only central function and provide the starting point of modern central place networks. The main attraction in this theme was the question of market cycles and the spatio-temporal relationship. Here, different quantitative methods were applied in most of the recent studies.

There is a large amount of literature available on periodic markets and marketing from all parts of the world. However, such studies are rarely available in Sri Lanka. In Bromly's comprehensive bibliography on periodic markets, only one study on this theme is mentioned. The earliest remarks on periodic markets in Sri Lanka are found in Kusuma Gunawardana's unpublished Ph.D. dissertation "Service Centres in Southern Sri Lanka" and in one of her papers "A Conventional Study of Ambalantota.[35] The first impressive study on the periodic markets in Sri Lanka (central Sri Lanka) was written by the anthropologist Jackson, D.W. in 1977.[36]

Until today, very little attention has been paid by the Sri Lankan writers to this theme, although periodic markets (Pola) were identified as a device for rural development, socio-economic development in urban areas and as an important medium of primary goods outlets to the urban consumer by the Sri Lankan government as early as the 1970s.[37] Among the hitherto written works, Rasak's M.A. thesis is the most comprehensive on this theme ever written to-date.

A periodic market is an authorised public gathering of buyers and sellers of commodities meeting at an approved place at regular intervals (Hodder 1965). Besides being points of economic contact, these markets have also been noted to be places of social and cultural activities.

---

35 Gunawardana, K.B., 1964. & 174.

36 Jackson, D.W., 1977.,Dicke:Badulla,1987;Bührlein:Nuwara-Eliya,1991.

37 High emphasis was given to the development of periodic markets in rural areas as well as in urban areas during the Srima Bandaranayaka Government.

Diag. 15: Lay-Out, Structure and Ground Differentiation after offered Commodities - Daily Market, Matara Kotuwegoda, Jan. 18, 1987

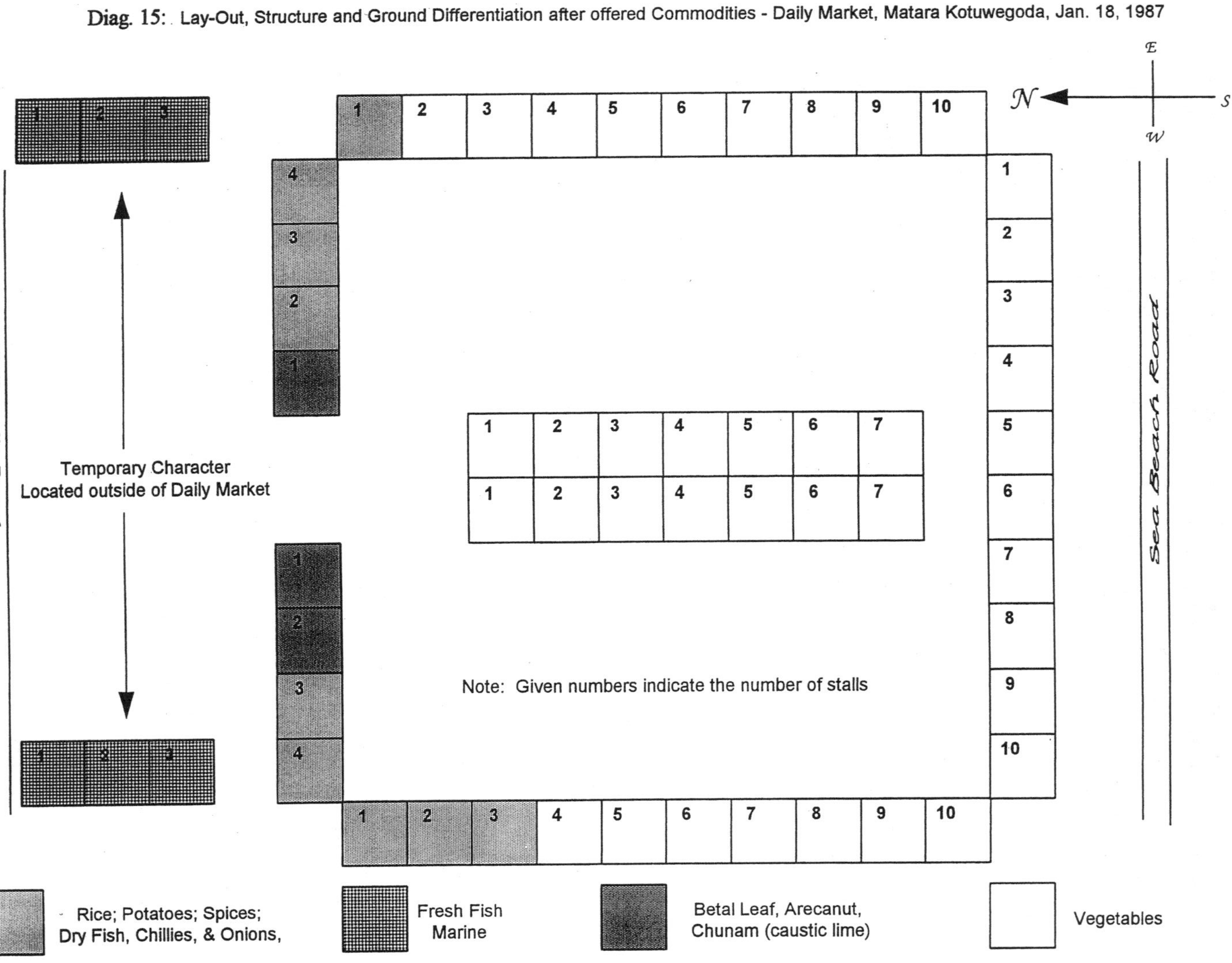

Some of these centres were granted urban status[38] in the recent past (mostly in the dry zone), for these were the only central places in some regions. In Sri Lanka, where periodic markets were known as Polas, the open ground on which they meet is usually provided with either temporary thatched or permanent cement shelters. The other common facilities are a well and a latrine on the Pola premises. These physical conditions of the Polas are determined by their owners. The Polas which are run by the local authorities are in better condition than those of private owners. The Polas of the private owners are mostly made of temporary thatched shelters and well and latrine facilities are absent.

Formerly the majority of these Pola grounds were privately owned but in the recent past most of these have been taken over by local authorities because they are a lucrative source of income. They are seen as money making operations by both sectors. Today, some Polas are administered directly by the owning authority, others are given out on tender to the private sector.

The tender revenue of the local bodies from the Polas have been increasing at a high rate. In 1987 it went up 200% due to the high competition of private owners. Although private owners pay a large amount of money to own a Pola, the net profit of the private owners is estimated to be 50%.[39]

These markets are the only outlets easily available to the rural producers to dispose of their surplus produce and craft products. It is also the centre from where they purchase various daily need items and imported products (Table 35).

Table 35
The medium of outlets, which the agricultural producers use to dispose of their produce.

Farm	Periodic Market Pola	Government Marketing Institutions	Collectors	Agent	Retail Rural Shops	Other outlets
10.5%	42.5%	9.2%	9.2%	04.6%	13.1%	10.9%

Source: Economic survey of lower UVa region 1981
D.P.A. Consultants Ltd. and Agro Skills Ltd.

As the above table shows, almost 43% of the total producers have chosen Polas to dispose of their agricultural products followed by the rural retail shops with 13.1%. The collectors and the government institutions play a minor role in this context. Although the origins of the Polas can be regarded as a provisioning mechanism for the urban centres of an export oriented economy, through the Polas many people of Sri Lanka receive a goodly proportion of the goods they need and use.

38 Gunawardana, K.B., 1964. & 1971.
Rasak, M.M.A., 1984.

39 Rasak, M.M.A., 1984.

The goods sold in these Polas and their arrangement on the ground vary. The majority of sellers deal in vegetables. Fruits, betel leaves, arecanut, and spices are also common commodities in the Pola. Rice and paddy which, in the past, were largely sold in the Pola have decreased to a great extent since 1974, when the government stepped-up its campaign to control and centralise this trade. Dry grains such as kurakkan (Eleusine Coracana = Dry Gram) and mung (Phaseolus Aures = Green Gram) are sold abundantly in the Polas which are located in the dry zone.

The low country vegetables, which constitute almost 95% of the Polas total vegetables, come predominantly from shifting cultivation, and to a lesser extent from home gardens, while the other 5% come from market gardens in the hill country.

Many Polas do both wholesale and retail trade, but most primarily exist for retail selling to consumers. The wholesale[40] trade occurs the night before or early in the morning of the retail sale day.

The wet zone, the highly urbanized region in the country comprising only 23% of the island's total land area, holds 53% of the total islands periodic markets, while the dry zone, the less urbanized region in the country comprising 77% of the islands total land area, holds only 47% of the total periodic markets (Pola). The rich fertile soil, favourable climatic conditions, good road networks, large urban population and high population densities are responsible for the high concentration of Polas in the south-west. The markets in this region mostly cater to the daily needs of the urban inhabitants who are not engaged in primary sector activities. The smaller number of Polas in the dry zone is mainly attributed to the unfavourable climate conditions, less fertile soil, bad accessibility, low urban population, and low population density.

Colombo, the most urbanized district in the wet zone with the highest population density (1,000 - 3,000 persons per square kilometre) holds the largest number of Polas (93), while Nuwara-Eliya, which also lies in the wet zone but in the hilly region in 2,000 m, where the major part of the land area is under cash crop (tea), poor accessibility and less population densities (300 - 500 persons per square kilometre) are found, has only 6 Polas.[41] The self-sufficient economy in the estate sector could probably be the main reason for the lack of Polas in this district.

The above stated facts indicate that the growth of the Polas were influenced by climatic and soil conditions, land use pattern, accessibility, population distribution and the level of urbanization in these regions.

In 1975, the Matara district had the fourth highest number of periodic markets (38) on the island. Matara "Pola" can be regarded as the highest order market in the periodic marketing system in the Matara district. This is the major centre for import and export and also of regional consumption and distribution. Other Polas are connected to Matara periodic market by some form of transport and are located so as to be convenient

---

40 The Wholesale in Sri Lanka means an amount of five pounds or more.

41 Ref. Bührlein, M., 1991.

points for the bulking of rural products. These Polas (bulking centres) are co-ordinated with the urban centre of Matara as well as with higher urban centres such as Colombo and Kandy.

The periodic market of Matara town, which is located on the right bank of the Nilwala river, is run by the Matara urban council. The explanation for the evolution of this periodic market is merely economic need, like almost all the periodic markets in Sri Lanka, in contrast to Indian periodic markets or some African and south American periodic markets , which were the result of economic need supported by religious motives[42]. The days on which the Pola is held (Wed. and Sun.) are not traditional.

There is no evidence that religion has had any impact on the market periodicity in the town or in the Matara district, as opposed to, for example, in countries such as Nigeria, in the four emirates of northern Nigeria, where Friday was selected as meeting day due to Islamic influence, or Ecuador, where the weekends are chosen as the day of trading due to the influence of Christianity[43].

When comparing the volume of the trade on these two days (Sun. & Wed.), Sunday can be regarded as the major market day (Table 36).

Table 36
The amount of tax revenue from the people's Pola, and the number of sellers, people's Pola
Matara town, 1987 Nov.

Periodicity	Tax Revenue (Rupees)	No. of Sellers
01.11.87 Sun	1448.50	-
04.11.87 Wed	1124.50	208
08.11.87 Sun	1590.50	322
11.11.87 Wed	1136.00	-
15.11.87 Sun	1605.50	-
18.11.87 Wed	1227.00	-
22.11.87 Sun	1673.00	-
25.11.87 Wed	1244.00	210
29.11.87 Sun	1611.00	331
TOTAL	12661.50	

Source: People's Pola tax register, 1987, Matara U.C.
People's Pola Bill book, 1987, Matara, U.C.

According to the above table,63.2% of the total tax revenue was collected from the Sunday Pola, while it is also seen that the number of sellers in the Sunday Pola is larger than in the Wednesday Pola. The physical condition of the Pola is not satisfactory, but better than the other periodic markets in the Matara district. Seventy percent of the total stalls in the market are permanent structures. They are of cement

[42] Deshpande, C.D., 1941, pp. 327 - 338.
[43] Hill, P. & Smith, R.T.H., 1972, pp. 45 - 355
Bromley, R.J., 1975.
Wanamali, S., 1975.

construction and roofed with corrugated iron sheets. Ten percent are temporary wooden stalls. The sellers who have no stalls (10%) pile their food on the floor[44] (Diag.16).

The rent for these stalls varies according to their structure and size. For permanent stalls, which are about 1.3 to 2 square meters in size, are rented for 12 Rupees a day while the smaller ones are rented out for 7 to 7.50 Rupees a day. The rent for temporary stalls ranges between 5 to 7 Rupees. The fee for the sellers who have their goods on the floor is fixed by estimating the quantity of goods. These fees are collected by a collector from the Matara urban council.

The goods sold in the Pola are separated by type. The heavier and bulk goods such as pottery, coconut and fresh fish are sold at the entrance of the Pola area where it is convenient for transportation.

Preference of association with friends and fellow caste members[45] on the ground is observed. Fish sellers from the "Karawa caste" have their caste members close to them. Some banana sellers from the Gowigama caste (farmer's caste) had their stalls close to each other while the pottery sellers (Badahala caste) had their caste companions close by. The vegetable sellers from Hakmana, Akuressa and Kamburupitiya area preferred to have the stalls of their friends from the same area close to them.

The number of sellers in the Pola varies between 208 and 331. The highest number of sellers are found at the Sunday Market. In contrast to the West African periodic markets, where the sellers are predominantly women, in Sri Lanka it is men who make up the majority of the sellers. During his visit to the Pola, the author observed that almost 85% of the total sellers consist of men. A small percentage of women sellers is engaged in the trade of such items as betel leaves, baskets (woven out of cane) and coir yarn products.

According to an investigation, it was observed that 60% of the sellers in the Pola were under 40 years old.[46] The people's Pola of the Matara town is opened for trade at five in the morning and lasts until six in the evening. There are identifiable variations during the market activity. The "assembling" of the sellers starts as soon as the market opens at 5 o'clock until 7 o'clock in the morning, although some sellers from the distances come with their goods a day before the Pola begins. They spend the night on the Pola premises. The buyers start coming to the Pola at about 8 o'clock in the morning. The busiest hours in the Wednesday and Sunday Polas are observed to be between 9 o'clock and 11 o'clock. The morning buyers in the Pola are mostly women (about 80%) who come to the Pola as soon as the house work is done and hope to go back home before the noon sun shines[47]. Polas in the evening on Wednesdays (after 4 o'clock) and in

---

44 This ground separation was observed during my visits to the Pola in 1987 & 1991.

45 This investigation was done during my visit to Pola in 1987, 1989, & 1991.

46 This data is based on an interview survey in 1987. (A sample survey of 10%).

47 In Sri Lanka, the daily needs of the household are still provided by women although this is changing.

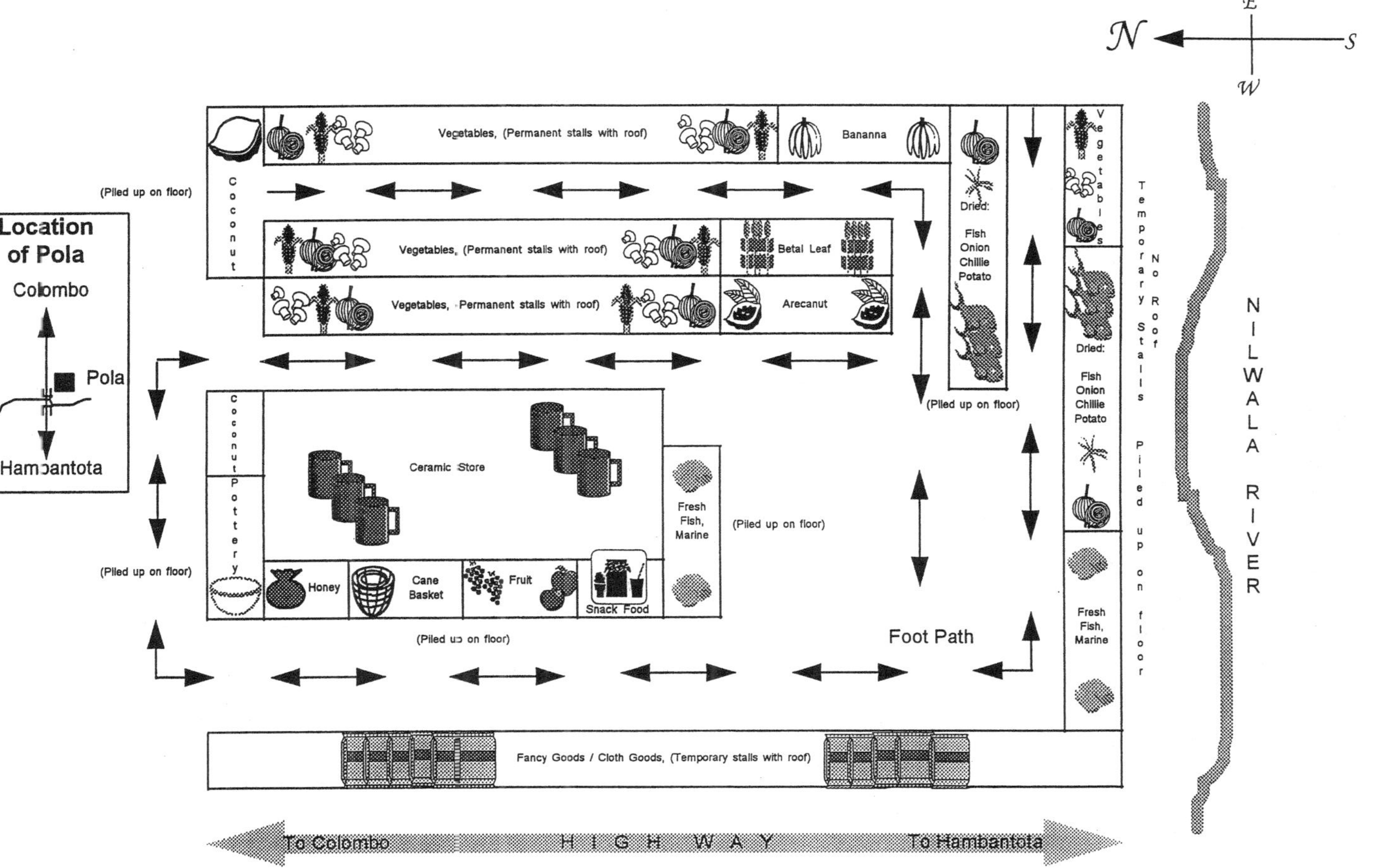

Diag. 16: Lay-out of Matara-Kotuwegoda Pola, (Periodic Market), after offered commodities, 1987.

the morning on Sundays are visited by substantial numbers of men buyers[48]. The areas where the buyers and sellers come from will be discussed in the Chapter 6.

Although the Pola is open until 6 o'clock in the evening, market activity starts decreasing after 11 o'clock. For example, during the day the selling of agrarian produce is the major activity in the first half of the market meeting, whereas in the second half, the purchase of urban goods from the urban shops becomes the more important activity of the periodic market sellers and the visitors. There is no sign of the existence of any barter system in the Pola. The bargaining over prices takes place in case of all commodities.

The goods sold in the Pola can be divided into two major groups described as primary and secondary goods. The primary goods constitute about 80% of the total goods for sale in the Pola, while secondary goods constitute only 20%. The goods in these two categories are given below.

Primary goods are considered to be the daily needs of human beings:

1) Vegetables
2) Fruit
3) Fresh fish (98% marine fish)
4) Relatively non-perishable items such as potatoes, dry onions, dry chillies, spices, dry fish and tea.
5) Dry grain.
6) Prepared snack foods and sweets.
7) Betel leaf, Arecanut, Chunam or Hunu (caustic lime) and tobacco leaf.

Vegetables are the most important commodity in this category. This constitutes about 70% of the total primary goods. The vegetables sold in the Pola can be divided into two groups:

1) low grown vegetables.
2) high grown vegetables.

Low grown vegetables which come mostly from the home gardens and the chena or hena land (shifting cultivation) of the surrounding areas and hinterland areas of the Matara town constitute 96% of the total vegetable supply of the Pola. They are grown by local farmers in very traditional and primitive methods. Chemical fertilisers and insecticides are rarely used in these vegetable gardens. The low grown vegetables, which are abundantly found in the Pola are brinjals[49], gourds, pumpkins, drumstick (Murunga), beans (mekaral), chillies, loofah (vatakolu), occra (lady fingers or bandakka), cucumbers,

---

48 The male workers come to Pola after office work at 4 o'clock in the evening. As Sunday is a non working day men come to Pola, letting their wives stay at home to do domestic work.

49 Brinjals, gourds, pumpkins, beans, chillies, loofah, occra, cucumbers and tomatoes are mostly grown in Chena Lands.

tomatoes (takkali) and leaves (Gotukola, Mukunuwanna, and Pala are the most common leaves, found in the Pola).

The supply of these vegetables (quantities) to the Pola vary with the seasons. February and March are the most prosperous months in the year. They form the peak season when the Maha harvest[50] comes in.

The vegetables which are grown in the hinterland of Matara are brought to the bulking centres (Polas) by producers and collectors by carts, tractors, bicycles and on heads. These vegetables drain to urban markets (Matara, Colombo, Kandy) through the wholesale dealers and petty traders. They buy these vegetables from the bulking centres not by weighing, but by just estimating the quantity of the commodity.

The demand for the low country grown vegetables is higher than that for the high country grown vegetables for the following reasons:

A) The low price.
B) The supply of chena crop depends on the seasons while the high country grown vegetables are available throughout the year.
C) The buyers of today in Sri Lanka are more conscious than ever of what they are eating. It is known to the buyers that in market gardens in the highland, where the nice vegetables come from, chemical fertilisers and insecticides are used.

The high country grown vegetables which constitute only 4% of the total vegetable supply in the Pola are grown by specialists in areas of concentrated market gardening. The most common vegetables are beetroot, cabbage, radishes, carrots, and leeks. The marketing of these vegetables is highly commercialized. Most growers use commission agents to sell their produce in urban markets. In contrast to the low country grown vegetables, these are sold to wholesale dealers according to weight.[51] Individual retailers in the urban markets do not find that they can get lower prices or better produce by dealing with the farmers directly. Due to this reason the high country grown vegetables are sent directly to the urban markets without going through the bulking centres or local Polas.

There are few high grown vegetable wholesale dealers in Denipitiya, a village that lies in the vicinity of Weligama and is famous for its Pola and the market gardening, and Matara who bring these products from the hill country and sell to the retailers.

The fruits sold in the Pola are almost all low grown. The most common fruits are banana, papaya, mango, and pineapple. These are grown in home gardens as well as in fruit gardens and are brought to the Pola from all parts of the country. The supply of these fruits to Pola varies with the seasons.

---

50 Maha =Great:Chena crops are sown in August-September and reaped in February-March.

51 Weitzel, k., pp. 170 / 71

Marine fish constitute 98% of the fish supply in the Pola. Only a few fishermen are engaged in inland fish trade.Inland fish species are rarely consumed in coastal areas. The fresh fish is brought to the Pola from the surrounding areas as well as from the town itself. King prawns, crabs and lobsters are rarely sold in the Pola because they are bought by the beach Mudalali (collectors) as soon as they are brought to the beach by fishermen (compare with Gläser, 1983). These marine species are very expensive[52] and are sold directly to the tourist hotels.

The relatively non-perishable food items such as potatoes, dry onions, dry chillies, and spices are often sold with dry and salted fish (Karawala and Umbalakada). These items are locally produced as well as imported. Dry grains such as Mung, Tala[53] (Seasem), Kurakkan are grown in the chena land. The quantity of supply to the Pola depends on the season. In Maha season the dry grains are abundantly found in the Matara Pola.

Tea is a very insignificant commodity in the Pola as this item is highly commercialised. The tea flows from the producer to the factory and then to wholesale and retail dealers in urban areas. Prepared snacks are sold in very small quantities in the Pola. Betel leaves are sold in combination with arecanut, chuman and tobacco leaves as well as separately.

Through the Pola, many people in the Matara town and surrounding areas receive a goodly proportion of the primary commodities they need. The Pola has a larger selection of vegetables than any other market in the town. The quality of these primary goods is, in general, good and the prices are lower than those of the city counterparts due to the lower overhead costs. The prices are more elastic. The chance for a bargain on a commodity is more possible and successful in the Pola than any other market in town.

Secondary Goods: "Secondary goods" are a conglomerate category, composed of all other goods sold in the Pola, as given below:

A) Pottery: village made, unglazed utilitarian pots for kitchen use.
B) Coir and cane products: coir ropes, coir mats, cane baskets.
C) Manufactured Goods: glassware, pins, ribbons, cloth goods (sarong, sarees, women and men's underwear, children's garments), costume jewellery (fancy goods), books and religious lithographs.

The pottery goods and coir products sold in the Matara Pola are mostly locally made. They come from the town itself (coir yarn products) and from the hinterland of

---

52 Until recent times the marine species such as lobster and crabs were not popular items of food among the Buddhist population in the region as these species are to be cooked alive. These were eaten mostly by the fishermen themselves and were rarely sold in the Pola as there was no demand. As tourism began to develop, sale of these species became a lucrative source of income. Today, the prices are so high that the local people cannot even think of buying them. In 1987, 1 kg of lobster was sold at 400 Rupees (16 DM) at Ginigasmulla beach (situated in Matara U.C. area) while 1 kg of Lobster was sold for 600 Rupees (24 DM) at St. Johns Fish retail and wholesale market in Colombo in Jan. 1991.

53 Tala (Seasem) yields an oil for medicines.

Matara. Instead of through an integrated redistributive hierarchy, pottery and cane yarn products reach the consumer through a simple solar flow pattern. The goods move directly from points of production to a single point of retailing. These goods are brought to the Pola either by collectors or the producers.

The manufactured goods have the same type of marketing system. They are not bulked and redistributed through the rural marketing system. For these goods Polas serve only as many separate retail sales points. These products drain directly from urban areas to the rural Polas. Colombo is the most important supplier in this regard. According to some interviews with the sellers, the author has come to know that the majority of the manufactured goods that sellers purchase, come directly from Colombo[54]. This shows Colombo's domination as supplier of manufactured goods on the island. That Colombo prices, even increased by transportation costs, can compete so widely with local sources of supply is a reflection of a highly centralised distribution system.[55]

The quality and selection of these goods in the Pola are very low. The factory seconds and rejects are sold in the Pola as items considered in perfect condition. The prices for the manufactured goods in the Pola are mostly lower than those of the counterparts in town but they are poor in quality. Due to this reason the consumers would prefer to buy these goods from the city shops .

In the case of secondary goods Matara periodic market (Pola) plays a minor role as a supplier of manufactured goods to the town and its surrounding population.

As discussed earlier, the marketing system of periodic markets in this region is basically dendritic and solar (Diag. 17).

The goods move through the Matara Pola in three basic types of routes:

1. in from the local area around the Pola and then back out to the same local area (low grown vegetables and fish).
2. in from the local area and then out to other, different areas (low grown vegetables and fish).
3. in from outside areas and then out to the local areas (high grown vegetables and manufactured goods).

On Pola days (Wednesday and Sunday) the marketing activities of the other two daily markets is very low. The buyers are more willing to go to the Pola than to the other markets, due to the larger selection of commodities and the lower prices. In addition to this, it provides for more fun with recreational, social and cultural activities. The majority of the sellers in the other two markets sell their goods in the Pola on these two days instead of going to the daily markets.

---

54 These interviews were performed in Jan. 1987. Only few sellers have bought their goods from Matara and Galle.

55 Jackson, D.W., 1977, P. 71.

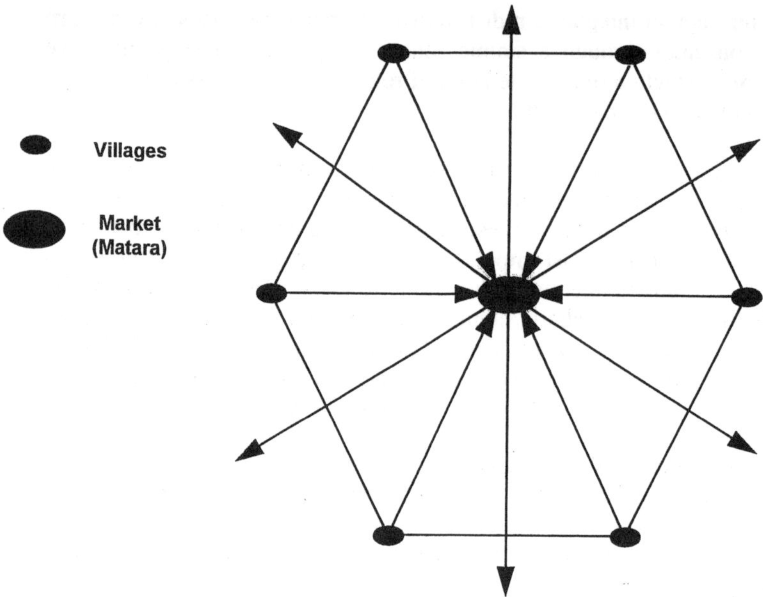

The simple Solar Marketing System

1. Villages
2. Periodic Markets
3. Minor Market Centers
   (Weligama, Akuressa, Dondara, Deniyaya, etc.)
4. Major Market Center
   (Matara)

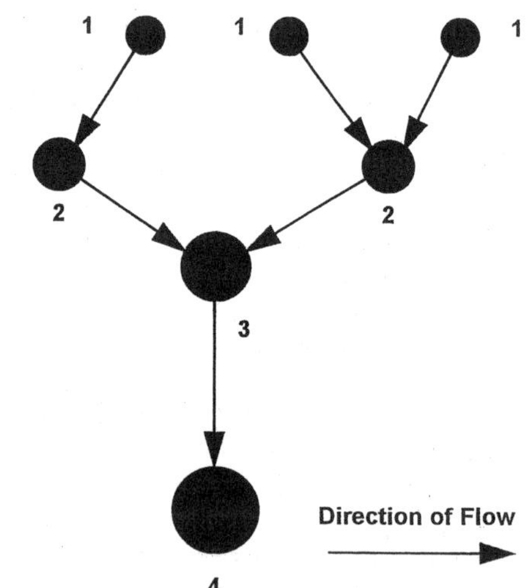

The Dendritic Marketing System

Diag. 17: Marketing system of periodic Markets in Matara District

In contrast to the two daily markets, the marketing activity of the other urban shops, which sell urban consumer goods, become more intensive. The buyers and sellers from the surrounding areas, as well as from long distance areas, purchase their urban consumer goods from the permanent shops.

3.4.2. The Central Business District of Matara

A survey was performed by the author in 1987 to identify the central business district of the town and its functional structure. All the commercial units along the major roads within the C.B.D. were taken into consideration. On the basis of these data a map has been drawn to depict the spatial structure and diversity of trade of the C.B.D. area (Map 22, in pocket). In this survey, information on the age of the commercial units, number of floors, ownership, ethnic affiliation of the owners, number of employees and monthly tax for commercial units were collected and analysed.

The identification of the C.B.D. of the town involves demarcation of an area where activities related to commercial, administrative, institutional, communication, and recreational requirements are concentrated. In Matara town, an area covering roughly Wards 2, 6, 7 (Kotuwegoda, Mainstreet, Kadeeweediya) and parts of Wards 1 and 5, (Fort and Uyanwatta) form the town core or C.B.D.

The total land area under commercial use accounts for 4.21% (33.93 ha)[56] the towns total land area. Seventy-nine percent (79% - 26.84 ha) of this total lies in the C.B.D holding 74% of the total commercial units of the town.

To demarcate the C.B.D. from other areas, the following criteria have been taken into consideration:

A. land values
B. commercial land use
C. density of shops
D. building heights
E. accessibility

A. The <u>land values</u> in the C.B.D. area are very much higher than those of other areas. They range between 8,000 -10,000 Rupees.[57]

B. The <u>commercial</u> land use in this area is very high. As mentioned earlier, 79% of the total area under commercial land use is found here. The striking feature in this regardis the high population density in the C.B.D.,(In the industrial countries, the population densities in the C.B.D.areas is very low as the area is used mainly for commercial purposes and not for residential). The Wards 2, 6, 7 (Kotuwegoda, Mainstreet, Kadeeweediya) which cover the C.B.D. have the highest population densities of the town, with 93.15, 85.50, 58.70 (Chapter 2) persons per hectare.This is a good example to indicate that

56 These Data are based on preliminary report, Structure Plan Matara,1981.
57 This information was obtained from the private owned land and property sales office, 1987.

the two functions,living and working in one place, is a predominant feature in the third world, although it is decreasing at a much lower rate.

C. Density of Shops - A very high frequency of shops and the highest shop density are found in this area. The compactness and the woven texture of the buildings is found here. Where compactness discontinues, it is only in the width of one house. These units are mostly very small in width due to partitioning of land into very small pieces[58], but large in number.The extension of the C.B.D. along the major roads varies. The C.B.D. area extends along the Mainstreet and Broadway Road approximately 670 meters, while it extends along the old Tangalle Road by approximately 600 meters. The shortest extension of the C.B.D. is found along the Hakmana Road with approximately 480 meters.

The shop density along the major roads is given below.

Table 37
The Density of Shops along the Major Roads
in the C.B.D. - 1984 - Matara U.C.

Road	Length c/a meters	No.of Shops	Density per 100 meters	% of Total Units	Remarks
Broadway	670	160	24	26	The 2nd cross street,
Mainstreet	670	97	14	20	3rd cross street and
Old Tangalle	600	116	19	17	the Station road
New Tangalle	600	125	20	23	connect Broadway road
Hakmana	480	53	11	09	and Main Street.
TOTAL	3020	551	18	95	
4th cross street	-	06	-	01	The high density of shops along the New Tangalle road is mainly contributed
3rd cross street	-	13	-	02	to the newly built, small commercial units in front of Post Office by Matara, U.C.
Station Road	-	13	-	02	
TOTAL	-	583	-	100	

Source: 1984 Survey.

According to the above table the highest shop density is found along Broadway road with 24 units per 100 meters, followed by New Tangalle road with 20 units. These roads are relatively new in comparison to Mainstreet and Old Tangalle Road. They were

[58] The customs and the laws of the Sri Lankan society permits the division of the land within the family.

built in the later British period as the traffic problem became more apparent on these two roads (Old Tangalle Road and Mainstreet) which connected Matara to Colombo and Hambantota. As soon as these two roads were built, they became the major and most important transport routes in Matara town. This led to quick growth of commercial units along these roads.

The third highest shop density is found along the Old Tangalle Road with 19 units per 100 meters, followed by Mainstreet with 14 units.

These were the ancient, major routes and the only routes prior to the British period which connected Matara to the ancient port Mantota (Mannar) in the north and the east. The ancient Bazaar of Matara was situated along this route (Chapter 1). The roads fell into disuse as transport routes as soon as the new roads were built and no buses are driven on these roads today. This led to stagnation of commercial activities along these roads. In addition to that, the lack of space also contributed to stagnation. Hakmana, the major road which connects Matara to the northern interior parts of the district, is fast developing, although it still has the lowest level of shop density, with 11 units per 100 meters, in the C.B.D. area.

D. Building Heights Multi-storey buildings are rarely found in the medium size towns of Sri Lanka. Only few such buildings are found in the Matara U.C. area. All of these are situated in the C.B.D. area of the town. The majority of the commercial buildings are one storey buildings,roofed with curved clay tiles. The front doors of these buildings are open to the street. According to the author's survey in 1985, 78.28% of the total commercial buildings in the C.B.D. area were one-storied, 19.82% were two-storied, and 1.5% were over two storeys.[59]

E. Accessibility The C.B.D. area of the Matara town is well connected to the other areas of the town by major and minor roads. A large proportion of land in this area is used for roads (no pavements) in contrast to the other areas of the town. The total land area under road is only 4.55 of the town's total land area, but the land area under roads in the C.B.D. area is 20%.

The road network in the C.B.D consists of 5 major roads and 7 minor roads. The length of these roads all together is about 6,187 meters[60]. The road density per one hectar in the C.B.D. area is 47 meters. The C.B.D. area can be reached by vehicles from any

---

59 The tallest buildings in the town (Wijeweera and S.K.) have only three floors.

60 The length of roads is calculated (measured) with the help of the Map of Matara town, scale one inch to 8 chains, reprinted in 1969. The major roads in C.B.D.are Broadway road, Mainstreet, Old Tangalle road, New Tangalle road and Hakmana road. The minor roads are Station road, Batuta road, Kalidasa road, First, Second, Third and Fourth Cross street, Elliot road, Sea Beach road and Pennyquick road.

part of the town within 5 to 10 minutes. The vehicle flow within the C.B.D. area, especially on the major transport routes such as Broadway Road, New Tangalle Road, and Hakmana Road is very high.

According to the bus plan (timetable) of Matara Ceylon Transport Board (C.T.B.) in 1985, there were about 118 buses which were driven 538 times a day through the C.B.D. area.[61] According to the private bus enterprise office of Matara there are about 353 private buses driven 671 times a day through the C.B.D. area.[62]

The daily influx of people into the C.B.D. area by buses accounted for 23,000 persons a day.[63] The data for pedestrian flow in the C.B.D is not available. The number of pedestrians is greater on the periodic market days.

The Nilwala river divides the C.B.D of Matara town into two parts (Map 22 in pocket). Therefore the spatial concentration ratio of activity represents a discontinuity and a scattered form of locational character. The Nilwala river is a great hindrance to the growth of the C.B.D. area into one compact form.

3.4.2.1. The Commercial Activities and the Functional Specialisation in the C.B.D Area of Matara Town.

The commercial units along the main roads in the C.B.D area accounted for 583 in May 1984. This was 76% of the total commercial units in the C.B.D. area in 1981. These units were categorized into 9 major groups (Chapter 3.4).

1) Primary goods: included are all the units dealing with food.

2) Secondary: all the units dealing with mid and long term needs such as textile shops, shoes, leather goods, watches, clocks, jewellery and books.

3) Household appliances: units dealing with chinaware, electrical goods and furniture.

4) Construction goods: units dealing with building materials.

5) Transport: units dealing with bicycles, other vehicles,and spare parts.

6) Manufacturing: some small industrial units dealing with production, as well as sale of imported goods.

7) Service: all kinds of service units, garages, repair units, restaurants, picture halls, private hospitals, private offices of lawyers

---

61 Bus Schedule, C.T.B., Matara, 1985.

62 Bus Schedule, Private Bus Company (Office), Matara, 1985.

63 Structure Plan - Matara Town, 1980 / 81.

8) Warehouses.
9) Other: wholesale shops dealing with cinnamon, rubber, and the units dealing with fertiliser and tractors.

An examination of the commercial units in the C.B.D. area of Matara shows some of the same functional characteristics as in the C.B.D. areas of the industrial world, although these are not clearly visible. Similar to the industrial world, a high concentration of service sector activities and long and mid-term related commercial units are found in the C.B.D. area of Matara town. According to the table below, the service sector is 34%, and with 199 units, is the major commercial activity in the C.B.D, followed by the commercial units which deal with mid and long term needs, with 29% (170 units). The frequency of primary goods related shops in comparison to the above two sectors is low, it takes third place with 14% (81 units) of the total commercial units in the C.B.D. (Table 38 & Diag.18).

Table 38
The Commercial Units in the C.B.D.
area Matara U.C. 1984

	Type of Units	No. of Units	%
1	Primary consumer Goods	81	14.0
2	Secondary Consumer Goods	170	29.0
3	Household Goods	36	6.00
4	Construction Related Goods	42	7.00
5	Transport Related Goods	26	04.0
6	Manufacturing cum Sales	10	02.0
7	Service and Service cum Sales	199	34.0
8	Warehouses	04	01.0
9	Other Units	15	03.0
	Total	583	100.0

Source: Survey, May 1984

Diag. 18: Type of Commercial Units, C.B.D. area of Matara, 1984

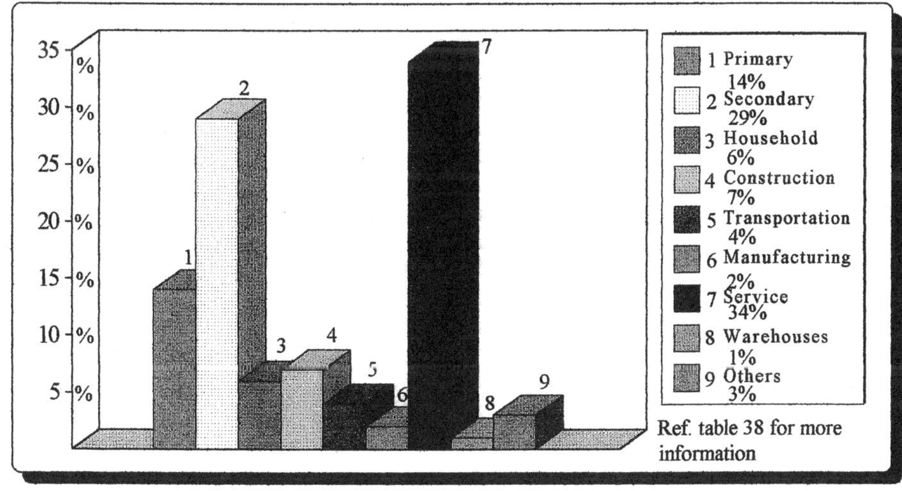

With relevance to the physiognomy and the internal structure of the C.B.D area of Matara, it bears more resemblance to the C.B.D areas of African towns in Tanzania (Vorläufer; 1972),Ghana (Mahn; 1980), Kenya (Henkel; 1979), Uganda (Kade; 1969) Portuguese Guinea and south-west Angola (Matznetter; 1963),than any other C.B.D areas in the European countries.

The following similarities in the physiognomy and the internal structures of the C.B.D. of Matara and in the C.B.D. areas of African towns are hereby identified:

A) The streets, which are basically narrow and without sidewalks, are encroached by the informal sector.

B) The shops are clustered only along the major roads and have compact form and woven texture.

C) The shops are mostly single and two-storey buildings whose front doors open on to the street.

D) High population densities are found in the C.B.D. areas of the town, as the commercial units are also used as places of residence. The rear area of the first floor of these buildings is often used for this purpose.

E) Special kinds of functional districts have not been developed in the C.B.D. areas. Educational institutions (schools), health facilities (hospitals, dispensaries), and public and private administration establishments are scattered over the entire town.

F) The goods sold and the services offered in the C.B.D.areas are basically mixed and lack specialization. However, it is also found, that the shops are clustered on the basis of the nature of goods sold and services offered, giving rise to a functional specialization of the segments of the streets.

G) There is no strict division between the wholesale and retail trade. Both of these activities take place in the same unit.

H) The C.B.D. areas are congested and dirty. The environmental conditions (water and air) are bad.

As indicated in Table 38, the most intensively used commercial area in the C.B.D is found along the Broadway Road (Map 22 in pocket & Photo 21). The commercial activities in this area are mixed, hardly any kind of specialization can be found in any activity. The commercial activity ranges from petty traders in hosiery, apparel, electrical articles and restaurants, etc., to large wholesale traders in provisions, grains, oils, building materials, hardware, furniture, etc. and the formal daily and weekly markets. There are a number of private offices and quite a few banks. Private offices consist of district or regional level services such as real estate, construction and other professional establishments and also the administrative centres of the distributors of agro-products like rice, cinnamon, palm oil, etc. A few auto/car dealers are also found in this area. While the Broadway Road shows a combination of all kinds of commercial activity, it contains to a small extent a concentration of banking facilities and private offices. According to the author's survey in 1984, 80% of the commercial units in this are oriented to the secondary needs of the town's population.

The New Tangalle Road is also characterized by mixed commercial activities, like Broadway Road, and there is found no specialization of any kind of activity (Map 22 in pocket). The commercial units, which deal with provisions (retail and wholesale), textiles, leather goods, shoes, hardware, motors, spare parts, restaurants, tea shops, and one of the daily markets are located here. A high concentration of tea shops and restaurants are found close to the C.T.B. (Ceylon Transport Board) and private bus terminals. According to the author's 1984 survey, there were 35 tea shops in the C.B.D. area. Fifty one percent (18 units) of this total were located in this area. The restaurants and tea shops cater mostly to passengers, tourists, and pilgrims who travel from other parts of country to the religious centre Kataragama (in Monaragala district), archaeological sites Tissa, Mulgirigala, Sithulpahuwa (in Hambantota district) and the Yala national park (in Monaragala district) through Matara. A high concentration of garages, outside the C.B.D., were identified along this road. There were 18 garages in town in 1984. Out of this total, 44.6% (10 units) were located along the New Tangalle Road, but outside the C.B.D. area. According to the survey, 68% of the total commercial units in this area offered mid-term and long-term goods to the town and surrounding area population, while 32% dealt with primary goods.

The Mainstreet is characterised by the presence of jewellery, textile and footwear shops, and a few shops of hardware, motor spare parts and auto/car dealers (Map 22&Photo.22). A concentration of small shops and simply assembled wooden stalls (temporary and semi-permanent structures) dealing with primary goods such as fruits and food items is found at the junction of Broadway Road and Mainstreet. The location of the General hospital at this point led to the growth of these commercial activities. These shops are oriented to the needs of the patients (Photo 23). According to the 1984 survey, 93% of the commercial units along the Mainstreet deal with mid-term and long-term goods, while only 7% of the total commercial units deal in the trade of primary goods.

Old Tangalle Road shows a concentration of hardware, ceramics, building materials, provision shops and general stores. According to the survey there were 32 hardware and building material shops in the C.B.D. area in 1984. Out of this total, 68% (22 units) were found here. Some of these units were established as early as 1944, due to the favourable location. Until 1960 this road was considered to be the major transport route which connected Matara with Hambantota district. Today Old Tangalle Road is used as a one-way street (Photo 24). In addition to the aforesaid commercial units, there were some retail and wholesale units dealing with tobacco and primary goods such as dry fish, dry onions, and potatoes. According to the survey, the majority of the commercial units (55%) in this area dealt with secondary goods, but a high percentage of commercial units (45%) were dealing with primary as well.

Hakmana Road is fast developing and may attain a high level of commercial activity in the near future. Some commercial offices (e.g. insurance co-operation) and banks (peoples) are already established there. A concentration of wholesale commercial units in the trade of cinnamon, rubber and arecanuts are found there. Seventy-nine percent of the commercial units in this area deal with long-term and mid-term goods, while only 21% deal with primary goods (Map 22 in pocket).

The Station Road has been chosen by large scale regional distributors, especially the government controlled ones such as petro-products, building materials depots, and food products (C.W.E.). This is the warehousing centre in the town, which is used for collecting and distributing of consumer goods for the whole region.

A concentration of service sector activities (administrative and public sector) is found in the Fort (this part of the Fort belongs to the C.B.D.). The major public sector administrative unit (Kachcheri) of the district is located here. There is also a concentration of private offices of lawyers and notaries around the courts (in the Ward Fort) . It should also be mentioned that there is a concentration of tourist hotels, tourist inns and guest houses in the Ward Polhena.[64] The average number of rooms per hotel is 12 and the average number of employees per hotel is also 12.[65] The calm beach, caused by the coral reef, is the major attraction in this development.

3.4.2.2. The Trade Activities in the C.B.D according to Ethnic Affiliation

As discussed earlier in this chapter, the C.B.D area extends along the major roads. There is no clear subdivision into Sinhala, Muslim or Tamil centres in Matara like in Kitale, a town in the trans Nzoia plateau in north Kenya, where European, Asian and African shop centres are found (Henkel, 1979, p 192). The shops of the Muslims and Singhalese are mixed, although the shops of some roads are predominantly owned by one of these two groups. The Tamils play a very insignificant role as businessmen in the C.B.D. area of Matara with only 1% in comparison to Badulla, in the eastern part of the hill country of Sri Lanka, where 60% of the shops were owned by Tamils in 1983, prior to the communal riots (Dicke 1987, p. 282). See the following table.

---

64 The tourist hotels which are found in the Polhena area are Polhena Guest House, Polhena Beach Hotel, Chilean Hotel and Sea View Restaurant. The largest hotel among these four is the Polhena Beach Hotel, which has 20 rooms and 40 beds. There are 30 employees in the hotel.

65 Structure Plan, Matara Town 1980 / 81.

Table 39
Number of Shops along the Major Roads in the C.B.D. area, by Ethnic Affiliation - Matara U.C. 1984

Road	No.of Shops	Ethnic Group S	M	T	% of total units per Ethnic Group S	M	T	Population by major Ethnic group 1981 and % of shop owners of the total population of each group: Population	%
Broadway	160	113	47	-	71	29	-	Singhalese 34,846	1.0
Mainstreet	97	44	53	-	45	55	-	(89%)	
Old Tangalle	116	45	67	4	39	58	03	Muslim 3,673	6.2
New Tangalle	125	81	44	-	65	35	-	(9.3%)	
Hakmana	53	42	11	-	65	35	-	Tamil 410	0.9
1st Cross St	06	02	04	-	33	63	-		
3rd Cross St	13	01	12	-	92	08	-		
Station Road	13	12	01	-	92	08	-		
TOTAL	583	340	239	4	60%	39%	01%	39,162	

Legend: S = Singhalese; M = Muslim; T = Tamils
Source: 1) Survey 1984.
2) Statistical book Matara district 1983.

According to the above table, the shops in the C.B.D. area are predominantly owned by the Singhalese with 58% followed by the Muslims with 41%. The Tamils own only 1% of the total C.B.D. area shops (Map 23 & Diag.19).

A comparison of the total population of each ethnic group with shop ownership of each group shows that Muslims are small in population size but the percentage of Muslims who are engaged in trade activities is higher than that of the Singhalese. Although the Muslims account for only 9.3% of the town's population, 6.2% of this total population own commercial units in the C.B.D. area. The shops owned by the Singhalese represent only 1% of its total population (89%). This uneven distribution of shops among the two ethnic groups is most probably attributed to their past history.

The Muslims, who came to Sri Lanka as traders, settled down in the shop centres or bazaar centres of medieval Sri Lanka and engaged in trade activities more than anything else. The Singhalese, who were mostly peasants, had very little to do with trade prior to the Colonial Period. This can be considered as a new and strange field of economic activity for them. Although the infiltration of Singhalese capital into business began during the Dutch period, up until the Post Colonial Period the trade in the urban as well as in the service centres of the island was dominated by the Muslims[66]. The figures of the shop owners from these major ethnic groups reflect a struggle for economic predominance between Sinhalese and Muslims.[67]

Diag. 19: Trade according to Ethnic Affliation, C.B.D.area, Matara, 1984

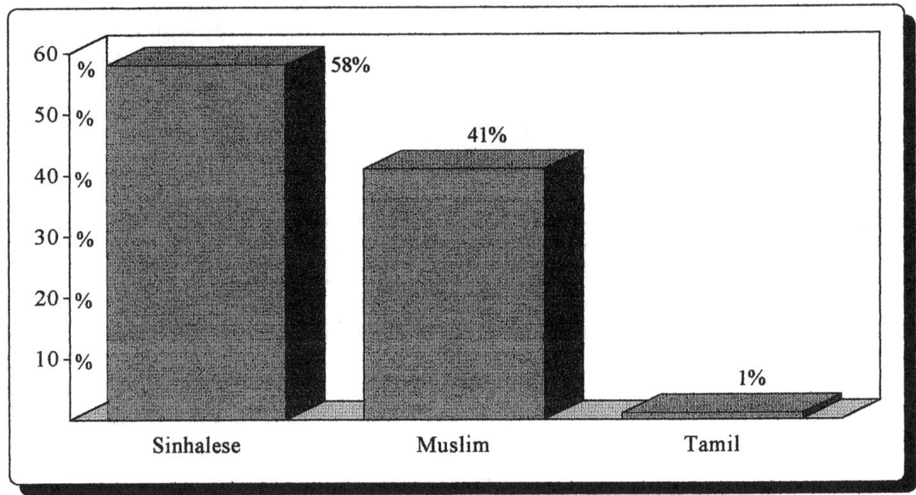

The main reason for the animosity between these two groups was neither religious nor cultural but based on economic aspects. The commercial riots between two groups in Matara as well as in other urban centres of the island in 1914 and 1981 were mainly based on this aspect. This problem was a major contributor to the division of Matara U.C. into 11 wards in 1956 (Chapter 1). A high concentration of Muslim shops is found along the ancient transport route Old Tangalle Road and Mainstreet. Fifty-eight percent of the total shops along Old Tangalle Road are owned by Muslims while they also own 55% of the total shops along Main Street. The medieval Muslim traders occupied this area since the days when the Sinhalese had very little experience in trade, but it is apparent from the above mentioned figures that the Singhalese, with time, have gained ground on business. Today they are only slightly behind the Muslims, occupying 39% and 45% of all the shops along the two roads. The shops along the other relatively newly built roads (Broadway, New Tangalle and Hakmana Roads) are predominantly owned by Sinhalese. The political, social and economic environment in the Post British era was more favourable for the Sinhalese entrepreneur than the minorities in the islands (Chapter 1). The trade along these roads was occupied by the Sinhalese as soon as the roads were built. The shops along the 3rd Cross Street and 1st Cross Street are

---

66 Kumari Jayawardana, 1986.

67 In some centres, e.g. Badulla, there was a keen competition for economic predominance between Tamils and Sinhalese prior to ethnic unrest in 1983. (Dicke, S., 1987.).

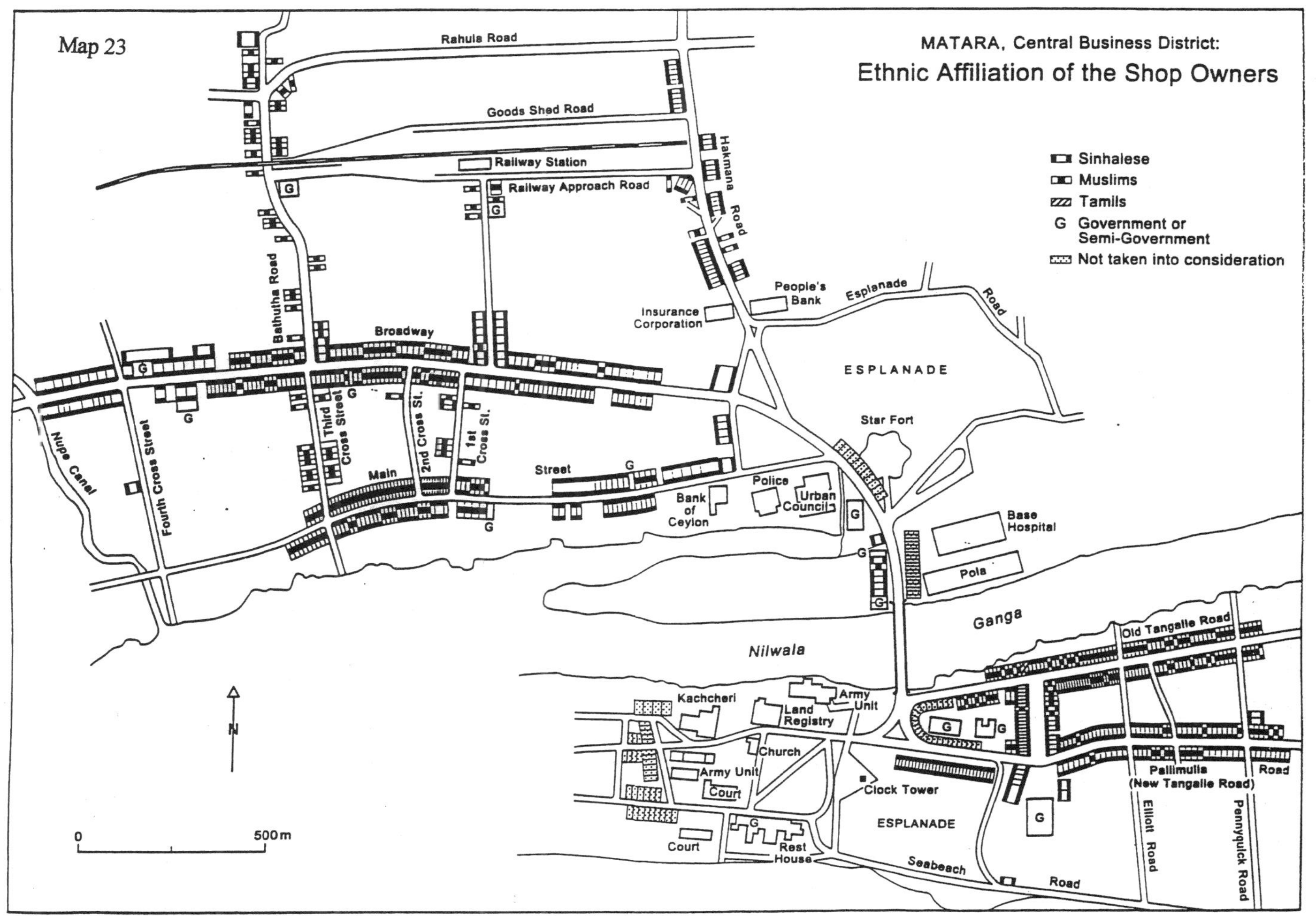
Map 23
MATARA, Central Business District:
Ethnic Affiliation of the Shop Owners
Sinhalese
Muslims
Tamils
G Government or Semi-Government
Not taken into consideration
Rahula Road
Goods Shed Road
Railway Station
Railway Approach Road
Hakmana Road
Insurance Corporation
People's Bank
Esplanade
Road
ESPLANADE
Star Fort
Base Hospital
Pola
Ganga
Nilwala
Police
Urban Council
Bank of Ceylon
Broadway
Main
Street
1st Cross St.
2nd Cross St.
Third Cross Street
Bathutha Road
Fourth Cross Street
Nupe Canal
Old Tangalle Road
Pallimulla Road
(New Tangalle Road)
Elliott Road
Pennyquick Road
Army Unit
Land Registry
Kachcheri
Church
Army Unit
Court
Court
Rest House
Clock Tower
ESPLANADE
Seabeach Road
N
0
500m

predominantly owned by Muslims while the majority of the shops along the Station Road are owned by Sinhalese.

Table 40
Number of Jewellery, Textile Other Mid-term needs, Footwear, Building Material, Daily Needs Shops and Restaurants According to Ethnic Affiliation - Matara C.B.D. Area, 1984

Road	Daily Needs Retail Shops			Mid-term Needs (MG)			Jewellery			Textile			Footwear			Building Material			Hotel,Tea Shop Restaurant			Total
	M	S	T	M	S	T	M	S	T	M	S	T	M	S	T	M	S	T	M	S	T	
Mainstreet	2	1	-	2	5	-	15	13	-	13	6	-	3	2	-	2	-	-	2	2	-	68
Old Tangalle	-	7	-	10	8	-	-	8	-	11	12	-	1	-	-	18	3	2	1	9	1	86
New Tangalle	6	12	-	5	2	-	-	2	-	4	5	-	1	-	-	3	4	-	5	29	1	79
Broadway	5	6	-	6	7	-	-	1	-	2	5	-	1	3	-	4	1	-	4	3	-	48
Hakmana	5	6	-	1	5	-	-	-	-	-	-	-	-	1	-	1	1	-	4	6	-	30
1st Cross St.	-	-	-	-	-	-	-	-	-	-	-	-	-	-	-	-	-	-	-	-	-	-
3rd Cross St.	4	3	-	5	-	-	-	-	-	-	-	-	-	-	1	1	-	1	-	4	-	19
Station Road	1	1	-	-	-	-	-	-	-	-	-	-	-	-	-	-	-	-	3	2	-	7
TOTAL	23	36	-	29	27	-	15	19	-	30	28	-	6	6	-	29	10	2	20	55	2	337

Source: Survey 1984
* Daily Need retail shops all deal with spices, rice, dry fish, dry chillies, onions.
* Mid-Term need shops all deal with personal need items such as toothpaste, brushes, cream.
*M = Muslim, S = Singhalese, T = Tamil, MG = Urban manufacture goods.

An examination of the ethnic composition of the shop owners shows that Muslims are overrepresented in the trades of mid-term needs, urban manufactured goods (29 of the 56 shops = 52%) and building material (29 of the 41 shops = 71%). The jewellery trade, which was one of the most specialised trades of the Muslim and the Tamils[68] in the past, was taken over by the Sinhalese. The trade of building materials is also one of the major and well-known commercial activities of Muslims and Tamils. These two groups are highly represented in this trade in every urban area of the island. The Muslims, occupying 71% of these shops, hold a dominating position in the C.B.D area, while the Sinhalese and the Tamils own only 24% (10 of 41 shops) and 5% (2 shops) play a minor role in this trade.

The Sinhalese are over represented in the trade, retail trade of daily need commodities (35 of 59 shops = 61%), jewellery (19 of 34 shops = 56%) and hotel trade (55 of 77 units = 71%). The Sinhalese hold a very high dominating position in the hotel

[68] Tamils play a very insignificant role in the trade of Matara town. They do not own a single jewellery shop in this town. But in most of the urban centres of the Island they take a very active part in the trade and are well represented.

and restaurant trade, occupying 71% of these units. The Singhalese who infiltrated into the bakery industry during the Dutch period had broken the monopolistic position of the Muslims in this trade, which they held in the pre-Dutch era[69].

3.4.3. Sub-Commercial Centres

In addition to the commercial core area, there are seven sub-commercial centres within the boundary of Matara town (Map 24). They provide the daily needs of the population who live outside of the commercial area and in the peripheral areas of the town. Some of these centres offer not only short-term and mid-term related consumer goods but also the long-term related consumer goods, such as radios and televisions. In some of these centres, service units such as hair salons, repair units (car and cycle), photo studios, laundries and tailor shops are also located. The structure of the shops in these centres is mostly permanent, but semi and temporary characteristics are also found. The number of the shops in these centres according to the count in 1990 ranges between 6 to 45.[70] The following are the important sub-commercial centres in Matara town:

3.4.3.1. Hunukotuwa sub-commercial centre
3.4.3.2. Issadeen town sub-commercial centre
3.4.3.3. Walpola sub-commercial centre
3.4.3.4. Peakwella sub-commercial centre
3.4.3.5. Rahula sub-commercial centre
3.4.3.6. Pamburana sub-commercial centre
3.4.3.7. Maddawatta sub-commercial centre

3.4.3.1. Hunukotuwa Sub-Commercial Centre.

Hunukotuwa Centre is the largest sub-commercial centre in Matara town with 45 commercial units. This centre lies at the road crossing of Batuta Road and the Rahula Road (Map 24 & photo 25). The growth of this centre mainly contributes to the Hunukotuwa daily market which was established in the British era. This daily market is the major supplier of fresh food items (vegetables and fish) to the town's population who live in the north western part of the town (Chapter 3.4.1). The other commercial units in this centre deal with short-term, mid-term and long-term (two radio and television shops) related consumer goods and services, such as repair work (car and cycle, 5 units), tailoring (3 units) and hair cutting (2 hair salons). This centre is developing very fast due to its close proximity to the commercial core area. In the very near future this centre will join with the commercial core area of the town along the main roads.

---

69 Chandra Prema, C. A., 1985

70 The author visited all these centres in Jan. 1990.

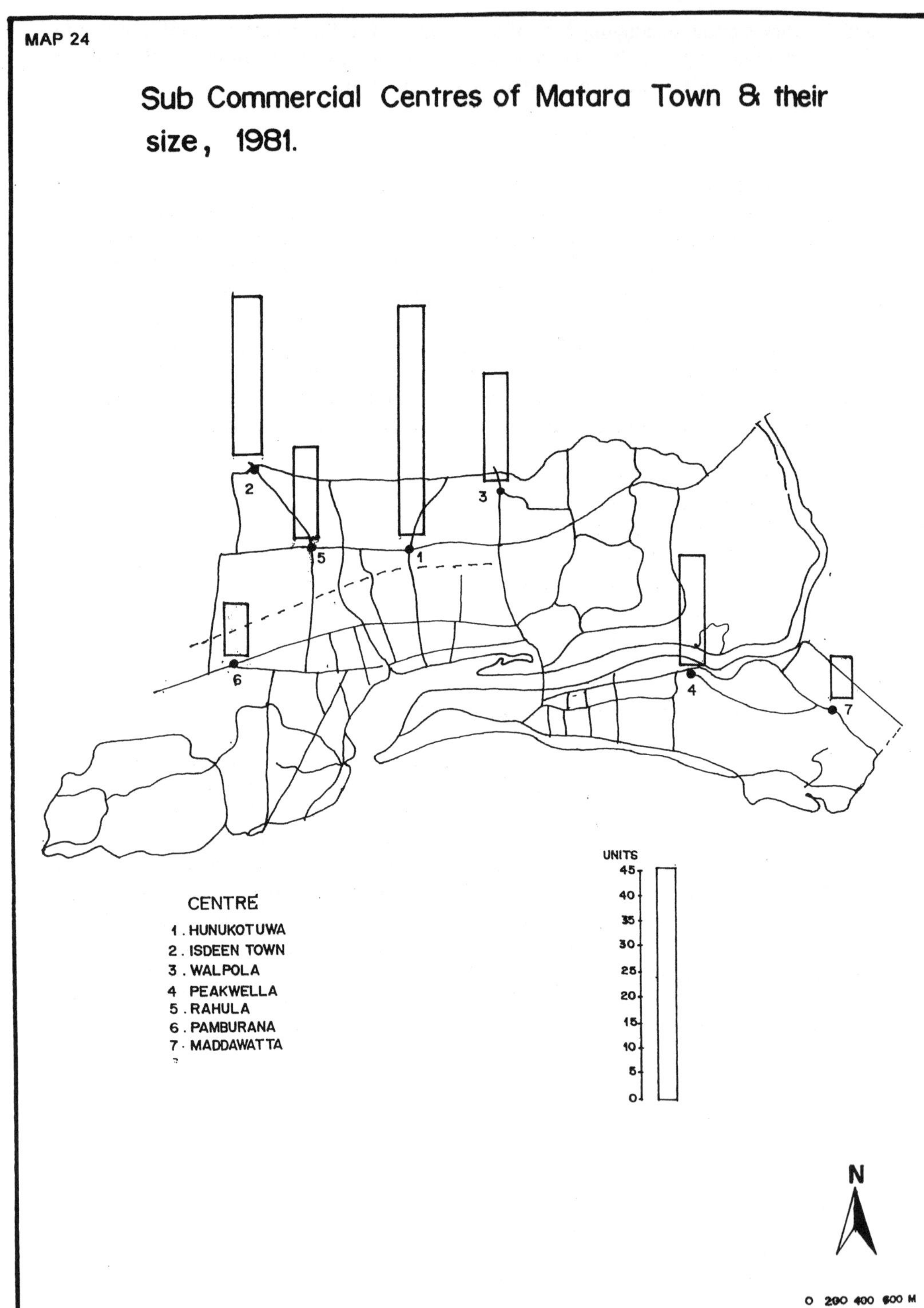
MAP 24
Sub Commercial Centres of Matara Town & their size, 1981.
1
2
3
4
5
6
7
CENTRE
1. HUNUKOTUWA
2. ISDEEN TOWN
3. WALPOLA
4 PEAKWELLA
5. RAHULA
6. PAMBURANA
7. MADDAWATTA
UNITS
45
40
35
30
25
20
15
10
5
0
N
0 200 400 600 M

3.4.3.2. Issadeen Town Sub-Commercial Centre.

Issadeen Town Centre is the second largest sub-commercial centre in the Matara town with 32 commercial units. It is situated at the road crossing between Matara - Akuressa major road and the minor road Weliweriya (Map 24 & photo 26). The growth of this centre contributed to the annexation of Issadeen town to the Matara U. C. in 1971. The majority (95%) of the commercial units deal with short-term and mid-term related consumer goods while a few of the units deal with long-term consumer goods (e.g. radio and television shops). There are five car and cycle repair workshops, two hair salons and one tailor shop located there. This sub-commercial centre provides services to the people who live in the extreme north western part of Matara.

3.4.3.3. Walpola Sub-Commercial Centre.

Walpola Centre is the third largest sub-commercial centre in the town with 23 commercial units and lies along the Hakmana Road in the northern part of town (Photo 27). The majority (95%) of the commercial units in this centre deal with short-term and mid-term related consumer goods. The service units such as repair workshops for car and cycle (2 units), hair salons (2 units), laundry (1 unit) and tailor shops (1 unit) are also located here. Walpola Sub-Commercial Centre provides services to the northern part of the town. This sub-service centre could also join the commercial core area of the town along the Hakmana Road in the near future due to its close proximity to the Matara town's commercial core area.

3.4.3.4. Peakwella Sub-Commercial Centre

Peakwella Centre is the fourth largest sub-commercial centre of the town with 22 shops. This centre lies along the old Tangalla Road on the south-eastern part of the town (Map 24). All of these shops are temporary in structure. Twenty out of 22 total shops in this centre deal with vegetables which are grown on the right bank of the Nilwala river. The vegetables are brought to the centre by small boats which are plying on the Nilwala river. According to information from one shop owner, two of these vegetable shops were established 50 years ago and continue to exist until today in spite of high competition. The other two shops deal with short and mid-term related consumer goods. This centre provides services to the town's population in the south-eastern part of the town.

3.4.3.5. Rahula Sub-Commercial Centre.

Rahula Centre is the fifth largest sub-commercial centre in the town with 18 commercial units. This centre lies between the road crossing Akuressa and Batuta Roads and Elavella and Batuta Roads (Map 24 & photo 28). The growth of this centre is mainly attributed to the Rahula College, which is one of the most famous schools in the southern western part of the island. Ninety-five percent of these shops deal with short and mid-term related consumer goods. The service related workshops such as repair service (3 car and cycle repair work shops) and one photo studio are located in this centre. This centre caters to the north-western part of the town.

3.4.3.6. <u>Pamburana Sub-Commercial Centre.</u>

Pamburana Centre is one of the smallest commercial sub-centres in the town with only ten units. Seven out of ten total shops in this centre deal with short and mid-term related consumer goods while the other units deal with services such as car and cycle repair (two units) and a petrol service station. This centre gives service to the extreme south western part of the town.

3.4.3.7. <u>Maddawatta Sub-Commercial Centre.</u>

Maddawatta Centre is the smallest sub-commercial centre in the town with only eight commercial units. This centre lies at the connecting point of Tangalle and Kekanadura Roads. Seven out of eight shops in this centre deal with short and mid-term related consumer goods, while the last one is a cycle repair shop.

3.4.4. <u>Evaluation of the Commercial Activities in the Town.</u>

The total commercial units comprising nine major categories (9 types) accounted for 1,698 in 1986 (Table 32). The majority of those units are located in the C.B.D. area of the town, while the others are located in the sub service centres. The relationship between the commercial units and the town's population (39,162 people in 1981) amounts to 0.04 units per person.

The primary goods related shops comprising 19 % (318 units) of the total commercial units (Table 32) is sufficient to provide for most of the important basic needs of the town and surrounding area. However, the uneven spatial distribution of these units cause three-quarters of the town's population to come to the town's core area in order to get these commodities. The most important commercial units in this category are the weekly and the two daily markets.

Secondary consumer goods are composed of various kinds of urban manufactured goods. These are provided to the town's consumers by 382 commercial units (24 % of the total urban shops). Within this category, the shops which sell a variety of urban manufacture goods[71] (glassware, pans, ribbons, costume jewellery, soap, garments & cosmetic goods) are predominant with 209 units; followed by textile shops, jewellery shops and footwear shops with 66, 49 and 26 respectively. These shops are in a position to meet the demands of the town's and district's population. The household, construction and vehicle related units consisting of 3.0% (55 units), 2.0% (40 units) and 4.0% (71 units) respectively, provide goods to the town's and the district's population.

The manufacturing cum sale units, consisting of 8.2% of the total commercial units, are in a position to provide services to the whole district. The most important units in this category are rice mills (2 units), bakery (20 units) and metal manufacturing and processing units. The town's rice and coconut mills, not only process these agricultural products but also distribute the finished goods to the whole region. The bakery units

---

71 These shops are called "Sappu Badu Kade" by the Sinhala population.

supply bread to the town and surrounding areas. The metal manufacturing and processing units provide services to the whole district. The service cum sale units consisting of 30% (507 units) of the total commercial units are the major commercial sector in the town. The highest number of establishments in this category (121 units) are related to repair workshops (cars and motorcycles) followed by barber salons, bicycle repair, tailor shops, radio repair,printing press and photo studios, consisting of 55, 38,32, 17 and 29 units respectively. They are in a good position not only to serve the town's population but also to serve the surrounding areas.

The hotel sector in this category, consisting of 45 restaurants, 130 small tea shops and eight hotels, provides refreshments for the town's population and the pilgrims and travellers who travel through Matara as well as to the buyers who come from other areas to Matara to buy consumer goods or services.

The bed capacity for the local travellers is well provided for by the Matara Resthouse which has 20 rooms and 25 employees. Spending nights in hotels is not common in Sri Lankan society. The travellers always try to find a house of a relative or a friend for this purpose. In addition to this, there are another 7 hotels which provide board and lodgings for locals as well as for tourists. The average number of rooms and employees for each unit was 12 in 1981. The average number of guest nights accounted for 330 foreigners and 43 locals.[72] The inadequacy of rooms for foreigners has drawn inhabitants of the town to turn the residential houses into guest houses. This has led to the uncontrolled development of tourist activities. However, since 1982 there has been a very sharp decline of tourist arrivals to Sri Lanka due to the civil unrest. The tourist arrivals have declined from 407,230 in 1982 to 230,106 in 1986[73]. This led to a decrease in the number of guest nights, the room occupancy rate and earnings from the tourist sector. However, the economy of Matara was not badly effected by this decline like centres such as Hikkaduwa, Unawatuna which are solely dependent on tourism.

The warehouses which constitute 11.0% (180 units) of the total commercial units are a good example for the storing and distribution function of Matara town

The above facts show that the commercial sector of Matara is established well enough to fill the requirements of the town's inhabitants and the district's population.

3.4.5. The Future Development of Matara Town.

An examination of the population in the town shows a typical expansion of population with high birth rates (26%) and a rather rapidly decreasing death rate (6.4%). The population above 18 years increased from 54.7% in 1971 to 61.7% in 1981 (Table 2 & 5). So the potential workforce increased by 7% during this period.

The economy of the town is mainly based on the service and commercial sector activities while the secondary sector plays a very insignificant role.

---

72 Structure Plan - Matara Town, 1981,(see under "Tourism").

73 Economic review, 1987, May

Community, social and personal service sectors offering 36.1% of the total employment for the urban settlements of the Matara district, takes first place followed by the trade sector with 24.6%. In contrast to these two sectors, the secondary sector offers only 7.8% of the total employment(Table 19 & 20). A high percentage of employment in this category is provided by the government and semi-government institutions. Fourty percent of the total employment in the urban settlements of the Matara district are offered by the public sector institutions. Eighty-six percent of the professional workers, 45% of the managerial workers and 86% of the clerical workers in this category are attached to the government and semi-government institutions.

The private sector employment in this category is insignificant. The growth of employment in these two sectors between 1971 and 1981 was very low. The community, social and personal sector employments and the commercial sector employments during this period has increased only by 3.4% and 1.9% while secondary sector employment decreased by 1.3%.

The revenue collected as taxes by the local authority, the Urban Council, is not sufficient to meet the expenses incurred by the authority. According to the analysis of income and expenses of the Matara U.C. in 1990, the total income of the local body in 1990 was 42,058,660 Rupees of which only 68.05% was derived from taxes and 31.95% was derived from government grants. The total expenses incurred by the local body in 1990 was 42,058,170 Rupees[74] (Table 41 and Diag.20).

Table 41
Analysis of income, Matara U.C. 1990.

Type of income	Amount(in Mill R.P.)	%
Government Grants	13.4	31.95
Rates	02.0	04.76
Tax	26.6	63.29
Total	42.0	100.00

Source : Budget Report, Matara U.C., 1990.

These figures show that the existence of this local body is impossible without the financial help of the government. The main reason for this low tax income is the low tax rates which are imposed on the small scale (low capital investments) commercial units. These small scale commercial units constitute almost 95% of the total commercial establishments of the town. In addition to this, it was revealed that there are many small scale shop owners who do not regularly pay their rates to the local body.

---

[74] Budget Report, Matara U.C. 1990

Diag.20: Analysis of Income, Matara U.C., 1990

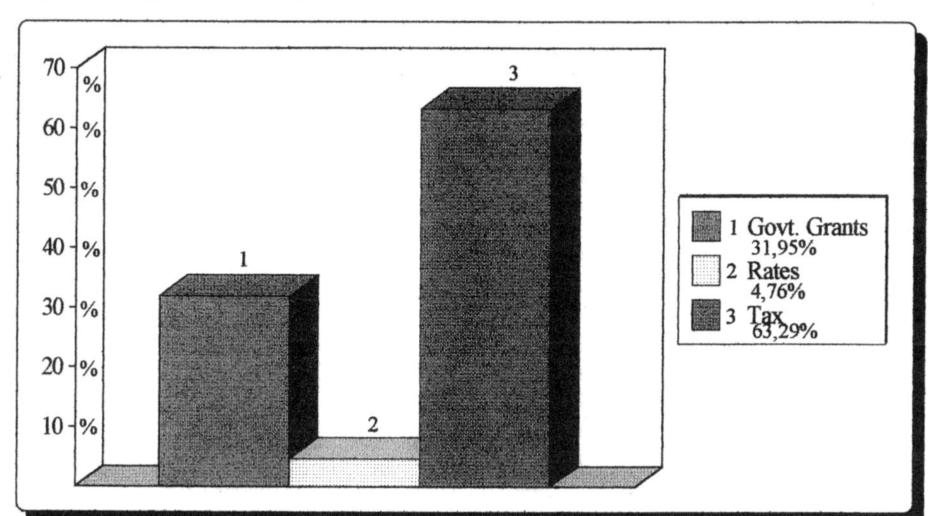

According to the 1990 budget report of Matara Urban Council, 92.20% of the total income was spent on the non-productive service sector (to pay wages, salaries, repair water wells and roads) while only 7.8% was invested that yielded returns[75] (Table 42 and Diag.21).

Table 42
Analysis of Expenditure, Matara U.C., 1990.

Type of Expenditure	Amount (Mill.Rp.)	%
Maintenance	31.0	73.66
Capital Expenditure	03.3	07.80
Public Administration	77.5	15.39
Financial Management	01.2	03.00
Others	00.0	00.15

Source. Budget Report, Matara U.C., 1990.

This shows the precarious economic situation of the town. The out migration which occurs due to the unfavourable socio- economic conditions of the town can be stopped in the future only by improving the aforesaid economic sectors .

The expansion of the primary sector activities in town is limited. However, intensification of the limited resources can substantially contribute to the solution of underemployment and financial problems of the town. In addition to the intensification

[75] Ibid.

Diag.21: Analysis of Expenditure, Matara U.C., 1990

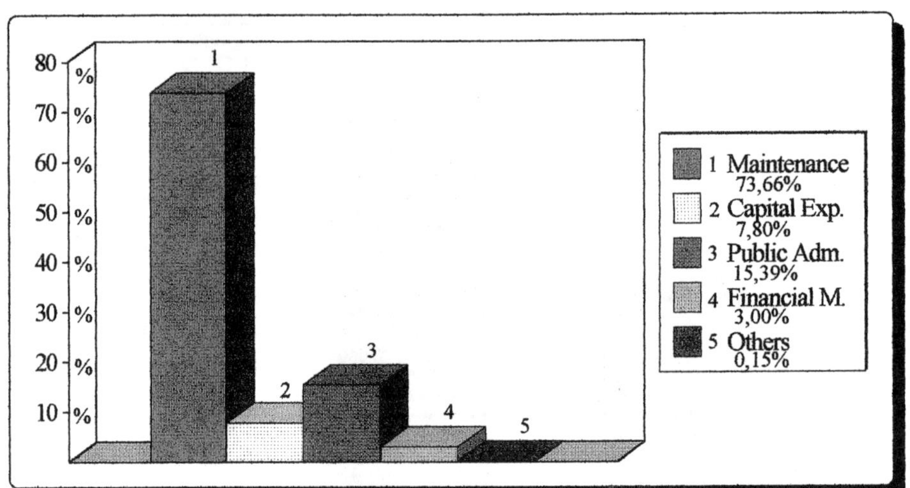

of the agricultural sector, poultry farming should be emphasised to the agricultural sector as a means of supplementary income to the households.

The creation of job opportunities in the community, social and personal sectors in the future is limited due to the fact that the availability of employment in these sectors is low (e.g. Kachcheri, hospitals and other government and semi-government offices). The decentralisation of these sectors further curtails the employment opportunities in this area.

The growth of Matara town as the district capital will increase the commercial activities of the town. This invariably brings more job opportunities for the town's population but it is questionable whether this growth can keep pace with the population increase in town. The commercial units which have sprung up so far are very small units with low investments. According to the 1984 survey, the average number of employees for a commercial unit in the C.B.D. area was only 2.

The employment generating capacity in the tourist sector of the town is limited. This is mainly due to the lack of scenic beaches, sites of archaeological values and other physical constraints. However, the improvement of physical constraints and the development of the two islets, namely Parey Duwa and Galagodiyana Duwa, which are still in disuse, as tourist centres could attract tourism which invariably creates more job opportunities for the town's population.

The secondary sector has a greater potential for creating employment than any other sector in town. However, this development is not based on the service cum manufacturing related industrial units such as garages which have sprung up like mushrooms over the last decade, but rather on the agro-based industries. The textile and influential open economic policy, have increased the employment opportunities for the fast expanding workforce. It is noteworthy to mention in this context, the newly established food producing industrial unit at Polhena. According to an Urban Council higher officer, this unit offers an estimated 150 jobs to the town's population, while at the same time, the textile industries absorb most of the female workforce, who were previously employed in the coir yarn industries at low wages.

The financial help, entrepreneurship and departure from the rentencapitalistic behaviour are vitally important to develop this sector. Although the development of industries is a key element in the government's economic policies, the government expenditure in this sector is still much lower in comparison to the agricultural sector. The government expenditure in this sector in 1986 was only 3.2% (106 million Rupees) of the total expenditure (3,296 million Rupees). The expenditure on the agriculture sector accounted for 13.5% (446 million Rupees). In contrast to the government expenditure, the commercial banks of Sri Lanka in 1986 gave 22.8% (9.3 million Rupees) of the total loans (40 million Rupees) to the industrial sector while giving only 10.3% to the agricultural sector[76]. The government's limited investment in the industrial sector can be attributed to its present policies for industrial development.

Currently, the government perceives its role in industrial development as mainly providing the necessary economic climate and the basic infrastructure. The private sector bears the major share of the burden in developing a viable industrial structure in Sri Lanka. However, an interview with a Bank of Ceylon's manager in 1987 revealed that a high percentage of the loans in Matara District were given to the agricultural sector. Nevertheless, it is noteworthy to mention that Peoples Bank and the Indian Oversee Bank at Matara gave loans to the producers who were involved in the production of Maldive fish (dried fish = Umbalakada) at Nilwella, Polhena and Totamuna. This sector provides seasonal employment and lucrative alternatives for the low price sale of tuna fish (Balaya) in the glut period.

The improvement of the existing agro-based industries (20 units), the cottage industries (940 coir yarn industrial units, 131 carpentry units and 19 textile units) and the establishment of new small-scale industries with large capital investments are vitally important to solve the unemployment problem of the town. In this regard, the government investments and the bank loans are very important to a country like Sri Lanka to improve this sector due to the lack of capital among the private sector entrepreneurship. In addition, the provision of other incentives are important to stimulate investments by private enterprises.

---

76 Review of the Economy, 1986, p. 252 - 301.

CHAPTER 4

4. Social Services and the Service Network of Matara Town

Under social services education, health facilities, recreational facilities and other community services are taken into consideration. Under the service network transportation, water supply, electricity supply and sewage are discussed.

4.1. Social Services

4.1.1. Education

Matara was said to be an important educational centre prior to the Colonial Period (Chapter 1). The history of the existing educational establishments of the town go back to the Roman Catholic and Protestant missionaries during the British period. The oldest existing schools in town, namely St. Servets College and St. Thomas College, were built by the British in 1894 and 1844 respectively.

Currently, there are eight different types of educational institutions in Matara and they are as follows:

1) Pre-schools (data pertaining to numbers is not available)
2) Primary schools (13 units, public sector)
3) Secondary schools (10 units, public sector)
4) Pirivens (Cloister schools)
5) Private schools (data pertaining to numbers is not available)
6) Polytechnic schools (1 unit, public sector)
7) Teachers training school (1 unit, public sector)
8) University of Ruhuna (Faculty of Arts and Science, public sector)

Educational facilities in the town are well distributed. In almost every ward there is at least one school. In addition, all the schools are within walking distance from the residential areas. Although the Matara Urban Council area has much better educational facilities than the other areas of the Matara district, they are still short of providing quality service to the school-going population of the town. These deficiencies can be attributed to the poor physical conditions of the schools as well as the shortage of school personnel as given below [1].

A) Fifty-seven percent (57%) of all the schools in town are primary schools. This leads to an overcrowding of the secondary schools.

B) The shortage of teachers is a considerable problem in the education system. According to the Education Department of Matara, the student/teacher ratio in the public schools of Matara in 1984 was 27:1.

---

[1] This information is based on the information of the Education Department, Matara & Structure Plan Matara 1981.

C) About nineteen percent (19%) of the secondary schools in town have no commercial and science education.

D) The majority of the schools which have science education cannot provide quality service to the students due to the lack of laboratory facilities and equipment.

E) Fifty percent (50%) of the schools lack toilet facilities.

F) As many as twenty schools in the town lack play ground facilities.

The opening of the University of Ruhuna in Matara (1981) can be described as a historical leap forward in the educational development in this region (Photo 29). The educational institutions in Matara play a crucial role in the development of the town.

9.1.2. Health Facilities

The health care units of the town of Matara can be categorised into eight (8) groups as follows:

Table 43

Medical Institute	Type of Medicine	No of Units
1) District hospitals	Western medicine	1 Unit
2) Private clinics	Western medicine	4 Units
3) Ayurvedic clinic	Indigenous medicine	1 Unit
4) Private dispensaries	Western Medicine	6 Units
5) Private Ayurvedic Dispensaries	Indigenous medicine	7 Units
6) Public Health Clinics	Western Medicine	3 Units
7) Dental Clinics	Western Medicine	3 Units
8) Pharmacies	Western Medicine	5 Units
Total		30 Units

The ratio of the town's population to health care institutions is 1,263:1. The most important health care institutions among these units are the more popular western medicine institutions. The history of western medicine in the town goes back to the Dutch period. The first hospital, which no longer exists, was built by the Dutch in Fort between 1720-1745 to treat the soldiers and Dutch officials (Chapter 1). The oldest western medicine institution, which still exists today, is the Matara District Hospital (base hospital). It was built by the British in 1936 on the right bank of the Nilwala river.

The spatial distribution of the health facilities shows a high concentration in the commercial core area (C.B.D.), namely Uyanwatta and along the Mainstreet while there is a marked lack of such facilities in certain areas of the town such as: Weragampitiya, Walpola, Polhena, Isdeen Town, and Welegoda (Map 25).

MAP - 25 Distribution Pattern of Health Care Units - Matara Town, 1980.

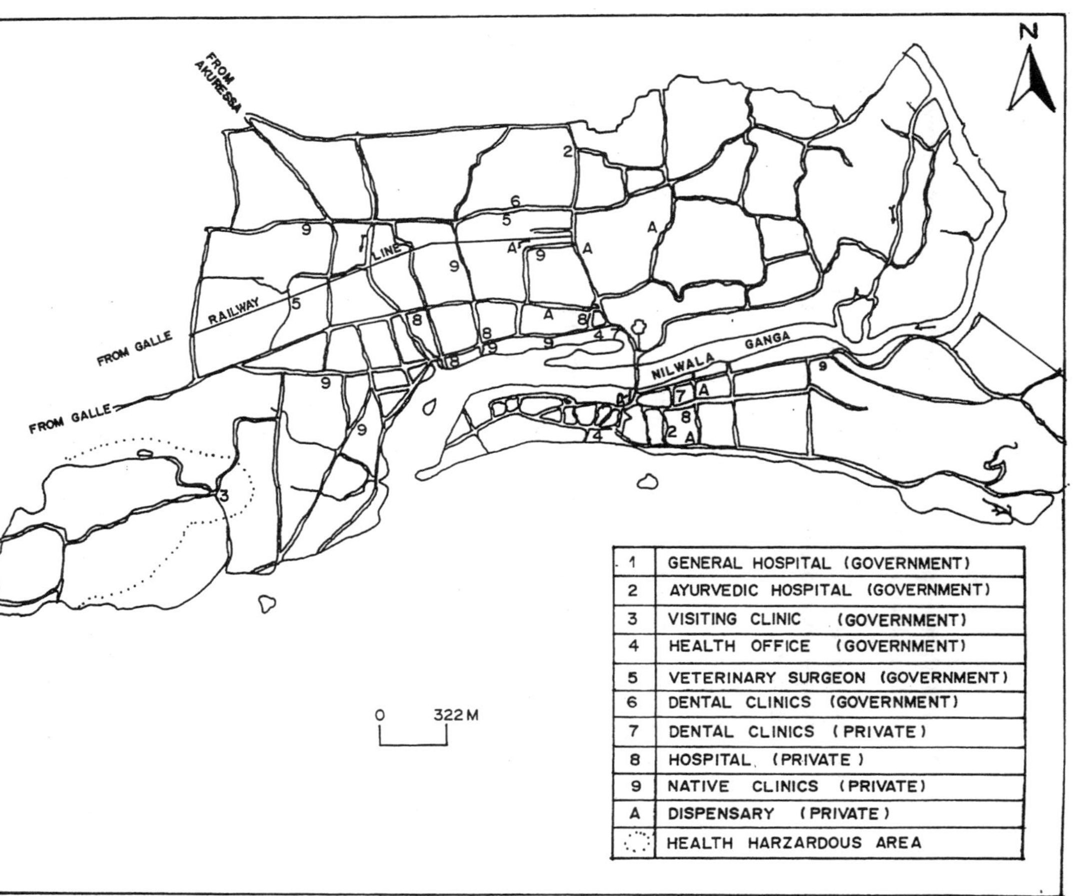

9.1.2.1. The Matara Base Hospital[2]

This hospital, run by the government, is strategically located and has easy access to the other rural and major hospitals (Photo 30). It is considered to be the best equipped health institution of the district, possessing forty percent (40%) of the district's total hospital beds, seventy-two percent (72%) of the total number of qualified doctors and seventy-two percent (72%) of the total district's nurses. Even though it is considered the best, often the replacement and addition to the stock of equipment and supplies is not met, causing major gaps in the quality of service provided.

One such deficiency is a pathological laboratory. Requirements for special pathological examinations must be sent away, resulting in delayed diagnosis and treatment. The hospital capacity is fully utilized throughout the year. The problems of over crowding are felt as the area serviced by this hospital is very large. The average number of people treated as out patients per day was 800.[3] There are many patients who lie on the floor or under the beds because the bed capacity of the hospital is not sufficient.

Some private clinics and nursing homes in the town have inpatient facilities. On the average, one hundred and fifty (150) patients visit these medical institution each day.[4]

The Ayurvedic Cinic, which is run by the Matara Urban Council is in a run-down, deteriorating state. An average of one hundred and five (105) patients seek medical attention in this clinic each day.[5] The three health clinics which are located at Polhena, Star Fort, and at the Medical Office of Health, carry out the immunisation against polio, tetanus, diphtheria, whooping cough, and tuberculosis. There is an anti-filaria unit in the Urban Council health office which, besides taking blood tests in the field, also carries out insecticide spraying operations.

4.1.3. Recreation Facilities

An acute lack of public spaces is one of the major problems in town. The existing open space ratio per one thousand (1000) inhabitants is only 0.2 hectares. Though there are vast open areas in some wards of the town, they are not suitable for public use as they are generally low lying and water-logged . The major organised public open spaces in the town are Uyanwatta Esplanade and Kotuwegoda Esplanade which are of Dutch origin and measure approximately 6.49 hectares. Both of these public spaces are located in the town centre. Six (6) out of the eleven (11) wards of the town do not have organised public open spaces.

Due to the institutional encroachment of public spaces during the last two (2) decades,such as the construction of a cricket stadium in the Uyanwatta Esplanade and the

---

2 This is the main health care institution which offers health care services to the population of Matara as well as to the Hambantota district.

3 Matara, Final Report ,Urban Development Authority, 1982, p. 58.

4 Structure Plan, 1980/81.

5 Ibid

occupation of half of the Kotuwegoda Esplanade by the Ceylon Transport Board Terminal, the available organised open spaces for the public have been further reduced (Photo 31). With the occupation of the Kotuwegoda Esplanade by C.T.B. Bus Terminal the town lost part of a fine recreational space. Furthermore, the beach to the south of the bus terminal is separated both physically and visually from the area north of the Kotuwegoda Esplanade. This has led to misuse of the beach. A number of small commercial units have established themselves around the bus terminal. In addition, this occupation has been the cause of many conflicts in traffic, namely at the junction north of the terminal, of the bridge along Mainstreet and Pallimulla Road (Photo 32).

This indicates that there is a direct conflict between recreational and other uses of the land. Presently, priority has been given to other services, as the administration considers the other services (commercial) to be more important to the public than the need for recreational facilities. This can be attributed to the fact that Matara is still a medium size town which has less congestion of industrial and commercial activities with domination of rural characteristics in most of the Urban Council areas. Therefore, it can be assumed that there is no great demand for recreational facilities such as open spaces from the town population itself.

It is noteworthy to mention that the Urban Council of Matara has become more conscious of the environmental condition of the town during the last few years. Kotuwegoda Beach, especially along the Beach Road, was once used as a dumping ground for urban trash in 1984, was converted into a garden by planting pine trees in 1991 (Photo 33).

Much greater emphasis should be given to the potential use of the beach as a natural heritage in Matara town because it has a greater potential to serve as a main recreational area.

4.1.4. Housing Schemes

As discussed in Chapter 2, there is a great housing shortage in town, especially in qualitative terms. To combat the housing shortage the government has implemented several steps. The National Housing Department (N.H.D.A) and the Urban Council of Matara play an important role in the housing projects in the Matara Urban Council area.

The low income groups of Matara are given preferential treatment when it comes to building housing projects. Matara has four low income housing schemes which are located in Walpola, Kadeweediya, Polhena, and Mainstreet. There is also a police headquarters housing scheme along the Sea Beach Road in Kotuwegoda (Photo 34). A certain degree of basic services such as roads, water supply and electricity are provided in these housing schemes. It is noteworthy to mention that the environmental improvement scheme at Totamune, which was inaugurated by the Urban Council of Matara and Urban Development Authority, improved the condition of about thirty-five (35) shanties by providing basic services and amenities such as water, toilets and garbage containers.

4.1.5. Other Community Facilities

The police headquarters of the Matara district is located on Mainstreet and the main jail in Fort. The main post office and telegraph office, which are located in Kotuwegoda, are in close proximity of each other. There are five (5) sub-post offices. They are located in the wards of Forts, Meddawatta, Uyanwatta, Welegoda, and Polehena (Ward nos. 1, 3, 5, 8, 10). The public telephone company, delivery facilities, and telegraph facilities exist only at the main post and telegraph office. The town hall and the public library are located in Ward 6, on Mainstreet.

Two of the best known cultural organisations on the island, Young Men's Buddhist Association (Y.M.B.A), and the Young Women's Christian Association (Y.W.C.A.), are also established in Matara.

4.2. Service Network

4.2.1. Transport Network

As discussed in Chapter 1, there was a track which connected Matara to Manthai, the ancient port of Sri Lanka, and to the other important political centres of the country, prior to the colonial powers. With the development of the spice trade, especially cinnamon during the Dutch period, this track was improved and better connected Matara to the other important sea ports, as well as to the Dutch military posts on the island. In addition, new tracks have been built in order to connect the interior parts of this region to Matara. The first track to Hakmana and to Akuressa were constructed during this period and later these trails were further improved and turned into roads by the British.

The British developed the road network and also introduced the railway system connecting Matara with Galle and Colombo. Through the development of the roads and the railway system, Matara has become the major urban centre, as well as the major commercial centre in the Matara district, thus connecting it with the other urban centres of its hinterland and coastal areas. According to the structure plan of 1980/81, the road network of Matara consists of one hundred and sixty-eight (168) roads which are different in quality and occupy 8.02% of the total land area of the town. The total length of these roads is approximately 51 miles (81.6 km). From this total, 33 miles have tar and metal surfaces. The remaining roads consist of sand and gravel.

The road network of the town is comprised of a distinct hierarchy where the truck routes, i.e., the coastal highway (A class road), Hakmana and Akuressa (B class roads) function as principal roads, Rahula Road, Uyanwatta Circular Road and Mainstreet as major roads, while all other roads inter-link different areas of the town with minor streets (Map 26). The Colombo-Hambantota Coastal Highway, which consists of Broadway Road and New Tangalle Road, passes through the central areas of the town, connecting the town with important service centres in the Hambantota District on the east and Galle and the other important service centres on the west. The Akuressa and Hakmana Road, which links Matara to the interior part of the Matara district, also passes through the central areas of the town.

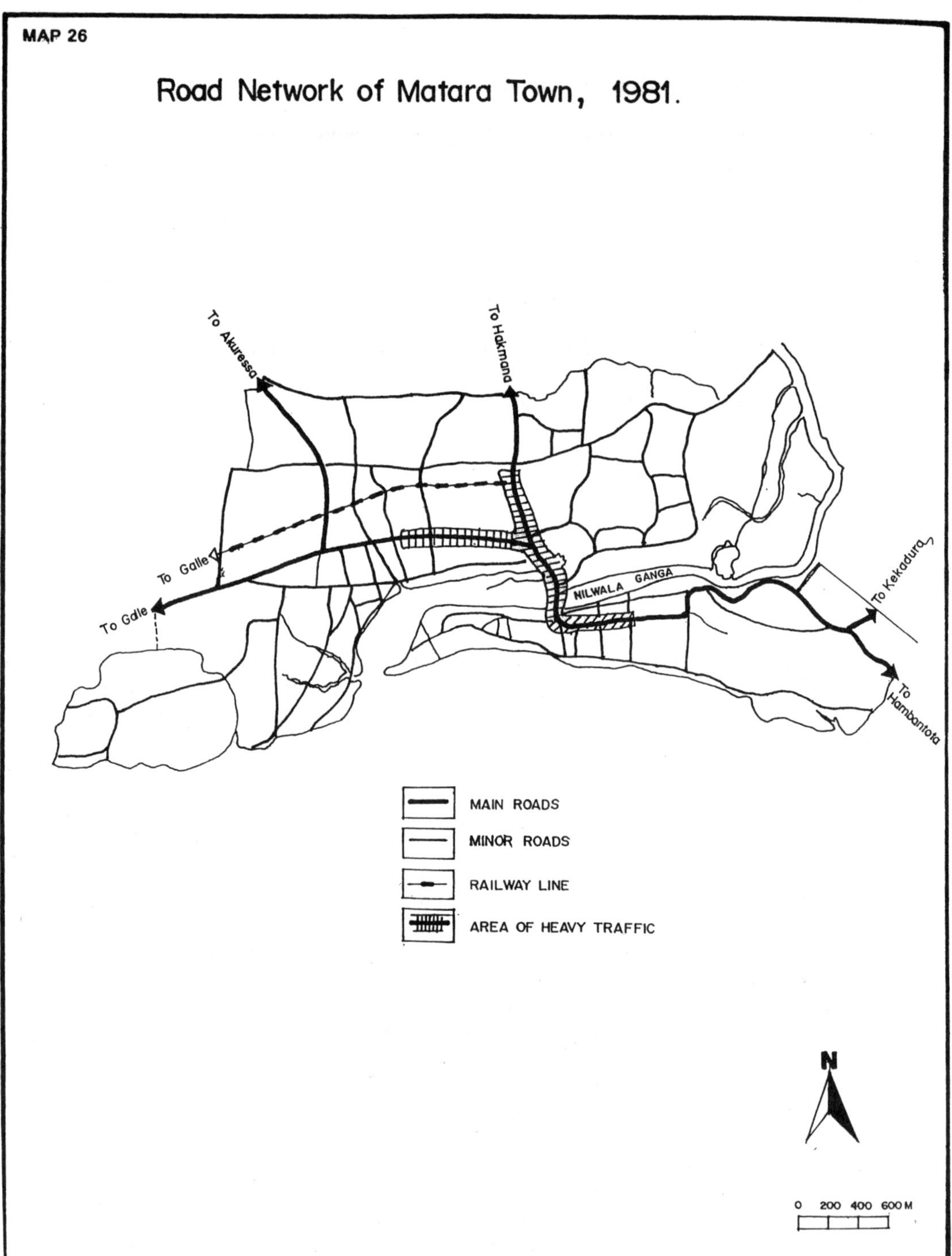

MAP 26
Road Network of Matara Town, 1981.
To Akuressa
To Hakmana
To Galle
To Galle
NILWALA GANGA
To Kekadura
To Hambantota
MAIN ROADS
MINOR ROADS
RAILWAY LINE
AREA OF HEAVY TRAFFIC
N
0 200 400 600 M

The spatial distribution of the road network shows that the major institutional and residential areas of the town are well inter-inked with the truck routes,except some areas of the wards of Polhena, Walpola and Meddawatta,due to physical constraints as discussed earlier in the Chapter 2. The major problem in the road network of the town is the congestion of roads in the commercial core area. The following facts have contributed to the problem of congestion.

A) The establishment of commercial and industrial activities that generate traffic, either through their need for constant servicing of provisions and wholesale establishments or through the nature of the activity, i.e. workshops, garages and various mills, has resulted in curb side parking for long durations, thereby contributing to congestion on the following roads: Broadway, Mainstreet, Pallimulla Road (New Tangalla Road) and Hakmana Road.

B) Roads such as Mainstreet and Old Tangalle Road, though designated as one-way roads, are used for two-way traffic, resulting in low flow of traffic and congestion.

C) The Nilwala river which divides the town into two parts, has a bridge at only one point, linking most of the roads on either side.

D) The administrative centre of the town in Fort, the daily market at Kotuwegoda, the periodic market on Mainstreet, and the Main Bus Terminal, private and C.T.B.bus terminal at Kotuwegoda, are located just off the bridge. These generate the heavy traffic at the southern part of the bridge, which is in the commercial core area (C.B.D.).

E) One of the principle transportation problems in the town occurs due to quality of the roadways. Most of these roads were built early in this century during the British period and in the post colonial period to cater to very low traffic flows.

According to the Structure Plan - Matara town , 1980/81 , 99% of the roads in the town are less than 9.9 meters in width. The widest road is the coastal highway, measuring 6-6.6 meters, followed by the Akuressa and Hakmana Roads, both measuring 4.2-5.4 meters. Many of these roads have passed through a period of severe neglect due to the lack of finance and materials (Pallimulla Road, Hakmana Road, Sea Beach Road, Mainstreet, Photo 35).

F) The soil of the town mainly consists of red and yellow podzolic soils, alluvial soils and regosol soils which are resistant to the water percolation. The water which is retained on the top of the clay layer causes severe damage to the roads, causing high maintenance expenses.

G) The lack of foot paths or pavement has led to the spilling over of pedestrians onto the already congested roads. This results in constriction of the traffic flow and accident hazards due to mix of modes. According to a study done by the police department (traffic) in 1987, the daily influx of vehicles into Matara was approximately 5,000, while the daily influx of people was approximately 40,000.

The occurrence of accidents in Matara town is much higher than in other centres of the Matara district. In 1987, there were 187 accidents in the administration area[6] of the traffic department of Matara, seven (7) of them were fatal accidents. Eighty percent (80%) of the total accidents took place in the town of Matara.[7] The reasons for the high occurrence of accidents, according to the officer in charge of traffic (OIC), were the narrow roads and the high volume of traffic.

An examination of the daily influx of vehicles into Matara shows that the highest number of vehicles (2,341) enter the town on the coastal highway from the western region of the Matara district, where large commercial and urban areas, such as Galle, Moratuwa, Mt. Lavinia and Colombo, are found (Chapter 6 & Diag 22). This is an indicator that the highest intensity of transactions is found in the western regions of the town. The second highest volume of communication is found in the eastern region of the Matara district, where the low level of urbanisation and large agricultural areas are found. The daily influx of vehicles on the coastal highway, from the eastern region of Matara, was 1,906 (Table 44). The lowest number of vehicles entered the town on the Akuressa and Hakmana Road from the northern region of the Matara district, where the major and minor cash crops are grown. This is due to the fact that Matara has lost its role as the centre for reloading the estate sector inputs and outputs (Chapter 6).

Table 44

Daily Influx of Vehicles by Type, Matara, 1.2.88

Road and direction of Influx	Type of Vehicles.				
	Cars	Buses	Trucks	Motorcycle	Total
Coastal Highway from west	543	679	689	433	2341
Coastal Highway from east	412	663	517	314	1906
Akuressa and Hakmana Road from the North	295	346	418	522	1581

Source: Department of Highways, Colombo, 1.2.1988.

The above discussion has proven that Matara is an important traffic nodal point between the coastal zone in the south and the hilly region in the north.

6 Jurisdiction area of the Traffic Department of Police at Matara is about 15 Km. radius. It is limited to Malimboda on Akuressa, Thihagoda on Hakmana Road and Kekanadura on Yatiyana Road.

7 Traffic Department of Police, Matara, 1987.

From North

Cars	295
Buses	346
Trucks	418
Motorcycles	522
Total	1581

MATARA

From West

Cars	543
Buses	679
Trucks	689
Motorcycles	433
Total	2341

From East

Cars	412
Buses	663
Trucks	517
Motorcycles	314
Total	1906

No. of Vehicles

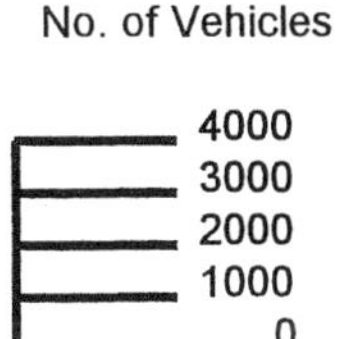

Diag.22: Daily influx of vehicles, (number of vehicles), into Matara, 1.2.1988

4.2.2. Water Supply

The Nilwala river is the only source of water for the town. The main elements in this system include the bank side intake on the Nilwala river at Nadugala, which is located 6 miles (10 km) north of the town. The treatment plant has a current capacity of 1.5 million gallons(6.8 million litres) per day. The existing raw water intake suffers from salinity of the Nilwala river at certain times of the year. The river level at Nadugala is influenced by tidal action, since the bed level is below mean sea level. Consequently, when very high tides coincide with low river flow, salinity invades within the tidal reach of the river upstream of the Nadugala intake. Under these conditions the water quality becomes unacceptable with more than 1000mg/1 total dissolved solids on occasions[8] and the intake pumps have to be switched off. This problem does not occur every year, although it may occur on several successive days leading to limitations of water supply. The present water supply to consumers in Matara is by means of standpipes and metered house connections. It is available to the consumers only 10 hours a day, namely 4 hours in the morning, 3 hours in the mid day and 3 hours in the evening.

An examination of the number of housing units with water service in the town show that only thirty-nine percent (39%,in 1971 it was only 23.3%) of the total housing units, comprised of 16,135 persons, have water service at home, while the majority of the residents depend on stand posts which are located throughout the town or other sources of water supply, such as wells and rivers (Photo 36). A high portion of this treated water is consumed by the domestic sector, which is 87.50% of the total water consumption. The water consumption by the other sectors is very low with only 12.5% of the total (Table 45).

Table 45
The Daily Water Consumption
Matara Town 1980

Sector	Consumption (Gallons)	%
Domestic	1312071 (5904319 litres)	87.5
Other sectors	188329 (847480 litres)	12.5

Source: Structure plan Matara town, 1981.

The spatial distribution of the water supply network shows that most areas of the town are fairly covered while some areas, such as Isdeen Town, remain unserviced and depend on other sources. The average per capita water consumption in town, of 150 litres per day, is much lower than the accepted international standard of 180 litres set by the World Health Organisation. The existing shortcomings and other problems (salinity) in the water supply network in town could be solved to a certain extent with the completion of the Kadduwa raw water intake plant which lies 5 miles (8 km.)upstream of Nadugala.

---

8 Matara Water Supply Project, Appraisal Report, 1983, p. 8

4.2.3. The Electricity Supply

The Ceylon Electricity Board supplies electricity to Matara Town. The distribution centre at Matara provides electricity to Matara as well as some outside centres such as Weligama, Weherahena and Dondara. The electrical network of Matara consists of 3.3 kv and 11 kv. Although the major part of the town is provided with 11 kv supply, there are certain parts of the town such as Broadway, Issadeen Town, Piladuwa and Meddawatta, which are still connected to the old 3.3 kv supply and subject to frequent breakdowns.

The spatial distribution of the electrical network shows that the areas in the town centres are well connected to the electrical network while the peripheral areas are poorly connected[9]. The street lighting is mostly confined to the centre of town. According to the structure plan of Matara in 1984, the Matara Urban Council alone consumed 42.8 % of the district's electricity supply.

The residential units which have electricity have increased from 45.2% in 1971 to 68.2% in 1981[10]. Although electricity is the main source of energy which is consumed by a large percentage of the population in the Urban Council area, 31.8 % of the total housing units still use kerosene oil and wood as sources of energy. These substitutions are used primarily by the low income groups of the town .

The prevailing consumption pattern in the town is shown in Table 46.

Table 46

The Consumption of Electrical Power
Among Various Sectors, 1981

Sector	% of Total Consumption
Commercial	09.99
Industrial	08.32
Institutions	17.24
Domestic	56.17
Religion Institutions	01.21
Street Lighting	07.07
Total	100.00

Electricity Department, Matara, 1981.

According to the above table, the domestic sector is the highest consumer of electrical energy, followed by the institutions. The relatively low industrial consumption is due to the fact that major industries such as Harischandra Mills and Odiris Silva Mills are direct consumers, obtaining their requirements from the Ceylon Electricity Board and not from the Matara Urban Council's distribution grid.

---

9 Final Report , Matara.,1982.

10 Electricity Dept., 1981.

4.2.4. Surface Drainage and Waste Water Disposal

4.2.4.1. Surface Drainage

The surface drainage network in the Matara town is as poor as in the other urban settlements, such as Badulla and Galle of Sri Lanka (ref. Dicke, S., 1987; Wellmer, H., 1989). The poor drainage network in the Matara Urban Council areas is mainly attributed to the unfavourable topographic conditions. As discussed in Chapter 2, a substantial portion of the Matara Urban Council area lies below the mean sea level. Construction of a good drainage network is very costly.

The first surface drainage network, which still exists today (Nupe canal and other small canals), was the work of the Dutch (Photo 37). They were constructed not only to prevent the floods, particularly in the Monsoon period, but also to dispose of the domestic waste water. The network of surface drains along the major roads which were constructed of masonry to carry the surface runoff, had come into existence during the British period and continues to exist today.

This network of drains is connected to a number of outlets (Elas) through which the water is let into the Nilwala river or the sea, depending upon the topography.

The acute problems which prevail in this surface drainage network are given below.

A) The cemented canals along the major roads are not well maintained and are not cleaned regularly. This leads to the disturbance of the slope and water stagnation for long periods.

B) The canals which are dug in the earth and not cement formed by the side of the roads, silt the Elas into which they carry the surface run-off from the roads. This results in the flooding of areas, particularly on the banks of the Elas, as well as low lying areas such as Uyanwatta Walpola, Polhena, Meddawatta, and Isdeen Town, during the Monsoons for long periods of time.

C) The Elas (canals) which are supposed to be used for surface drainage, are used for the soaking of coir by the people engaged in making coir products, particularly in Polhena and in Totamuna, which leads to the stagnation and pollution of the water, as well as pollution of the air.

D) The surface drainage network, which is subjected to stagnation and pollution of water, is a favourable breeding place for the mosquitoes Culex Fatigans and Anopheles, which are considered to be the vector of filariasis and malaria.

4.2.4.2. Sewerage

There is no sewerage network in the town. Septic tanks and pits are used to dispose of the human waste. All the human waste disposal systems (tanks, pits) in the town are lacking sanitary measures and provide breeding places for the pathogenic agents.[11]

However, a high percentage of the town's population does not have access to methods of hygienic disposal of night-soil.[12] Therefore, it must make use of the coastal and low lying areas in the vicinity of their settlements. According to the census of the population and housing in 1981, 25 % of the total population of the town did not have toilet facilities in their homes . Almost all of these housing units are occupied by low income groups, namely fisherman. Although the septic tank and pits are used for the disposal of fecal excrement, the domestic waste water remains in the surface drains by the side of the roads(photo.38). The stagnation of the waste water in these canals due to slope disturbances, provides favourable breeding grounds for the mosquito Culex Fatigans and other insects, just a few metres away from the dwellings. The introduction of Guppie fish into these canals to control the larva population was not always successful because of the strong pollution of water in some canals.

The largest industrial establishments in town, Harischandara Mills and Oidiris Silva Mills, let waste water into the Nupe Canal, while the Base Hospital Matara disposes of its waste water into the Nilwala river, resulting in water and air pollution.

4.2.4.3. Garbage Disposal

The garbage disposal of the town is the responsibility of the Matara Urban Council. Currently, four tractors, six bullock carts and four handcarts are used to collect the garbage. However, garbage collecting programs cannot be carried out properly due to the old vehicles which are not always in working order. The collection and dumping of garbage within the Matara Urban Council area, particularly in Fort (along the Nilwala river bank), Kotuwegoda (along the Nilwala river bank) and Polhena, pollute the river water as well as the air. This leads to great health hazards in the town, contributing to the increase of epidemic intestinal tract disease such as dysentery, typhoid, bacillary and porta-typhoid.

---

11 Wellmer, H; Galle, 1989.

12 Compare with Wellmer , H., Galle, 1989.

CHAPTER 5

5. Land Use Pattern of the Matara U. C. Area

The total land area of the town is 808.64 hectares. This area is bound by Tudawa Boundary Road to the north, Nilwala river and part of Brown Hill Road to the east, Polhena Boundary Road and Pamburana - Welegada Road to the west and the coast to the south. The Nilwala river divides the town into two parts. The southern part being about one-third of its northern counterpart, resulting in a discontinuity in spatial concentration of commercial activities.

Eighty-five percent (85%) of this total land area is owned by the private sector. Followed by the government and urban council with 12.7% and 2.3% respectively[1].

According to the land use pattern of the Matara urban council area as presented in Table 47, the largest area is occupied by the residential sector with 40.32%, followed by cultivated land area, roads, marsh land, flood prone areas, religious area, educational institutions, vacant land, commercial, industrial, infrastructure, private and public administration, play grounds, social services, cemeteries, health and recreational facilities, with 24.04%, 8.02%, 7.76%, 3.43%, 2.99%, 2.71%, 2.58%, 2.49%, 1.38%, 0.98%, 0.84%, 0.67%, 0.51%, 0.48%, 0.48% and 0.33% respectively (Map 27 & Diag.23).

Diag.23: Land Use Pattern, Matara, 1981

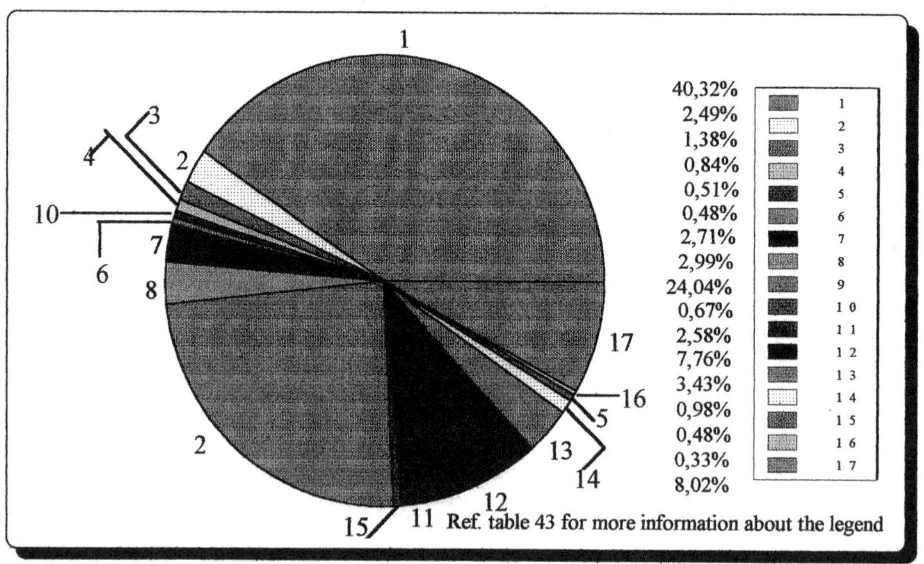

---

[1] Structure Plan, Matara, 1981.

Table 47
Matara Town - Existing Land Use Pattern
and Area Distribution, 1981.

Type of Land Use		Area (ha)	Percentage (%)
1. Residential			
- High Income	50.52 ha		
- Middle Income	161.44 ha		
- Low Income	114.06 ha	326.02	40.32
2. Commercial		020.12	02.49
3. Industrial		011.12	01.38
4. Private and Public Administration		006.72	00.84
5. Social Services		004.12	00.51
6. Health (public & private)		003.86	00.48
7. Educational Institutions		021.92	02.71
8. Religious Area			
- Buddhist temple	20.43 ha		
- Church	00.78 ha		
- Mosque	02.91 ha	24.12	02.99
9. Green Area (Cultivated Land)			
- Paddy	012.23 ha		
- Coconut	162.22 ha		
- Other Crops	020.00 ha		
		194.45	24.04
10. Playground		005.42	00.67
11. Vacant Land		020.93	02.58
12. Marsh Land		062.79	07.76
13. Flood Prone Area		027.73	03.43
14. Infrastructure		007.82	00.98
15. Cemeteries		003.96	00.48
16. Recreational Facilities		002.67	00.33
17. Roads		064.87	08.02
Total		808.64	100.00

Source: Structure Plan - Matara Town, 1980/81., Vol. 1

The striking feature in the land use pattern of Matara urban council area is the high utilization of land by agriculture (24.04%) in contrast to the low utilization of land by the industrial and commercial sector. In addition, there is a presence of a large area of marsh land which is categorised as underdeveloped. The development of this area into built-up areas is very costly (Table 48).

MAP 27

Existing Land Use Pattern of Matara Town, 1981

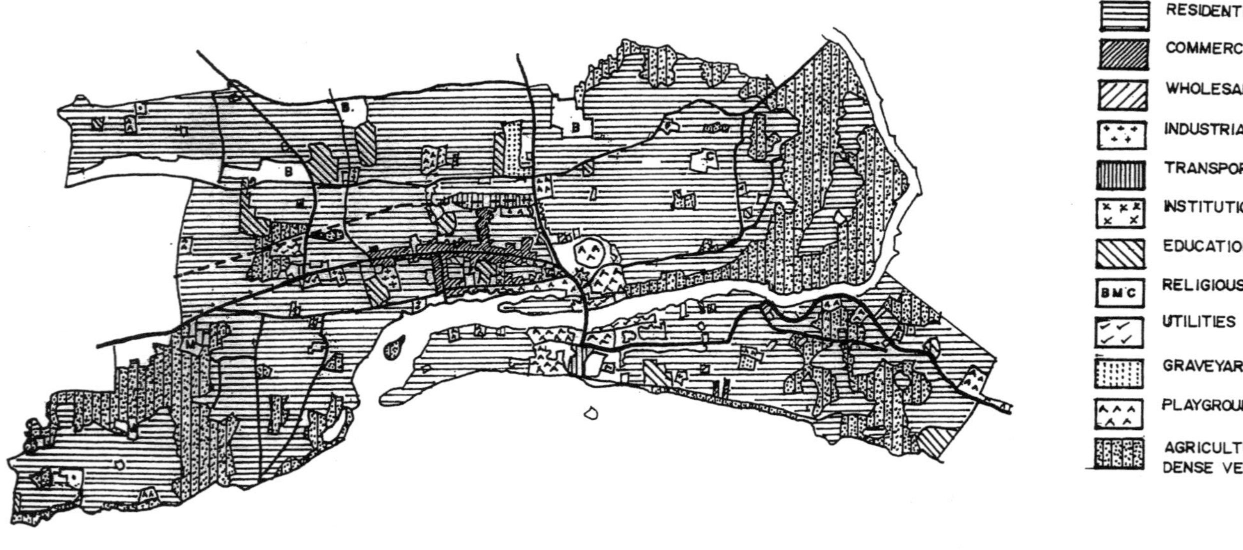

Source:- Final Report, Matara, Urban Development Authority, 1982.

Table 48
The Division of the Urban Council Area by Developed,
Under Developed and Undevelopable Land Area, 1981.

Type of Land use	Area (ha)	Total Area	% of the total Land Area (ha)	Total %
Developed Land Area				
1. Residential	362.02	--	40.32	--
2. Commercial	020.12	--	02.49	--
3. Industrial	011.12	--	01.38	--
4. Administration	006.72	--	00.84	--
5. Social Service	004.12	--	00.51	--
6. Health Care	003.86	--	00.48	--
7. Educational	021.92	--	02.71	--
8. Religion	024.12	--	02.99	--
9. Recreational	008.09	--	01.00	--
10.Roads	064.87	--	08.02	--
11.Cemetries	003.96	--	00.48	--
12.Other Infrastructures	007.82	502.74	62.20	
Undeveloped Land Area				
1. Cultivated Land Area	194.45	--	24.04	--
2. Vacant Land Area	020.93	--	02.58	--
3. Flood Prone area	027.73	243.11	30.05	
Undevelopable Land Area				
1. Marsh Land	--	062.79	--	007.75
Total	--	808.64	--	100.00

Source: This divisional categorization is based on the data of Structural Plan - Matara Town, 1980/81.

The division of the Matara Urban Council area into developed, under-developed and undevelopable land areas as presented in Table 48, shows that 62% of the total land area consists of developed land while 30.0% is under-developed land. This land could be used for expanding the built-up area. The flood prone areas which are included in this category, currently can be used only seasonally. However, it is expected that this land could be used for cultivation throughout the year as soon as the Nilwala river project is completed .

Marsh lands which consist of 7.75% of the town's total area, are low lying areas along the Nilwala River and expand into the interior in the Piladuwa area in the eastern part of the town. Therefore these two areas, with 11.19% of the total land area, are currently considered as the physical constraint areas in terms of spatial direction.

A comparison of the developed land area of Matara town with the other adjoining district capitals such as Galle, Hambantota and Ratnapura, shows that Galle has the highest developed land area of the district capitals in the southern province with almost 68% of the total land area followed by Matara with 62% (Table 49).

Table 49
The Land Use Pattern of the Developed Area in Matara, Galle, Hambantota and Ratnapura (in percentage) and the Average Values
for the Sri Lanken Urban Settlements.

Type of Landuse	Matara 1980	Galle 1981	Hambantota 1982	Ratnapura 1981	Average Values
Residential	65.7	72.6	48.9	70.0	61.9
Commercial	4.1	2.1	3.3	2.0	2.8
Industrial	2.2	2.6	9.3	0.8	3.4
Public & Semi-Public	13.3	9.4	16.5	10.5	15.4
Parks & Playgrounds	1.7	2.8	4.6	0.5	4.9
Roads & Railway	13.0	10.5	17.4	16.2	11.2
Developed area as % of the total area.	61.8	67.8	30.2	19.2	60.2

Source: Menike, 1983, p. 113.

Hambantota has the lowest developed land area in the southern province with only 30.2%. This is because 47% of the total land area of the Hambantota town consists of sand dunes, marsh and water bodies. Ratnapura has the lowest developed area among the four district capitals with only 19.2%. This is because 75% of the total land area of Ratnapura consists of plantation and other dense vegetation. The developed, residential, commercial and the transportation land areas of Matara town lie above the national level, while the values of the other sectors lie below the average national level.

5.1. Developed area

5.1.1. Residential Land Use

An examination of the land use pattern by different sectors shows that residential land use is the single largest land use in the town, covering 362.02 hectares which is 40% of the total town area. This is about 66% of the total developed area and is higher than the national level (61.9%). The residential land areas are distributed all over the town, the highest percentage occurring in Welegoda and Weliweriya (Wards 8 and 11). Fort and Mainstreet (Wards 1 and 6) have minimum coverage under this land use. The structure plan of Matara, 1980, subdivides the residential area into three categories, in terms of the income level of the households. The income levels are not given in the structure plan.

The highest percentage of the residential land area is used by the middle income groups with 49.52% of the total, followed by low income groups with 35.02%[2]. The high

---

2 Structure Plan, Matara, 1981.

income residential area with 15.4% in comparison to the other two categories is very low. This reflects the socio-economic conditions of the urban population.

The high income group mainly consists of professionals and businessmen living in the Fort along the main thoroughfares along the North Uyanwatta Circular Road, Sirimangala Road, the Esplande Road, Akuressa Road, Hakmana Road, Rahula Road and in Issadeen town and in Meddawatta in Browns Hill. Their houses mainly consist of bungalows, street houses and Walawwa .

The middle income group mainly consists of small scale traders and government servants. The residential areas of this group mainly occupy the old city wards of Kotuwegoda, Mainstreet, Kadeweediya, the southern part of Uyanwatta, some pockets around Issadeen town and areas along the Rahula Road and Akuressa Road . In addition, Walpola and Polhena also have a few isolated pockets of the middle income groups. Their houses consist mostly of row houses and farm houses.

The low income group consists of fisherman, labourers, domestic servants and agricultural workers. The low income residential areas are found where accessibility is poor and the problems of drainage, sanitation and flooding exist. These residential areas are mainly found in Totamuna, Polhena, some areas along old Tangalla Road, Broadway Road (Dahrmapala Mawatha close to Nupe), Mainstreet (Kumarathunga Mawatha) at Station Road and Uyanwatta Circular Road. Their houses mainly consist of cluster houses and Palpaths, jerry-built houses, slums and shanties.

5.1.2. Industrial Land Use

As far as the industrial sector is concerned, Matara utilizes a very low share of land for this purpose, similar to other towns on the island. The industrial land use, which measures only about 11.12% hectares, comprises all the service industries and various agro-based industries in the town. There are 138 small scale industries and 2 large scale industries (Chapter 3). The industrial sector occupies only 1.38% of the total land area and 2.2% of the total developed area of the town, which is lower than the national average of 3.4% and it offers only 7% of the total employment to the urban residents. This reflects its insignificant role in the spatial concentration as well as in the urban economy of Matara town. This situation is mostly attributed to the non-availability of raw materials for the development of industries as well as the traditional and renten-capitalistic behaviour of the entrepreneurs which hinder the employment generation and expansion of industries.

The industries in Matara town are scattered all over the town reflecting the absence of planning. It seems they were established wherever it was convenient or permitted. However, a high concentration of industries (57%) is found in the Commercial Core Area (C.B.D.) where the land for expansion is limited.

The small scale industries are scattered randomly and tend to be tied to the town centre, while large scale industries such as Harischandra mills and Odiris Silva mills are located in the transitional zone between the town core area and the residential area, where land is still available for expansion. The factors which have influenced the location of industries in Matara seem to be power (better electricity and water services in the town centre), transport (better transport facilities in the town core area) and the market (close proximity to the consumer). In addition, the coir yarn industry of the town, which is tied to its raw material, coconut husk, is located in Polhena where this resource is found.

5.1.3. Tertiary Sector Land Use

In contrast to the industrial sector, the tertiary sector plays an important role in terms of land utilization as well as in the economy of the town. The tertiary sector, which consists of commercial, health, educational, administration and social services, occupies 7% of the total land area and 11% of the developed land area of the town and offers about 75% of the total urban employment (Chapter 3).

5.1.3.1. Commercial Sector Land Use

The commercial sector, occupying 2.49% of the total land area and 4.1% of the total developed land area of the town, offers 24.6% of the total employment (Chapter 3). An examination of the spatial distribution of the commercial units shows that the commercial core area covering roughly the wards Kotuwegoda, Kadeweediya, Mainstreet and some parts of Fort and Uyanwatta occupies 74% of the total commercial land use area and possess 74% of the total commercial units of the town (Chapter 3). The rest of the commercial units are found isolated in the urban land use area or clustered in the sub-commercial centres of the town.

The Commercial Core Area (C.B.D.) of Matara, as in the towns of other developing countries such as Bungoma, Webuye and Kitale in western Keniya[4], Yendi and Thamala in Ghana[5] and Badulla[6] and Galle[7] in Sri Lanka is characterised by concentrations of mixed functions (primary, secondary and tertiary).

Although special kinds of functional districts have not developed in the C.B.D. area (Central Business District) of Matara, it is found that there is a functional specialization to some extent along some segments of the roads. Mainstreet is characterized by the presence of jewellery, textile and footwear shops. The old Tangalle Road is characterized by the presence of hardware, ceramic and building material stores. Hakmana Road is characterized by concentrations of cinnamon and rubber wholesale establishments. The Station Road is characterized by the presence of warehouses. Although Broadway Road shows no specialization of any activity, a concentration of banking facilities and other private offices of district and regional level services is found

---

4 Henkel, R., 1979.
5 Mahn, Chr., 1980.
6 Dicke, S., 1987.
7 Wellmer, H., 1988.

there. A concentration of lawyers and notaries is found in Fort, where the Supreme Court, District Courts, Magistrate Courts and additional courts are located. A concentration of tourist hotels is found in the Polhena area where beautiful beaches are available.

5.1.3.2. Health Sector Land Use

The health sector occupies only 3.86 hectares (0.48%) of the total land area and 0.76% of the total developed area of the town, but plays a very significant role in providing the special medical care facilities for the whole region (Chapter 6). There are 30 medical care units in town. The most important unit in this sector is the base hospital of Matara. It occupies 1.78 hectors (46%) of the total land use area, which is under the health sector landuse.

The health care institutions of the town are unevenly distributed over the urban area. A high concentration of these facilities is found in the town centre, while there is a marked lack of such facilities in the peripheral areas (Chapter 4).

5.1.3.3. Educational Land Use

The location of large numbers of schools and the utilization of a considerable amount of land for educational purpose is a predominant component in the land use pattern of Matara town. Educational facilities comprise 26 public sector institutions and other private institutions occupy 2.71% of the total land area and 4.36% of the total developed land area of the town (Chapter 4). Educational facilities are well distributed over the urban land area. There is a school in almost every ward in town and these are located within walking distance from the residential areas.

Although the majority of the schools in the town are located outside the Commercial Core Area, there is a substantial number of schools which are located in the Commercial Core Area. This hinders the expansion of commercial activities in the town centre and leads to land utilization conflicts between the commercial sector and the social service sector.

The opening of Ruhunu University campus on the eastern side of town would lead to growth of commercial as well as educational activities towards the eastern direction. The educational facilities in Matara town, which attract the student population from all over the region, continue to play a crucial role in the development of the town (Chapter 6).

5.1.3.4. Administration Sector Land Use

As discussed earlier in Chapter 3, all the major administrative functions of the district are located in Matara town. The most important unit in this respect is the head office (Kachcheri) of the administrative head (the government agent) of the district, which is located in the ward Fort (1). The entire Matara district is served by these activities in the context of government administration. The administrative functions of the town can be treated as one of the key functions that affects the future potential of the town's development. The public and private administration sector occupies 0.84% of the total land area and 1.3% of the total developed land area of the town. Although the concentration pattern of these activities show a scattered manner and there is a new development of the location of administrative units taking place northwards from the Fort, a high concentration of activities is still located in the Ward Fort.

5.1.3.5. Social and Community Services

The social and community services, comprising public library, town hall, post office, police station and other social service units, occupy 0.51% of the total land and 0.8% of the total developed land area of the town. The areas of these services reach far beyond the town boundaries. Their contribution to the development of Matara as a service centre for the whole region is immense (Chapter 6).

5.1.4. Religious Area

Religious area occupies 2.99% of the total land area and 4.79% of the developed land area. Some religious centres in the town such as the Peakwella Buddhist Temple, the Rajamaha Vihara Buddhist Temple, St. Mary's Church, and the Kotuwegoda Mosque dominate the human life of the towns population as well as the district's population by fostering social values (Chapter 6).

Buddhist temples, comprising 27 in number, occupy almost 85% of the total religious land area. This reflects again the religious composition of the towns population (Chapter 2). Mosques (4 units) occupy only 12% of the total religious area of the town followed by churches (3 units) with only 3.2%.

Most of the Buddhist temples are located away from the town centre while churches and mosques are located mainly in the town centre. Religious areas can be indicated as rigid areas which cannot be utilised for other purposes.

5.1.5. Transportation Land Use (Roads)

The transportation sector covers 64.87 hectares i.e., 8.02% of the total land area and 13.0% of the total developed area of the town. This is higher than the national average level of 11.2%. Out of this total hectarage, about 37 hectares (57%) is under the railway system, the Ceylon Transport Board (C.T.B.) central terminal and the C.T.B. depot. The high utilisation of land area by the transportation sector reflects the major role, which Matara town plays in terms of transportation and communication in the southern region (Chapter 6).

5.1.6. Recreational Land Use

The recreational sector, consisting of public parks, play grounds, cinema halls and sport clubs, occupies 1% of the total land area and 1.7 % of the developed land area of the town. This is much lower than the national average level of 4.9 %. The most significant units in terms of land utilisation in this sector, are two public parks, namely Uyanwatta Esplanade and Kotuwegoda Esplanade. They occupy almost 79% of the total land area under recreational land use. Both of these public parks are located in the town centre and are subject to encroachments by the commercial sector activities (Chapter 4).

5.1.7. Graveyards

Graveyards utilise only 0.48% of the total land area of the town. Graveyards for different religious groups, namely Buddhist, Muslims and Christians, are located in five different wards of the town.

5.2. Underdeveloped Land Area

5.2.1. Cultivated Land Area

The agricultural activities hold the second major place in the land use of the town. It accounts for 194.25 hectares (i.e., 24.04%) of the total town area. This is also one of the major factors that reflect the dominance of rural characteristics in Matara town. Coconut alone occupies 83% of the total cultivated area, followed by other crops (mainly vegetables) and paddy with 10% and 6% respectively. Although the coconut lands are found throughout town, large areas of coconut cultivation are found in Meddewatta, Walpola and Polhena, while the other crops, paddy lands and market gardening areas are confined to Piladuwa area, which lies on the eastern part of the town along Nilwala river (ref. Chapter 3).

5.2.2. Vacant Land

The vacant lands which occupy 2.58% of the total land area of the town can be found in residential areas and close to the town centre. These lands can be used for any functional purpose in case of demand for land in the future.

5.3. Undevelopable Land Area

Marsh lands occupy 7.75% of the total land area of the town. These lands lie in the eastern part of the town along the Nilwala River in Piladuwa area and in the south-western part of the town, Polhena. These low lying areas are currently regarded as undevelopable. The transformation of these lands into developed lands, if needed, would be costly.

CHAPTER 6

6. Centrality

6.1. The Commercial Hegemony and the Catchment Areas of Matara Town

6.1.0. Commercial Hegemony

Matara, the district capital of the Matara district offers many different short-term, mid-term and long-term commodities and services more than any other urban centre or service centre of the district. This attracts not only the town's population, but also the district's population towards it. The commercial hegemony as well as the economic predominance of Matara town can be proved by analysing the following indicators.

6.1.1. The Number of Commercial Units and Their Types in the Four Towns of the Matara District.
6.1.2. The Number of Current Accounts and Amount of Deposits in the Major Banks of the Town.
6.1.3. The Number of Telephone Units used for Commercial Purposes.
6.1.4. The Towns Revenue.

6.1.1. The Number of Commercial Units and Their Types in the Four Towns of the Matara District.

Matara district had 2,632 commercial units in 1986 which were distributed among the four urban settlements namely Matara (U.C.), Weligama (U.C.), Akuressa (T.C.) and Dondara (T.C.). Out of this total 1,657 (63%) were located in the Matara town while 16%, 19% and 2% of the total commercial units were located in Weligama, Akuressa and Dondara respectively (Table 50 and Map 28).

Table 50
Distribution pattern of commercial units by type in urban settlements of Matara district, 1986.

Type of units		Matara No.of units	%	Weligama No.of units	%	Akuressa No.of units	%	Dondara No.of units	%
Daily need consumer goods		329	50	139	21	157	24	31	5
Mid-Term & Long-Term consumer goods		658	78	121	14	67	8	2	-
Services		563	61	138	15	207	22	15	2
Others		107	52	32	16	62	30	4	2
Total	1986	1657	63	430	16	493	19	52	2
Total	1981	1698	60	466	17	588	21	52	2

Source: This calculation is based on Tax Registers at Matara U.C., Weligama U.C., Akuressa T.C., Dondara T.C., 1986.

MAP 28

Distribution pattern of commercial units by type & their size among the urban settlements of Matara district, 1986.

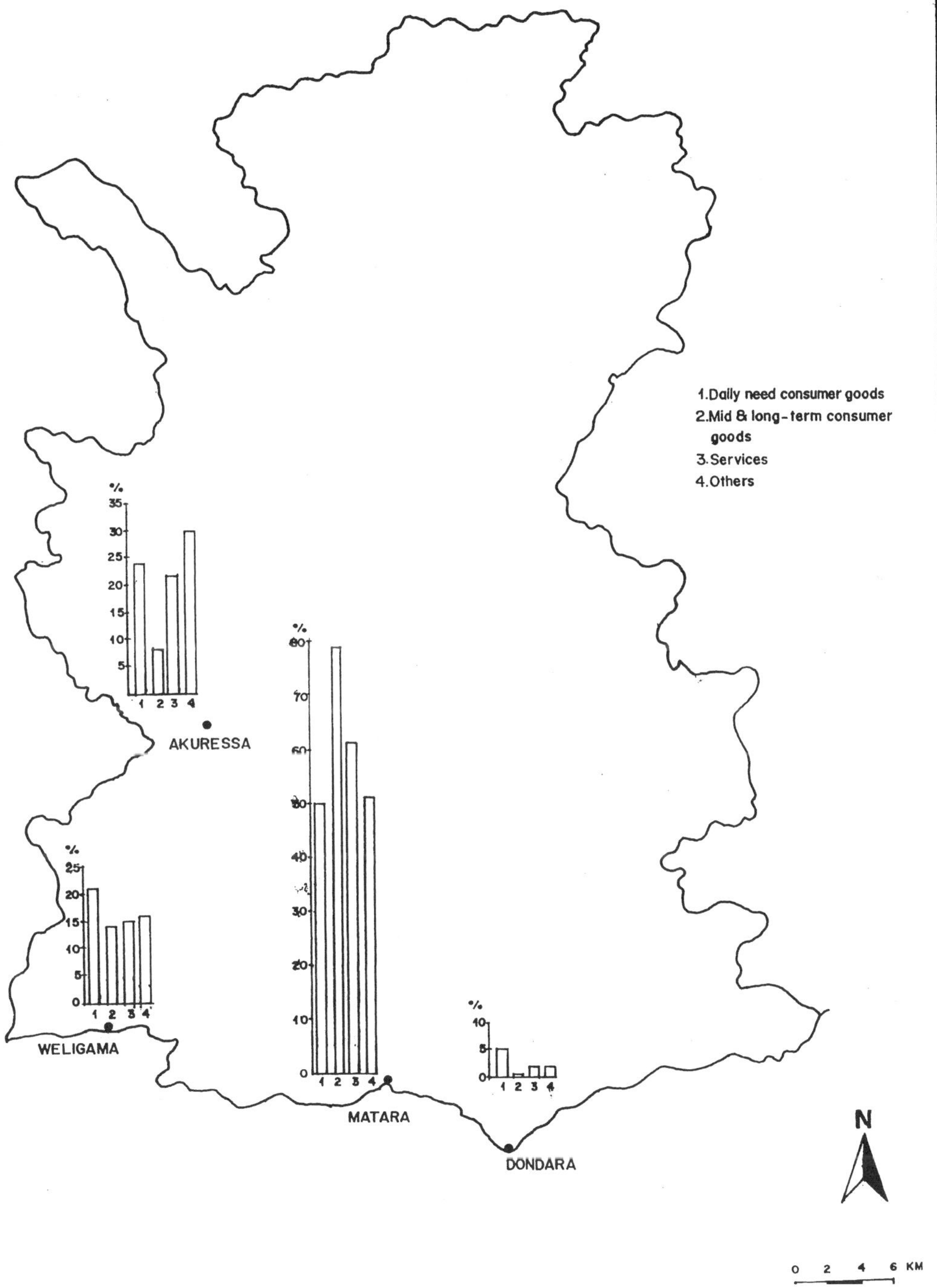

1. Daily need consumer goods
2. Mid & long-term consumer goods
3. Services
4. Others

AKURESSA

WELIGAMA

MATARA

DONDARA

N

0 2 4 6 KM

As Table 50 indicates, the majority of the commercial units in each of the groups daily need related units 50%, mid and long term related units 78% and service sector related units 61% are located in the Matara Urban Council area.

A comparison of the total commercial units in the urban settlement of Matara district in 1981 and 1986 has revealed that the number of commercial units has declined from 2804 to 2632 units. This decline has taken place in every urban settlement of the district except Dondara (Matara by 41 units, Weligama by 36 units, Akuressa by 95 units. The total number of decreased units accounts for 172).

6.1.2. Current Accounts and Deposits in the Major Banks

An examination of the current accounts and the amount of deposits in the major banks, Bank of Ceylon and the Peoples Bank in Matara town and in the other urban centres, proves its hegemony over the other centres (Table 51). The banking until recently is not a common practice in the Srilankan general population. This could be either due to the low income level, lack of trust of the monetary system or lack of liquidity. Banking facilities are mostly used by the merchants.

Table 51
The number of accounts and the amount of deposits in bank of Ceylon and Peoples Bank, 1982.9.30.

Centre	No. of Accounts		%	Amount of Deposits		%
	Peoples Bank	Bank of Ceylon		Peoples Bank	Bank of Ceylon	
Matara	--	3786	76	20009000	43812177	90
Weligama	--	481	10	2555000	1577193	6
Akuressa	--	277	5	346900	1524465	3
Dondara	--	418	8	113000	991444	1
Total	--	4952	100	23023900	47905279	100

Source: Statistical Book, Matara District., 1983.

Table 51 shows the Matara towns predominance in the commercial sphere processing 76% of the total number of current accounts followed by Weligama with only 10%. In regard to the current deposits, Matara becomes first in the rank with 90% followed by Weligama with only 6%.

6.1.3. Commercial Telephones

A comparison of the total commercial telephones found in Matara district as against the adjoining districts shows the predominance of Matara district in the commercial sphere. According to the telephone directory, Matara district had 758 commercial telephone units in its service centres and urban settlements while the adjoining districts of Hambantota and Ratnapura, have had only 150 and 45 units respectively[1].

Again, this pattern shows the dominance of the urban centre of Matara versus other urban centres of the Matara district. So the percentage of telephone units in the Matara Urban Council area in 1984 amounted to 68% followed by 8% in Weligama Urban Council area.

6.1.4. Town's Revenue

The annual revenues collected by local authorities can be regarded as a crude measure of their relative prosperity, thus indicating the wealth of the inhabitants of their respective localities. Out of the total revenue collected by the urban settlements of the Matara district in 1986, Matara comes first with 80% followed by Weligama with 15%. The per capita revenue collected by the Matara U.C. in 1986 was 891 Rupees (approximately 33 German Marks) followed by Weligama with 375 Rupees (Table 52).

Table 52
Annual income of the urban settlements of Matara district, 1986.

Centre	Annual income	%	Population	Per Capita dues (in Rupees)
Matara U.C.	34929555	80	39162	891
Weligama U.C.	6705840	15	17872	375
Akuressa T.C.	1596342	4	6885	231
Dondara T.C.	385313	1	7628	50
Total	43517050	100	71547	1547

Source: Budget Reports of Matara U.C., Weligama U.C., Akuressa T.C., Dondara T.C., 1986.

6.2. The Catchment Area of Matara Town (Centrality)

After discussing the town's commercial and economic hegemony over the minor centres, it is important to look into the centrality of Matara compared with the other centres. Centrality is the measure of importance of a place in terms of its functional capacity to serve the needs of the people in the surrounding areas. The centrality however depends only upon the central functions. These functions have a certain range beyond the limits of the place and serve to the needs of the surrounding region. The six centrality indicators which are taken into consideration in this study are given below.

6.2.1. The towns connection to the road network.
6.2.2. The administration.
6.2.3. The school facilities (Education).
6.2.4. The medical facilities.
6.2.5. The trade.
6.2.6. The social, religious and cultural functions

---

1 Telephone Directory of Sri Lanka, 1984.

6.2.1. The Towns Connection to the Road Network

The road network which is the functional link is vitally important in the relationship between the town and its surrounding areas. The transport of goods and passengers between these two entities is a major component in the sector of transportation and communication.[2]

The road network of the Matara district has a length of approximately 565 miles (910 Km) and density of 1.25 miles per square miles (2 km per 2.559 km^2)[3]. The quality of these roads varies.[4] A considerable portion of these roads are tarred but badly maintained. Some have deteriorated to the extent that they are impassable in the wet season or can only be used by tractors, vehicles with four wheels or ox carts of which 784 were registered in the Matara district in 1981.[5] This is a further factor in accelerating the deterioration of already neglected roads. Some narrow winding stretches of these road ways along the rivers are liable to inundation and destruction. The spatial distribution of the road network shows that there is a higher level of connectivity in the southern coastal and central zones than in the northern zone of the district. The north zone is less well served and some areas are relatively inaccessible. Although Matara district has a comparatively dense road network which is higher than the national average, enabling easy transportation of agricultural products for marketing in the region, this advantage is counterbalanced by the above mentioned shortcomings in quality of the road network. The important roads which connect Matara town to other urban centres and the service centres are given below:

A. The coastal highway (A class road) from Matara to Colombo via Galle, south west direction.
B. The coastal highway (B class road) from Matara to Kataragama via Hambantota, south east direction.
C. The main road (C class road) from Matara to Deniyaya via Akuressa, north west direction
D. The main road (C class road) from Matara to Deniyaya via Kamburupitiya, north east direction.
E. The main road (C class road) from Matara to Beliatta and Walasmulla via Hakmana, south east and north east direction.

According to the Statistical book of Matara District,1981, the most important transport medias in Matara district are the government owned bus service (C.T.B = Ceylon Transport Board), private bus services, private lorry service and the railway service.

---

2 Compare with Dicke, S., Badulla, 1987.

3 Integrated Rural Development Project, Matara District, Status Report, 1981,p. 83.

4 These roads are categorised into 5 classes such as A, B , C, D,& E by the Department of Highway according to their qualities. The criteria for this classification is not given. The D & E class roads are said to be Gravel & Earth roads.

5 Statistical Book, Matara District, 1983.

Even until 1987 the C.T.B. buses played a very important role in the transportation of goods and passengers even though they were having a very high competition with the private bus services. In 1987, Matara Depot was operating 120 buses a day and sold 11,509,312 tickets a month while the goods transported weighed 334,792 tons (Table 53).

Table 53
Tickets sold and goods transported by C.T.B.
1987 March, Matara Depot.

Type of Tickets & Goods	No. of Tickets	Transported Goods in Tons
Regular Tickets	11364312	-----
Season Tickets	145000	-----
Goods	--------	334792

Source: C.T.B. Depot, Matara

According to the 1987 bus time-table (schedule) of Matara C.T.B., these 120 buses travelled 538 times a day within Matara and to other centres. Three hundred and sixty two (362) out of the total 700 journeys were within a radius of 19.2 Km which connected 40 centres to Matara. The rest of the journeys connected Matara to the middle and long distance areas (Map 29). The spatial interpretation of these journeys shows a high frequency to the south-west axis along the coastal highway from Matara to Colombo where the highly urbanised areas are found. In this regard Galle is the most important centre to Matara with 74 journeys a day followed by Weligama and Colombo with 35 and 29 respectively (Map 29&30)[6]. The second most important connections to Matara lies in the south east direction. There are about 51 journeys a day from Matara to Kataragama via Dikwella, Tangalla, Ambalantota and Hambantota. The high frequency of journeys to Kataragama shows its importance as a religious centre to Matara. The other important centres in this axis are Gandara, Dikwella and Tangalla with 25, 23 and 39 journeys a day.

In contrast to the above said two directions, the north axis, north-west axis and north-east axis, where mostly rural settlement are found, have a lesser passenger flow. A high frequency of journeys in these axis are limited to the central zone. In the north zone bus journeys become less frequent. Yatiyana and Kamburupitiya are the most important centres with 44 and 31 journeys a day, which lie on the north-east axis in the central zone. Akuressa is the second most important centre with 30 journeys a day which is located on the north-west axis in the central zone. The third most important centre is Hakmana with 23 journeys a day. This centre is located on the north-east axis in the central zone. There is a very low passenger flow between Matara and the minor service centres such as Deniyaya, Morawaka and Kotapola, which are located in the northern zone. Morawaka and Kotapola enjoy the highest number of journeys in this respect with 12, followed by Deniyaya with only 7 journeys a day. In addition to these, there are some bus routes which connect with far lying urban centres such as Amparai with 4 buses a

---

6 The number of buses given in this study are only the direct buses which travel daily to these centres. In addition to these buses, passengers could also travel to Weligama and Galle by buses which travel to Colombo.

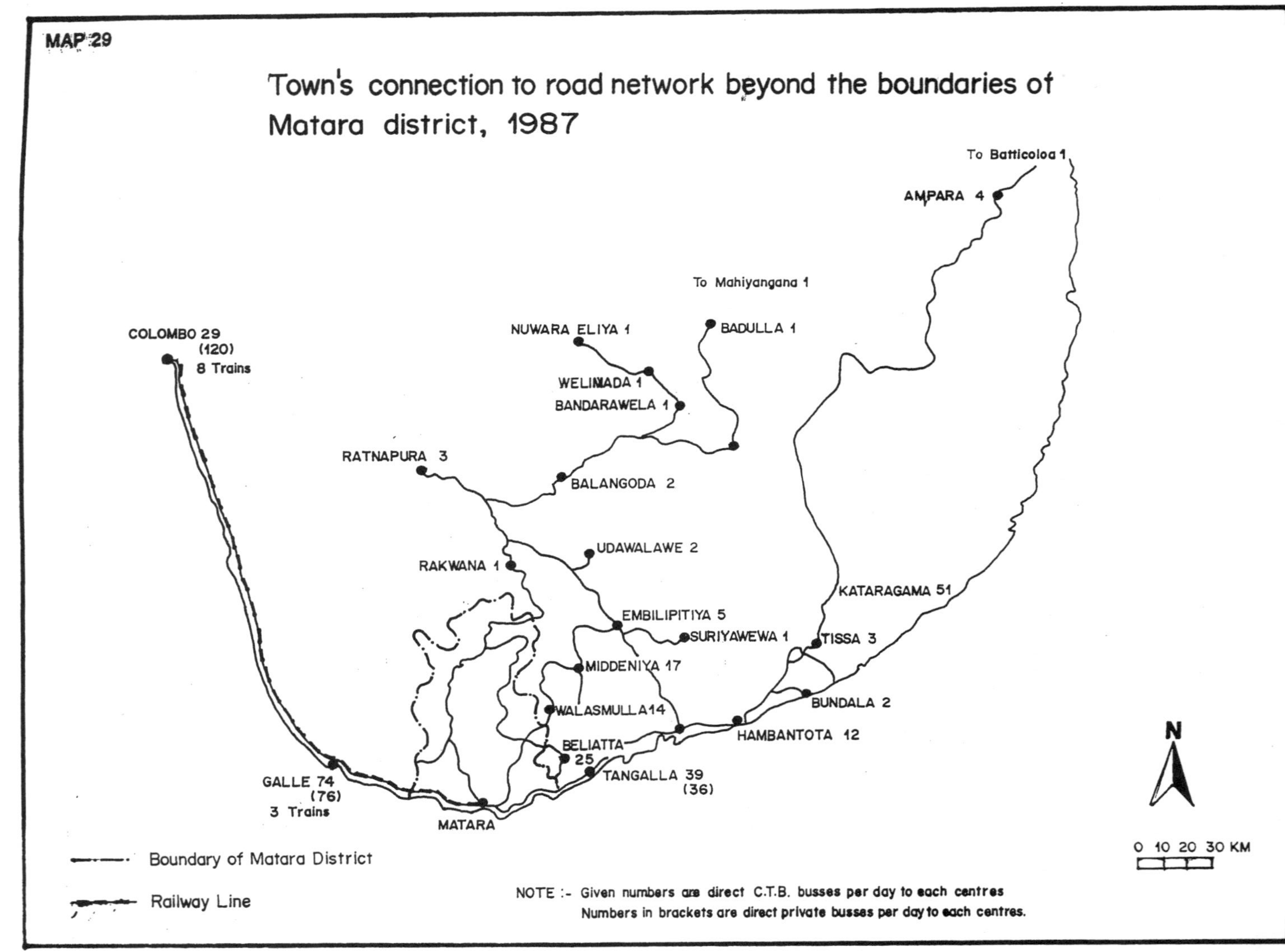
MAP 29
Town's connection to road network beyond the boundaries of
Matara district, 1987
To Batticoloa 1
AMPARA 4
To Mahiyangana 1
COLOMBO 29
(120)
8 Trains
NUWARA ELIYA 1
BADULLA 1
WELIMADA 1
BANDARAWELA 1
RATNAPURA 3
BALANGODA 2
UDAWALAWE 2
RAKWANA 1
KATARAGAMA 51
EMBILIPITIYA 5
SURIYAWEWA 1
TISSA 3
MIDDENIYA 17
BUNDALA 2
WALASMULLA 14
HAMBANTOTA 12
BELIATTA
25
GALLE 74
(76)
3 Trains
TANGALLA 39
(36)
MATARA
N
0 10 20 30 KM
Boundary of Matara District
Railway Line
NOTE :- Given numbers are direct C.T.B. busses per day to each centres
Numbers in brackets are direct private busses per day to each centres.

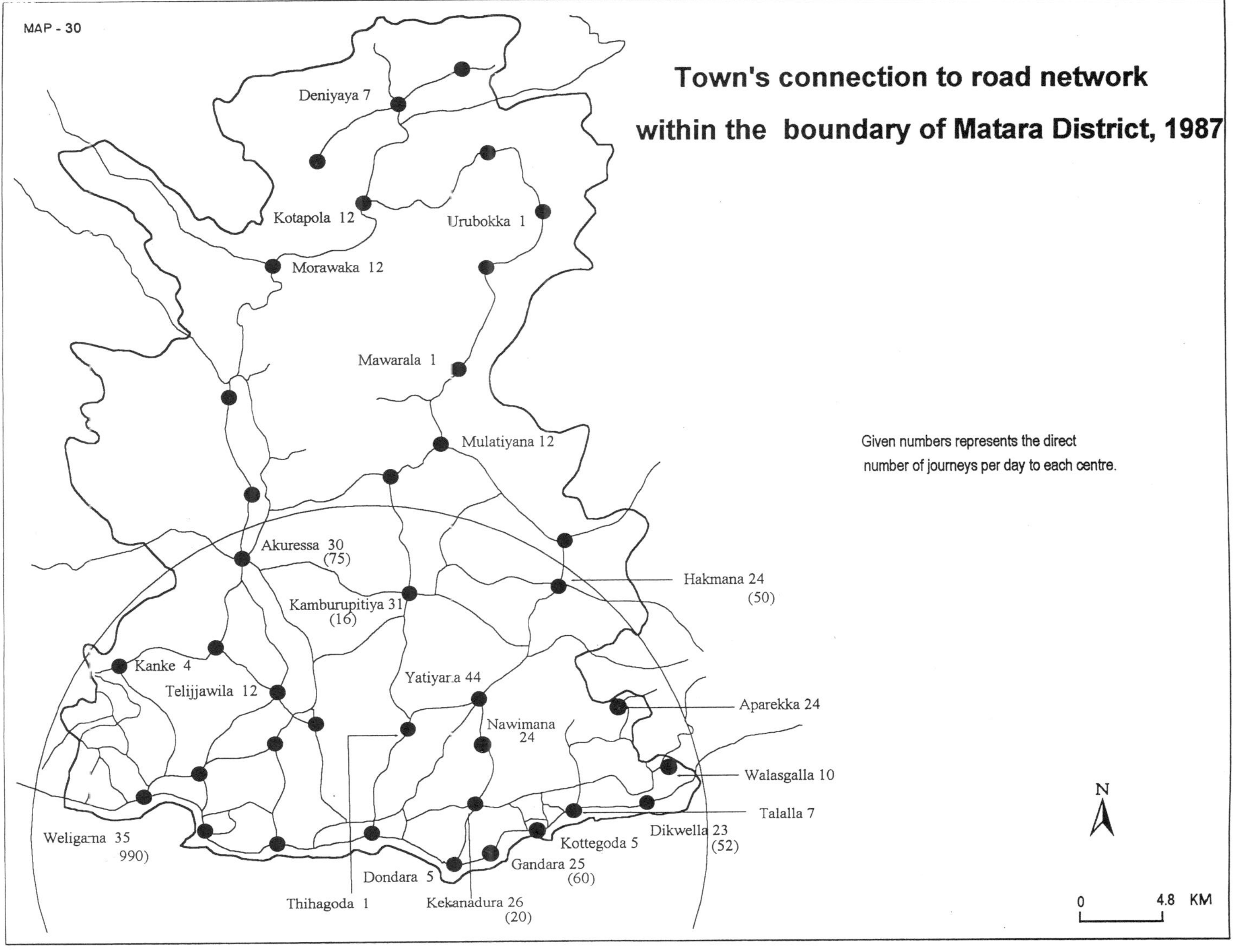

MAP - 30
Town's connection to road network
within the boundary of Matara District, 1987
Given numbers represents the direct
number of journeys per day to each centre.
Deniyaya 7
Kotapola 12
Urubokka 1
Morawaka 12
Mawarala 1
Mulatiyana 12
Akuressa 30
(75)
Kamburupitiya 31
(16)
Hakmana 24
(50)
Kanke 4
Telijjawila 12
Yatiyana 44
Nawimana
24
Aparekka 24
Walasgalla 10
Talalla 7
Dikwella 23
(52)
Kottegoda 5
Gandara 25
(60)
Weligama 35
990)
Dondara 5
Thihagoda 1
Kekanadura 26
(20)
N
0
4.8 KM

day, Batticoloa with 1 bus a day, Bandarawela with 1 bus a day and Nuwara-Eliya with 1 bus a day to Matara.

The private bus services which compete with the C.T.B. show a some what different pattern of spatial distribution of journeys. According to the time-table of private bus companies, they operate 320 buses a day to transport passengers. These buses travel 671 times a day up and down Matara with the other centres. They totally avoid the uneconomic routes in the northern region of the district such as Matara-Kotapola, Matara-Deniyaya and Matara-Morawaka as well as the long distance uneconomic routes such as Amparai, Bandarawela, Baticoloa and Nuwara-Eliya.

The highest frequency of journeys is found in the south western axis as indicated in the C.T.B. bus time-table. The most important centre according to the private bus schedule, is Colombo with 120 journeys a day followed by Weligama and Galle with 90 and 76 journeys respectively. The second most important connections are located in the south-eastern axis. The most important centre in this area is Gandara with 60 journeys a day followed by Dikwella and Tangalla with 52 and 36 journeys respectively. Matara private companies do not operate bus services to the religious centre of Kataragama nor to the northern zone of the district, most probably due to the unprofitability of these routes. Their services are exclusively limited to the central zone. Akuressa is the most important centre in the northern axis with 75 journeys a day followed by Hakmana, Kekanadura and Kamburupitiya with 50, 20 and 16 respectively.

The Ceylon Railway, which played a very important role in the transportation of passengers and goods in this region in the first half of the century during the British era and in the first decade of the post colonial era had lost its major role to other transport media. The Ceylon Government Railway (C.G.R) Department which was set up in 1864, still to this day, controls the entire service.

According to the train time-table (schedule) of the Matara railway station in 1987, the C.G.R. operated 11 trains a day to connect Matara to the other centres. Eight trains out of 11 connected Matara to Colombo while the other three trains connected Matara to Galle. The train service in the Matara district is exclusively limited to the coastal area as there are no railway lines either in the eastern part or northern part of the district. The important service centres in the Matara district which are connected to Matara by railway are Weligama and Kamburugamuwa.

The diminishing importance of the railway as a transport media can be proved by the following table. The importance of the railway, which held a dominant position in the transportation of goods and passengers in the British era and early post-British era, has been decreasing, due to the growth of other transport media. This can be proved by Tables 54,55 & 56.

Table 54
Passengers Statistics 1979, 1983, 1986 March.

Destination	Tickets Sold at Matara and Colombo Railway Station		
	1979 March	1983 March	1986 March.
Matara to Colombo	14,299	5,633	5,838
Colombo to Matara	19,159	14,278	11,318
Sri Lanka	3,229,113	2,082,944	1,916,458

Source: Ceylon Government Railway Department, Colombo (unpublished data).

According to Table 54, the passenger flow by train for all Island decreased from 3.2 Million in March 1979 to 1.9 Million in March 1986 while the passenger flow between Matara and Colombo decreased from 33,458 in March 1979 to 17,156 in March 1986.

The transported goods from Matara to Colombo decreased from 128 tons in January 1980 to 25 tons in January 1985(Table 55).

Table 55
Transportation of Goods by Train (in Tons)
1980, 1983, 1984, 1985 January.

Destination	1980 Jan.	1983 Jan.	1984 Jan.	1985 Jan.
Matara to Colombo	128	25	24	25

Source: Ceylon Government Railway Dept., Colombo (unpublished data).

The C.W.E. (Co-operative Wholesale Establishment), one of the major food suppliers to the Islands population, delivered only 28.5% of its total despatch to Matara by train in 1987.

Table 56
C.W.E.'s (Co-Operative Wholesale Establishment)
despatches to Matara by Train and Lorries, 1987.

Train	Lorry
2,704(tons)	6,791(tons)

Source: C.W.E., Colombo, 1987 (unpublished data).

The under utilisation of the railway service as a transport medium in the last two decades is attributed to the following reasons:

A. The inconvenient location of the railway station for the passengers. The railway station of Matara is located outside of the commercial area and far away from the bus terminal. This causes more expenses to the traveller.

B. Occurrence of long delays due to one way line.
C. The slow travel of trains due to the dilapidation of the line. The buses take only 3 to 3.30 hours to complete this journey while trains take more than four hours.

Other services are insignificant as sources of transportation.

6.2.2. Administration

All the major administrative functions of the district are located in Matara town as this is the capital of Matara district. The administrative head of the district, the government agent, is appointed by the ministry of public administration and local affairs and has his head office (Kachcheri) in the Matara Urban Council area. The government agent co-ordinates the government activities in the district and acts as the deputy head for many departments pertaining to work in the district. To facilitate his task, the Matara district is subdivided into 11 assistant government agent divisions. These divisions are administered by the assistant government agents who are also appointed by the ministry of home affairs (Map 31). Each A.G.A. division is further subdivided into "Gramasewaka Division", which is the lowest level in the hierarchical order of administration. There are 207 such Gramasewaka Divisions in Matara district. They are:

No.	A.G.A. Divisions	Gramasewaka Divisions
1	Kandaboda Pattuwa west	14
2	Wellaboda Pattuwa east	17
3	Gangaboda Pattuwa south	14
4	Wellaboda Pattuwa west and four Gravets	37
5	Weligama Korale south	14
6	Morawaka Korale	12
7	Morawaka Korale west	16
8	Weligama Korale north	32
9	Kandaboda Pattuwa east	13
10	Weligama Korale west	20
11	Gangaboda Pattuwa north	18
Total		207

The most important government departments, state sector corporations and state sector services, are located in the Matara Urban Council area, and some of the administrative heads who are responsible for district wide activities, are given below.

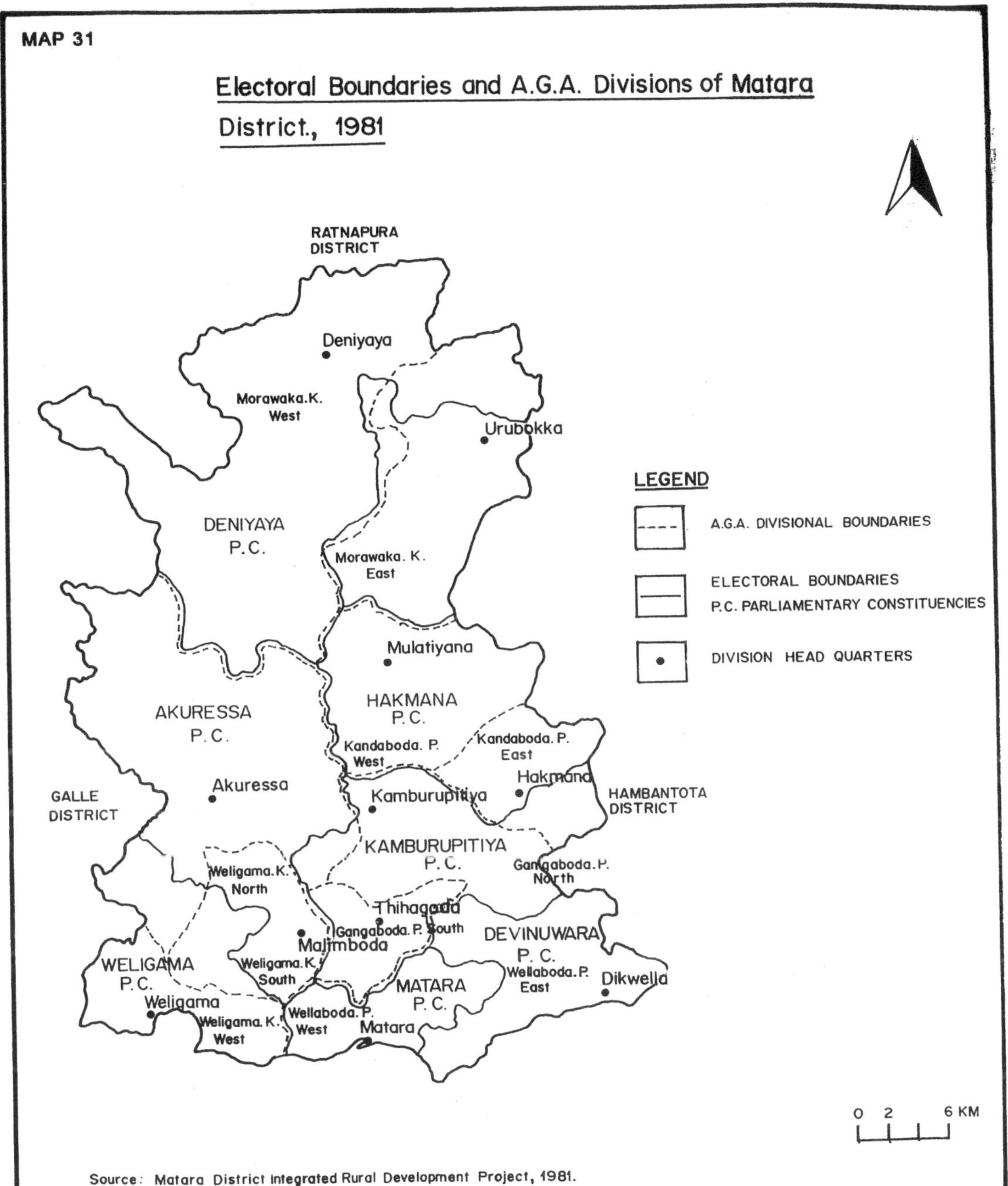
MAP 31
Electoral Boundaries and A.G.A. Divisions of Matara District., 1981
RATNAPURA DISTRICT
Deniyaya
Morawaka.K. West
Urubokka
DENIYAYA P.C.
Morawaka. K. East
Mulatiyana
HAKMANA P.C.
AKURESSA P.C.
Kandaboda. P. West
Kandaboda. P. East
Hakmana
Akuressa
GALLE DISTRICT
Kamburupitiya
HAMBANTOTA DISTRICT
KAMBURUPITIYA P.C.
Gangaboda. P. North
Weligama. K. North
Thihagoda
Gangaboda. P. South
DEVINUWARA P.C.
Malimboda
WELIGAMA P.C.
Weligama. K. South
MATARA P.C.
Wellaboda. P. East
Dikwella
Weligama
Weligama. K. West
Wellaboda. P. West
Matara
LEGEND
A.G.A. DIVISIONAL BOUNDARIES
ELECTORAL BOUNDARIES
P.C. PARLIAMENTARY CONSTITUENCIES
DIVISION HEAD QUARTERS
0 2 6 KM
Source: Matara District Integrated Rural Development Project, 1981.

Chart 1
Administrative and State sector services,
Matara U.C. area, 1984 .

Departments	Department heads
Provisional Administration	Government Agent
Registrar Generals	District Registrar
Local Government	Asst. Commissioner of local government
Small Industries	Asst. Director of Small Industries
Industrial Development Board	Regional Manager
Textile	Assist. Director
Ceylon Transport Board	Regional Manager
Agriculture and Lands	District Agri. Extension Officer
Agrarian Services	Assist. Director
Tea Authority(Tea small holding-Corporation)	Regional Manager
Land Commission	District Land Officer
Forest Department	District forest Officer
Irrigation Department	Chief Engineer
Highway Department	Chief Engineer
Marketing Department	Asst. Comm. Marketing
Food Commission	Asst. Controller of Food
Co-operative Development Board	Asst. Comm. of Co-operative Development Board
Education Department	Director of Education
Health Department	District Medical Officer
Labour Department	Asst. Comm. of Labour
Post (regional mail sorting centre)	District Post Officer
Supreme Courts	-------------
Magistrate Courts	---------------
District Courts	---------------
Additional Courts	---------------
Co-Operative Wholesale Establishment	Regional Manager
Ceylon Electricity Board	Chief Engineer
National Water Supply and Drainage Board	Chief Engineer
Building Materials Corporation	Regional Manager
Telecommunication	Chief Engineer
Ruhunu Television Corporation	Chief Engineer
Insurance Corporation	Regional Manager
Prison	Asst. Superintendent of Prison
Police	Asst. Superintendent of Police (A.S.P.)
Central Bank (regional office)	Regional Officer
Bank of Ceylon	Regional Officer
Peoples Bank	Regional Officer
Sampath Bank	Regional Officer
National Savings Bank	Regional Officer
Bank of India	---------------

Source: Matara District Integrated Rural Project, 1981.
Telephone Directory, 1984.

In addition, the Urban Council (U.C.) oversees the administration, social services and development of Matara town. The Urban Council consists of 11 members who are elected by the residents of the Matara U.C. area. The chairman, who is the head of the Urban Council, is elected by the members of the Urban Council. The administrative activities of the Urban Council are strictly limited to the Urban Council area.

The district is also divided into seven constituencies for the purpose of parliamentary elections. They are Matara, Dondara, Weligama, Kamburupitiya, Akuressa, Hakmana and Deniyaya. According to the above discussed facts, Matara town is a centre of administration which has six hierarchical orders. The administrative functions of each hierarchical order are clearly delineated by the existing political and administrative boundaries as given below:

1. Gramasewaka Division: This is one of the lowest areas at the administrative level. These small administrative areas(207)are administered by the Gramasewaka (service men or head man of the village) and assist the government agent in his task of administering the district.
2. Matara Urban Council: The administrative functions of the Matara Urban Council are limited to the Urban Council area, the second smallest administrative area (808 ha.) in the hierarchical order.
3. A.G.A. Divisions: There are 11 A.G.A. Divisions in the district. The administrative functions of the assistant government agents are confined to their particular areas. The Matara U.C. area is situated in the A.G.A. Division Wellaboda Pattuwa west and four Gravets.
4. Parliamentary Constituencies: The Matara district is divided into 7 political boundaries. The members of Parliament are involved in all kinds of activities pertaining to their electorates. The heads of the government institutions are mostly influenced by them.
5. The Government Agent: His administrative functions extend to the whole district.
6. The administrative areas of the government institutions and the state sector corporations extend to the whole Matara district.

6.2.3. A)Education -Schools

General education in Sri Lanka is provided within the formal school system which is subdivided into university education and technical education.

Matara district possessed 4.7% of the total number of schools, 4.6% of the total number of students, and 5.1% of the total number of teachers of the island in 1982. See the following Table.

Table 57
Number of schools, teachers and students
Matara District and Sri Lanka, 1982.

No.of Schools/Students/ Teachers	Sri Lanka	Matara District	%
Number of School	9901	467	4.7%
Number of Students	3484661	158575	4.6%
Number of Teachers	133802	6886	5.1%

Source: 1) Review of the economy, 1986, p. 99
2) Statistical book Matara District, 1983, p. 60.
3) Matara District integrated rural development project, 1982, p. 6:1.

The student-teacher ratio in the Matara district with 23:1 is somewhat lower than the national level of 26:1. An analysis of the schools facilities does not reveal any noteworthy differences between Matara and the rest of the country.[7]

An examination of the census of statistics in 1981 revealed that the number of government schools was fairly evenly distributed over the geographical area of the Matara district.

Evaluation of the questionnaires in the author's survey in 1987 revealed that 58.7% of the total students had a high school within 2 km from their residence while 18.9% had such a school in a distance between 3.2 km and 6.2 km. The rest 23.2% came to school from areas which were located beyond 6.4 km (Table 58)

Table 58
The number of respondents (students) in the university entrance classes (grade 12) at the selected 9 schools, the distance between the schools and home, and the mode of travel.

Name of school and the location	No. of respond-ants	Distance from school to home			Mode of travel			
		0-2	2-4	over 4	walk	bus	bicy-cle	oth-ers
Deniyaya Cent., Deniyaya	100	48	30	22	51	44	05	0
Urubokka Cent., Urubokka	100	68	27	5	76	10	14	0
Morawaka Cent., Morawaka	100	50	04	46	58	38	04	0
Godapitiya Cent., Akuressa	100	33	25	42	26	57	17	0
Methodist Cent., Hakmana	100	68	24	08	61	26	13	0
Narandeniya Cent., Kamburupitiya	100	50	22	28	50	44	06	0
Thalpawila Cent., Dondara	100	83	04	13	82	11	05	2
Dikwella Cent., Dikwella	100	61	14	25	51	42	07	0

(contd. in the following page)

7 Integrated rural development project, Matara District 1981, p. 6.1.

Siddarta Cent., Weligama	42	36	09	07	21	04	14	3
Total	842	487	159	196	476	276	85	5
Percentage(%)	100	57.8	18.9	23.2	56.5	32.8	10.1	0.6

Source: Questionnaire Survey, 1987.

An examination of the data revealed that some students must travel long distances to attend a particular school, due to the inadequacy of science education in the schools which are located closer to their residence.

Although the number of schools are fairly distributed over the geographical area, the distribution of qualified teachers and the better qualified schools are highly distorted in favour of the urban over the rural areas. Many students in the rural areas are denied the opportunity of advanced secondary education which is afforded to their urban counterparts. This applies particularly to science education.

An inquiry into the standard of the schools in the district reveals that the Matara education circuit[8] alone possesses 42.8% of the "A" grade schools, 20% of the "B" grade schools and 14.6% of the total "C" grade schools of the district(Table 59).

Table 59
Classification of schools by standard.
1982.03.01 - Matara District.

Educational Circuit	1A Grade	%	1B Grade	%	1C Grade	%
Matara	03	42.8	03	20.0	12	14.6
Total	07	100.0	15	100.0	82	100.0
Educational Circuit	2nd Grade	-----	3rd Grade	-----		
Matara	07	4.1	18	12.1		
Total	167	100.0	148	100.0		

Source: Statistical book, Matara district 1983.

Reference: 1A schools have 11 and 12 grades in science education with hostel facilities.
1B schools have 11 and 12 grades in science education without hostel facilities.
1C schools have commerce and arts education up to 11 and 12 grade without hostel facilities.
Second grade schools have classes from only the first grade to tenth grade.
Third grade schools have classes from only the first grade to fifth grade.

An inquiry into the education personnel shows that 22% of the districts total graduate teachers (37% of the total physics graduates, 37% of the total biology graduates and 47% of the total mathematics graduates of the district), 20% of the total trained

---

8 Detailed data for school and teachers in Matara town is not available. The Matara education circuit covers the whole Matara constituency including the Matara U.C area. According to the information of the education department of Matara, all the A and B schools and some of the C grade schools are located in Matara town.

teachers (30% of the English teachers, 28% of the science teachers and 27% of the mathematics teachers of the district) alone were found in the Matara educational circuit.[9] See the following table.

Table 60
No. of Qualified Educational Personnel in Educational Circuit of Matara and Matara District, 1981.

Educational Circuit	No. of. Graduate Teachers	%	No.of. Trained Teachers	%	No.of. Qualified Teachers	%
Matara	262	21.5	833	20.1	107	7.0
Total	1216	100.0	4142	100.0	1525	100.0

Source: Statistical hand book, Matara district, 1983.

The facts discussed offer strong evidence to prove the mal-distribution of the education facilities in favour of the urban areas. The urban schools, with better educational and other facilities, have become the most prominent schools in the region.

Prominence in examination results, better sport facilities and the advantages in the job market tend to attract students to these schools from all over the region. To be educated in such a school is a source of pride to the Sri Lankan general population (photo 39).

The data on enrolment of students in schools indicates that, in addition to serving the student population of the town, these schools also cater to the needs of the student population from "Umland", "Hinterland" and "Einflussgebiet".

Statistics available from the educational officer, Kachcheri, Matara indicate that there were 18,602 students enrolled in the town's schools in 1980/81. Out of this total 9,602 students (52%) were from the surrounding areas and commuted daily to the schools in the town. To find out the catchment areas of the education service of the Matara town, five famous schools, the Technical School and the University of Ruhuna were taken into consideration. At first, an inquiry into the school will be made followed by the Technical School and the University respectively.

The five schools which are chosen for this study are the best A and B grade schools in the whole Matara district. The number of students and the teachers in these schools in 1984 accounted for 10,242 and 381 respectively. So the student: teacher ratio was 26:1 (Table 61).

According to the school records in 1984, 56% of these students had their place of residence between 0 km and 3.2 km, while 21.9% lived between 3.2 km and 8 km away. The students who commuted from areas over 8 km accounted for 22.1% (Table 62).

9 The size of the educational circuit is only 3.9% (19 sq.miles) of the district's total land area (481.25 sq.miles). The school going population in this circuit in 1981 was 13.9% (22,048) of the district's total (158,575). The teacher's population was 18.3% (1,63) of the district's total of 6,886. The student teacher ratio was 17:1 which was much lower than the average ratio of 23:1.

Table 61
Five famous schools in the Matara town by:
year of opening, number of students
and the number of teachers.

Name of School	Opening Year	No. of Students	No. of Teachers
St. Thomas(boys school)	1844	2028	76
St. Servets(boys school)	1894	1542	66
Rahula(boys school)	1925	900	30
Mahamaya(girls school)	1924	2657	108
Sujatha(girls school)	1925	3115	101
Total		10242	381

Source : The school records, 1984.

Table 62
Catchment areas of the students in the five prominent schools
of the Matara town, 1984, April.

0 - 3.2 km	%	3.2 - 8 km	%	over 8 km	%	Total
1280	14.0	418	4.5	330	3.5	2028
839	9.0	377	4.0	326	3.5	1542
Not av-ailable.	-----	---	---	---	---	----
1402	15.0	520	5.6	735	7.9	2657
1703	18.0	735	7.8	677	7.2	3115
Total	56.0	2050	21.9	2068	22.1	9342

Source: The school records, 1984.

In addition to the school records, the school season tickets sold by the C.T.B. (Ceylon Transport Board) for the month of April 1984 were checked to verify the catchment areas of the towns schools. An inquiry into the monthly bus season tickets can be regarded as one of the best methods to find out the commuting areas of students, as the majority of the students travel by bus. According to the questionnaire survey, which is presented in Table 58, 32.8% of the total students who commuted to the towns schools, travelled by bus. Almost all the students who travelled by bus held season tickets due to their low price. The number of students who come by cycles, cars or carts is low. According to the survey, there were only 10% of the total students who travelled to the schools by cycles while only 0.6% used other transport media (Table 58).

In the period between 1984 and 1987, the C.T.B. operated 32 school buses a day (morning and afternoon) up and down Matara to transport students.[10] According to the monthly season ticket register at Matara C.T.B. Depot, the C.T.B. sold 3,126 schools season tickets in the month April 1984 to the students who travelled from other areas to

---

10 C.T.B.Depot Matara, 1987.

the town. Although the places of residence are not given in the register, the distances are given as presented in the following Table 63.

Table 63
The Catchment areas of the students by the distance and the monthly season tickets sold for the month April 1984.

The distance km.	The number of monthly season tickets sold	% ---
00 - 05 km	589	18.84
05 - 10 km	1287	41.17
10 - 15 km	570	18.23
15 - 20 km	471	15.06
Over 20 km	209	6.70
Total	3126	100.00

Source: Monthly School Season Ticket Register 1984, Ceylon Transport Board, Matara.

The catchment areas of the school services is smaller than that of the health services. The season tickets sold to students living in an area between 0 km and 5 km was only 18.84% of the total tickets. This is good evidence to show that the majority of the students who live close to school either walk or use transport media such as cycle and carts. The highest number of tickets (1287 = 41.17%) was sold to students who live in an area between 05 km and 10 km. In this context, the area between 0 km and 10 km can be regarded as the "Umland" of the town's school services with 60% of the season tickets sold.

The number of season tickets sold decreases rapidly beyond the 10 km bus circuit. The area between 10 km and 20 km can be regarded as the "Hinterland" with 33.29% of the season tickets sold. The "Einflussgebiet" lies beyond 20 km with only 6.7% of the total season tickets sold.

B)Polytechnic Institute

The Polytechnic Institute of Matara provides a variety of full and part-time courses in engineering, technical and commerce including short-term programmes in masonry, carpentry and tailoring for the school leavers who lack technical skill. The improvement of technical skills would, to some extent, help to solve the unemployment problem of the school leavers. Although there were 43 such schools in mobile training centres in 1981, which offered technical courses to the district's population, they were poorly equipped in comparison to Matara Technical School and were inadequate to cater to the demand throughout the district.[11]

In 1987/88, 467 students were admitted to the technical school at Maddawatta, Matara, of which 95% (443) were full time and 0.5% (24) were part-time. An inquiry into the place of residence of these student reveals that only 22% of the total admitted students came from the town itself while the rest (78%) came from other than the Matara urban council area (Table 64 and Map 32).

[11] Integrated rural development project, status report, Matara district, 1981,pp. 33-94.

Table 64
The Catchment areas of the admitted students to
Technical School Matara, 1987/88.

Location	No.of Students	% of the total	% of the total Students who live in other areas than Matara U.C.
Matara.U.C.	105	22.4	------
00 - 10 miles (0 - 16 km)	227	48.6	62.7
10 - 20 miles (16 - 32 km)	73	15.6	20.2
over 20 miles (over 32 km)	62	13.4	17.1
Total	467	100.0	100.0

Source: Data is based on the student admission register of technical school Matara, Maddawatta, 1987/88.

A high concentration of places of residence for these students is found between 0 and 10 km as in the afore mentioned school services. This area with 62.7% of the total number of students can be regarded as the "Umland" area of the Technical School. The "Hinterland" lies between 10 km and 20 km with 20.2%. The "Einflussgebiet" with 17.1% lies beyond the 20 km line.

An analysis of the place of residence by districts showed that 95% (443) of the total students came from Matara district itself, while only 5% came from other districts with Hambantota district providing 16 students, Galle providing 7 students, and from Monaragala providing 1 student.

C)University of Ruhuna

Matara town, as an educational centre, is further strengthened by the founding of the Southern University Campus of Ruhuna in 1978.

Seven hundred and thirty-two new students were admitted for the academic year 1986/87, of which 45 (6.1%) were agriculture, 344 (47%) were social science, 101 (13.8%) medicine and 242 (33.1%) were science.[12] This was 16.4%, 18.7%, 20.9% and 16.0% of the total university entrants of the island (Table 65).

12 Student enrolment register of 1986, Ruhuna Campus, Matara

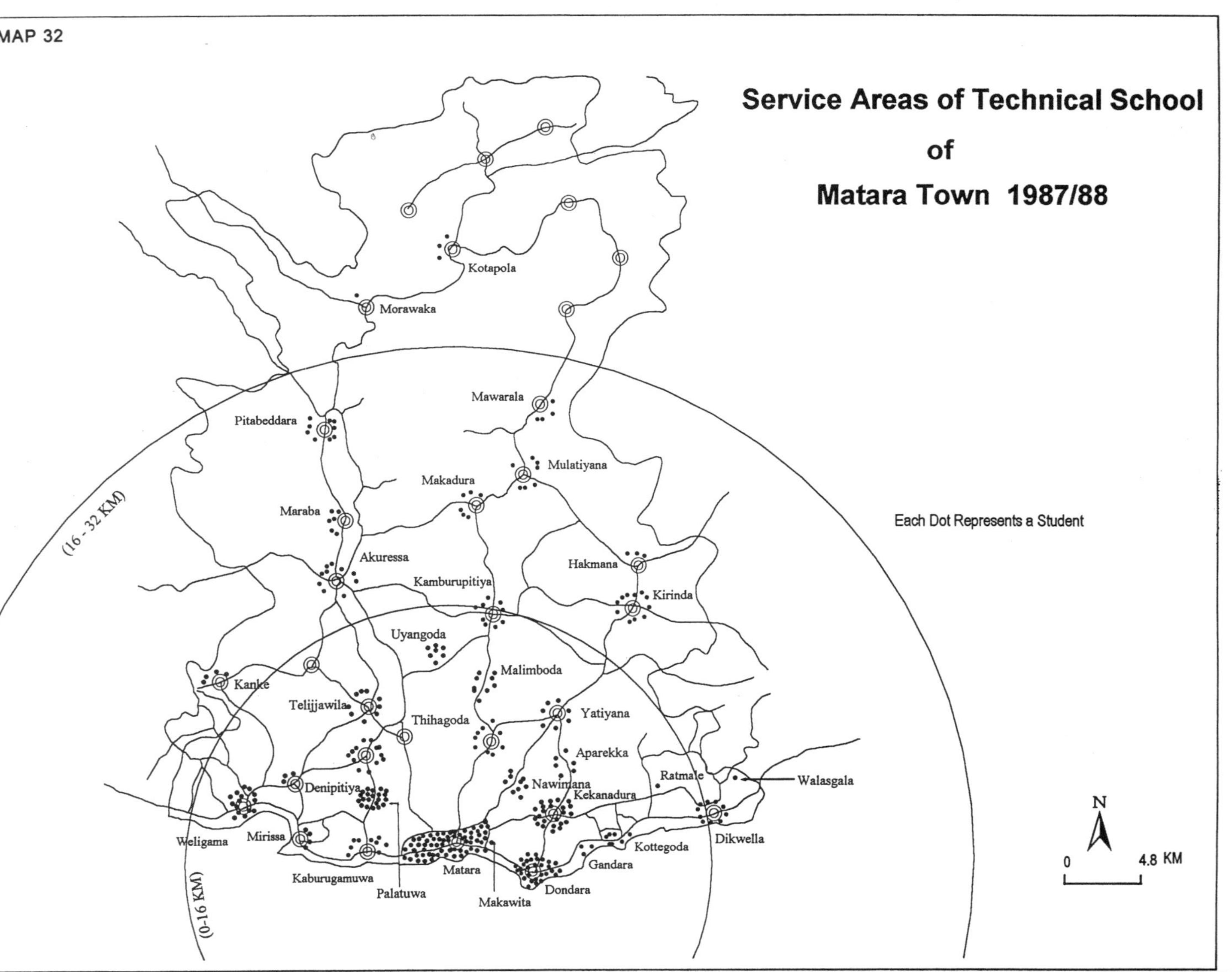
MAP 32
Service Areas of Technical School
of
Matara Town 1987/88
Each Dot Represents a Student
N
0
4.8 KM
(16 - 32 KM)
(0-16 KM)
Kotapola
Morawaka
Mawarala
Pitabeddara
Mulatiyana
Makadura
Maraba
Akuressa
Kamburupitiya
Hakmana
Kirinda
Uyangoda
Malimboda
Kanke
Telijjawila
Thihagoda
Yatiyana
Aparekka
Ratmale
Walasgala
Nawimana
Kekanadura
Denipitiya
Weligama
Mirissa
Kottegoda
Dikwella
Gandara
Matara
Kaburugamuwa
Palatuwa
Dondara
Makawita

Table 65
Undergraduate Entrants in Higher Education Institution
by Course (Agriculture, Social Science, Medicine, and
Science, Sri Lanka and Ruhuna Campus Matara, 1986/87.

	COURSE	OF STUDY		
	Agriculture	Social Science	Medicine	Science
Sri Lanka	275	1843	482	1510
University of Ruhuna.	45	344	101	242
Percentage(%)	16.4%	18.7%	20.9%	16.0%

Source: Review of the economy, 1986, p. 101.
Student admission register, University of Ruhuna, 1986 / 87.

An analysis of the data of the university entrants for the academic year 1986/87 by districts reveals that the catchment area of the university is larger than that of the other school services and the health services of the town. The 732 enrolled students for the academic year 1986/87 were from 17 districts out of the total number of districts (22) of the island (Table 66 and Map 33).

Table 66
New Admissions - 1986/87 Classified
by District of Origin.

District	No.of Students	%
Amparai	15	2.0
Anuradhapura	10	1.0
Badulla	39	5.0
Batticoloa	--	---
Colombo	31	4.0
Galle	194	27.0
Hambantota	121	17.0
Jaffna	--	---
Kalutara	21	3.0
Kandy	01	---
Kegalle	04	---
Kurunegala	18	2.0
Mannar	--	---
Matara	203	28.0
Matale	--	---
Monaragala	19	3.0
Nuwara Eliya	03	---
Polonnaruwa	05	---
Puttalam	04	---
Ratnapura	42	6.0
Trincomalee	02	---
Vavuniya	--	---
Total	732	---

Source: Admission Register 1986/87, University of Ruhuna, Matara.

Absence of entrants from Jaffna, Mannar, and Vavuniya districts which lie in the northern part of the island and of which the majority of the inhabitants are Tamils,

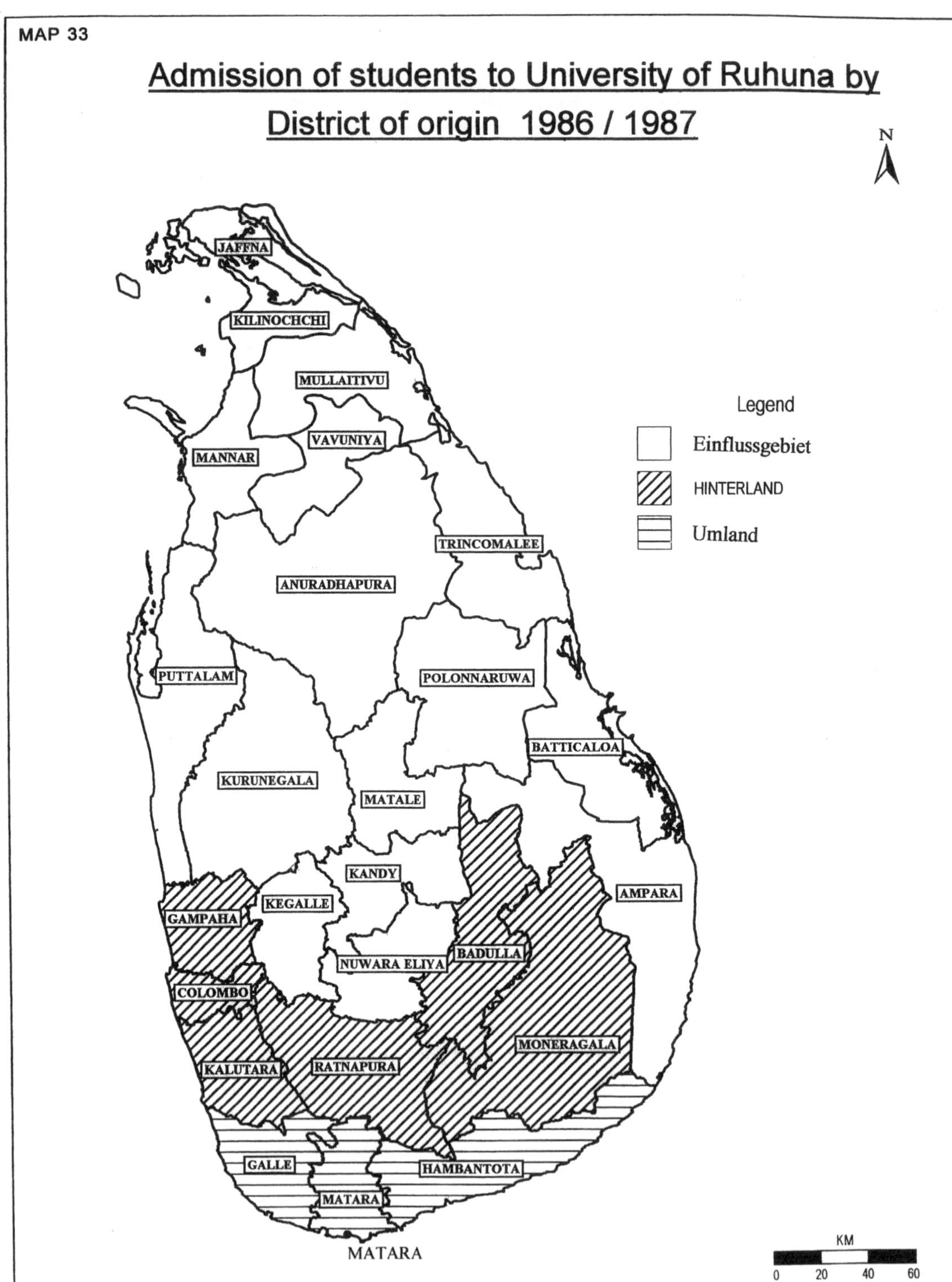
MAP 33
Admission of students to University of Ruhuna by District of origin 1986 / 1987
N
JAFFNA
KILINOCHCHI
MULLAITIVU
VAVUNIYA
MANNAR
TRINCOMALEE
ANURADHAPURA
PUTTALAM
POLONNARUWA
BATTICALOA
KURUNEGALA
MATALE
KANDY
AMPARA
KEGALLE
GAMPAHA
BADULLA
NUWARA ELIYA
COLOMBO
MONERAGALA
KALUTARA
RATNAPURA
GALLE
HAMBANTOTA
MATARA
MATARA
Legend
Einflussgebiet
HINTERLAND
Umland
KM
0
20
40
60

probably contributed to the existence of a university in Jaffna which absorbs the students from these areas. Absence of the students from the district Batticaloa and the very small number of students from the districts such as Trincomalee (2 students), Polonnaruwa (5 students), Amparai (10 students) which lie in the eastern part of the island, is most probably due to the newly established university in Batticoloa, which absorbs the students from these areas. Absence of entrants from Matale district and the very few entrants from Kandy (1 student), Nuwara Eliya (3 students), and Kegalle (4 students) districts is probably due to the existence of the most famous university at Peradeniya in Kandy.

Although Colombo district possesses the highest number of universities on the island with four out of nine, University of Colombo, University of Kelaniya, University of Vidyodaya at Udahamulla, and the newly established Open University at Nugegoda, there were 31 entrants from Colombo district. This is probably due to the inadequacy of the facilities in these institutions to meet the demand throughout the island.

An examination of these figures reveals, the university of Matara attracts students from all over the island. However, a high percentage of the facilities offered are used by the students living in the south-western quadrant of the country. The highest number of entrants to this university for the academic year 1986/87 was from the Matara district itself with 28% followed by Galle and Hambantota with 27% and 17% respectively. In this context, the area which covers Galle, Matara and Hambantota districts can be regarded as the "Umland" area of the university of Matara with 71% of the total entrants. The area which covers Colombo, Kalutara, Ratnapura, Badulla and Monaragala districts with 21% of the total entrants can be delimited as the "Hinterland" area. The area beyond these districts comprises the "Einflussgebiet" with only 8% of the total entrants.

6.2.4. Medical Facilities

The health services in Sri Lanka are organised into two types: western medicine and indigenous medicine. Indigenous medicine is called Ayurveda. These two types of services are provided through state controlled medical institutions, private nursing homes and government registered western, Ayurvedic and homeopathic practitioners. However, state run medical institutions provide the greater part of the health services, with the private sector merely providing supplementary care.

Several problems exist in the medical service in Sri Lanka. One problem is the lack of medical equipment, another is the inadequately trained manpower. The manpower situation is worsened by the exodus of trained medical personnel to other countries due to political unrest and low salaries offered to doctors. Statistics show that the number of qualified doctors (western medicine)decreased from 2,822 in 1984 to 2,217 in 1986[13].

Matara district possesses 4.5% of the total number of state owned western medical hospitals, 3.57% of the western medical dispensaries, 2.37% of the qualified

---

13 Review of the economy, 1986.

western medical doctors, 2.68% of the qualified western medical nurses, and 3.27% of the total existing Sri Lankan western medical hospital beds (Table 67).

Table 67
Existing government health care facilities (western medicine), Matara District and Sri Lanka, 1983.

	No. of Hospitals	%	No. of Dispensaries	%	No .of qualified Doctors	%
Matara	23	4.65	12	3.57	67	2.37
Sri Lanka	494	100.00	336	100.00	2822	100.00

	No. of Nurses	%	No. of Beds	%
Matara	194	2.68	1443	3.27
Sri Lanka	7216	100.00	41513	100.00

Source: Review of the Economy, 1983
The sound of nutrition, 1983.

Matara State Hospital is the base hospital which provides specialised medical facilities to an entire region which includes the Matara district (population 644,231), Hambantota district (population 424,344), Monaragala district (population 273,570) and the Ratnapura district (population 797,087). There are major gaps in the provision of services to such a large region and the population therein. An explanation of the table, "Health Services, Matara District, 1985", shows that the extremity of the health care situation is second only to that of the need for food.

According to the table there are only 35 state operated health care units in the Matara district. If the Matara district alone is served, these units possess 1,443 beds, 67 qualified doctors, 39 assistant medical practitioners, 7 medical specialists, 8 dental surgeons, 194 nurses and 211 midwives to provide health services to a population of 644,231. When the numbers of staff and the population are examined, the ratio of qualified doctors, nurses, and beds to the population is: 1:9,615, 1:3,320, and 1:446, respectively.

The health care situation and problems in Matara are typical of those of Sri Lanka as a whole, except for a lower incidence of malaria in the Matara district. Many of the medical ailments in the district and country are preventable through improved water quality, hygiene and sanitation conditions. An effective preventive medicine program would result in relief of pressure on the Matara district hospital and allow it to offer an improved service to needy cases and concentrate on medical cases of a more specific nature.

A specific topic for preventive medicine arises upon examination of the type of housing units found in the Matara Urban council area. A substantial percentage of the housing units in the Urban council area in 1971 consists of semi-permanent and improvised units (28.2%) while 25.1% have no latrine facilities and 76.7% have no treated water facilities(ref. chapter 2).[14]

Due to a lack of sanitary measures, the sewage serves as a very nutritious medium for propagation of pathogenic agents and insects. Under such circumstances, inhabitants are exposed to the dangers of polluted soils and vegetables which are grown in these areas.

This discussion would not be complete without mention of the so called urban type filariasis, alias wuchereria bancrofti or elephantiasis which occurs in the coastal areas of the Matara district. Again this parasitic disease is due to the unsanitary environmental conditions. A high occurrence of this disease is found in Matara Urban Council area, particularly in the ward Polhena, where the husk pits are found in close proximity to the living quarters. These husk pits are the most favoured breeding places of the mosquito Culex fatigans, which is considered to be the vector of wuchereria bancrofti.[15]

The main reason for the attraction of the health services in the district's capital such as Matara in Sri Lanka is the mal-distribution of health services and facilities over the region. Generally the mal distribution of health personnel is turning into a major problem not only in Sri Lanka, but also in other fast developing countries like South Korea.[16] Since there is not any data available for the employees in the private sector health institutions, the data of the employees in the state owned base hospital is used to show the imbalance of the health personnel and facilities over the region. An analysis of the medical facilities in the Matara base hospital shows that this hospital possesses 81% of the district's total qualified doctors, 100% of the specialists, 36% of the dental surgeons, 72% of the total nurses and 40% of the district's total hospital beds[17]. Although the state-owned hospitals are still concentrated in the major towns, steps have been taken in the recent past to decentralize these services since the health care policy of the government is not based on profit,but rather on social welfare (Map 34).

The ratio of the health personnel and beds to the town population is much lower than that of the district. So the ratio of qualified doctors (specialists and dental surgeons are included), nurses, and beds to the town's population in 1983 was 1:1087, 1:279, and 1:68 respectively. If the private sector medical personnel were taken into consideration, the ratio would be much lower.

According to information from the District Medical Officer (DMO) of the Matara Base Hospital, in 1987 Matara Base Hospital had many medical units, which most of the other hospitals in this region did not have. These units were: Dental unit, Dermatology unit, Eye, Nose and Throat (ENT) unit, Venereal disease unit, Surgical unit, Paediatric unit, Nutrition/Malnutrition unit, X-Ray unit, Cardiac unit, Physiotherapy unit, Sterilisation unit, Blood banks, Anti-malaria and Anti-filaria units.

---

14 Ref. Population Census 1981

15 Schweinfurth, U., 1983, 1984.
Samarawickrema, 1982.

16 Compare with Soh, C.T., Korea, 1980.

17 Ref. Statistical Handbook, 1983

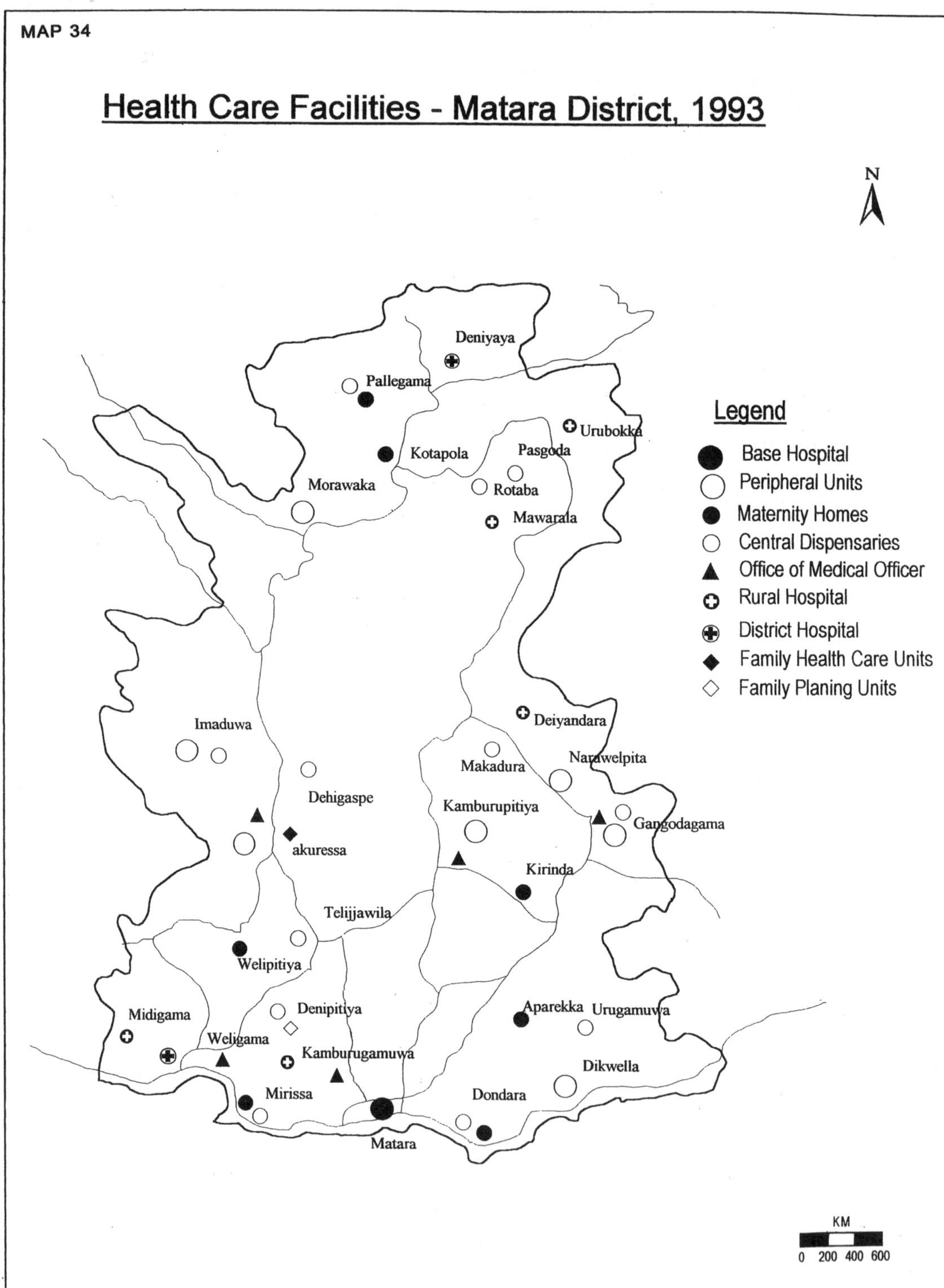
MAP 34
Health Care Facilities - Matara District, 1993
N
Legend
Base Hospital
Peripheral Units
Maternity Homes
Central Dispensaries
Office of Medical Officer
Rural Hospital
District Hospital
Family Health Care Units
Family Planing Units
Deniyaya
Pallegama
Urubokka
Kotapola
Pasgoda
Morawaka
Rotaba
Mawarala
Deiyandara
Imaduwa
Makadura
Narawelpita
Dehigaspe
Kamburupitiya
Gangodagama
akuressa
Kirinda
Telijjawila
Welipitiya
Denipitiya
Aparekka
Urugamuwa
Midigama
Weligama
Kamburugamuwa
Dikwella
Mirissa
Dondara
Matara
KM
0 200 400 600

Lack of these units outside of Matara Base Hospital gives strong evidence that distribution of medical personnel as well as the medical equipment are highly distorted in favour of the urban over the rural areas.

The four private clinics in Matara town are fairly well equipped to undertake minor surgical operations such as hernia operations, family planning and obstetrical operations.

The above discussed facts prove that the Matara Base Hospital is the major and the only clinic which provides special treatments for the whole region, Matara district, Hambantota district, Monaragala district and Ratnapura district. According to the patient's admission register of the Matara Base Hospital, 3,235 patients were admitted to this hospital in the month of December 1983. The average number of patients per day during this period was 104. An inquiry into the places of residence of the patients (which are presented in Table 68, a 10% sample and in Map 35) shows that 76.92% of the patients treated at the Matara Base Hospital during this period, came from outside the Matara Urban Council Area. So Matara's state owned health care centre, Base Hospital provided treatment not exclusively to the local residents, but also to the inhabitants of the other areas. An examination of the figures in the table 68 shows a varying degree of intensity in health care provided by the Matara Base Hospital over the region.

This treatise employs Schöller's classification scheme, i.e., Umland, Hinterland and Einflussgebiet to classify the service by degree of intensity. This delimitation is not based on the hierarchical order of the services as in Schöller's work, but merely on the degree of the intensity of any kind of service which the town provides.[18] In this paper, Umland is considered to be the area with a high degree of intensity of influence followed by Hinterland with a medium degree of intensity of influence. Einflussgebiet is the area with the least degree of influence.

Table 68
Catchment area of the Patients, Base Hospital, Matara,
Period between 1.12.83 and 31.12.83.

Functional range (Km)	No. of Patients	%	% of the total Patients who live other than Matara U.C. area
Matara U.C. area	78	23.2	-------
00.0 - 12.8 km.	88	26.0	33.8
12.8 - 25.6 km.	63	18.6	24.2
25.6 - 38.4 km.	38	11.2	14.6
38.4 - 51.2 km.	29	08.6	11.2
Over 51.2 km.	42	12.4	16.2
Total	338	100.0	----

Source: Patients Register, Base Hospital Matara, 1983. The functional range is based on a sample of 10%.

According to Table 68, the "Umland" area of the Matara Base Hospital is located between 0 km and 12.8 km, with 33.8% of the total admitted patients from the outside area of Matara U.C. The "Hinterland" is located between 25.6 km and 12.8 km with

18 Compare with Schöller, P., 1953.

24.3% of the total patients who were admitted to the hospital from outside areas of the Matara U.C. The "Einflussgebiet" of the health care services of the Matara Base Hospital covers a very large area of the Matara district and extends into the adjacent districts. This area is located outside the 25.6 km line. The patients admitted to the hospital from this area account for 53.5% of the total patients. They are not concentrated in any particular location, but are dispersed all over the region (Map 35).

An observation of the places of residence which are presented on the map shows that the residential areas of the patients are highly concentrated in the northern and eastern parts of the district, while there are few patients from the western area. This could be attributed to the fact that Galle, a large town which lies in close proximity to Matara (40 Km) in the west, provides the inhabitants with more specialised and better health care services than Matara. However, this speculation could not be proven by the questionnaire survey in 1987 which shows consumer behaviour of the Matara district population. There were only two out of forty-eight respondents in Weligama, close to Galle who mentioned that they go to Galle in case of a serious illness or injury. However, it is possible that patients are forced to go or transferred to the Galle Base Hospital due to the inadequacy of medical equipment in the base hospital of Matara.

In addition to an examination of the patients' admission register, a survey was conducted in 1987 to find out the area of influence of Matara town and the consumer behaviour of Matara district's population. This information is of crucial importance to delimit the various urban spheres of influence. In this context, 900 questionnaires were distributed to the school principals of nine central schools which are dispersed over the Matara district. The principals were asked to get these questionnaires filled out by their 11th grade students who were preparing for the university entrance examination, without influencing their point of view. Of 900 questionnaires given to the school principals, 858 were returned, a response rate of 95%.

The analysed data from the questionnaire (question 20 and 21), " Where do you go for medical treatment?"

a. For minor injuries or diseases.
b. For more serious illness are given in the table number 69.

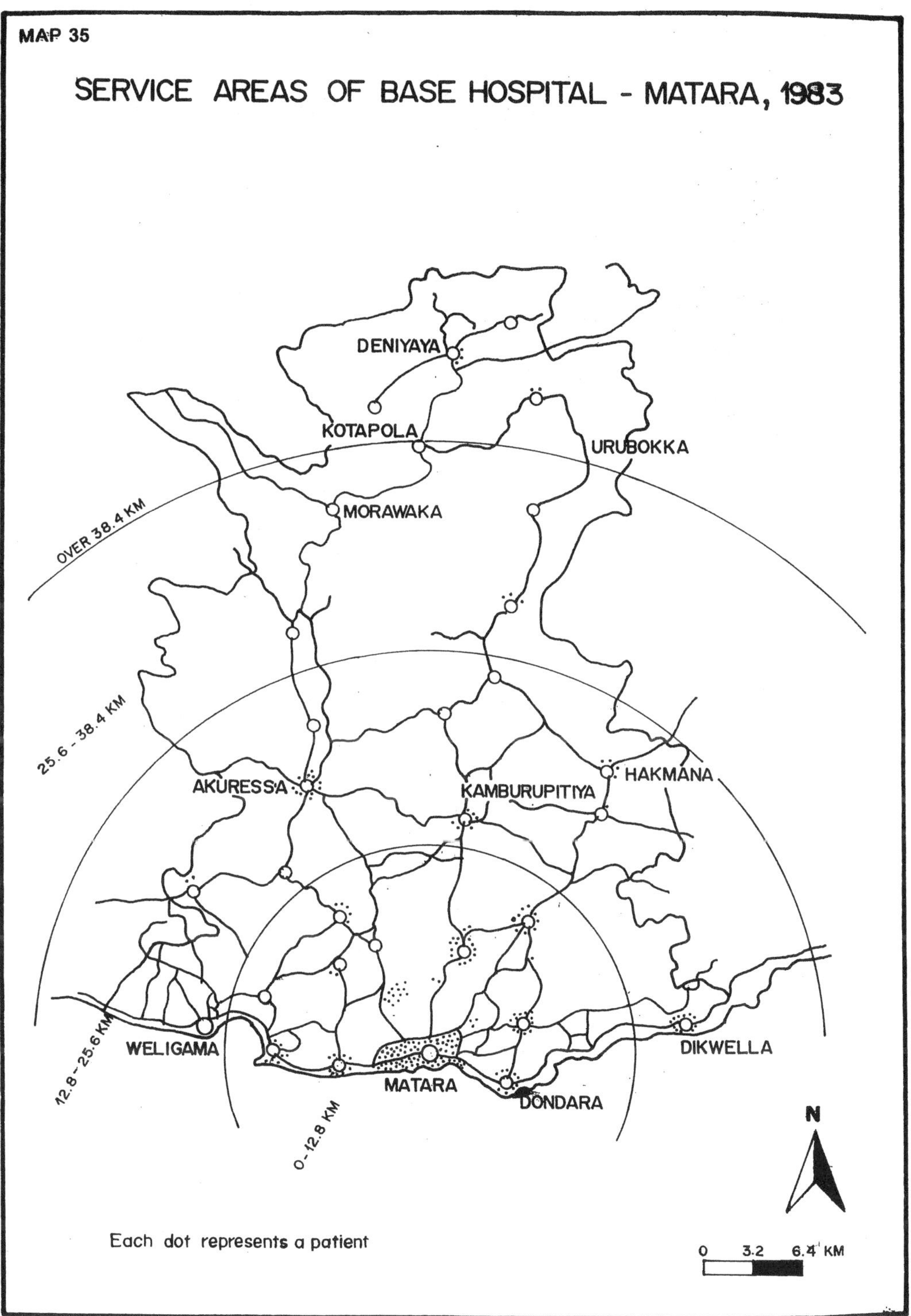
MAP 35
SERVICE AREAS OF BASE HOSPITAL - MATARA, 1983
DENIYAYA
KOTAPOLA
URUBOKKA
MORAWAKA
OVER 38.4 KM
25.6 - 38.4 KM
AKURESSA
KAMBURUPITIYA
HAKMANA
12.8 - 25.6 KM
WELIGAMA
MATARA
DONDARA
DIKWELLA
0 - 12.8 KM
N
Each dot represents a patient
0 3.2 6.4 KM

Table 69
The important health care centres of the study area according to the frequency of entries in questions 20 and 21 of the questionnaire.

Akuressa (Central School)

Question No. 20	Frequency of entries	Question No. 21	Frequency of entries
Akuressa Govt.P.H.*	66	Matara.B.H.*	66
Matara B.H.	1	Akuressa Govt.P.H.	27
Others	33	Galle. B.H.	1
		Others	6
Total	100		100

Hakmana (Methodist Central School)

Question No. 20	Frequency of entries	Question No. 21	Frequency of entries
Hakmana Govt.C.D.*	88	Matara B.H.	89
Others	12	Hakmana Govt.H.*	5
		Others	6
Total	100		100

Deniyaya (Central School)

Question No. 20	Frequency of entries	Question No. 21	Frequency of entries
Deniyaya Dist.H.*	87	Deniyaya Dist.H.	60
Others	13	Matara B.H.	30
		Colombo	2
		Others	8
Total	100		100

Morawaka (Central School)

Question No. 20	Frequency of entries	Question No. 21	Frequency of entries
Morawaka Govt.P.H.	68	Matara B.H.	72
Others	32	Deniyaya Dist.H.	7
		Galle B.H.	9
		Akuressa Govt.P.H.	7
		Morawaka Govt.P.H.	5
Total	100		100

Urubokka (Central School)

Question No. 20	Frequency of entries	Question No. 21	Frequency of entries
Urubokka Govt.R.H.	89	Matara B.H.	74
Others	11	Deniyaya.Dist.H.	16
		Urubokka.Govt.R.H.*	2
		Others	18
Total	100		100

Weligama Siddarta (Central School)

Question No. 20	Frequency of entries	Question No. 21	Frequency of entries
Weligama Govt.D.H.	39	Matara. B.H.	24
Others	3	Weligama Govt.D.H.	15
		Galle. B.H.	1
		Others	2
Total	42		42

(contd. in the following page)

Dondara (Central School)

Dondara Govt.D.*	59	Matara. B.H.	92
Matara. B.H.	28	Others	8
Others	13		
Total	100		100

Dikwella (Central School)

Dikwella Govt.P.H.	69	Matara. B.H.	88
Matara. B.H.	31	Dikwella.Govt.P.H.	12
Total	100		100

Kamburupitiya (Central School)

Kamburupitiya Govt.P.H.	84	Matara. B.H.	84
Matara. B.H.	1	Kamburupitiya.Govt. P.H.	9
Others	15	Galle. B.H.	2
		Others	5
Total	100		100

Source: Questionnaire Survey 1987.
Remarks: B.H. = Base Hospital
Govt.P.H. = Government Peripheral Hospital
Govt.C.H. = Government Central Dispensary
Govt.Dist.H. = Government District Hospital
Govt.R.H. = Government Rural Hospital
Govt.D. = Government Dispensary

An examination of the data in the above table shows that in case of a minor injury or illness the majority of the respondents (75%) would go for treatment at the government hospital or health care centres which are located close to their place of residence. The closer the respondents lived to Matara, which has a well developed transportation system and lower bus fares, the greater the preference to go to Matara rather than going to the inadequately equipped health care centres which lie closer to their residence. As support for this conjecture, 28% of the total respondents in Dondara area and 22% of the total respondents in Dikwella area prefered to go to the Matara Base Hospital for treatment.

According to the analysed questionnaires, the health care units are well dispersed over the region, so that 68% of the respondents could reach a health care unit in 30 minutes walking time. Seventy-five percent of the respondents walked to these medical centres, the remainder traveled by bus or bicycle.

In case of a serious injury or illness, the majority of the respondents (76%) would go directly to the Matara Base Hospital for treatment without visiting the other health care centres (Map 36). However, in the areas where somewhat better equipped hospitals are found such as Deniyaya which has a district hospital with 50 beds, a high percentage of the respondents would go first to these hospitals. The percentages of the respondents who go to these hospitals in case of serious injury or illness are 60% and 36% respectively.

MAP 36

Importance of Base Hospital - Matara in case of serious illness or injury for the district's population.

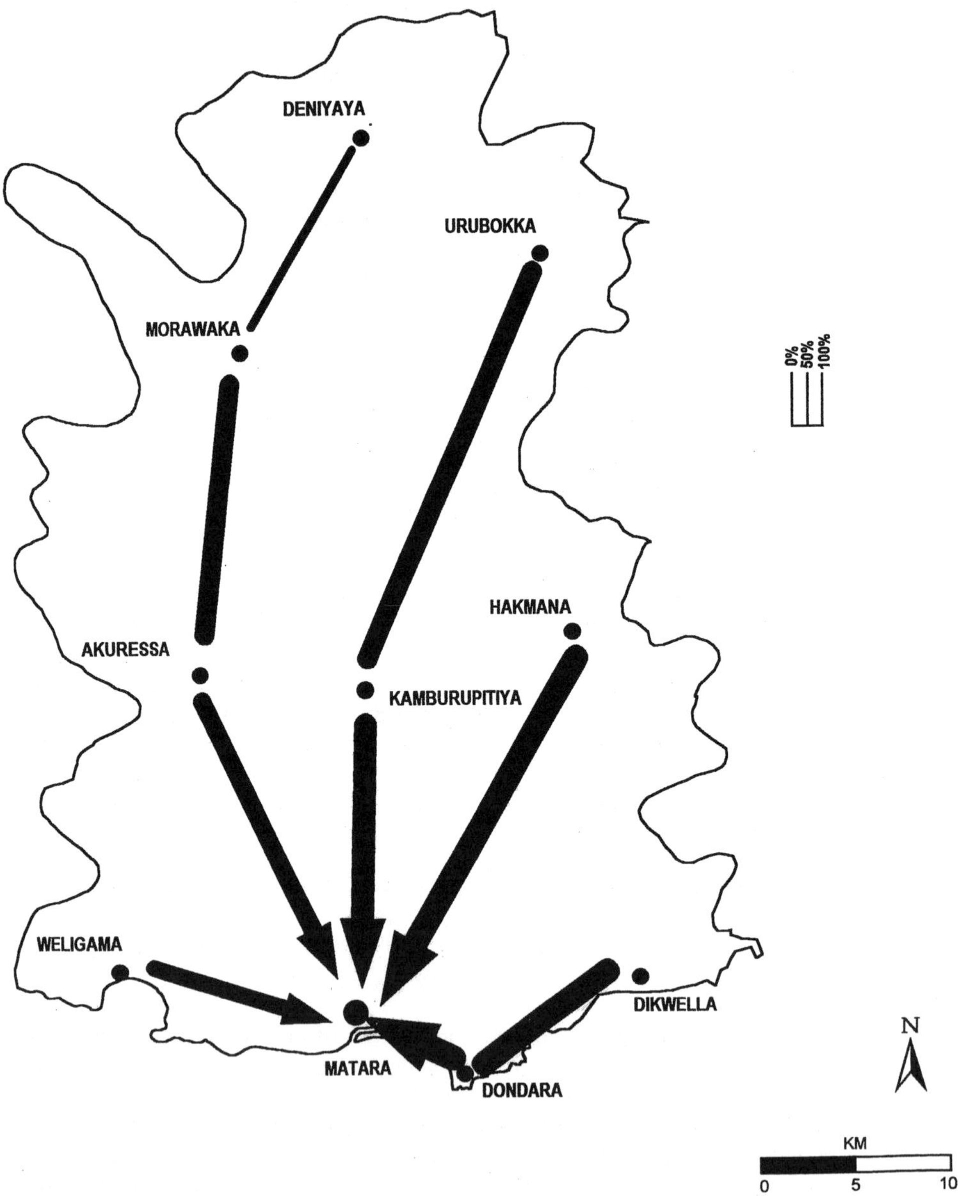

Only a few respondents mentioned private medical institutions in their questionnaires. This could be attributed to the fact that only a few private health care institutions are located in those areas and the high charges in the private sector institutions may prevent the use of these centres by the population in general.

The question concerning the patient's behaviour in reference to health care institutions shows that the Matara Base Hospital has the district's largest catchment area for serious injury or illness.

The private sector health care units provide the remainder of medical services to the population in this region. In contrast to the state run free charge hospitals, the private hospitals are patronised by medium and high income groups since the charges for the treatments are high. These private hospitals are not overcrowded like the government hospitals and are clean. There is a shorter waiting time for treatment or consultation by a specialist in comparison to the government hospitals. Most of the specialists who staff the private hospitals are government doctors who are compelled to work in the private hospital in their free time due to the low government institution salaries.

As mentioned earlier, there were four western medicine private hospitals, six western type private dispensaries and three dental clinics in the Matara Urban Council area in 1984. One out of five private hospitals was investigated in this work to find out the areas of influence of the private hospitals. Mohotti hospital which was established in 1958 is considered to be one of the best private hospitals, not only in the Matara U.C. areas, but also in the entire region.

The average patient load per day at the OPD during the period of 01.09.87 to 31.12.87 was 100. According to the "indoor general admission register", 209 patients were admitted to this hospital during the period between 01.09.87 and 31.12.87. An inquiry into the place of residence of these patients showed that 26.2% of the total admitted patients were from the town itself (Table 70 and Map 37).

Table 70
Catchment area of the patients - Private Hospital "Mohotti"
Matara, From 1.9.1987 to 31.12.1987.

Functional range	No. of patients	% of total patients	% of total patients who live other than Matara U.C. area
Matara U.C. area	56	26.2	----
00 - 12.8 Km	77	36.0	48.7
12.8 - 25.6 Km	22	10.2	13.9
25.6 - 38.4 Km	20	9.3	12.7
38.4 - 51.2 Km	4	1.9	2.5
Over 51.2 KM	35	16.4	22.2
Total	214	100.0	100.0

Source: Indoor Patients Admission Register 1987.,
Private Hospital "Mohotti", Matara.

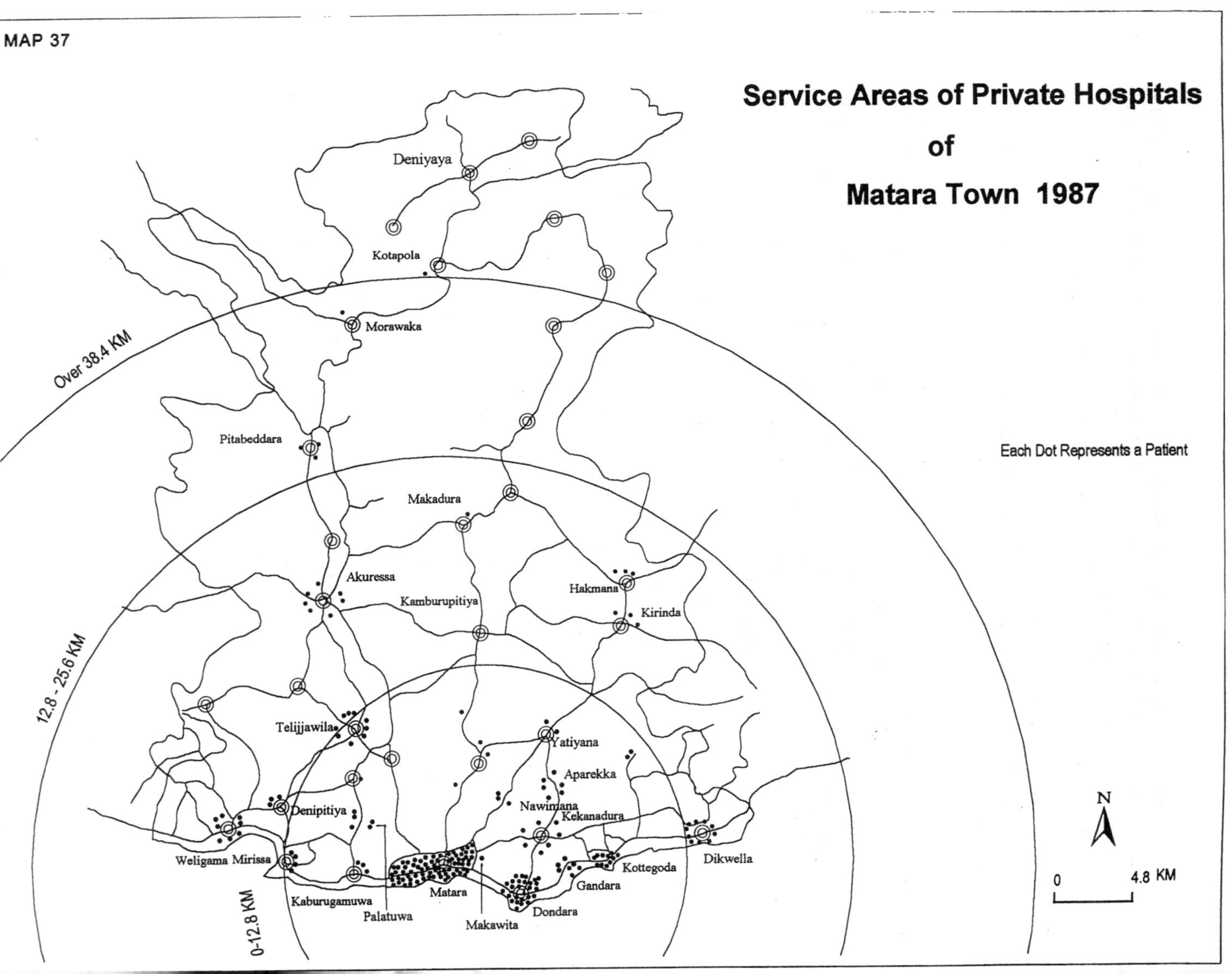
MAP 37
Service Areas of Private Hospitals
of
Matara Town 1987
Each Dot Represents a Patient
N
0
4.8 KM
Over 38.4 KM
12.8 - 25.6 KM
0-12.8 KM
Deniyaya
Kotapola
Morawaka
Pitabeddara
Makadura
Akuressa
Kamburupitiya
Hakmana
Kirinda
Telijjawila
Yatiyana
Aparekka
Nawimana
Kekanadura
Denipitiya
Weligama
Mirissa
Kaburugamuwa
Palatuwa
Matara
Makawita
Dondara
Gandara
Kottegoda
Dikwella

The "Umland area" of the private hospital Mohotti is compatible with the Umland area of the Matara Base Hospital. It is located between 0 km and 12.8 km. The "Hinterland" area of the private hospital is larger that that of the base hospital. It extends from 12.8 km to 38.4 km. "The Einflussgebiet" of the private hospital extends to the adjacent districts like the "Einflussgebiet" of the base hospital. An examination of patient admissions shows that 80% (172 patients) of all the patients were from the Matara district itself followed by Hambantota district with 17% (36 patients). The number of patients admitted from other adjacent districts was low. There were only two patients from Galle district, one patient from Monoragala district, one patient from Ratnapura and one patient from Amparai district (Map 38).

The above discussed facts proved that private hospitals of the Matara U.C. area have large catchment areas because of the mal-distribution of health care facilities throughout the region.

6.2.5. Trade

The centrality of trade and the town's relationship with its surrounding areas are investigated by taking its commercial services into consideration as given below.

6.2.5.1.A) MATARA as a centre of important and easily available outlets to the rural producers as well as to other traders to dispose of their goods and a market place from where to purchase various goods urban goods (local and imported).

6.2.5.2.B) MATARA town as a collector and redistributor of local agricultural products.

6.2.5.3.C) MATARA as a reloading point for the estate sector imports and exports.

6.2.5.4.D) MATARA as a centre for consumption of agricultural raw materials.

6.2.5.5.E) MATARA as a major centre of food distribution to the district's population as well as to the population of the adjoining districts.

6.2.5.6.F) MATARA as the sole distributor of petro products and one of the major building material suppliers for the whole region.

6.2.5.7.G) MATARA as an important place of refreshment and lodging for commercial travellers, businessmen, tourists and pilgrims as well as a place for honeymoons of newly married couples from the Matara and Hambantota districts.

6.2.5.8.H) MATARA as a place of work and employer of the rural surplus labour.

6.2.5.1.A) MATARA as a Centre of Important and Easily Available Outlet to the Rural Producers as well as to other Traders to Dispose of Their Goods and a Market Place from where to purchase Various Urban Goods (Local and Imported).

As discussed earlier in Chapter 4, Matara is the major commercial centre for the whole Matara district possessing 63% of the total registered commercial units of the district. An inquiry into the type of commercial units in 1986 has also revealed that Matara town processes 50% of the total short-term consumer goods related shops, 78% of

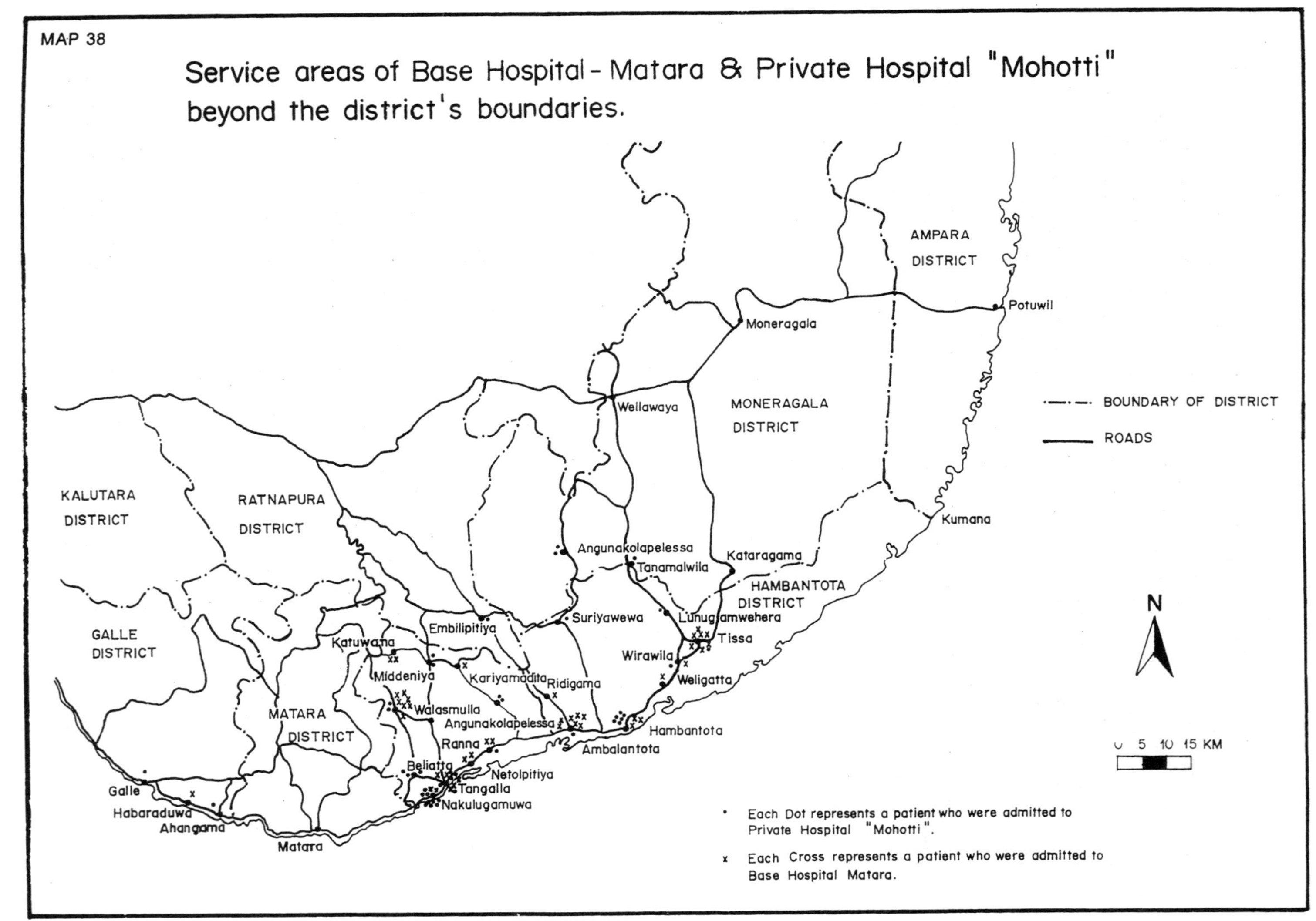
MAP 38
Service areas of Base Hospital - Matara & Private Hospital "Mohotti"
beyond the district's boundaries.
AMPARA DISTRICT
Potuwil
Moneragala
Wellawaya
MONERAGALA DISTRICT
BOUNDARY OF DISTRICT
ROADS
KALUTARA DISTRICT
RATNAPURA DISTRICT
Kumana
Angunakolapelessa
Tanamalwila
Kataragama
HAMBANTOTA DISTRICT
Embilipitiya
Suriyawewa
Lunugamwehera
Tissa
GALLE DISTRICT
Katuwana
Wirawila
Middeniya
Kariyamaditta
Ridigama
Weligatta
Walasmulla
MATARA DISTRICT
Angunakolapelessa
Hambantota
Ranna
Ambalantota
Beliatta
Netolpitiya
Tangalla
Nakulugamuwa
Galle
Habaraduwa
Ahangama
Matara
N
0 5 10 15 KM
• Each Dot represents a patient who were admitted to Private Hospital "Mohotti".
x Each Cross represents a patient who were admitted to Base Hospital Matara.

the total mid-term and long-term goods related shops and 52% of the other consumer goods and the service related shops (Table 50 and Map 28). The high concentration of different types of shops in Matara town offers a higher selection of various goods to the consumers than any other centre of the district. This tends to attract the people to Matara from the whole region.

In regard to the collection and redistribution of the local agricultural products, the weekly and the two daily markets in town can be considered as the most important trade institutions (Chapter 4). According to the questionnaire survey in 1987, 90% of the total respondents go twice a week to the weekly market (periodic market or pola) to buy their day to day needs.

An investigation into the place of residence of the sellers in these three markets shows that all the sellers of the two daily markets come from the town itself while the sellers of the weekly market come from all over the region.[19] Through an interview of 100 sellers out of 232 in January 1987, it was revealed that 95% of the sellers came from the Matara district itself, while only 5% of the total sellers came from the adjoining district, Hambantota. In contrast, it was found that 30-40% of all the sellers of the periodic market in the Hambantota district were traders of the Matara district[20].

This is an indication that Matara is profiteering from the underdevelopment of the Hambantota district. The other striking feature in this regard was that there were no traders in the Matara Pola from Galle district. This can be attributed to the fact that the sellers of the Galle district, which is more urbanized than the Matara district , find the Galle Pola more lucrative and attractive than Matara Pola.

According to a sample survey conducted by the author in 1987,15% of all the sellers came from the town itself while 46% of the sellers came from an area which lies between 0 and 12.8 km radius. The rest of the sellers (29%) came from the area which lies beyond 12.8 km radius. The "Umland area" of the pola, in regard to the sellers, lies between 0 and 12.8 km, with 46% of the total sellers (Map 39).

The answers to the question why they came to sell their goods at Matara Pola instead of going to the Polas at a closer proximity to their homes are given below:[21]

A) The volume of business in the Matara Pola is higher than that of other Polas in the district.
B) The goods can be sold very fast,saving time so that they can go home early.
C) The goods can be sold at a higher price than at any other Polas making higher profits, even though transport charges are incurred.

Sellers in the Matara Pola consist of professional and producer sellers. The ratio of professional sellers to producer sellers was 50:50. The producer sellers are mostly

---

19 Matara Urban Council, 1987.

20 Rasak, M. Periodic Markets in the Hambantota district, M.A. thesis, University of Ruhuna, Matara, 1984.

21 The author is greatly indebted to his cousin Raju de Silva who helped him collecting data.

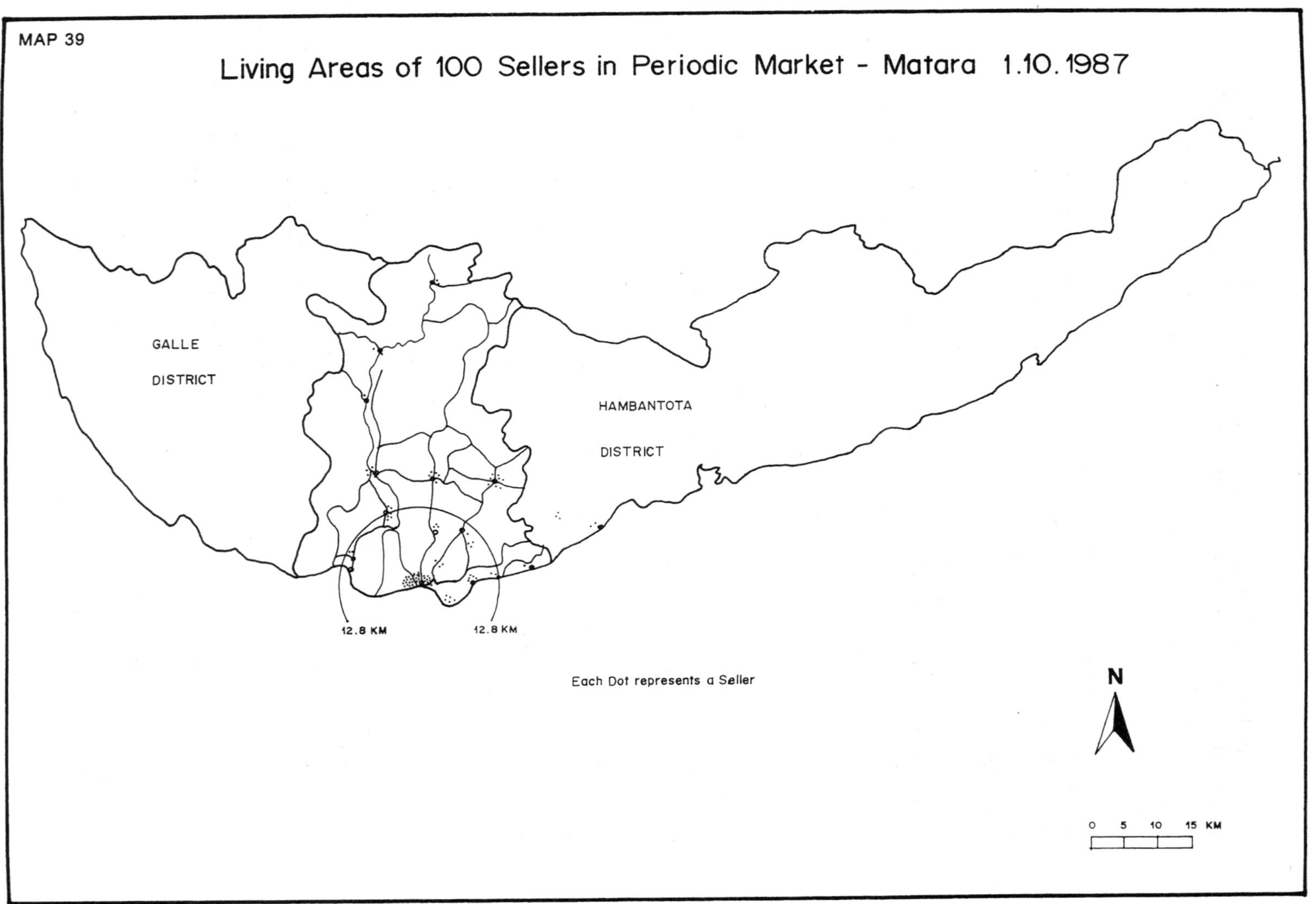
MAP 39
Living Areas of 100 Sellers in Periodic Market - Matara 1.10.1987
GALLE DISTRICT
HAMBANTOTA DISTRICT
12.8 KM
12.8 KM
Each Dot represents a Seller
N
0 5 10 15 KM

farmers who live in close proximity to town. Their products are mostly grown in home gardens and in small market gardens. The living areas of these producer sellers do not exceed a distance of 16 km from Matara town (Map 40). Their products are brought to the Pola by carts, bullock carts, tractors, bus, cycles, pingos or on their heads. Some residential areas of these producer sellers are given here: Piladuwa (vegetable), Bandattara (vegetable), Kapuduwa (vegetable), Batuwita (vegetable), Makawita (vegetable), Yatiyana (vegetable), Gandara (fish), Kottegoda (fish), Dondara (fish), Totamuna in Matara Urban Council area (fish) and Ginigiamulla in Matara Urban Council area (fish).

After selling their goods, the producer sellers spend some of their money to purchase urban goods.

The professional sellers, mostly the shop owners of town, bring a large quantity of their goods either by vehicles, or by buses. They come from all over the district.

The answer to the question, "Where do the professional sellers buy their goods?", is presented in the following table.

Table 71
Location of Polas, opening days and districts
from where sellers buy goods, 1987.

Location of Pola	District	Holding days
Ambalantota	Hambantota	Monday & Wednesday
Agunacolapalassa	Hambantota	Sunday & Wednesday
Beliatta	Hambantota	Daily
Deiyandara	Matara	Tuesday & Friday
Debokkawa	Hambantota	Thursday
Hakmana	Matara	Daily
Hungama	Hambantota	Friday
Middeniya	Hambantota	Friday & Monday
Monaragala	Monaragala	Saturday & Tuesday
Pannegamuwa	Hambantota	Thursday & Friday
Ranna	Hambantota	Tuesday & Friday
Tissa	Hambantota	Daily
Suriyawewa	Hambantota	Saturday & Tuesday
Weeraketiya	Hambantota	Saturday & Monday
Wadigala	Hambantota	Thursday & Sunday
Wallasmulla	Hambantota	Tuesday & Friday
Tangalla	Hambantota	Sunday
Wellawaya	Monaragala	Saturday & Sunday

Source: Interview Survey of 1987.

According to the above table, the majority of the periodic markets (82%) where the professional sellers buy their goods lie in the Hambantota district, where Chena cultivation (shifting cultivation) is highly practiced, followed by Monaragala district (Map 40). This particular behaviour of the seller is attributed to the following facts:

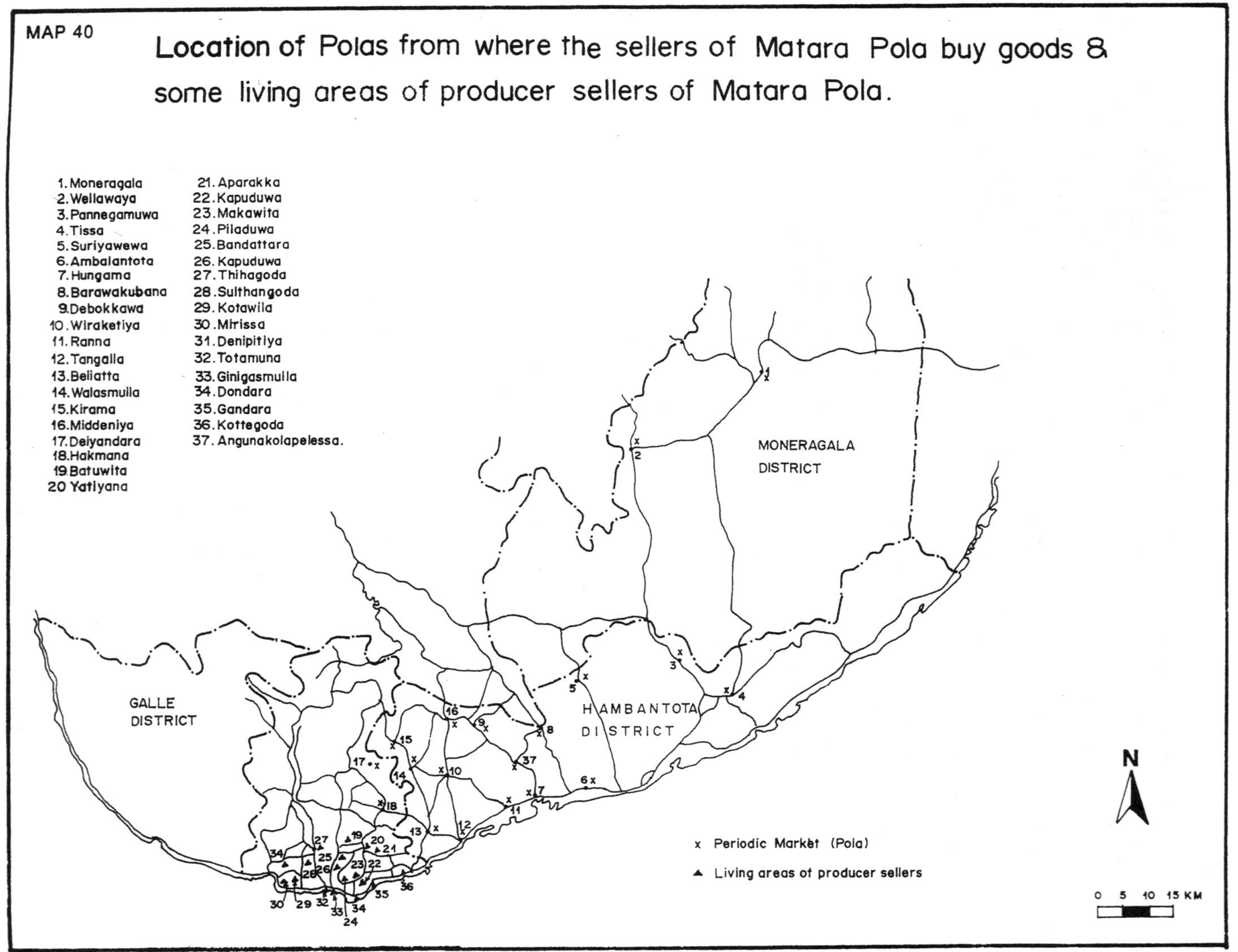
MAP 40
Location of Polas from where the sellers of Matara Pola buy goods &
some living areas of producer sellers of Matara Pola.
1. Moneragala
2. Wellawaya
3. Pannegamuwa
4. Tissa
5. Suriyawewa
6. Ambalantota
7. Hungama
8. Barawakubana
9. Debokkawa
10. Wiraketiya
11. Ranna
12. Tangalla
13. Beliatta
14. Walasmulla
15. Kirama
16. Middeniya
17. Deiyandara
18. Hakmana
19. Batuwita
20 Yatiyana
21. Aparakka
22. Kapuduwa
23. Makawita
24. Piladuwa
25. Bandattara
26. Kapuduwa
27. Thihagoda
28. Sulthangoda
29. Kotawila
30. Mirissa
31. Denipitiya
32. Totamuna
33. Ginigasmulla
34. Dondara
35. Gandara
36. Kottegoda
37. Angunakolapelessa.
MONERAGALA DISTRICT
HAMBANTOTA DISTRICT
GALLE DISTRICT
x Periodic Market (Pola)
▲ Living areas of producer sellers
N
0 5 10 15 KM

A) The most important agricultural products such as vegetables, cereals and fruits, which are largely consumed by Buddhist Sinhalese, are not usually cultivated in the Matara district. The area under such agricultural cultivation is only 7.2% (vegetable 2.3%, fruit 1.5%, cereals .02%, and other agricultural products 3.4%) of the total cultivated land area of the district. In contrast to the small amount of land area under the above said agricultural cultivation,a high percentage (51.56%) of the cultivated land area of the district produces cash crops,with major cash crops at 41.10% and minor cash crops at 10.46%[22]

B) Although the land area under homestead accounts for 37.7% of the total cultivated land area of the district,the production of vegetables, fruit, and cereals in the home gardens is very low. This cultivation is mostly done on a subsistence level and consumed by the households.

C) The price of the agricultural products (vegetables,fruit, cereals) in the Matara district is much higher than in the Hambantota district due to higher urbanisation and scarcity of the goods. The agricultural products in the Hambantota district are grown on Chena land and mostly brought to the Pola by producers.These products are much cheaper for the sellers of the Matara district, although transport costs are incurred.

As shown above Matara district does not produce sufficient food for its inhabitants and is highly dependant on Hambantota district for its basic needs.

The highland vegetables and fruit, which constitute only 4% of the total vegetables and fruit in the Pola, are brought by three professional wholesale traders in Denipitiya, which lies closest to Weligama and Matara town itself . These are brought from Haputale, Nuwara Eliya, Kanda Pola, and Bandarawela and sold to the retailers on a commission basis.[23]

Food items such as dry chilli, dahl, onions, salt-fish (Karawala) and dry fish (Umbalakada) are brought to the Pola by wholesale traders from C.W.E. (Co-operative Wholesale Establishment) at Colombo and Matara and sold to the retailers on a commission basis. The rice is brought to the Matara pola by collectors of Hakmana area. The collecting areas of rice are located in the Hambantota and Monaragala districts which are considered to be the least urbanised and underdeveloped districts in the southern region of the island.

Fish is brought to Pola from the surrounding areas of the Matara town. The most important fishing centres are Ginigasmulla (in the Matara U.C. area), Totamuna (in the Matara U.C. area), Kottegoda (which lies 12.8 km from Matara), Dondara (4.8 km from Matara), Gandara (8 km from Matara) and Dikwella (19.2 km from Matara). Fish from

---

22 Statistical hand book, Matara district,1983, Land use map of Galle and Matara districts 1983, High land crops and livestock statistics , Matara district, 1981, Rural development project, 1981).

23 Weitzel, K., 1970.

Mirissa and Weligama are very seldom brought to Matara as they have a ready market in Colombo.

The methods of transportation of fish to the Pola are cycles and other vehicles. The areas from which some particular agricultural products and commodities come to Pola are presented in the map 41.

According to information gained through the interviews and from the tax collectors of the Pola, 90% of the buyers came from the town itself while the rest, 10%, came from an area which does not exceed a 6.4 km radius. This is strikingly similar to service areas of the Pola in central Sri Lanka (6 km radius) as well as to the service areas recorded for other agrarian societies such as China and Guatemala (5.8 km radius).[24] This indicates that Matara periodic markets (Pola) predominantly provide services to the town's population. The service area of the Pola is confined to the areas which lie in close proximity to the town.

This is mainly because of the following facts:

A) The Pola offers merely short-term related goods to the buyers which can be bought from the centres where they live.
B) These goods are much cheaper in other service centres than in a more urbanised area.
C) The buyers feel that it is not worth time and money going to Matara to buy these goods.

This can also be proven by the questionnaire survey of 1987 as presented in the table 72.

Table 72
The Polas to which the respondents go to buy their primary goods; the transport media which they use, and the time which they need to go to Pola (Matara district, 1987).

Area of Pola	Location	No.of. respondents	Transport Media			The Time		
			Walk	Bus	Others	0-30	30-1	Over 1hour
Deniyaya*1	Pallegama	80	-----	----	--------	-----	-----	-------
Kotapola		10	-----	----	--------	-----	-----	-------
Beralapanatara		5	-----	----	--------	-----	-----	-------
Morawaka		5	-----	----	--------	-----	-----	-------
Total		100	35	41	24	50	35	15

(contd.in the following page)

24 Skinner, G.W., 1964
Dicke, S. 1987.
Jackson, W.D., 1977.

Urubokka*2	Urubokka	98	-----	----	--------	-----	-----	-----
Bengamuwa		1	-----	-----	-----	-----	-----	-----
Matara		1	-----	-----	-----	-----	-----	-----
Total		100	69	23	8	42	50	8
Morawaka*3	Morawaka	75	-----	-----	-----	-----	-----	-----
Dangalla		13	-----	-----	-----	-----	-----	-----
Pitabeddara		2	-----	-----	-----	-----	-----	-----
Kotapola		5	-----	-----	-----	-----	-----	-----
Opatha		5	-----	-----	-----	-----	-----	-----
Total		100	52	31	17	57	33	10
Akuressa*4	Akuressa	75	-----	-----	-----	-----	-----	-----
Pitabeddara		7	-----	-----	-----	-----	-----	-----
Kanka		2	-----	-----	-----	-----	-----	-----
Makadura		1	-----	-----	-----	-----	-----	-----
Opatha		1	-----	-----	-----	-----	-----	-----
Matara		2	-----	-----	-----	-----	-----	-----
Total		100	21	59	20	65	31	4
Kamburupitiya*5	Kamburupitiya	59	-----	-----	-----	-----	-----	-----
Deiyandara		8	-----	-----	-----	-----	-----	-----
Matara		5	-----	-----	-----	-----	-----	-----
Thihagoda		4	-----	-----	-----	-----	-----	-----
Bengamuwa		3	-----	-----	-----	-----	-----	-----
Kadduwa		1	-----	-----	-----	-----	-----	-----
Mawarala		5	-----	-----	-----	-----	-----	-----
Karaputugala		5	-----	-----	-----	-----	-----	-----
Makadura		8	-----	-----	-----	-----	-----	-----
Pasgoda		1	-----	-----	-----	-----	-----	-----
Hakmana		1	-----	-----	-----	-----	-----	-----
Total		100	48	33	19	62	35	3
Hakmana*6	Hakmana	95	-----	-----	-----	-----	-----	-----
Walasmulla		3	-----	-----	-----	-----	-----	-----
Beliatta		2	-----	-----	-----	-----	-----	-----
(contd. in the following page)								
Total		100	55	37	8	49	37	14
Weligama*7	Weligama	28	-----	-----	-----	-----	-----	-----
Kamburugamuwa		1	-----	-----	-----	-----	-----	-----
Kanka		2	-----	-----	-----	-----	-----	-----
Galbokka		2	-----	-----	-----	-----	-----	-----
Welipitiya		5	-----	-----	-----	-----	-----	-----
Denipitiya		4	-----	-----	-----	-----	-----	-----
Total		42	24	8	10	27	11	4

(contd.in the following page)

Dikwella*8	Dikwella	51	-----	-----	-----	-----	-----	-----
Walasmulla		27	-----	-----	-----	-----	-----	-----
Ratmale		14	-----	-----	-----	-----	-----	-----
Gandara		1	-----	-----	-----	-----	-----	-----
Matara		3	-----	-----	-----	-----	-----	-----
Wattegama		1	-----	-----	-----	-----	-----	-----
Dondara		2	-----	-----	-----	-----	-----	-----
Radampola		1	-----	-----	-----	-----	-----	-----
Total		100	53	30	17	73	23	4
Dondara*	Dondara	8	-----	-----	-----	-----	-----	-----
Matara		61	-----	-----	-----	-----	-----	-----
Kumbalgama		22	-----	-----	-----	-----	-----	-----
Others		9	-----	-----	-----	-----	-----	-----
Total		100	26	58	16	75	22	3
Total		842	383	320	139	500	277	65
Percentage (%)		100	45,5	38,0	16,5	59,4	33,3	7,7

Source: Questionnaire Survey 1987.

Remarks:

*1 Deniyaya is 77 km from Matara in the northern region of the Matara district. The bus fare to Matara from Deniyaya was 10 Rupees. The time needed to reach Matara was 3 to 4 hours.

*2 Urubokka is about 64 km from Matara in the northern eastern region of Matara district. The bus fare was 8 Rupees. The time needed to reach Matara was 3 to 4 hours.

*3 Morawaka is 51 km from Matara in the northern region of Matara district. The bus fare was 7.25 Rupees. The time needed to reach Matara was 3 to 3.30 hours.

*4 Akuressa is about 22 km from Matara in the central region of Matara district. The bus fare was 4 Rupees. The time needed to reach Matara was 1.30 hours.

*5 Kamburupitiya is about 21 km from Matara in the central region of Matara district The bus fare was 3.50 Rupees. The time needed to reach Matara was 1.30 hours.

*6 Hakmana is about 24 km from Matara in the central region of Matara district. The bus fare was 4.25 Rupees. The time needed to reach Matara was 1.30 hours.

*7 Weligama is about 10 km from Matara in the coastal zone of Matara district. The bus fare was 2 Rupees. The time needed to reach Matara was 45 Minutes.

(contd. in the following page)

*8 Dikwella is about 19 km from Matara in the coastal zone of the Matara district. The bus fare was 3.75 Rupees. The needed time to reach Matara was 1 hour.

*9 Dondara is about 5 km from Matara in the coastal zone of the Matara district. The bus fare was 1 Rupees. The time needed to reach Matara was about 20 minutes.

As in the above table, the consumers buy their goods from the Polas which lie in close proximity to their living place (Map 42). Forty-six percent (46%) of all the respondents walk to the Pola while 38% travel by bus and 17% go by cycles. The time needed to go to Pola was only 0-30 minutes for 59.38% of the respondents, followed by

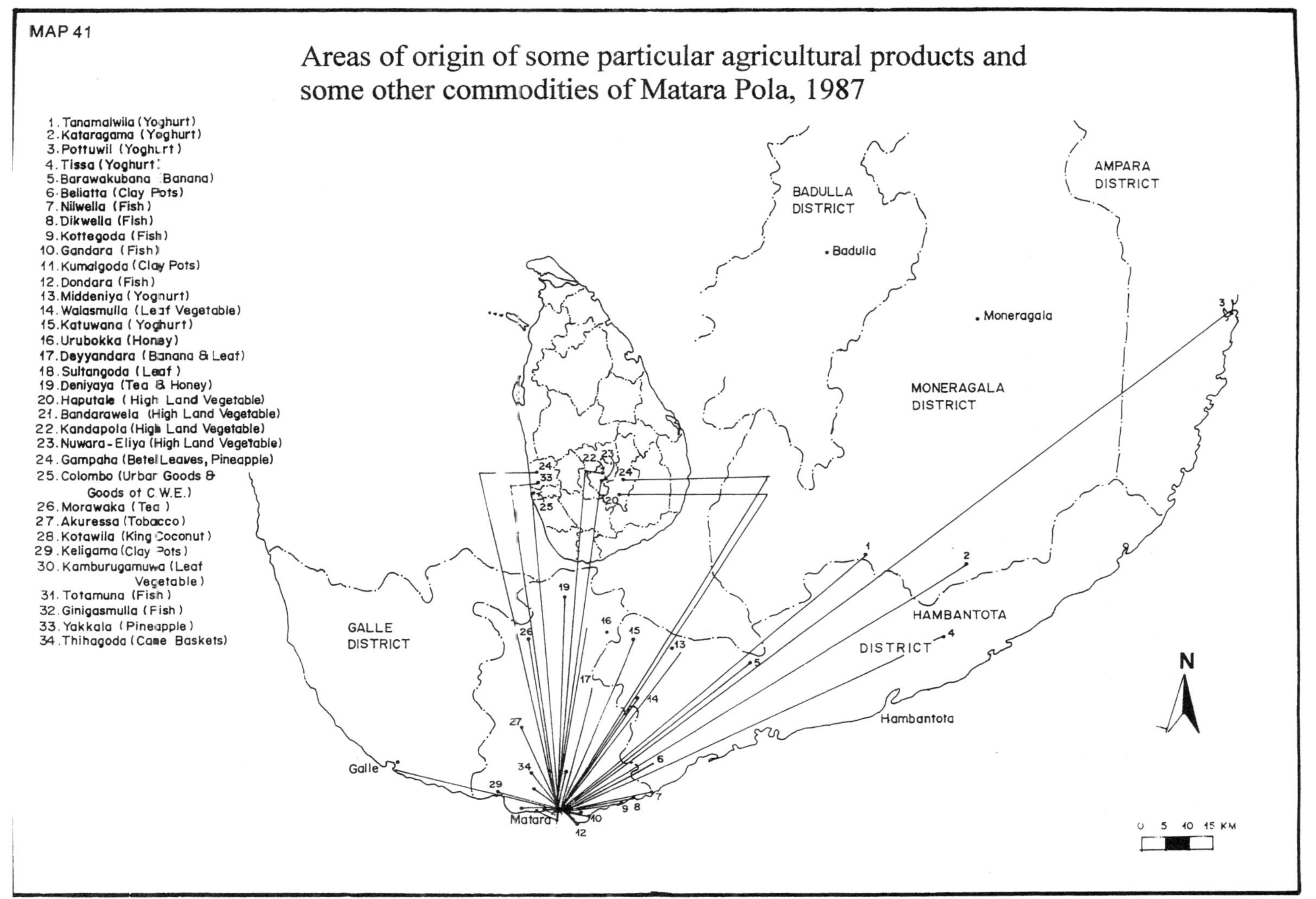
MAP 41
Areas of origin of some particular agricultural products and some other commodities of Matara Pola, 1987
1. Tanamalwila (Yoghurt)
2. Kataragama (Yoghurt)
3. Pottuwil (Yoghurt)
4. Tissa (Yoghurt)
5. Barawakubana (Banana)
6. Beliatta (Clay Pots)
7. Nilwella (Fish)
8. Dikwella (Fish)
9. Kottegoda (Fish)
10. Gandara (Fish)
11. Kumalgoda (Clay Pots)
12. Dondara (Fish)
13. Middeniya (Yoghurt)
14. Walasmulla (Leaf Vegetable)
15. Katuwana (Yoghurt)
16. Urubokka (Honey)
17. Deyyandara (Banana & Leaf)
18. Sultangoda (Leaf)
19. Deniyaya (Tea & Honey)
20. Haputale (High Land Vegetable)
21. Bandarawela (High Land Vegetable)
22. Kandapola (High Land Vegetable)
23. Nuwara-Eliya (High Land Vegetable)
24. Gampaha (Betel Leaves, Pineapple)
25. Colombo (Urban Goods & Goods of C.W.E.)
26. Morawaka (Tea)
27. Akuressa (Tobacco)
28. Kotawila (King Coconut)
29. Keligama (Clay Pots)
30. Kamburugamuwa (Leaf Vegetable)
31. Totamuna (Fish)
32. Ginigasmulla (Fish)
33. Yakkala (Pineapple)
34. Thihagoda (Cane Baskets)
BADULLA DISTRICT
Badulla
AMPARA DISTRICT
Moneragala
MONERAGALA DISTRICT
HAMBANTOTA DISTRICT
Hambantota
GALLE DISTRICT
Galle
Matara
N
0 5 10 15 KM

30 minutes to 1 hour for 33%. The respondents who came from a longer distance which took more than one hour amounted to 7.7% of the total.

According to the above table, only 8.2% of all the respondents, who live in areas other than Matara Urban Council area, came to the Matara Pola. A close examination also reveals that 86% of these respondents live in close proximity to the Matara town. They came from the Dondara area which lies only 5 km from Matara.

The reason why they come to Matara Pola instead of getting their commodities from Dondara weekly market rests on the following facts:

A) Close proximity. Dondara lies only 3 miles (5 km) from Matara and the bus fare from Dondara to Matara is only 1.50 Rupees. The time needed to reach Matara from Dondara by bus is only 30 minutes.

B) Matara has a larger selection of short-term, mid-term and long-term goods than Dondara. The place of residence of the other few respondents who mentioned Matara as a place of market for the short-term related goods (Akuresa 2, Kamburupitiya 5 and Dikwella 3) is 19 km to 24 km from Matara. The bus fares are between 3 to 5 Rupees while the time is over an hour.

The reasons why they came to Matara Pola from a long distance to buy short-term related goods instead of going to the other Pola or shop centres in their living areas are probably the following :

A)Caste prejudices are still present, particularly in rural areas and are capable of creating service centres in contravention of all rational considerations. There was a case where a new fair was opened within a stone's throw of an existing one merely because of caste rivalry.[1]

B) The high concentration of a larger selection of consumer goods in Matara than at any other centre of the Matara district. Through conversations with some residents of Hungama, which lies 96 km from Matara in the Hambantota district and Morawaka, which lies 51 km from Matara in the Matara district, it was revealed that some consumers tend to go to Matara to buy short-term related goods on special occasions such as marriages,funerals and other ceremonies because they can buy large quantities and different types of desired goods in one place,instead of going to several places. It was also revealed that the quality of the goods and the prices of items such as dahl, onions, salt-fish, dry fish and potatoes, sugar and canned foods were much better and lower priced in Matara than in other centres.[2] It seems it is much cheaper to go to Matara to buy these goods than to go to several places which costs more money and time.

---

1 Gunawardana, K.A.: service centres in the Southern Ceylon, unpublished Ph.D. dissertation, 1964, University of Cambridge.

2 These conversations were conducted in 1990, January, with some relatives of the author who live in Morawaka and Hungama.

Desire Lines for Periodic Markets (Pola) - Matara District

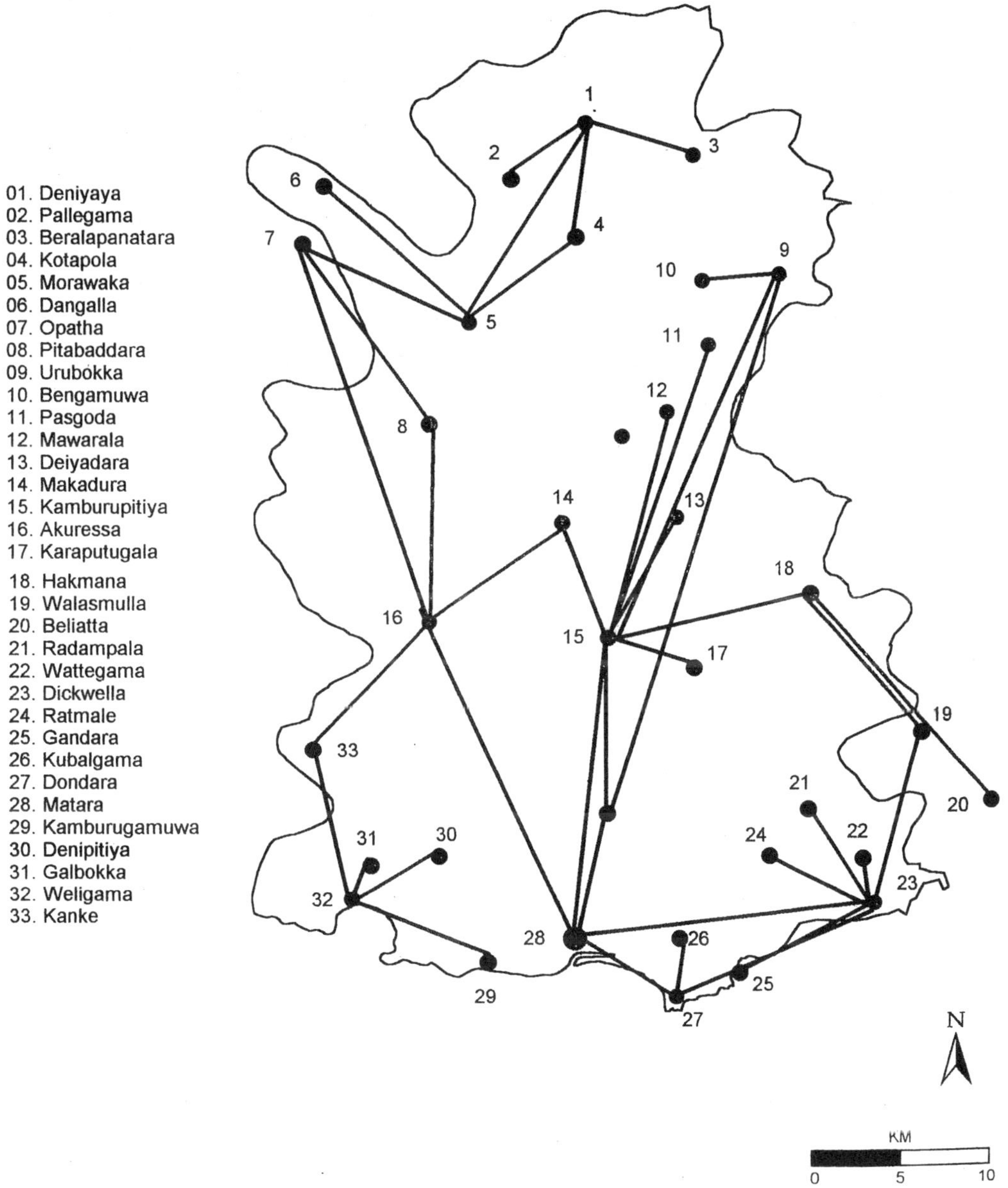

01. Deniyaya
02. Pallegama
03. Beralapanatara
04. Kotapola
05. Morawaka
06. Dangalla
07. Opatha
08. Pitabaddara
09. Urubokka
10. Bengamuwa
11. Pasgoda
12. Mawarala
13. Deiyadara
14. Makadura
15. Kamburupitiya
16. Akuressa
17. Karaputugala
18. Hakmana
19. Walasmulla
20. Beliatta
21. Radampala
22. Wattegama
23. Dickwella
24. Ratmale
25. Gandara
26. Kubalgama
27. Dondara
28. Matara
29. Kamburugamuwa
30. Denipitiya
31. Galbokka
32. Weligama
33. Kanke

N

KM
0 5 10

The above discussed facts have proven that the service area of the Matara Pola is much smaller than the service areas of the other services of the town. The "Umland" area of the Matara Pola lies within the 6.4 km radius.

According to the questionnaire survey almost all the respondents bought their short-term and mid-term consumer goods, in addition to the Pola, either from the small shop centres such as Beralapanatara, Waralla, Pasgoda, Kotapola, Mulatiyana, Pitabaddara, Yatiyana and Thelijjawila which lie close to their residential areas or from the larger commercial centres such as Deniyaya, Urubokka, Morawaka, Akuressa, Kamburupitiya, Hakmana and Weligama. In contrast to the short and mid-term goods, the long-term consumer goods of Matara town are more attractive to people who live in far away areas (Table 73 & Map 43). The most important goods in this regard are motor spare parts (73% of the total respondents) followed by vehicles, motorcycles and cycles, agricultural equipment, jewellery, electrical goods, construction goods and furniture, with 69%, 56%, 44%, 40%, 27%, and 16%, respectively. This is because of the following factors:

A) In some centres goods such as vehicles, agricultural equipment and electrical goods are not available at all.

B) The quality and prices of these goods in the Matara town is much better and lower than in the other centres.

C) There is a larger selection in Matara than other centres.

Table 73
Catchment area of the Long-term consumer goods of Matara, 1987.

Residence area of Respon-dants*1	G O O D S					
	Furniture		Electrical		Construction	
	Respon-dants (Total)	People who would come to Matara to buy Furniture	Respon-dants	People who would come to Matara to buy E.T.G.	Respon-dants	People who would come to Matara to buy C.G.
Urubokka	100	4	42	23	82	20
Deniyaya	100	4	64	4	95	8
Morawaka	100	3	59	18	83	6
Akuressa	100	2	75	14	80	6
Hakmana	100	12	44	21	85	22
Kamburu-pitiya	100	11	73	17	81	22
Weligama	42	3	39	5	42	9
Dikwella	100	11	62	27	93	24
Dondara	100	86	100	93	100	84
Total	842	136	558	222	741	201
%	100	16	100	40	100	27
	Jewellery		Vehicles		Motor Spare Parts	
1.	75	35	40	24	52	44
2.	91	11	81	50	68	50
3.	82	25	54	15	48	10
4.	77	24	40	36	40	28
5.	80	51	47	28	42	25
6.	81	40	72	51	72	65
7.	42	3	24	10	24	6
8.	95	33	47	38	45	35
9.	100	98	96	92	96	92
Total	723	320	501	344	487	355
%	100	44	100	69	100	73

(contd. in the following page)

Agricultural Equipment

1.	52	46
2.	68	12
3.	50	13
4.	12	7
5.	43	8
6.	40	23
7.	15	8
8.	53	34
9.	100	93
Total	433	244
%	100	56

Source: Questionnaire Survey, 1987.

Remarks:*1 The respondents are the number of students who answered to these particular questions.

6.2.5.2.B) <u>Matara Town as Collector and Redistributor of Local Agricultural Products</u>.

In this regard the trade activities pertaining to cinnamon and rubber are taken into consideration as these are the most important trade activities of the town.

There are some wholesale establishments in the town which collect cinnamon and rubber from local areas and resell them to the traders of Colombo for distribution and export. Four of these major establishments are located along the Hakmana Road, which is developing fast.

These agricultural products are grown in the central zone of the district. The most important areas are Nawimana, Makadura, Hakmana, Akuressa, Yatiyana. The middle man or collector- intervention in this trade is very low. The producers themselves bring their products to Matara by tractors and bullock carts. The cinnamon harvest is brought to these establishments twice a year while the rubber harvest is brought throughout the year.

In addition, there are eight shops in Matara town located in Kotuwegoda along the new Tangalla Road, which collect dry grains such as mung (green grains), kurakkan, cow-pea, tala and peanuts from local areas and resell most grains (90%) to the town's population and to other inhabitants of the district. Their trade activities are involved in retail as well as wholesale. Grains are brought to the shops by collectors as well as the shop owners.

Some areas where these grains are collected are given below:

Pepper: Akuressa, Hakmana, both lying in the central zone of the Matara district, and Middeniya in the Hambantota district

Mung: from Middeniya, Walasmulla of Hambantota district, Hakmana from the Matara district, Wellawaya and Embiliyapitiya from the Monaragala district.

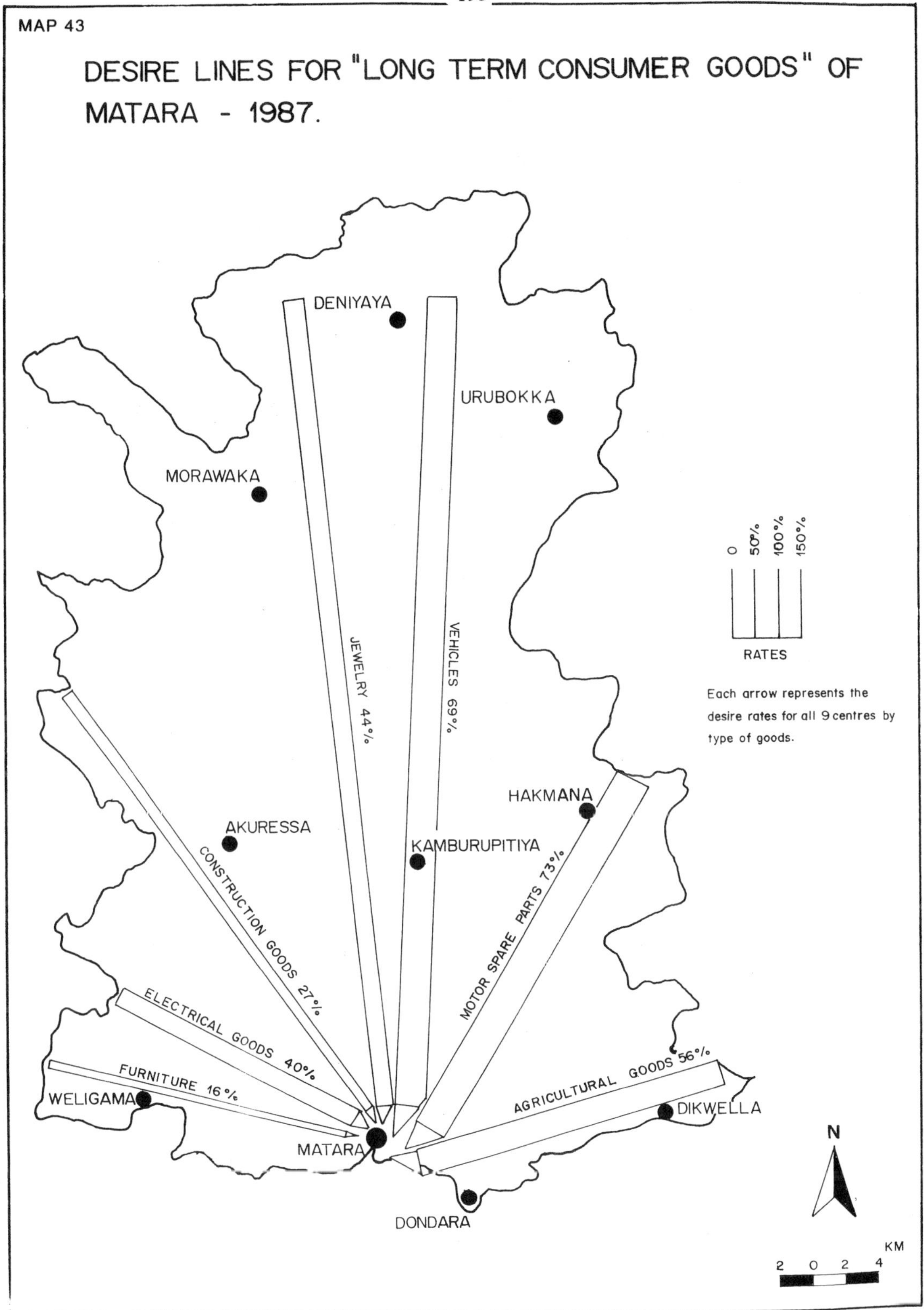
MAP 43
DESIRE LINES FOR "LONG TERM CONSUMER GOODS" OF MATARA - 1987.
DENIYAYA
URUBOKKA
MORAWAKA
AKURESSA
KAMBURUPITIYA
HAKMANA
WELIGAMA
MATARA
DIKWELLA
DONDARA
JEWELRY 44%
VEHICLES 69%
CONSTRUCTION GOODS 27%
MOTOR SPARE PARTS 73%
ELECTRICAL GOODS 40%
FURNITURE 16%
AGRICULTURAL GOODS 56%
0
50%
100%
150%
RATES
Each arrow represents the desire rates for all 9 centres by type of goods.
N
KM
2 0 2 4

Thala: Embiliyapitiya and Wellawaya from the Monaragala district.

Cow-peas and peanuts: Wellawaya, Embiliyapitiya and Buttala from the Monaragala district.

6.2.5.3.C) Matara as a Reloading Point for the Estate Sector Imports and Exports.

With the introduction of the plantation economy of tea, rubber in the northern zone of the Matara district during the British era, a planned transport network had come into existence. It linked Matara to the northern zone of the district as well as to the island's capital, Colombo. Since then, Matara became the reloading point for the imports and the exports of the plantation sector. The agricultural imports such as fertiliser, insecticide, agricultural equipment and food items which are consumed by the estate workers were brought from Colombo to Matara and distributed to the estates. The processed tea and rubber were brought to Matara from the northern and central zone of the district and sent to Colombo for exportation. The main transportation medium during this period was the railway.

However, as discussed earlier in Chapter 6.2.1, with the development of the other transport media, the railway lost its predominant role in the transportation of goods. Presently, the consumer goods and the imports of the plantation sector are bought by the plantation owners from the centres which are located close to the plantations and where reasonable prices are offered.

The processed tea and rubber are no longer brought to Matara for reloading but are sent to Colombo by lorries via Akuressa, Imaduwa and Galle without even touching Matara.[3]

6.2.5.4.D) Matara as a Centre for Consumption of Agricultural Raw Materials

In this regard, three of the most important agro-based industries in town, Harischandra Mills and Company, Odiris Silva and Company and Timber Corporation were studied.

D_1)Harischandra Mills

Harischandra Mills is the major industrial employer in town which offers 420 job opportunities to the town surrounding area's population (Chapter 3). Almost all products in this establishment are based on the agricultural raw materials.

---

3 This information is based on conversations with an ex-superintendent of Deniyaya Tea Estate, the largest tea estate in the Matara district, and the chief accountant at the Tea Smallholding Authority, Matara, 1987.

According to the annual audit report of 1987, this establishment used 76 million Rupees worth of raw materials (imports) for the production of consumer goods during the year 1989.

An examination of the areas where these inputs came from has revealed that 15% of the total expenditure was spent to buy raw materials from Colombo, the capital of Sri Lanka, which lies 100 miles (160 km) from Matara while 60% of the total expenditure was spent to buy inputs from an area which lies within a radius of 25 miles (40 km). The rest, 15%, of the total expenditure was spent on raw materials which came from beyond the 25 mile (40 km) radius.

These inputs are brought by lorries from the far-lying areas while the inputs from the close lying areas are transported by tractors and bullock-carts.

Soap is one of the major products in this establishment. The coconut, which is the most important raw material for this production, is brought from the coastal zone of the district. The other inputs (grains) such as mung, kurakkan, tala and rice, which are used to produce different types of food items, are brought from the central zone of the Matara district as well as from the Chena cultivation (shifting cultivation) areas of the adjoining Hambantota and Monaragala districts. The production of citronella oil in this establishment is highly dependent on the citronella harvest in the central zone of the district and Hambantota district. Tea is brought to this industry from Deniyaya Kotapola and Morawaka, which are located in the northern zone of the district.

Although the major catchment area of the inputs in this industrial establishment are confined to an area which lies within a radius of 25 miles (40 km), the whole catchment area extends to Colombo, Hambantota and Monaragala districts. Seventy percent (70%) of the products in this establishment are sent to Colombo and Kurunegala districts.

D_2)Odiris Silva Mills and Company

The Odiris Silva Mills and Company, which is the second largest industrial establishment of Matara town, produces only coconut oil. The catchment area of the inputs lies in the coastal zone of the Matara, Galle and Hambantota districts. This area lies within a radius of 25 miles (40 km). The coconut oil which is produced in this establishment is sold island-wide.

D_3)State Timber Corporation

The State Timber Corporation is one of the major timber suppliers to the state institutions. The major buyers of these products are railway department for sleepers for the railway line, postal department for transmissions posts and Electricity Board for electrical posts. In addition to government corporations, the State Timber Corporation of Matara, also supplies timber to private institutions.

The Timber Corporation receives its timber predominantly from forests and, to a lesser extent, from home gardens. According to the Progress Central Report of 1986, the

State Timber Corporation of Matara acquired 8.8 million decametres of timber for the year 1986. The name of the forests, their locations and the quantities of timber are presented in the following Table and in Map 44.

Table 74
Production of Timber for the year 1986,
State Timber Corporation, Matara.

Name of the Forest	Location & District	Quantity (in Decimeter)
Dellama	Morawaka/Matara	1522930
Wellama	Akuressa/Matara	1181455
Beraliya	Akuressa/Matara	3731187
Diyadawa	Kotapola/Matara	710286
Horagalaparagala	--------/Matara	604466
Mulatiyana	Mulatiyana/Matara	440068
Elakanda	--------/Galle	88255
Kotawila	--------/Galle	19600
Polgahakanda	--------/Galle	43958
Gonadeniya	--------/Hambantota	60775
Maasmulla	Kamburupitiya/Matara	134183
Panilkanda	Urubokka/Matara	117926
Homadola	--------/Galle	158473
Total		8813562

Source: Progressive Report, Stc/Mic/Ms/9/86, State Timber Corporation 1986, Matara.

According to the above table, 96% of the total timber production was obtained from forests which are located in the Matara district, while only 3% and 1 %, respectively, were obtained from the adjoining districts, Galle and Hambantota. A close examination of these figures also reveals that a high percentage (62%) of this timber is not acquired from the northern zone of the Matara district where large forest areas are found, but from the central zone where forest are mostly exploited for cultivation. This is due to the fact that large areas of natural virgin forests such as Singha Raja Forest and Mulatiyana Forest in Kotapola, Panilkanda Forest and Rammale Kanda Forest in Urubokka in this zone are under preservation.[4]

6.2.5.5.E) Matara as the Major Centre of Food Distribution to the District's Population, as well as to the Population of the Adjoining Districts.

In this regard, the catchment areas of the most important food stuff distributors on the island, namely Co-operative Wholesale Establishment (C.W.E.) and Multipurpose Co-operative Society, are taken into consideration and investigated.

---

[4] Statistical Handbook, Matara, 1983.
Integrated Rural Development Project, Matara Dictrict, 1981.

MAP 44

PRODUCTION AREAS OF TIMBER - TIMBER CORPORATION MATARA, 1986

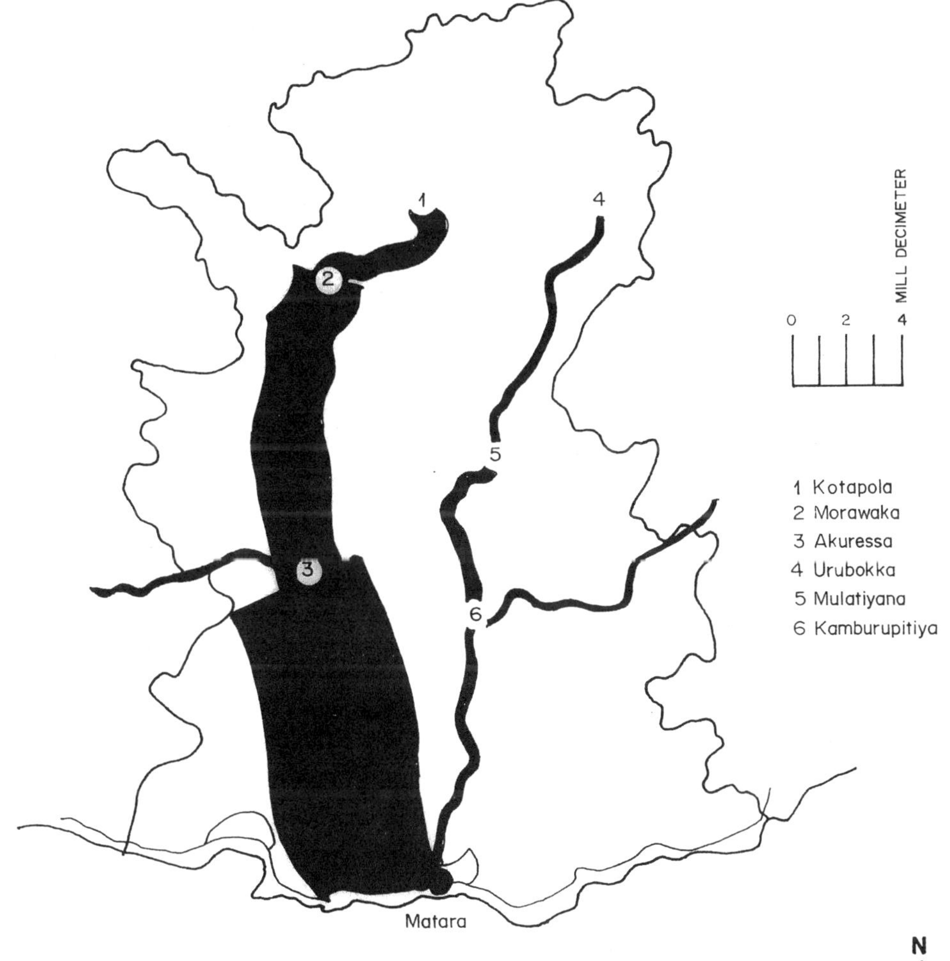

E_1)Co-operative Wholesale Establishment (C.W.E.)

The C.W.E., Matara, is one of the most important distributors of the essential consumer goods in this region. With a turnover of 11.5 million Rupees in 1987, Matara C.W.E. became the second largest distributor of food items among the other C.W.E. outlets on the island (Table 75 & Map 45).

Table 75
Total Turnover of the Co-operative Establishments of Sri Lanka, 1987.

Location of C.W.E. Stores	Turnover (in Rupees)
Matale	4105222
Anuradhapura	5121632
Polonnaruwa	4068429
Ratnapura	5215588
Baticaloa	1266632
Puttalam	2147566
Kandy	6168968
Monaragala	2403817
Chilaw	719770
Embilipitiya	1603436
Matara	11581326
Nawalapitiya	1364265
Kurunegala	8333463
Polgahawela	657329
Amparai	5115688
Colombo(at Maclam & 4th Cross road)	103168324
Bandarawela	2258364
Badulla	3472668
Galle	5982749
Total	179904896

Source: C.W.E. Office, Colombo, 1987.

A comparison of the C.W.E.'s turnover and the district`s population of Matara, turnover being 11.5 million Rupees and the district's population is 643,786 with the adjoining districts, Galle turnover being 5.9 million Rupees and the population is 814,531, Hambantota where there is no C.W.E. and the population is 424,344 and Ratnapura turn over being 5.2 million Rupees and the population is 797,087 shows that, although the Matara district has a smaller population than Galle and Ratnapura, it has the highest turnover compared with the other centres. The main reason is that the Matara C.W.E. has to distribute consumer goods not only to its district but also to the entire Hambantota district. In addition, it was revealed through an interview with the General Manager at the C.W.E. head office in Colombo in 1987 that Matara C.W.E. has better equipped storage facilities than the C.W.E. at Monaragala or Ratnapura. Because of this Matara C.W.E. has to supply some of the consumer goods to Monaragala and Ratnapura districts.

The above discussed facts have definitely proved that the service area of the Matara C.W.E. is not merely confined to the town's boundaries but extends beyond the district's boundaries.

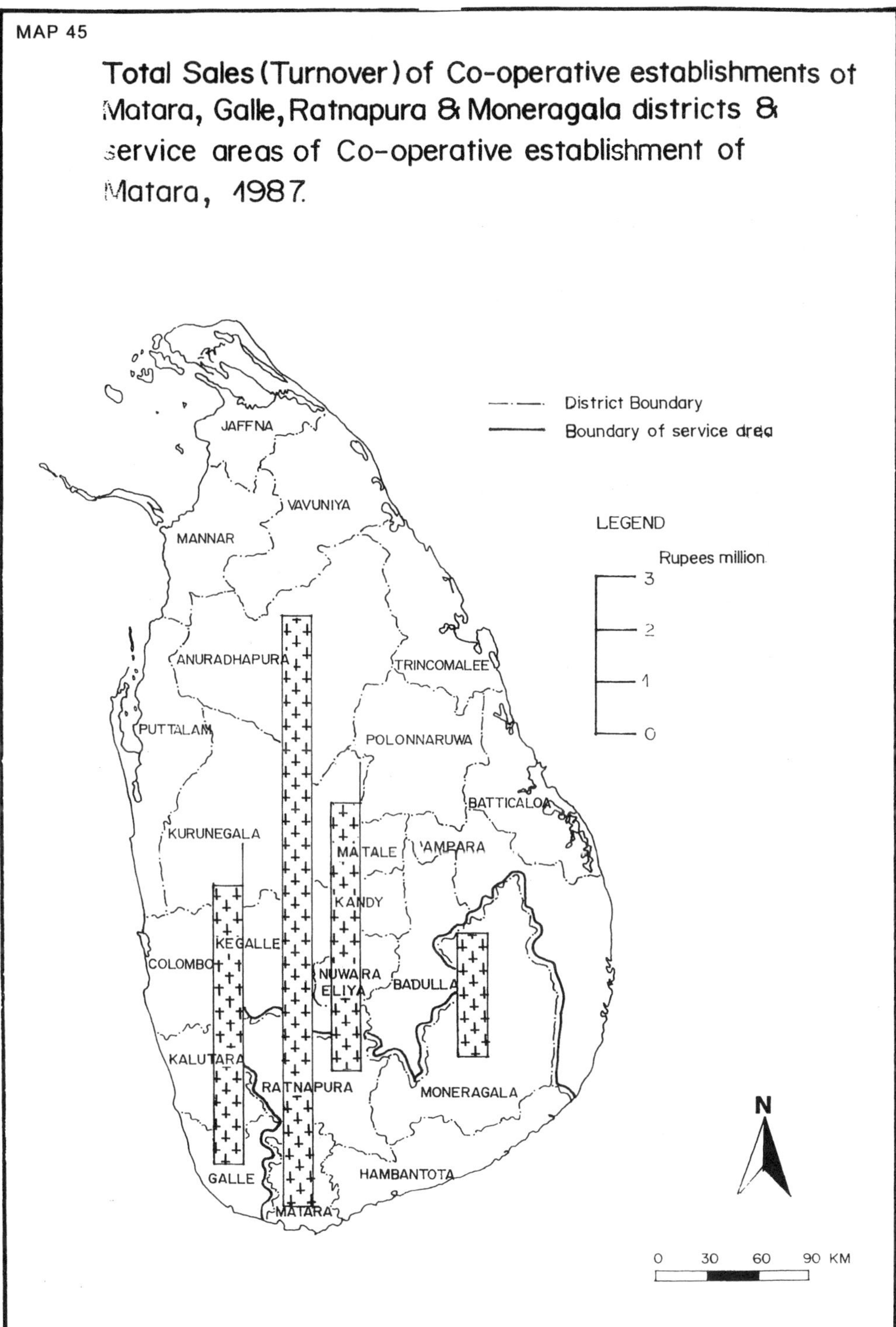
MAP 45
Total Sales (Turnover) of Co-operative establishments of Matara, Galle, Ratnapura & Moneragala districts & service areas of Co-operative establishment of Matara, 1987.
District Boundary
Boundary of service area
LEGEND
Rupees million
3
2
1
0
JAFFNA
VAVUNIYA
MANNAR
ANURADHAPURA
TRINCOMALEE
PUTTALAM
POLONNARUWA
BATTICALOA
KURUNEGALA
MATALE
AMPARA
KANDY
KEGALLE
COLOMBO
NUWARA ELIYA
BADULLA
KALUTARA
RATNAPURA
MONERAGALA
GALLE
HAMBANTOTA
MATARA
N
0 30 60 90 KM

E_2)Multi-Purpose Co-operative Society (M.P.C.S.)

Besides offering a retail service to the consumers and acting as a channel for the food stamp scheme, the Co-operative Society branches play an important role in the supply of agricultural inputs, notably fertilisers, agro-chemicals and paddy seeds. They purchase paddy from the farmers and finally resell it through their outlets. In spite of the diversification of their commercial activities due to changing market conditions, the M.P.C.S. still heavily rely upon the distribution of basic consumer items such as rice, flour and sugar under the Food Stamps Scheme (FSS).

The rationing scheme in these establishments necessitates registration with an authorised dealer and this has the tendency to create market areas for these commodities roughly corresponding to the administrative units.

The market areas of a Co-operative are determined when the Co-operative is first formed. This would indicate that, in this case, the market principle is not operative in the spontaneous manner indicated by Christaller. It was found, however, that people seek registration with the Co-operative store of an adjoining village because it happened to be located nearer, or there were cases where people did not change their dealer even when they changed their residence and were much nearer to another dealer in terms of distance. This inertia may be due either to the tediousness of the process which one has to go through in order to change one's registration for rationed commodities or to mere caste prejudices. The service area of the Matara Multi-Purpose Co-operative Society is smaller than the other services of the town. It does not exceed a radius of 5 miles (8 km)as depicted in the Map 46.

However, the range from where the food items are brought to these establishments extends to far lying areas. The collecting areas of rice are Hambantota and Monaragala districts. In addition, there were some collectors from the Hakmana area which lies in the central zone of the Matara district who bring grains such as mung (green grain), cowpea and peanuts from Monaragala and Hambantota district where the Chena cultivation is highly practised.

6.2.5.6 F) As the Sole Distributor of Petro Products in the District and one of the Major Building Material Suppliers to the Whole Region.

In this regard, the service areas of the Ceylon Petroleum Corporation and the Building Materials Corporation are taken into consideration and investigated.

F_1) Ceylon Petroleum Corporation

The Ceylon Petroleum Corporation, which is one of the most lucrative state corporations, still holds the monopoly on the importation and distribution of petro products on the whole island. There has been no change in this sector even today due to the non-existence of competition.

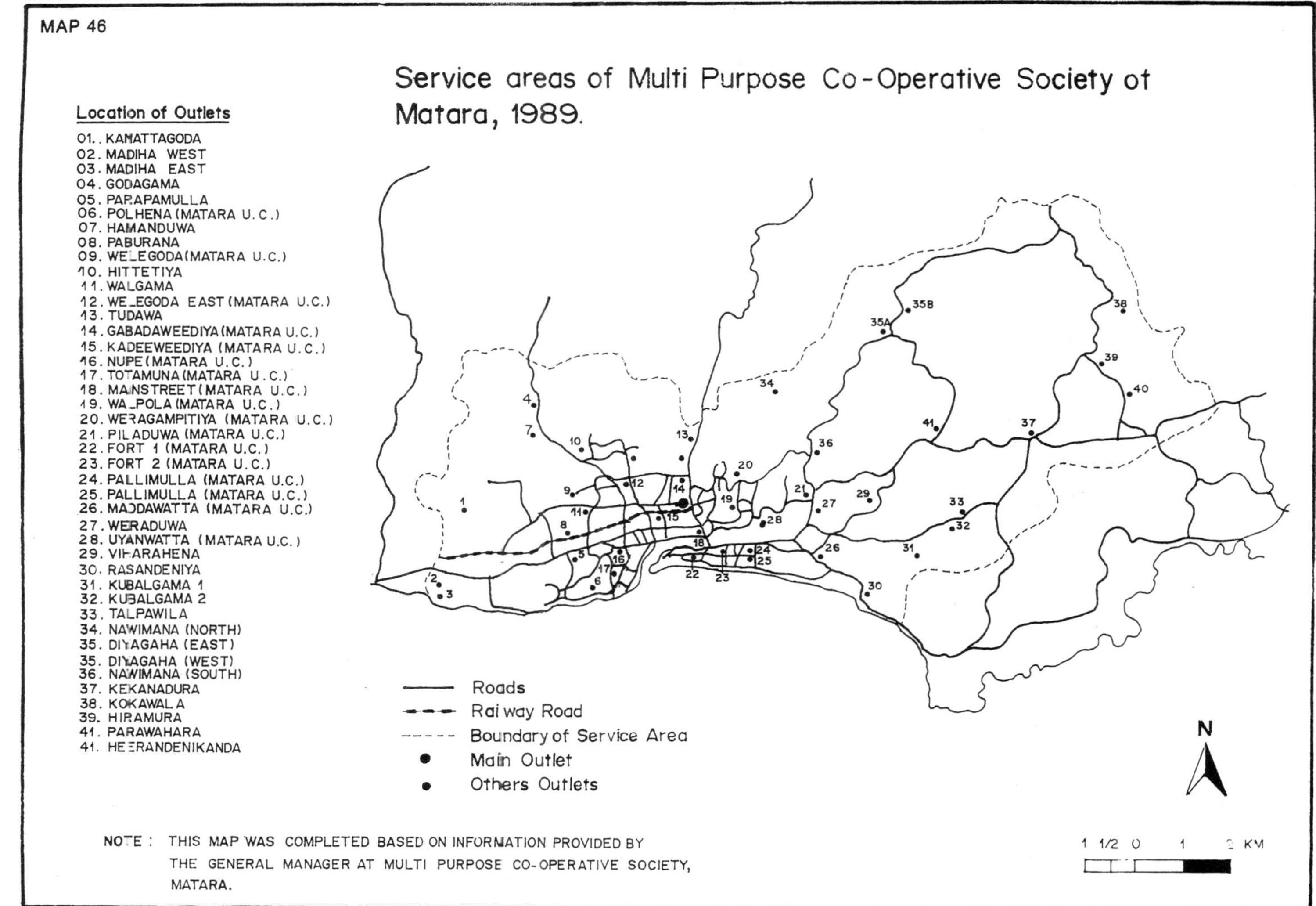
MAP 46
Service areas of Multi Purpose Co-Operative Society of Matara, 1989.
Location of Outlets
01.. KAMATTAGODA
02. MADIHA WEST
03. MADIHA EAST
04. GODAGAMA
05. PARAPAMULLA
06. POLHENA (MATARA U.C.)
07. HAMANDUWA
08. PABURANA
09. WELEGODA (MATARA U.C.)
10. HITTETIYA
11. WALGAMA
12. WELEGODA EAST (MATARA U.C.)
13. TUDAWA
14. GABADAWEEDIYA (MATARA U.C.)
15. KADEEWEEDIYA (MATARA U.C.)
16. NUPE (MATARA U.C.)
17. TOTAMUNA (MATARA U.C.)
18. MAINSTREET (MATARA U.C.)
19. WALPOLA (MATARA U.C.)
20. WERAGAMPITIYA (MATARA U.C.)
21. PILADUWA (MATARA U.C.)
22. FORT 1 (MATARA U.C.)
23. FORT 2 (MATARA U.C.)
24. PALLIMULLA (MATARA U.C.)
25. PALLIMULLA (MATARA U.C.)
26. MADDAWATTA (MATARA U.C.)
27. WERADUWA
28. UYANWATTA (MATARA U.C.)
29. VIHARAHENA
30. RASANDENIYA
31. KUBALGAMA 1
32. KUBALGAMA 2
33. TALPAWILA
34. NAWIMANA (NORTH)
35. DIYAGAHA (EAST)
35. DIYAGAHA (WEST)
36. NAWIMANA (SOUTH)
37. KEKANADURA
38. KOKAWALA
39. HIRAMURA
41. PARAWAHARA
41. HEERANDENIKANDA
Roads
Raiway Road
Boundary of Service Area
Main Outlet
Others Outlets
N
1 1/2 0 1 2 KM
NOTE : THIS MAP WAS COMPLETED BASED ON INFORMATION PROVIDED BY THE GENERAL MANAGER AT MULTI PURPOSE CO-OPERATIVE SOCIETY, MATARA.

The distribution areas of these products (gas, tar, kerosene oil) covers the whole Matara district, Hambantota district and some parts of the Galle district. These products are directly brought from Colombo by their own fleet of trucks and distributed through private outlets.

F_2) <u>Building Materials Corporation (B.M.C.)</u>

The Building Materials Corporation was the major importer and distributor of building materials until 1977. Since 1977 this corporation also had to compete with the private sector in retail trade. The total turnover of the state trading co-operations on the island decreased by 12% from 6,310 million Rupees in 1985 to 5,572 million Rupees.[5]

The Matara B.M.C. distributes its goods through the retail sales points which are located in Ambalantota (Hambantota district), Embilipitiya (Monaragala district) and Ratnapura (Ratnapura district).

According to the sales reports of the Matara B.M.C., the sales turnover for the year 1987 was 8.9 million Rupees (8,927,135 Rupees) of which 80% of the business was involved with the Matara district.[6]

This indicates, although the service areas of the Matara B.M.C. extend over the districts boundaries, the high intensity of its business is confined to the Matara district.

6.2.5.7.G) Matara as an Important Place of Refreshment and Lodging for Commercial Travellers, Businessmen, Tourists and Pilgrims as well as a Place for Honeymoons of Newly Married Couples of the Matara and Hambantota District.

In comparison to other urban and service centres of the Matara and the Hambantota districts, Matara has a larger selection of hotels and restaurants than any other centre. Matara Rest-house, which is of Dutch origin and managed by the Hotel Corporation, was one of the most famous rest-houses in this region from the Colonial period (Dutch and British) to the post Colonial period until the late 1970s. Its growth has been mainly achieved because of its favourable location on the beach and along the Colombo-Hambantota Highway.

The rest-house at Matara has been providing refreshment and night lodgings to commercial travellers, tourists and pilgrims who travel through Matara to religious centres such as Dondara in Matara district, Mulgirigala in Hambantota district, Kirinda in Hambantota district, Situlpahuwa in Hambantota district and Kataragama in Monaragala district. In addition, according to information from the manager, this rest-house was the most famous honeymoon centre for newly married couples in the Matara and Hambantota district until the late 1960s (Photo 40).

With the development of the tourist industry after 1966, several hotels and restaurants have sprung up in the other centres of the district which, in turn, led to the

5 Review of the Economy, 1988, p. 193.

6 Sales report, Matara B.M.C., 1987.

decline of business in the Matara Rest-house. However, an examination of the visitors' register of the Matara Rest-house, has revealed that it still plays an important role in the hotel industry services to a population who lives in areas other than the Matara Urban Council area.

According to the visitors' register there were 314 guests who spent nights in this rest-house in the month of December, 1987.[7] An examination of the areas where they came from revealed that 138 of all the guests (44%) came from 13 villages which are located in the Matara district, followed by Colombo district, Galle district and Hambantota district with 131 (42%), 20 (5%) and 12 (4%) respectively. A high percentage of the guests from the Matara and Hambantota districts were married couples who came to Matara to spend their honeymoon.[8] The rest of the guests were from the Badulla district (5 guests), Kandy district (2), Monaragala district (2), Kalutara district (2), Puttalam district (1) and Ratnapura district (1) (Map 47).

In addition, the Sport Club of Matara, which was one of the famous meeting places of the British in this region, planters in the northern region of the Matara district and government officials, lost its importance during the post-colonial period. Today this sport club is visited by a few government officials who live in the Matara Urban Council area.

6.2.5.8.H) Matara as a Place of Work and Employer of the Rural Surplus Labour.

In this regard, the monthly bus season tickets sold for the month of April, 1984 by the Ceylon Transport Board and the production process of the jewellery shops in the Matara town are taken into consideration and investigated.

As there was no detailed data available for the commuting area of the urban employees, the author was again compelled to look into the monthly season tickets which were sold to the employees who commuted daily to the Matara town. As the bus is the most popular mode of travel with 53% among the other transport media, an investigation into the monthly season tickets was justified to find out the catchment areas of the commuters. Almost all the employees hold season tickets as these are offered to them at a considerably lower price.

As discussed in Chapter 3, the employment generating capacity of the Matara town is very low and cannot absorb the rural surplus labour. It is not in a position to offer enough job opportunities to its workforce. According to the 1981 census of statistics, only 24% of the total workforce of the town is employed . In such a situation it is obvious that the number of commuting employees from other areas to urban areas is very low. Through an investigation, it was also revealed that only 10% of the total employees in the largest industrial establishment of Matara Harischandra Mills, came from areas other than the Matara Urban Council area. [9]

---

7 Visitors register, Matara rest-house, 1987.

8 This information is based on an interview with the rest-house manager.

9 This information is based on a conversation with the chief accountant and the personal officer at Harischandra Mills, Matara, 1987.

MAP 47

Service Areas of Matara Rest House and number of Tourists by District, 1987 November

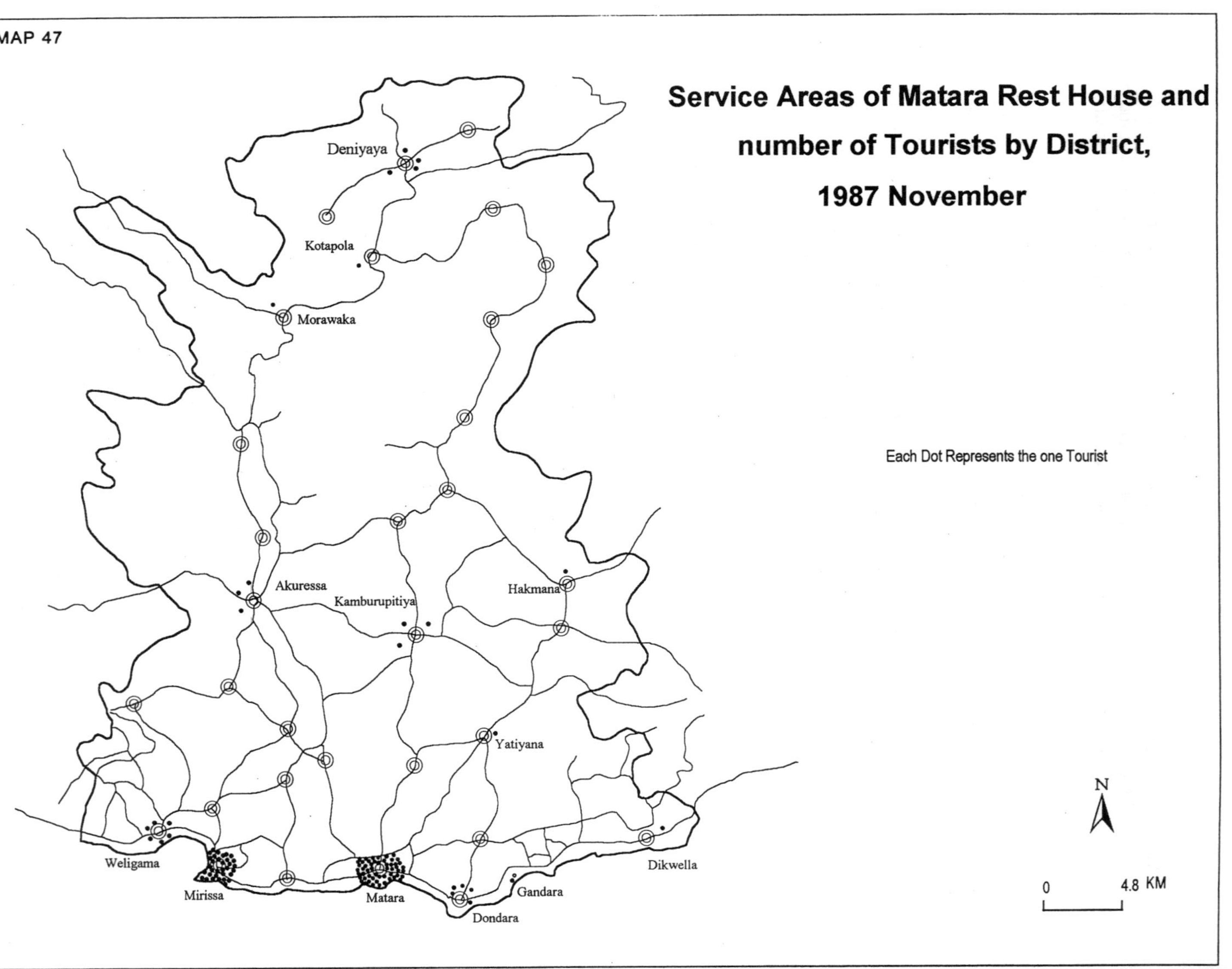

According to the monthly season tickets register of the Ceylon Transport Board (C.T.B.) Matara, 895 monthly season tickets were sold in the month of April 1984 to the employees who commute daily to Matara from other areas. An investigation into the areas where they came from revealed that the majority of these commuters (70%) came from areas which lie between 0 and 10 km away (Table 76).

Table 76
Commuters by distance (from residential areas to Matara), April 1984.

Distance (in Km & Miles)	No.of.sold tickets	%
00 - 05 Km (0 -3 miles)	50	28.00
05 -10 Km (3 -6 miles)	76	42.00
10 -15 Km (6 -9 miles)	20	11.00
15 -20 Km (9 - 13 miles)	22	12.00
20 -25 Km (13 -16 miles)	10	06.00
Over 25 Km (over 16 miles)	02	01.00
Total	180	100.00

Source: Monthly Season Ticket Register 1984, C.T.B. Depot, Matara. (A sample Survey of 20%).

A close examination of this area also reveals that the number of commuters who travel by bus to Matara from the areas which lie between 0 km and 5 km is lower (28%) than the number of commuters who travel by bus to Matara from the areas which lie between 5 km and 10 km. This is definitely due to the fact that the employees who live in the areas between 0 and 5 km walk to Matara or go by bicycle. After 10 kilometres, the number of employees who travel to Matara by bus decreases radically (see the above table).

H_1)Jewellery Trade

In 1984 there were 36 jewellery shops in the Matara town of which 19 (51.73%) were owned by Sinhalese and 17 (48.27%) were owned by Muslims. According to the information of the shop owners, these shops are visited not only by the residents of the Matara town but also by the residents of the whole Matara district, Hambantota district and Galle district. It was also revealed from the 1987 questionnaire survey that 44% of the total respondents would go to Matara to buy their jewellery (Table 73). The popularity of Matara as the best jewellery centre in the whole region rests on the following facts.

1) The quality and handicraft of the Matara products are much better than any other centre in the whole region.
2) The shop owners of Matara are more trustworthy than any other place in the region.

The most striking feature in this trade is not the service but the production procedures, which links Matara to its surrounding areas. According to information from a jewellery shop owner (The Southern Jewellery is located in the Mainstreet), only a few jewellery shop owners of the town have their workshop at the sales units. Almost 90% of this jewellery is produced by the skilled labourers in villages surrounding the town who belong to the Nawandan caste (jewellery makers).[10] Some production areas of jewellery are: Godauda (13 km) Belideniya (10 km), Kekandura (9 km), Talalla (9 km), Naotunna (11 km), and Prawahara (11 km). Almost all of these villages lie in the eastern part of the coastal zone .

6.2.6.I.) Matara as a Centre of Religious, Social, Recreational and Cultural Services.

In this regard, the religious places, movie theatres, public library and the newspaper and magazine circulation in town are taken into consideration and investigated.

I_1)Religious Functions

The location of religious places of worship in an area reflects the social composition and social aspirations of the community. The religious place is a kind of social service centre which dominates human behaviour by fostering social values. Matara has 27 Buddhist temples, three churches and four mosques which occupy 3% (24 ha) of the total land area of the town. The religious centres such as Peakwella Temple, Rajamahavihara Temple, St. Mary's Church and the Mosque of Kotuwegoda are historic monuments and were built in the colonial architectural styles of the Dutch and British. These centres have religious importance, attracting a considerable number of Buddhists, Muslims and Christians at different times of the year.

Therefore, in the context of the town's development, the leading social institutions and religious centres will take more responsibility in the future.

I_2)Social and Recreation Functions

I_{2-1})Movie Theatres

Prior to the introduction of television to Sri Lanka in the early 1980s, to visit a movie theatre was one of the most popular free time activities of the Sri Lankan general population, as there was limited access to other recreational activities. Television is considered to be more of an entertainment object than a mass medium in Sri Lanka.

The total number of TV's and radios registered in the Matara district in 1984 was 2,901 and 5,734, respectively[11]. The majority of these registered television sets and radios were confined to Matara town. The ratio of the televisions and radios to the district population was 1:222 and 1:112. These figures indicate the limitation of accessibility to the Sri Lankan general population of such a common service in developed countries. The service areas of the television sector are still mostly confined to the urban areas of the island.

---

10 Most of the Sinhalese jewellery traders and producers of the island belong to this caste. This is one of the lowest caste in the hierarchical order of the caste system in Sri Lanka.

11 Post Office, Matara, 1987.

In the Matara district there are six movie theatres, of which three are located in Matara town itself. The ratio of the districts population to a movie theatre in 1987 was 107,297:1 while the ratio of the town's population to a movie theatre was only 13,054:1.[12]

According to information from the theatre managers at S.K. Cinema and Broadway Cinema, a substantial number of the viewers of the morning shows (from 10:30 to 1:30) and the afternoon shows (from 2:30 to 5:30) are from the Umland and Hinterland areas of the Matara town which consists of the Matara and Hambantota districts.

The higher attraction of the movie theatres in Matara than the other theatres rest on the following facts:

A) The picture halls in the Matara town are well maintained and cleaned and therefore are nice to visit with the whole family.

B) Brand new movies are first shown only in the movie theatres in Matara town until the demand for these films is exhausted. Only then are these films sent to the Umland and Hinterland.[13]

I_3) School Activities

School functions such as graduation and sport meetings in Matara town are visited by the inhabitants of the district at different times a year. Two of the most important school feasts are the school sport meet and the cricket matches between the town's schools. The cricket match between the Rahula College and the St. Servets is one of the most exciting events of the year in the region. This cricket match is visited by cricket fans from all over the region.

I_4) Public Library

The literacy rate of 85.4% in Sri Lanka is among the highest in Asia.[14] In such a situation it is not an error to believe that Sri Lanka has a large reading population.

The library is the most important supplier of reading material to the Sri Lankan reading population. According to a sample survey conducted by the Marga Institute in 1972 it was revealed that 48% of the books read had been borrowed from libraries, while only 18% of the total number of books read had been directly purchased by the readers.[15] This result was mainly due to the limited purchasing power of the readers based on the low average income.

---

12 These calculations are based on 1981 Census.

13 Facts are based on the personal investigations.

14 Report on Consumer Finances and Socio-economic Survey 1980/82, Part 4, p. 58. (Central Bank of Ceylon).

15 The Sinhala Reading Public, Sri Lanka, Marga Research Studies, 1974,p. 55.

In a situation where the purchasing power of the reading public is severely limited, the establishment of a well distributed system of libraries becomes a major factor in expanding and developing the reading public.

The public library of Matara Urban Council is the largest library in the Matara district in comparison to the libraries at Weligama Urban Council, Akuressa and Dondara Town Councils. The available stock of books in 1987 is accounted for 19,032 which is constitued of Tamil, English, Sinhala novels and English, Sinhala literature books (Public Library ,Matara,1987).

The total number of members in this library for the year 1987 was 5,207 of which 347 were junior members and 4,860 were adult members.[16] Although there is no limitation for any person to use this library, the membership is confined to the urban council boundaries.

According to the visitor's register, there were 1,735 visitors in the month of November 1987. The average number of visitors per day was 58. Out of the total, the visitors who came from areas other than Matara Urban Council area were 350 (13%). These areas consisted of 47 villages which all were traced by the author on the topographic map of Matara district. According to this investigation the "Umland area" of the library service lies between 0 and 3.75 miles (6 km) from the Matara U.C. area with 68.6% of the total visitors, followed by the "Hinterland area" with 29.1% of the total visitors, which is located between 3.75 miles (6 km) and 9.3 miles (15 km). The "Einflussgebiet" of the town's library service with only 2.3% of the total visitors, is located beyond the 9.3 miles (15 km - Map 48).

I_5) The Newspaper Circulation

The newspaper is the most famous and easily accessible mass media to the Sri Lankan general population. The local newspapers are rarely available in Sri Lanka. The newspapers in Sri Lanka have a centralized marketing system. All the daily papers are printed in Colombo and distributed island-wide through agencies.

There were two newspaper agents in Matara town in 1990. According to their information, the distribution areas of the newspapers were confined to the town's boundaries as there are other newspaper agents throughout the Matara district.

The total number of newspapers sold per day through these two agents was 5,205. This indicates that 88% of the total households of the town (the total households in the town in 1981 was 5,939) buy newspapers every day.

Although the newspaper distribution areas of these two agencies are confined to the town's boundaries, they are the sole distributor of some monthly magazines such as Satara (Education), Kalpana (Imagination), and Rawaya (Sound) to outlying areas. One thousand copies of Satara are sent to Deniyaya, located in the extreme north of the Matara district and Tissa, in the Hambantota district, while 750 copies of Rawaya and

---

16 Membership register, public library, Matara, 1987

MAP 48

Service Areas of Public library - Matara, 1987

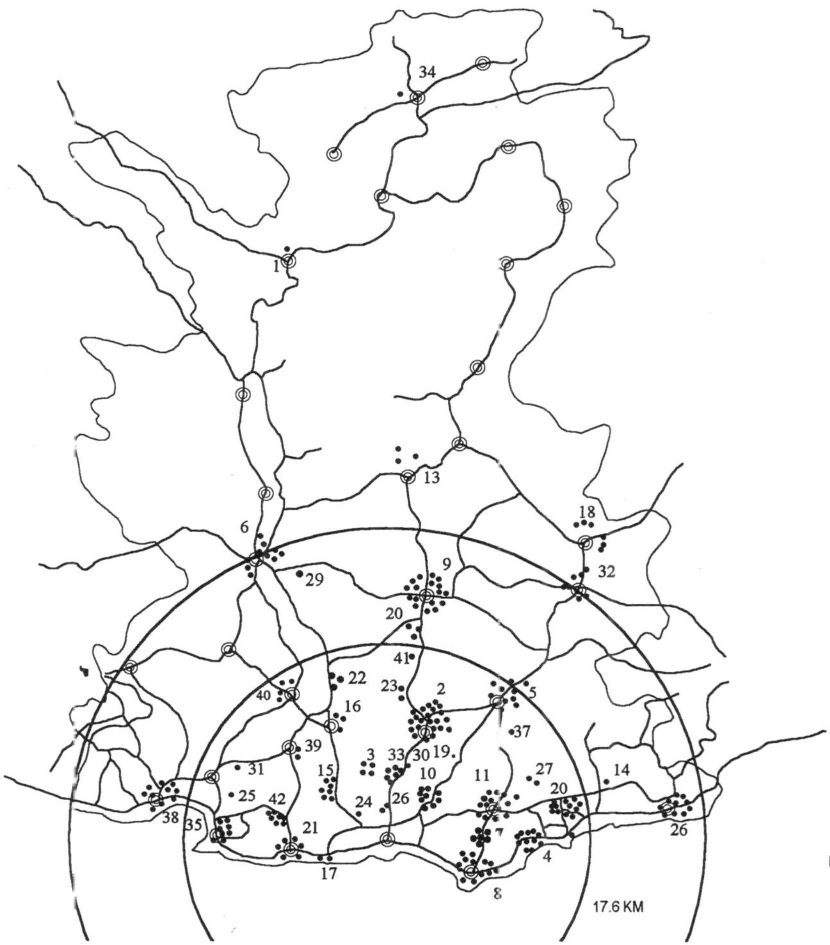

1. Morawaka
2. Thihagoda
3. Palatuwa
4. Gandara
5. Yatiyana
6. Akuressa
7. Kapugama
8. Dondara
9. Kamburupitiya
10. Naimana
11. Kekanadura
12. Kottegoda
13. Makadura
14. Ratmale
15. Godagama
16. Malimbada
17. Madiha
18. Hakmana
19. Diyag
20. Naotunna
21. Kaburugamuwa
22. Kitalagama
23. Witiyala
24. Hiththetiya
25. Polwatumodara
26. Tudawa
27. Parawahera
28. Akurugoda
29. Athuraliya
30. Bandattara
31. Warakaoitiya
32. Kirinda
33. Nadugala
34. Deniyaya
35. Mirissa
36. Dickwella
37. Aparakka
38. Weligama
39. Sultangoda
40. Telijjawila
41. Attudawa
42. Kotawila

Note :- Given numbers indicate the residential areas of visitors

17.6 KM

N

0 4.8 KM

Kalpana are sent to Weligama and Deniyaya in the Matara district, monthly through these two agencies of Matara.

6.3. The Hierarchical Order of the Important Service Centres of the Matara District.

After discussing the catchment areas of the town's central services and its relationship with the surrounding areas, an attempt is made to find out the hierarchical order of the most important service centres in the Matara district. The service centres which are taken into consideration are Matara, Weligama, Deniyaya, Akuressa, Dikwella, Kamburupitiya, Morawaka, Hakmana, Dondara and Urubokka (Map 49).

The other service centres in the district are much smaller in comparison and have limited central functions. The trade activities in these centres are mostly confined to the supply of short term related consumer goods. The service areas of these centres are much smaller than the centres mentioned above.

Since Christaller's introduction of the hierarchical order of the service centres in southern Germany in 1933 (Christaller, 1933), employing the telephone method, many attempts have been made by geographers employing different methods as well as modifying Christaller`s method. Christaller's method was found unsatisfactory and unemployable to other regions of the world due to different social and economic conditions[17] (Smailes, 1969, Manshard, 1961, Vorlaufer, 1971, Henkel, 1979, Misra, 1987, Ghapure and Pawr, 1987, Dicke, 1987).

In this treatise the hierarchical order of the important service centres in the district are identified by the available central services in them. Some central services which are employed by Smailes (Smailes, 1969) to find out the hierarchical order of British towns such as banks, high schools, movie theatres, hospitals, and the administration (government agents) are employed in this treatise, as the author believes that these are very suitable indicators for a country like Sri Lanka due to the following reasons:

A) Sri Lanka was under the British administration for 133 years (1815 - 1948). During this period the administrative system, trade pattern, and the urban planning were highly influenced by the British.

B) During this period Sinhalese took over some British habits and customs.

C) Even after independence there has been no marked change in these systems which had been moulded by the British and the Sinhalese are still adhering to some of the British habits and customs.

---

17 Neef has criticized the inapplicability of the telephone method to other regions of Germany in his paper in (Geogr. Mitt. 94, 1950, p. 6-17.)

In this treatise, first the central services are categorized into five groups. Assuming these five services have the same level of need and usage to the consumer, a weight of 10 points are given to each group as presented below:

Service Groups	Points
1) Administration	10
2) Commerce	10
3) Public Service	10
4) Social Service	10
5) Communication	10

Each of the major service groups consists of several single central services as follows:

1) <u>Administration</u>
   A) Local authority
   B) Central government authority
   C) Judicial service
   D) Protection

2) <u>Commerce</u>
   A) Bank
   B) Market
   C) C.W.E. (Ceylon Wholesale Establishment)
   D) M.P.C.C. (Multi-Purpose Co-operative Society)
   E) Tourism

3) <u>Communication</u>
   A) Post Office
   B) Bus service
   C) Railway

4) <u>Public Service</u>
   A) Health
   B) Education

5) <u>Social Service</u>
   A) Movie Theatre
   B) Library

The single services are again graded with a number between 1 and 5 and given 1 to 5 points defining the available level of services, as Fernando employed in his work, to identify the functional magnitude of the urban centres in southern Sri Lanka (Chart 2)[18].

Grade	Points
I	5
II	4
III	3
IV	2
V	1

18 Fernando, P.N., 1984

Chart 2
Grading of Services in the Service centres of Matara District.

Major Groups	Services	Grade.1	Grade.2
		Point 5	Point 4
1) Administration	1)Local authority	Municipal Council	Urban Council
	2)General Govt. administration	Govt.Agent ----------------	Asst.Govt. Agent
	3)Judical	supreme Courts	High Courts
	----------	Magistrate Courts District Courts	----------
	4)Protection	Superintendent of Police	Asst. Sup. of Police
2) Commerce	1)Bank	3 branches & over	2 branches
	2)Marketing	No. of Commercial Units over 1000 (Major Centre) --------------- --------------- ---------------	No. of Com-mercial units 500-1000 (Medium Centre)
	3)C.W.E.	Whole Sale Centre ---------------	Retail-outlets
	4)M.P.C.C.	Whole Sale Centre ----------------	Retail-outlets
	5)Tourism	Tourist Hotel	Local Hotel
3) Communication	1)Post Office	Head Post Office ---------------	Sup-Post Office
	2)Transport	Major Bus Depot ---------------	Terminal-Points
	3)Railway	Main Station ---------------	Minor - Station
4) Public Service	1)Health	Base Hospital ---------------	District-Hospital
	2)Education	University ---------------	Secondary-School
5) Social Service	1)Movie Theatre	More than one	One
	2)Library	Stock of books- More than 18000	Under 18000

(contd. in the following page)

Major Groups	Services ------	Grade 3 Points 3	Grade 4 Points 2	Grade 5 Points 1
1	1	Town Council	Village Council	-----------
--	2	Circuit Officer (Village Head)	Gramasewaka	-----------
--	3	Periodic Courts	--------------	-----------
--	4	Sub-Inspector	--------------	-----------
2	1	1 branch	2 Rural banks	1 Rural bank
--	2	100-500 (Minor Centre)	50-100 (Hamlet Centre)	less than 50 (HamletCentre)
--	3	------------	-------------	-----------
--	4	Retail outlets ------------	Retail outlets -------------	Retailoutlets -------------
	5	-------------	-------------	-----------
3	1	Post Boxes	Post Boxes	----------
	2	Bus Stops for express buses	Bus stops for regular buses	Bus stops for regular buses
	3	-------------	---------------	---------
4	1	Rural hospital	Peripheral Hospital	Central Dispensary
	2	Junior Schools	Primary School	----------
5				
	1	None	-----------	----------
	2	None	---------	---------

A final score is given to each service centre for the services available by multiplying the scores of the grade by the weight attributed to the particular service. The total score indicates the functional magnitude and hierarchical order of the important service centres of the Matara district (Chart 3).

According to the final score a hierarchy of service centres of five groups can be identified as given below:

Chart 3
Functional magnitude and hierarchical order
of the service centres of Matara district.

M A J O R G R O U P S of
S E R V I C E S & the P O I N T S

Service Centre - Population										
Groups*1		1				2				
Points		10	10	10	10	10	10	10	10	10
Services*2		1	2	3	4	1	2	3	4	5
Matara	39,162	40	50	50	40	50	50	50	50	50
Weligama	17,872	40	40	--	30	40	30	40	40	50
Akuressa	6,885	30	40	--	30	40	30	40	40	40
Dondara	7,628	30	40	--	--	40	20	40	--	--
Deniyaya	------	20	40	30	30	40	40	40	40	40
Kamburupitiya	------	20	40	--	30	40	20	40	40	--
Dikwella	------	20	40	--	30	30	20	40	40	--
Morawaka	------	20	40	50	30	30	20	--	--	--
Urubokka	------	20	40	--	--	30	20	--	--	--
Hakmana	------	20	40	--	30	40	20	--	40	--

Groups		3		4		5		Total
Services	1	2	3	1	2	1	2	Weight
Centre								
1.	50	50	50	50	50	50	50	780
2.	50	40	40	40	40	40	40	600
3.	50	40	--	20	40	--	40	480
4.	50	20	--	--	30	--	40	310
5.	50	40	--	40	40	--	40	530
6.	50	40	--	20	40	--	--	380
7.	50	40	--	20	40	--	40	410
8.	50	30	--	20	40	--	--	330
9.	50	30	--	30	40	--	--	240
10.	50	30	--	--	40	--	--	310

Source: Statistical Book, Matara district 1983
Population Plan, Matara district 1985
Road map of Sri Lanka 1987
Development Plan of Hakmana, Dondara, and Kamburupitiya (Hakmana, Dondara and Kamburupitiya Sanwardana Pragathiya), 1977, 1983, 1986.

Remarks: * 1 & 2: refer chart 2
Detailed population data for the service centres Deniyaya, Kamburupitiya, Dikwella, Morawaka, Urubokka, and Hakmana is not available in Population Census of 1981.

A Order Service Centre = Major Service Centre

Matara is the major service centre as well as the major urban centre with the highest score of the 780 points and with the largest urban population of 39,162 inhabitants (Diag. 24). The highest level of all the central functions are concentrated here. The service areas of these functions reach far beyond the district boundaries.

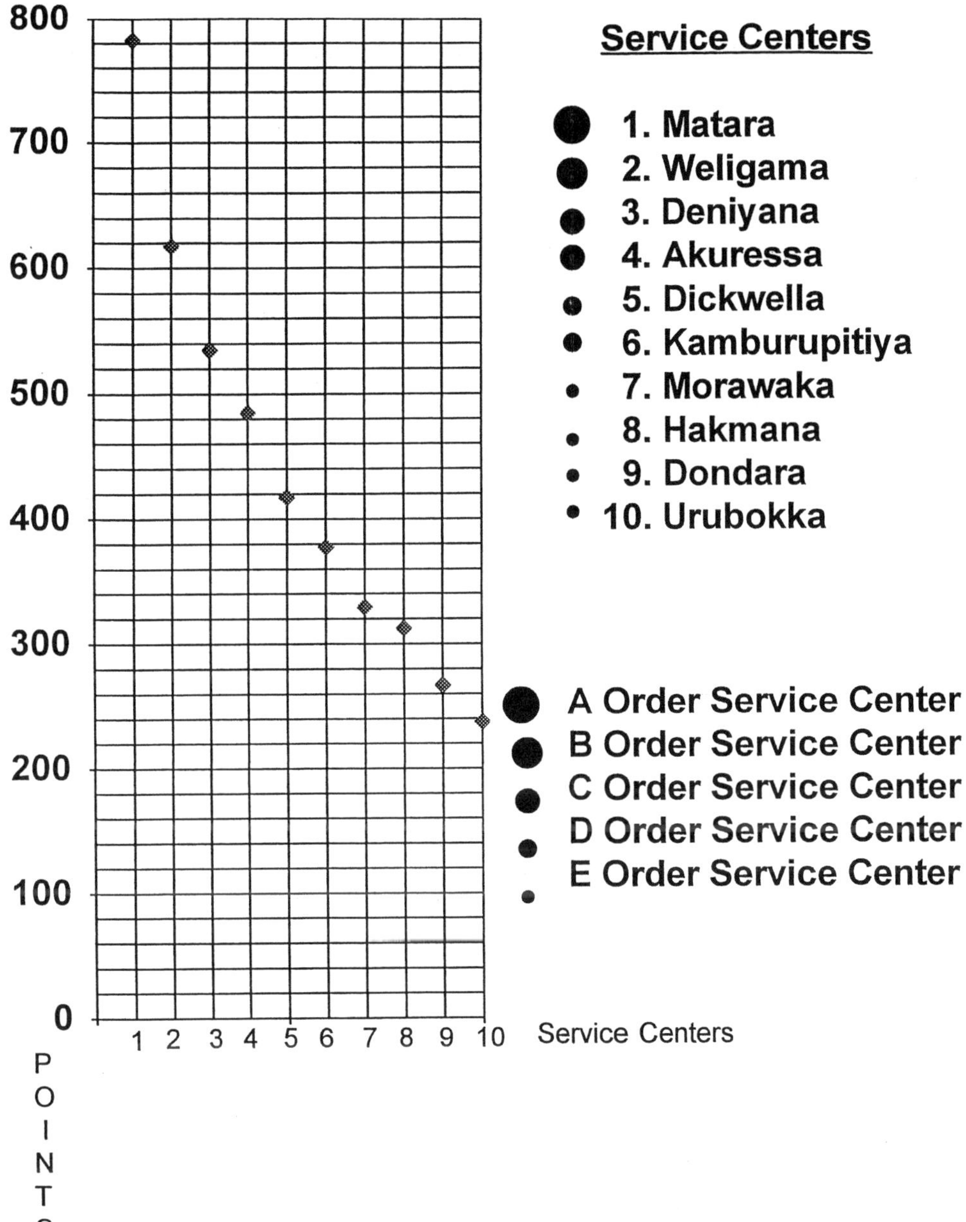

Diag. 24: Functional magnitude and hieracchical order of the important service centers of Matara District, 1987

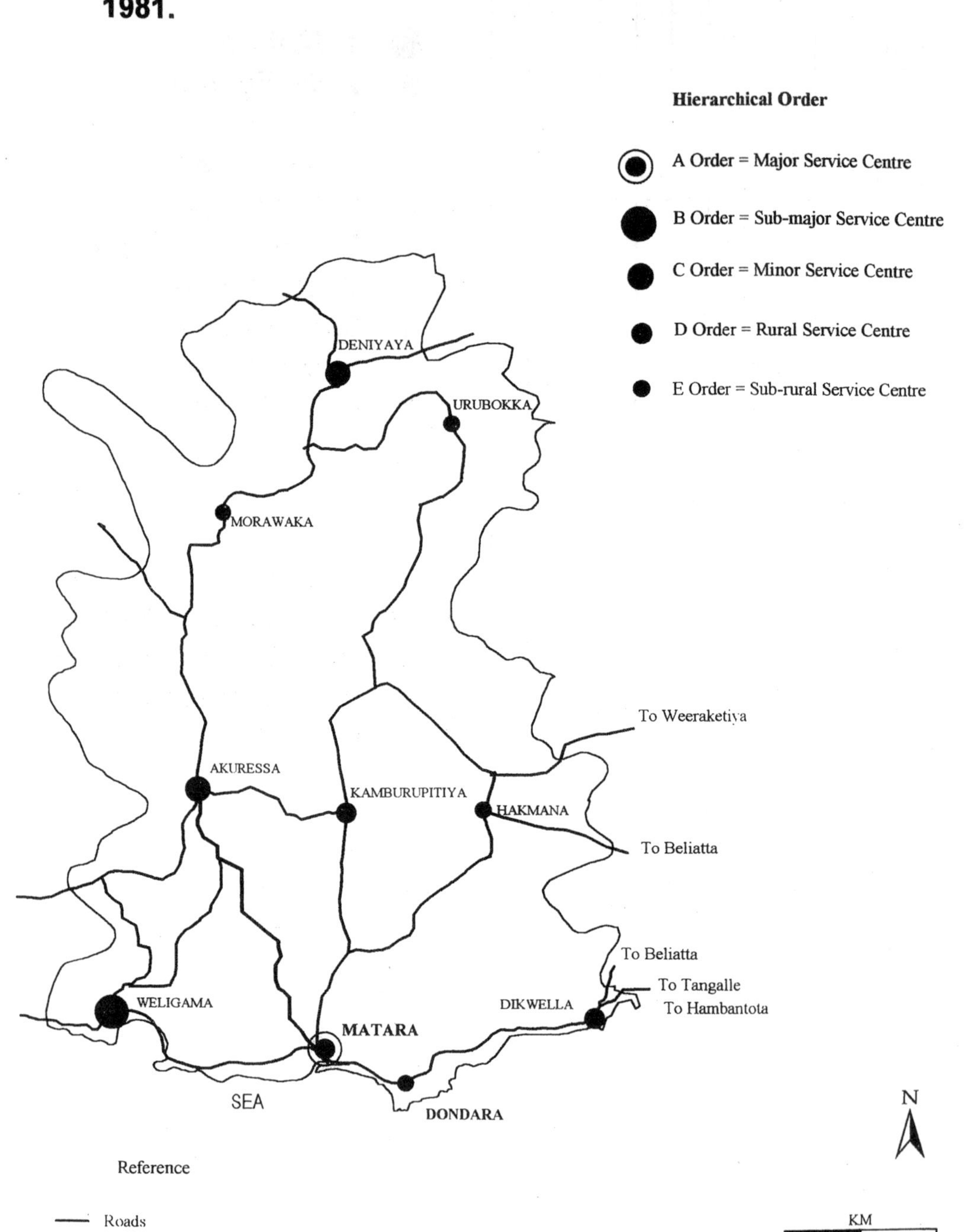
MAP 49
Hierarchical order of the Service Centres of Matara District 1981.
Hierarchical Order
A Order = Major Service Centre
B Order = Sub-major Service Centre
C Order = Minor Service Centre
D Order = Rural Service Centre
E Order = Sub-rural Service Centre
DENIYAYA
URUBOKKA
MORAWAKA
AKURESSA
KAMBURUPITIYA
HAKMANA
To Weeraketiya
To Beliatta
To Beliatta
To Tangalle
To Hambantota
DIKWELLA
WELIGAMA
MATARA
SEA
DONDARA
N
Reference
Roads
KM
0
5
10

B Order Service Centre = Sub-major Service Centre

Weligama is the sub-major service centre of the district with a score of 600 points. It is also the second largest urban centre of the district with 17,872 urban inhabitants. Although it has the same level of urban status (Urban Council), according to the Sri Lankan Urban hierarchical order, it has a lower grade of central functions, and a lower number of central functions as well as a lower number of residents than Matara. The trade sector in this centre is involved in short-term, mid-term as well as long-term commodities and services. The selection of the mid-term and long-term commodities in this centre is lower than Matara. The service areas of this centre are much smaller than Matara. The growth of this town as a major service centre is greatly hampered by the close location of the major service centres, Matara (6 miles or 10 km) on the eastern side and Galle (19 miles or 30 km) on the western side.

C Order Service Centre = Minor Service Centre

With total scores of 530 and 480, Deniyaya and Akuressa are the minor service centres in the district (Photo 41). The population of these two centres is 6,465 and 6,885 respectively. The most striking feature in this context is that Deniyaya, which lies in the extreme northern part of the Matara district, has not, even today, been granted the urban status although it holds more central functions than Akuressa, the urban centre (Town Council).

The growth of these centres as minor service centres is mainly due to their favourable location. Deniyaya lies 48 miles (77 km) from Matara along the highway Matara - Ratnapura at a road crossing in the northern zone, where the major cash crop of tea is extensively grown. This is the major service centre for the whole northern region of the district

Akuressa lies 14 miles (22 km) from Matara, along the highway Matara - Deniyaya at a road crossing in the central zone, where the major cash crops of tea and rubber as well as the minor cash crops of cinnamon, citronella and pepper are grown. This is the major service centre in the central zone of the Matara district.

Although the trade sectors in these two centres are involved in short-term, mid-term and long-term commodities, the selection of mid-term and long-term commodities is very limited. The service areas of these two centres are limited to the northern and central zones.

D Order Service Centres = Rural Service Centres

Dikwella and Kamburupitiya are the rural service centres of the district with total scores of 410 and 380. These two centres hold more limited and lower grade central functions than the above discussed C Order Service Centres. The population of these two centres is 10,146 and 1,476 respectively. The growth of these two centres as rural service centres is due to their favourable locations.

Dikwella is located 12 miles (19 km) from Matara on the eastern side, along the major highway Colombo - Hambantota in the coastal zone. This area is a well known fishing area of the district.

Kamburupitiya lies at the road crossing of Hakmana - Akuressa road and Matara - Urubokka road, 13 miles (21 km) from Matara in the central zone where minor cash crops are grown. The commercial activities in these two centres are predominantly involved with the short and mid-term consumer goods.

E Order Service Centres = Sub Rural Service Centres

The score of the E Order Service Centres or sub-rural service centres lies below 380 points. These are Morawaka (330 points), Hakmana (310 points), Dondara (310 points) and Urubokka (240 points).

Morawaka and Urubokka are located along the main roads on the northern zone of the district where the major cash crops of tea and rubber are grown. The population of these centres is 3,160 and 4,145, respectively.

Hakmana is located at a road crossing in the central zone where the minor cash crops of cinnamon, citronella and pepper as well as the major cash crops of rubber and coconut are extensively grown. The population of this settlement is not available in the census of 1981.

Dondara lies along the highway Colombo - Hambantota only 3 miles (5 km) from Matara on the eastern side in the coastal zone. This is a rich fishing centre in the Matara district. The population is 7,628. The growth of this centre is greatly hampered by its close proximity to Matara.

The striking feature in this context is that although Dondara is granted the urban status (Town Council), it has very few central functions and they are of the lowest grade.

CHAPTER 7

Summary

Urban studies are relatively scarce in Sri Lanka, and a preponderance of the few hitherto written works pertain mostly to larger urban settlements. This is true even though medium and small-sized towns have played a significant role in the economy of the island nation. Yet, the exact impact of the latter on the country's economy has rarely been investigated.

The present treatise (dissertation) is intended to provide a geographical analysis of a medium-sized town, Matara, which is located in the south-western quadrant of Sri Lanka. The town and its hinterland are jointly considered.

The dissertation is divided into two parts.

The first part describes the physical features ,history, population living characteristics, conditions,economy,social services and land utilization of the town.The second part, the main section of this treatise, deals with the centrality and the catchment areas (influential areas) of Matara town.

Matara is a settlement of ancient origin. The starting point for the development of this settlement is connected with its favourable location, favourable climatic conditions, and well established political organisation.

The favourable physiographic features and agro-climatic conditions for wet rice cultivation in the surrounding areas of Matara town stimulated the growth of settlements as early as the 3rd Century B.C.. Matara town's relative centrality and the easy access it provided to those areas in Matara district growing cinnamon, the most important export commodity during the pre-colonial and colonial periods, were central factors in attracting the first European colonialists, the Portuguese and Dutch. Later, these very same factors would also draw the occupying British to Matara. The British expanded cultivation to include rubber and tea. Prior to the first occupation of Matara by the Portuguese in 1505, Matara was a commercial centre of little consequence.

During the Portuguese and Dutch periods, Matara became one of the principal administrative centres and central collecting points for agricultural products. Matara also served as one of the major ports in the southern region of Sri Lanka. These factors led to the socio-economic stratificaion and diversification of this centre. Under the British, Matara was granted urban status and became the administrative and commercial capital of Matara district.

During and following the colonial eras, Matara began increasingly to provide services and goods to an area and population other than itself. The basic element of the "central place theory" became more visible(in this era)than ever before.

Growth of urban settlements in Sri Lanka has been a foreign element which had little influence on the settlement pattern of the Island. Among the colonial powers, it was the British who exercised greatest impact on how and where population centres developed.

According to both European and North American measurements, almost all towns in Sri Lanka except the commercial capital, Colombo, fall into the category of service centres.

The words, "town" and "village", may have somewhat vague appellations when applied in Sri Lanka, where the traditional economic heritage always has been agricultural. As a result, it becomes somewhat difficult to distinguish between urban and rural areas for statistical comparisons. Until today, a clear definition of "urban" is absent in the collection of census statistics.

The morphology of Matara town has changed from a simple linear pattern in the pre-colonial period to a grid pattern in the British era. The grid pattern exists even today. However, distinctive areas such as residential, industrial, and commercial are not as easily distinguishable, or as well-developed in Matara town as they may be in European countries. A functional mix of residence, trade, storage, and craft industry are inter-mingled in close, compatible associations.

Urbanisation of Sri Lanka has been a very slow process, and one which never has had as great an impact on the country as it may have had in other third world nations. It was also revealed that it was not the rural / urban migration which influenced urbanisation in Sri Lanka but the creation of new settlements through arbitrary annexations or horizontal expansion.

Matara town is predominantly inhabited by Sinhala Buddhist population while Muslims make up the largest minority. An examination of the population structure has shown that Matara town has a typical expanding population with high birth rates and decreasing death rates.

The quality of life of the town's inhabitants is poor. A large segment of the population is deprived of basic amenities such as treated water, electricity, toilets, and permanent houses. Due to the lack of these amenities and ignorance of general sanitation practices, parasitic diseases such as typhoid, dysentery, hepatitis, and filariasis are spreading in the town.

An examination of the residential areas shows that the majority Sinhalese tend to concentrate in the outer zone of the commercial core area, probably because of their cultural heritage, while the minorities prefer to live inside the commercial core area. In addition, an easily observed and declining social gradient, underscored by rapidly falling real estate prices and reduction of services, can be seen to exist toward the town's outer periphery. The central areas of the town, where real estate prices remain both stable and very high, are mostly occupied by the affluent, or privileged, classes drawn there by easy accessibility to all services.

An examination of the economy has revealed that the administrative and commercial sectors play major roles in the economy of Matara town while the industrial facet plays a very insignificant role. The slow growth rate of the industrial sector is mainly attributed to the lack of resources.

The C.B.D. (central business district) of Matara town was delimited by investigating land values, land-use patterns, density of commercial units, building heights and accessibility.

Mapping and analysis of the central business district of Matara displayed a remarkable diversity of trade with a rich assortment of goods in comparison to the other service centres of Matara district.

The integral and spatial structure of the C.B.D. of Matara shows that it has some of the functional characteristics found in the towns of European countries. However, C.B.D. of Matara bears more resemblance to those towns in the developing world which were also under British control.

The investigation also revealed that there is extremely high competition between the Sinhalese and Muslims for trade predominance. Competition from the Tamil element, such as found in many other Sri Lankan towns, is completely absent in Matara town, even in pre - 1983 times .

The slow growth of the economy in the town offers no entry points to the increasing population.

Out-migration and the unemployment problems in the town can be solved only by improving cottage and agro-based industries. In addition, improvement of agriculture and fishery would also contribute in large measure towards solving this problem.

In the last chapter, the commercial hegemony of Matara Town over the other service centres was investigated by comparing such basic indicators as the number of commercial businesses, number of bank accounts, and number of commercial telephones.

After proving the commercial hegemony of Matara town, the centrality and the catchment areas of Matara town were investigated taking communication, administration, medical facilities, educational facilities, social and cultural services into consideration. With regard to the commercial and health care services of the town, in addition to the available reports and data, a questionnaire survey was conducted by the author to find out the extent of the service area.

It became evident that Matara town is a traffic junction between the western and extreme eastern parts of Sri Lanka, servicing not only the local hinterland but also large feeding areas extending mainly to the east and to the north. The extension of service areas to the west is hampered by the location of a larger urban town, Galle.

A hierarchical order of the important service centres of the Matara district is identified by examining the central services, such as administration, commerce, public service, social service, and communication.

According to this investigation, it is found that there are five hierarchical orders of service centres existing in the Matara district. Matara dominates by being the major service centre in the hierarchical order.

Bibliography

Abayasekara, G. : Population growth and distribution in Sri Lanka. In : Population problems of Sri Lanka, edit: Demographic training and research unity, University of Colombo, 1976, pp. 1 - 26

Abeyagunawardana, T.H.D. : "A Regional Survey of Matara District", In: Bull., of the Ceyl. Geogr. Soc., Vol. 6, Colombo 1952, pp. 38-64.

Abeyasingha, T. : Portuguese Rule in Ceylon 1594-1612, Colombo 1966.

Abeyasundara, A.N.A. : Recent trends in Morbidity and Mortality. In: Populationproblems of Sri Lanka, edit: Demo. Tra. & Res. Unit. 1976,pp. 48-67.

Abele,G / Wolf,K. : Methoden zur Abgrenzung und inneren Differenzierung verschiedenrangiger Geschaftszentren. In: Bei. Z. dt. Landeskunde, Bd. 40, Bonn 1968, pp. 238-252.

Abhayaratna, O.E.R. / Jayawardana, C.H.S. : "International Migration in Ceylon". In: The Ceyl. Jourl. of His. & Soc. Studies., Vol. 8 Nos. 1/2, January/Dec. Colombo 1965, pp. 69-89.

Adams, F.D. : The Geology of Ceylon, Colombo 1929.

Agel, P. : Marginale Siedlungen in Urbanisierungsprozes: Das Beispiel Colombo / Sri Lanka: Ein Beitrag zur Analyse des sozialen wandels in Südasien. Frankfurter Wirt-U. Soz. Geogr. Schriften, Heft 43, 1982.

Agrawal, P.C. : Weekly Market size and service area in Bastar district (Madhya Pradesh, India). In: Ind. Geogr. Jourl. Vol. 43, 1968, pp 29 - 33.

Agrarian Research & Training Institute : Cinnamon Cultivation in the Matara district: Occasional Publication, No. 22., 1981.

Akbar, M.E. :"Matara Distrikkaye Muslim Janathawa" (Muslim population in Matara district). In: Matara Sahithya Dara (Litaratur of Matara district), Matara 1965., pp. 124 - 126.

Amarasingha, P. : Planing approach for districts in Sri Lanka, M.A. diss.,Institute of social studies, Hauge, 1983.

Arasaratnam, S. : Dutch Power in Ceylon 1658-1687, Amsterdam 1958.

Arasaratnam, S. : Francois Valentijn's description of Ceylon, London 1958.

Balasuriya, W / Siriwardana, D.E. : "Matara Nagaraye Aurudu Hathalihaka Palanaya" (Forty years of administration over Matara). In: Matara Distrikkaye Sahithya Dara. 1965, pp. 165 - 169.

Bandarage, A. : Colonialism in Sri Lanka. In: The Political Economy of the Kandyan Highlands, 1833 - 1866., Berlin 1983.

Barlett, A. : The Map Collectors issue, No. 38, London 1987. p. 17 - 21.

Bartz ,F. : Fischer auf Ceylon, Bonn Geog. Arb. H. 27, 1959

Bartz, F : "Die Insel Ceylon - Gesellschaft, Wirtschaft und Kultur- landschaft". In: Erdk. Vol. X1, Heft. 4, Nov. 1957, Bonn, pp : 249 - 266.

Bart, E. : Home gardens and Home gardening in the Matara district (a seasonal paper). Agrarian research institute, Colombo 1981.

Bechert, H. (edit) : Culture of Ceylon in Medieval times, Wiesbaden 1960.

Bechert, H. : Buddhismus und Landschaft. In: Erdkundl. Wissens, Heft 54, 1981, pp. 183-192.

B.M.C., Matara. : (Building Materials Corporation), Matara, Sales Reports 1987.

Bobek, H. : Grudfragen der Stadtgeographie. In: Geogr. Anzeig. 28 Jg., Gotha, 1927, 213-224.

Bobek, H. : Über einige funktionelle Stadttypen und ihre Beziehungen zum Lande. In: Comptes. Rendus du Congress Internationale de Geographie, Amsterdam 1938, Bd. 12, Arbeiten der Sektion 3a Kulturgeographie; Leiden, pp. 88 - 102.

Bobek, H. : Die Hauptstufen der Gesellschafts und Wirtschaftsentfaltung in geograpischer Sicht. In: Die Erde, Jg. 90, Berlin pp. 259-298.

Bohle, H.G. : Südindische Wochenmarkt systeme In: Erdkl. Wiss., Heft 82, 1986.

Boustedt, O. : Grundriss der empirischen Regionalforschung, Teil. 1, Bevolkerungsstrukturen, Hannover 1975.

Boustedt, O. : Bestimmung und Analyse zentralortlicher Erscheinungen in einer Grossstadt Hamburg in Zahlen, So. Heft. 1, 1970, pp. 1 - 10.

Boyce,J./ Ferreth,J. : Field Work in Geography. Cambridge, London 1984.

Brohier, R.L. : Ancient Irrigation Works in Ceylon., Colombo 1934.

Brohier, R.L. : Lands, Maps and Surveys., Colombo 1951.

Brohier, R.L. : Seeing Ceylon., Colombo 1957.

Brohier, R.L. : Food and People., Colombo 1975.

Brohier, R.L. : Links between Sri Lanka and Netherlands (A Book of Dutch Ceylon). Colombo 1970.

Bromly, R.J. : Markets in the developing countries. In: " A Review".,Geography. No. 56., 1971, pp. 124 - 132.

Bromly, R.J. : Periodic Markets, Daily Markets and Fairs (A Bibliography), 1974.

Bromly, R.J/ Symanski, R. : "Market Place Trade in Latin America", In: Latin American Rural Review, Vol 9, 1977, pp. 3-38.

Bührlein, M. : Die Bedeutung Nuwara Eliya als "hill station" im lichte moderner Kurortklimatologie, In: Erdkl. Wiss., Bd. 97, 989, pp. 169 - 207.

Bührlein, M. : Nuwara Eliya: " hill station " und zentraler Ort im Hochland der Insel Ceylon - Sri Lanka.,Beitr. Südasien - Forschung - Band 146, 1991.

Carter, H. : Einfuhrung in die Stadtgeographie., Berlin, 1980.

Cave, H. : The Ruined Cities of Ceylon. London, 1900.

Cave, H. : The Book of Ceylon. London, 1908.

Casie Chitty, S. : Church Mission. In: Ceylon Gazetter. Colombo, 1834.

Central Bank of of Ceylon : Five Years Development (Paswasaraka Pragathiya)- 1977 July - Ceylon: 1982 July. 1982.

Central Bank : Reports on consumer finances and socio-economic survey 1981 / 82. part. 1, 1984.

Central Bank : Rural savings mobilisation, occasional papers, No. 8,1984.

Central Bank : Review of the economy. 1986.

Central Bank : The Role of the Banking in Rural Development. Occasional papers, No. 14, 1986.

Central Bank : Central Bank of Ceylon. Bull., 1987 August.

Central Bank : Development of small scale industries. 1989.

Ceylon Gazetter : Island of Ceylon. 1934.

Chandraprema, C.A : "Ruhuna" (A study of the history, society and ideology of southern Sri Lanka). Colombo 1989.

Christaller, W. : Die zentralen orte in Suddeutschland. Jena, 1933. Darmstadt, 1968.

Clark,J. : The growth of capital cities in Afrika. In: Afrika Specktrum - Urbanisierung in Afrika, 2 / 71, Hamburg, pp. 33 - 40.

Codrington, H.W. : Ancient Land Tenure and Revenue in Ceylon. Colombo, 1938.

Codrington, H.W. : Notes on Ceylon Topography in the 12th Century.,In: The Ceyl. His. Jourl., Vol. 1V, 1954 & 1955, No. 1 - 4.

Cook,E.K. : Ceylon: Geography, Resources and People, London 1931.

Cooray, P.G. : An Introduction to the Geology of Ceylon. Colombo, 1967.

Cooray, P.G./ Vitanage,P.W. : A note on lime - burning in the Kegalle district. In: Bull. of the Ceyl. Geogr. Soc., Vol. 9, Nos 3 & 4, 1955, pp. 68 - 77.

Cordiner,J.A.M. : A Description of Ceylon, London, 1807.

Coward,J / Edwards,C./ Pollard,J. / Poole,M. : Worked excercises in Human Geography. Cambridge Univ. Press, Cambridge, 1983.

C.T.B.(Ceylon Transport Board) Matara : Bus Schedule of 1985.

C.T.B., Matara : Monthly School season tickets register of 1984.

Davis,K. : Urbanization in India. In: India's urban future, California, pp. 27 - 54.

Davy,J. : An account of the interior of Ceylon and its inhabitants with travels in that Island. London, 1821.

Dept. of Highways, Colombo : Traffic Records of 1988.

Dept. of Water Supply, Matara : Water Consumption Records of 1981.

Dept. of Electricity, Matara : Electricity Consumption Records of 1981.

Dept. of Traffic, Matara Police : Traffic Records of 1987.

Dept. of Irrigation, Colombo : Feasibility reports on multipurpose development of the Nilwala Ganga basin, Vol. 1 & 2, 1987.

Dept. of Fisheries, Matara : Annual Reports of the Production, 1987.

Deraniyagala, P.E.P. : A Carbonaceous Jurassic shale from Ceylon. In: Spol. Zey. XX1, pt. 3, 1939.

Deraniyagala, P.E.P. : The Pleistocene of Ceylon, National History Series, 1958.

Deshpande, C.D. : Market Villages and Periodic Fairs of Bombay Karnatak. In: The Indian Geogr. Jour l, Vol. XV1. No. 4., Oct. - Dec. 1944, pp. 327 - 339.

Deshmukh, P.W. : Periodic Markets and regional links in Sangli district. In: Kumbhar,A.P.,Deccan geographer,1975, pp. 327 - 339.

De Silva, C.R. : Ceylon under British Occupation 1795 - 1833., Colombo, 1962.

De Silva, K.M. : History of Ceylon, Vol. 111. Univ. of Ceylon, Peradeniya,1973.

De Silva, K.M. : The foundation of Sri Lankan history(The Classical era the Colonial era and the Independent era).In: Insight - Guides (Sri Lanka), Colombo 1991, pp. 32 - 55.

De Silva, K.M. : Nationalism and its impact. In: Ceyl. Jourl. of His Stud., Vol. 4 - 6, Colombo 1976,. pp. 62-72.

De Silva, S.B.D. : The political economy of underdevelopment, London, 1982.

De Silva, S.F. : The Cultural Evolution of Modern Ceylon. In: Bull. Ceyl. Geogr. Soc., Vol. 4., No. 1 - 3, 1949.

De Silva, S.F. : The Historical Geography of Ancient Cities in Ceylon. In: Bull. Ceyl. Geogr. Soc., Vol. 5, No. 2 & 3, 1950, pp. 124 - 135.

De Silva, S.F. : A Regional Geography of Ceylon. Colombo, 1954.

De Silva, S.F. : A Geographical Interpretation of Ceylon History. In: Bull. Ceyl. Geogr. Soc., Vol. 9, No. 3 & 4, 1955.

Dharmadasa, K.N.O. : Language Conflicts in Sri Lanka. In: Jourl. of Soc. Sc.,Vol. 4. , No. 2., Colombo 1982, pp. 47 - 66.

Dharmasene, K.M. : Fishing Industry at Mirissa - Matara District, (Marga Publication) 1983.

Dharmasena, K. : The Port of Colombo 1860 - 1939, Colombo 1973.

Dhiman, R.P.S. : Rural dependence on service centres in district Moradbad, In: The Geogr. Obs., Vol. 21., India, 1985, pp. 48 - 53.

Diamantha,S. : Land suitability evaluation of the Matara district, Colombo,1970.

Dias, J.N.S. : World market and marketing of spices. In: Economic Review, Colombo 1987.

Dicke, S. : Die Stadt Badulla., Zeitr. S.A.S. Forschung, Univ. Heidelberg, Bd. 114, 1987.

Dicke, S. : Badulla - Ein Zentraler Ort auf Ceylon, In: Edkl. Wiss. H.97, 1989, pp. 101 - 140.

Dixit, R.S. : Market centres of a backward economy, Hamirpur district (U.P.)9., In: Dec. Geogr., Vol. XX111, Oct - Dec. 1985., No.3 India 1985, pp. 127 - 143.

Domrös, M. : Untersuchungen der Niederschlagshaufigkeit auf Ceylon nach Jahresabschnitten. In: Jahrbuch d. Südasien - In d. Univ. Heidelberg, 11, 1967/68, Wiesbaden, 1968, pp.70 - 84.

Domrös, M. : "Wet Zone" und "Dry Zone"- Moglichkeiten einer klima- ökologischen Raumgliederung der Insel Ceylon. In: Erdkundl. Wiss., Heft 27, Wiesbaden, 1971, pp. 205 - 232.

Domrös, M. : Der Monsun im Klima der Insel Ceylon.In: Die Erde, Bd.102, Heft 2/3, 1971, pp. 118 - 140.

Domrös, M. : The Agroclimate of Ceylon. Geoecol. Res. 2, Wiesbaden, 102, 1974.

Domrös, M. : Sri Lanka: die Tropeninsel Ceylon. Wiss. Länderkunde, Vol.12.,Darmstadt,1976.

Domrös, M. : Der Jahres - und Tagesgang der Schwule im Tropenklima von Sri Lanka. In: Aachener Geogr. Arb. 14., 1981, pp. 123 - 138.

Domrös, M. : Studies on the Mountain Climatology and Geoecology of the Central Highlands in Sri Lanka. In: Erd.wiss. Forschg. Bd. XV111, 1984, pp. 99 - 114.

Drieberg, J.C. : Cinnamon - Historical sketch of the industry in Ceylon., In: Trop. Agri., vol. LXXXV11., No. 4, 1931. Oct.

Dutt, K.M./Armin, R. : Toward a Typology of South Asien Cities. In: The Nat. Geogr. Jourl. of India, Vol. 32, 1986 March, pp. 30 - 39.

Edirisingha, P.
Edirisingha, P. : Lankawe Kohulanu Karmanthaya (Coir Yarn Industry of Ceylon)., Vol. 1,2, Colombo 1956/ 1957.

Escher, A. : Can the traditional crafts pursued in Moroccan Towns be assigned to the "Informal Sector"? The example of the Mat weavers of Sale. In: Applied geogr. and development. (A biannual collection of recent German contributions), Vol. 33, Tubingen, 1987, pp. 93 - 107.

Evers, H.D. : Kulturwandel in Ceylon: Eine Untersuchung über die Entstehung einer Industrie-Unternehmerschicht, In: Soz.Wiss. Beitrage zur Entwicklung Forschung, Bd. 1, Baden - Baden, 1964.

Evers, H.D. : Monastic Landlordism in Ceylon: A traditional system in a modern setting. Repr. Series, No. 38, Yale Univ. 1969.

Farmer, B.H. : Pioneer peasent colonization in Ceylon, London 1957.

Farmer, B.H. : Ancient irrigation works in Ceylon, London 1964.

Farmer, B.H. : An introduction to South Asia. London 1982.

Fernando, L.G.D. : The Geology and Mineral Resources of Ceylon, In: Bull. Imperial Institute,Vol. XLV1, 1948.

Fernando, N.A. : A study of Tea Small Holdings in Deraniyagala (Matara district). In: Jourl. of the Nat. Inst. of Plant. Manag., Vol. 4., No. 1, 1984.

Fernando, P.N. : Towards a Strategy for Urban Renewal of the Urban Settlements of Sri Lanka, MSc Thesis, Univ. Moratuwa, 1984.

Fernando, S.N.U. : Progress of the Geological Survey of Ceylon. In: Bull. Ceyl. Geogr. Soc., Vol. 8, Nos. 1 & 2, 1954, pp.1 - 10.

Fernando, S.N.U. : Ceylon Soils, Colombo, 1967.

Fernando, S. : The impact of Buddhism on small scale fishery performence and development. In: Fisheries,Marga publication, special issue, Vol. 7, No. 2 & 3, 1984, pp. 110 - 162.

Fernando,T. : 100 days in Sri Lanka'87., Colombo 1988.

Fisher Länderkunde : "Südasien", Band 2, 1971.

Gamage, W. : Henagama and Mirissa South.: A comparison of some socio- economic indicators of development in an agricultural village and fishing village in Matara district. (Marga publication), 1982.

Gamage, W. : Henegama - An analysis of a Wetzone agricultural village in Southern Sri Lanka (Marga pub.) 1983.

Gamage, W. : Small Scale Fisheries (Sri Lanka): Some facts pertaining to fishermen Co-operatives in the Marine Fishery., Marga pub. 1980.

Freks, S./Sangers, S. : Home Garden and Home Gardening in Matara District - The present situation and fututre prospects, 1985. (Marga / Auw research project on popular participation in planned development at village level.).

Geddes, P. : Town planning in Colombo: A preliminary report, Colombo plan, 1921.

Geiger, W. : Culture of Ceylon in Medieval Times., Berchert, H. (edit), Wiesbaden 1960.

Ghapure, V.T./ Pawar, C.T. : Centrality and Hierarchy of Agro - Service Centres in the Pancha Ganga Basin (Maharasahtra), In: The Geogr. Vol. XXX1V, No. 1., India, 1987.

Gläser, T. : Die Insel Mannar - Zur Problematik der Fischerei im Nordlichen Ceylon. In: Erdkl. Wiss. H.54, 1981.

Gläser, T. : Fischerei und Fischereiwirtschaft im nordlichen Ceylon: Standort und Lebensraum der Fischer im Norden der Tropeninsel, Stuttgart, 1983.

Godakumbure, C.E. : Architecture of Sri Lanka., Colombo, 1976.

Goonawardana, K.W. : A new Netherland in Ceylon. In: The Ceyl. Jourl. of His. and Soc. Stud., Vol. 2., No. 2, 1959, pp. 228 - 231.

Goonawardana, T.P. : A survey of some of Sri Lanka's state aided development programmes in the fisheries sector, Marga pub. 1980 Oct. Government Gazette, No. 10, 821, Colombo, 1955 July 29.

Govt. Agent's Reports, 1872 : Colombo Museum Library.

Gormsen, E. : Market Distribution Systems, Mainzer Geographische Studien, 10, 1976.

Gormsen, E. : Weekly Markets in the Puebla region of Mexico, In: Smith, R.H.T. (Hrsq.), Market Place Trade - Periodic markets, Hawkers, and traders in Africa, Asia and Latin America, VanCouver 1978, pp. 240 - 253.

Gunasegaram, S.J. : Selected Writings., Colombo, 1985.

Gunasekara, H.M. : The Economy of Sri Lanka 1948 - 1973, In: The Ceyl. Jourl. of His. Stud., Vol. 4 - 6, 1976, pp. 73 - 83.

Gunawardana, K.M. : Service centres of Southern Ceylon. Ph.D. diss., Cambridge, 1964.

Gunawardana, K.M. : A conventional study of Ambalantota (Hambantota District.) Cambridge, 1974.

Gunawardana, K.M. : Some recent changes in the pattern of internal migration in Sri Lanka., In: Progress, Vol. 2., Issue. 2, Colo 1982- June, pp .7 - 11.

Gunawardana, K.M./ Silva, P. : The urban fringe of Colombo : Some trends and problems concerning its land use. In: Modern Ceylon Studies, Vol. 2, 1971.

Gunawardana, R. : War and Peace in Sri Lanka, Colombo, 1987.

Gunawardana, R. : A Lost Revolution (Sri Lanka), 1990.

Guruge, A. : Return to Righteousness, Colombo, 1965.

Hackel, E. : A visit to Ceylon 1882 (translated by Clara Bell). In: The Ceyl. His. Jourl. Vol. 23, Colombo, 1883.

Harischandra Mills, Matara : Annual Audit Reports of 1986.

Harris, B. : Rural - Urban Economic Transactions: A case study from India and Sri Lanka. In: S.W.R. de A. Samarasinghe (ed) Agriculture in the peasant sector of Sri Lanka, Peradeniya, 1976.

Harris, B. : The economic and spatial relations of transactions and its implication for rural indebtedness in Hambantota District of Sri Lanka. In: S.W.R. de A. Samarasinghe (ed), Agriculture in the peasant sector of Sri Lanka, Peradeniya, 1976.

Harris, C. : Functional classification of cities in the U.S.A., In: Geogr .Review, No. 33, 1945, pp. 86 - 89.

Harris, C.H.D./ Ullman, E. : The nature of cities., In: Ann. of the American Academy of Political and Soc. Sci. Vol. 242, Philadelphia, 1945,pp. 7 - 17.

Hauser, J.A. : Bevölkerungsprobleme der Dritten Welt. Bern, Stuttgart,1974.

Hausherr, K. : Traditionaler Brandrodungsfeldbau (Chena) und moderne Erschliesungsprojekte in der Trokenzone im SE Ceylons. In: Erdkl. Wissen, Heft. 27, Wiesbaden, 1971.

Hausherr, K. : Kataragama: das Heiligtum im Dschungel SE Ceylons - aus geographischer Sicht., Gottingen, 1978.

Heinritz, R.(edit.) : Zentralität und Zentraler Orte. Teubner Studienbücher, 1979.

Henkel, R. : Central Places in Western Kenya. Heidelberger Geogr. Arb., Heft. 54, 1979.

Henkel, R. : Periodic Markets in Western Kenya. In: Die Erde; Bd. 110. pp. 165 - 180.

Hettiarachchi, N. : Environmental Hygiene and Nutrition (Parisarika - Saukkya saha Poschnaya). In: Poshana Handa (Sound of Nutrition), 1985, pp. 30 - 40.

Heydt, J.W. : Heydt's Ceylon (Trans. by Ravenhardt, R.), Plates 70, 71, 72. Colombo, 1972.

Hewavitharana, R. : Rural Employment Creation in Sri Lanka; problems, programmes and strategy for the future, In: Sri Lanka Eco .Jourl., Vol. 2, No. 1, Colombo 1987, pp. 1 - 22.

Hilhorst, T./ Vanenk, G. : Home gardening. Agri. Univ. of Wagenigen, Netherland), Netherland, 1985.

Hill, P. / Smith, R.H.T. : The Spatial and Temporal Synchronisation of Periodic Markets- evidence from four Emirates in Northern Nigeria.,In: Eco. Geogr., Vol. 48 ,No. 5, pp. 346 - 355.

Hofmeister, B. : Stadtgeographie (Das Geographische Seminar), Braun-Schweig, 1976.

Hofmeister, B. : Die Stadtstruktur. In: Ertrage der Forschung, Bd. 132., Darmstadt, 1980.

Holden, L. : Ceylon., London, 1939.

Holmes, C.H. : The Grass Fern and Savannah Lands of Ceylon. Oxford, 1951.

Hossen, N. : Evaluation of the present agro - based industry and its future development in Matara district., Agrarian Research Institute, 1985.

Hulugalla, H.A.J. : Ceylon of the early travellers, Colombo, 1980.

Indrapala, K. : South Indian Mercantile Communities in Ceylon ca 950 - 1250. In: Jourl. of His. and Soc. Stud., New Series, Vol. 1, 1971 ,No. 2, pp. 101 - 113.

Indrarathna, A.D.V.de.S. : The Ceylon Economy. Colombo, 1966.

Interview Surveys : Periodic Market (Pola), 1987, 1991.

Jackson, D.W. : Polas in Central Sri Lanka (Some preliminary remarks on the development and functioning of Periodic Markets). In: Smarasingha, S.W.R. de.A (ed.), Agriculture in the peasant sector of Sri Lanka, Ceyl. Stud. Semi. Peradeniya, 1977.

Jamkar, A.G. : Spatial disposition and spatio - temporal analysis of Periodic market places in Dhula district(India). In: The Decc.Geogr.

Jayathilaka, K.M./ Spencer, R.T./Wu.Schu. : Buddhism and Science : In: Collected Essays, No. 3.,Colombo, 1969.

Jayawardana, K. : Ethnic and Class Conflicts in Sri Lanka, Colombo, 1986.

Jefferson, M. : The Law of the Primate City. In: Geogr. Rev. Vol. 29, New York, 1939, pp. 226 - 232.

Jeyasingham, W.L. : The Urban Geography of Jaffna., Ph.D. diss., Clark Univ.USA, 1958.

Joachim, A.W.R. : The Soils of Ceylon. In: Bull. Ceyl. Geogr. Soc., Vol. 8, Nos. 3 & 4 , 1954, pp .67 - 71.

Joachim, A.W.R. : The Soils of Ceylon. In: Trop. Agri., Vol. X, 3, 1955, pp. 161 - 172.

Johnson, B.L.C./ Scrivenor, M. : Sri Lanka; Land, People and Economy, London, 1981.

Jones, G.W./Selvarathnam : Urbanisation in Ceylon. In: Mod. Ceyl. Stud., Vol. 1 No. 2 , 1970, pp. 199 - 212.

Kade, G. : Die Stellung der zentrale Orte in der kulturlandschaftlichen Entwicklung Bugandas (Uganda). Frankfurter Wirt.- u. Soz. Geogr. Schriften, 6, 1969.

Kamburupitiye Wanarathna Himi (Buddhist Monk- Wanarathna of Kamburupitiya) : Matara Manawa Wamsaya ha Puravidyathmaka Ihihasaya (Anthropology and Archaeological History of Matara), Matara, 1950.

Karunatilaka, H.N.S. : Demographic Aspects of Unemployment in Sri Lanka, In: Population Problems of Sri Lanka. (edit): Demographic Training and Research Unit, Univ. of Sri Lanka, Colombo, 1976, pp. 146 - 169.

Karunatilaka, H.N.S. : Urbanisation of Sri Lanka. In: Sri Lanka Jourl. of Soc. Sci., Vol .4., No. 2, Colombo, 1981.

Karunatilaka, H.N.S. : The Economy of Sri Lanka, Colombo, 1987.

Karunatilaka, H.N.S, : Black Money in the Sri Lankan Economy. In: Sri Lanka Eco. Jourl., Vol. 2, 1987, pp. 22 - 32.

Klopper, R. : Der geographische Stadtbegriff. In: Geogr. Taschenbuch 1956 \ 57, Wiesbaden, 1956, pp .453 - 461.

Knox, R. : An historical relation of Ceylon. 1681 .Reprint. In: Ceyl. His. Jourl. 6, 1958.

Kotalawala, D.A. : Some aspects of social changes in the south west of Sri Lanka 1700 - 1833., In: Soc. Sci. Rev., No. 4, pp. 64.

Kularathnam, K. : A Concise Atlas of Geography of Ceylon, Colombo, 1971.

Kumbar, A.P. : Periodic Markets and Regional Links in Sangli District(India).In: Deccan Geogr. 1963, pp. 539 - 547.

Laping, J. : Aspekte der Stadt im altindischen Staatslehrbuch des Kautilya. In: Kulke, H (edit) Stadte in Südasien, Wiesbaden, 1982, pp. 1 - 16.

Leach, E.R. : Hydraulic Society in Ceylon. In: Past and Present, No 15, 1959.

Luu, P. : Les Systems Agroforestiers De La Zone Humide Sri Lanka: Agriculture Du Passe Ou D 'Avenir?, Ph.D. dissertation, 1989, Universite De Montpellier, Sciences Et Techniques Du Languedoc.

Mahn, C. : Periodische Märkte und Zentrale Orte in Nord Ghana. Heidelberger Arbeiten, 1980.

Manawadu, S. : Matara Grama Nama Saha Ithihasaya (Village names and their history - Matara district). 1991.

Manshard, W. : Die Stadt Kumasi (Ghana), Stadt und Umland in ihren funktionellen Beziehungen, In: Erdk. Bd. XV, Heft 3, 1961, pp. 162 - 179.

Marel, K. : Inter - und Intra - Regionale Mobilität, Schriftreihen des Bundesinstituts fur Bevolkerungslehre, Vol. 8,Wiesbaden, 1972.

Marby, H. : Die Tee Landschaft der Insel Ceylon. In: Erdkl. Wiss. Bd.27, Wiesbaden, 1971, pp. 23 - 101.

Marby, H. : Tea in Ceylon. Geoec. Research, Vol. 1, Wiesbaden, 1972.

Marga Publication : The Sinhala reading public, Sri Lanka, 1974.

Marga Publication : The informal sector of Colombo, 1979.

Marga Publication : An analytical description of poverty in Sri Lanka, 1981.

Marshall, H. : Ceylon: A general description of the Island and its inhabitants, London,repr. Dehiwala, 1969

Matara U.C. (Urban Council) : Register of Commercial Establishments, 1986.

Matara U.C. : Daily Tax Records (Kottegoda and Hunukotuwa Daily Markets), 1987.

Matara U.C. : Tax book of Peoples Weekly Market, 1987.

Matara U.C. : Budget Report of 1987.

Matznetter, J. : Das Enstehen und der Ausbau Zentrale Orte und ihre Netze an Beispielen aus portugiesichen Guinea, und Süd west Angola, Frankfurter Wirtschafts und Sozial Geographische Schriffen, 1967.

Mcgee,T.G. : The South Asian City, Prager, 1957.

Mendis, G.C. : Ceylon today and Yesterday, Colombo, 1957.

Mendis, M.W.J.G. : Urbanisation in Sri Lanka. In: Progress, Vol. 1, Issue 4, 1981

Mendis, M.W.J.G. : Small and Medium Towns in Sri Lanka. In: Eco. Rev., Dec.1982., pp. 27 - 32.

Mendis, M.W.J.G. : Large Towns in Sri Lanka. In: Eco. Rev. April 1982.

Mayhew, S. : G.C.S.E. Geography, Penguin books, London, 1984.

Menike, K.P. : A comparative analysis of land use in selected towns of Sri Lanka. Ph.D. diss., Univ. of Moratuwa, 1983.

Misra, K.K. : Identification of functional hierarchy of service centres in Hamirpur district(India).In: Decan. Geogr., Vol. XX1V, Oct / Dec. 1986, No. 3, pp. 98 - 109.

Montipa, M. : A study of production and marketing problems of coir yarn industry in Matara district.,A publication of Agrarian Research Institute, 1985.

Ministry of Higher Education : Directory of Technical Education 1986 / 87.

M.P.C.S.(Multi Purpose Co-Operative Society), Matara. : Buying and Selling Register 1987.

Muthumala, K : Urban Geography of Matara, M.A. Thesis, Univ. of Heidel berg, Geowiss. Fak., 1985.

Muller, K.P. : Rentenkapitalismus : eine geographische Erklarung fur Unterentwicklung., In: Geogr. Rundschau, 1984, Heft. 5.

Neef, E. : Das problem der zentrale örte. In: Pet. Geogr. Mitt. 94, 1950, pp. 6 - 17.

Netrakavesna, M. : A study of fisheries industry in Matara district. A publication of Agrarian Research Institute, 1985.

Niemeier, G. : Zur typologische Stellung und Gliederung der Indischen Stadt. In: Festschrift fur W. Maas, Gottingen, 1961.

Niemeier, G : Siedlungsgeographie. Geographisches Seminar, Braun - Schweig 1977.

Nyrop, R.F. : Area hand book for Ceylon., Washington, 1971.

Panabokka ,C.R. : Soil Science: The soils of Ceylon and use of fertilisers, Colombo, 1967.

Panditaratna, B.L. : Colombo: A Study in Urban Geography. Ph.D., London, 1960.

Panditaratna, B.L. : Colombo City: it's population growth and increase from 1824 - 1954., 1960

Panditaratna, B.L. : The Colombo Townscape: Some aspects of it's Morphology. In: Univ. of Ceyl. Rev., Vol. 19, No. 1, 1961.

Panditaratna, B.L. : The functional zones of Colombo City. In: Univ. of Ceyl.Rev., Vol. 19, No. 2, 1961, pp. 138 - 166.

Panditaratna, B.L. : A geographical description and analysis of Ceylonese towns. In: Ceyl. Jourl. of His. and Soc. Stu., 4, 1961, pp. 71 - 95.

Panditaratna, B.L. : The Port Capital City of Colombo: A geographical interpretation. In: Univ. Ceyl. Rev., Vol. 22,1964, pp. 135 - 159.

Panditaratna, B.L. : Some reflections on urban geographical research with special reference to Colombo. In: Ceyl. Geogr., Vol. 19, 1965, pp. 43 - 54.

Panditaratna, B.L. : Kandy Town: Functional areas and current trends of land use. In: Ceyl Jourl. of His. and Soc. Stud., Vol. 10, No. 1 & 2, pp. 103 - 113.

Panditaratna, B.L. : The urban field of Colombo. In: Bull. of the Ceyl. Geogr. Soc., Vol. 14, Nos. 1 - 4, 1960 Jan / Dec., pp. 26 - 36.

Patients Admission Register : Base Hospital, Matara, 1983.

Admission Register : Private Hospital "Mohotti", Matara, 1987.

Peebles, P. : Sri Lanka: A hand book of historical statistics, Boston, 1982.

Perera, N.P. : The ecological status of the Montane Grasslands (Patans) of Ceylon. In: Ceyl. Forrester.9, No .1 & 2, 1969, pp. 27 - 51.

Perera, S.G. : The Conquista of Queyroz; The only history of the Portuguese in Ceylon., Colombo,1925.

Perera, S.G. : The temporal and spiritual conquest of Ceylon, Colombo,1930.

Perera, S.G. : History of Ceylon for schools: The Portuguese and the Dutch 1505-1796. ,Vol. 1, Colombo, 1955.

Perera, S.G. : History of Ceylon for schools: The British period and after, Vol. 11, Colombo, 1959.

Perera, S.D.V. : Recent advances in Urban Geography. In: Ceyl. Geogr.Vol. 14, No. 1 - 4, Colombo, 1960.

Percival, R. : An account of the Island of Ceylon 1803. In: Ceyl. His. Jourl., Vol. 22, Colombo, 1975.

Phillipus,B. : Ceylon (1672) (Translated by Brohier). In: His. Jourl. Vol. V11, 1958, No. 1 - 4.

Pieris, K.R.S./ Doidge, C. : Colombo Shanty Housing. A publication of Univ. of Moratuwa., Sri Lanka, 1970.

Pieris, K.R.S./ Doidge, C. : Analysis of a shanty town (Univ. of Moratuwa), 1977.

: Future of shanty towns. (Univ. of Moratuwa), 1978.

Pieris, P.E. : Dutch Power in Ceylon. Colombo, 1970.

Pieris, P.E. : Ribeiro's History of Ceilao. Colombo, 1909.

Peiris, W. : Galle: The Southern Capital. In: Today, Vol. 8, No. 1, 1959.

Planing and Implementation Division, Matara District : Souvenirs published in connection with Mahapola.Weligama Sanwardana Pragathiya (The Development of Weligama), 1985
Dondara Sanwardana Pragathiya, 1987.
Kamburupitiya Sanwardana Pragathiya, 1987.
Hakmana Sanwardana Pragathiya, 1986.
Matara Sanwardana Pragathiya, 1986.

Post office Matara : Records of Television and Telephone registration, 1987.

Preu, C. : Coastal Erosion in Southwest Sri Lanka: Consequences of Human Interference, In Malaysian Jourl. of Trop. Geogr. Vol .20. Dec. 1989. pp. 30 - 41

Preu, C. : Zur problematik der rezenten Morphodynamik an den küsten Sri Lankas, Forschungen auf Ceylon III, Erdkl. Wiss. H.97,1989, pp. 23 - 42.

Public Library, Matara : Membership Register of 1987.

Puvanarajan, P. : Pattern and Process of Urbanisation. In: Population Problems of Sri Lanka, 1976.

Puvanarajan, P. : Growth Pattern in the process of Urbanisation: The case of Sri Lanka. In: Population Problems of Sri Lanka, 1979, pp. 150 - 162.

Questioner Survey : "Consumer Behaviour", Matara District, 1987.

Radkadahena Chandrajoti Maha Thero (Buddhist Monk of Radkadahena) : Buddhism its history and civilisation, Colombo, 1972.

Rajapaksa, J.(Rev.) : Matara disawe pathiri Landesi misanari meheya. (missionary activities of the Dutch in Matara district), in: Matara sahithya Dara, 1965.

Ralapanawa, S. : Sri Lankawe Bauthika Padanama (Physical Geography of Sri Lanka), Colombo, 1980.

Ranasingha, A.G. : Census of Ceylon, 1946, Vol. 1, Part. 1.

Ranasingha, P.C.H. : The Development of the Road System of Sri Lanka. In: Sri Lanka Jourl. of Soc. Sci. Vol 6, No. 1 and 2, 1983, pp. 115 ß 146.

Rankine, E. : The Port of Colombo. In: Ceylon Today, Vol. 4, No. 12, 1955.

Rao, S.L.N. : Mortality and Morbidity in Sri Lanka. In: Population Problems of Sri Lanka, 1976.

Rasak, M.M.A. : Hambantota Distrikkaye Sankramana Polawal (Periodic Markets of Hambantota District), M.A. Thesis. Univ. of Colombo, 1985.

Ratnayaka, K.L. : A Geographical Analysis of the Historical Development of Towns in Sri Lanka. Ph.D. Diss. Edinburgh, o.j. (1983).

Ravenhart, R. : Ceylon: History in Stone. Colombo, 1964.

Ravenhart, R. : Travels in Ceylon 1700-1800. Colombo, 1964.

Resthouse, Matara : Visitors Register, 1987.

Roberts, M. : The Ruin of Ancient Ceylon and Drift to the South West. In: The collapse of the Rajarata Civilisation and the drift to the south west (edit. Indrapala), Peradeniya, 1971, pp. 99 - 109.

Roberts, M. : Hogoblins, Low Country Sinhalese Plotters or Local Elite Chauvinists? Directions and Patterns in the 1915 Communal Riots. In: Sri Lanka Jourl. of Soc. Sic., Vol. 4, No. 2,1981. Dec., pp. 83 - 126.

Roberts, M. : Elite Formation and Elite's 1832-1931: Collective Identities, Nationalism and Protest in Modern Sri Lanka, Marga, 1979.

Roberts, M. : Ethnic Prejudice in Sri Lanka (A Lecture, given at the South Asian Institute, Univ. of Heidelberg, 1987.

Rosayro, R.A.de. : The Montane Grasslands. In: Trop. Agr. 101, 4, 102, 1 & 3,1945 / 46.

Rosayro, R.A.de. : Notes on the Ratanas of Ceylon. In: Bull. Ceyl. Geogr. Soc., 9, No. 3 & 4, 1955, pp. 35 - 43.

Rayan, B. : Caste in Modern Ceylon., New Brunswick, 1973.

Rayan, B. : Social-Cultural Regions of Ceylon. In: Rural Sociology, Vol. 15, No. 1, 1950, pp. 3 - 19.

Sahabandu, S.S. : Current legislation relation to urban councils in Sri Lanka. Marga publication, 1981.

Samaraweera, V. : Ceylon's trade relations with Coromandel during early British time. In: Mod. Ceyl. Stud., Vol 3. No. 1, 1972.

Samarawickrema, W.A. et al. : Significance of Coconut Husk pits as Larval Habitats of Culex quinque fasciatus (Say) in the Filariasis Endemic Coastal Belt of Sri Lanka. (Southeast As.j.Trop.Med. and publ. Health XIII, 4) Dec. 1982, pp. 590 - 595.

Sappiedeen, T.B. : Spices Industry in Sri Lanka. In: Economic Review, 1987.

Schafer, H. : A) Neuere stadtgeographische Arbeitsmethoden zur Untersuchung der innere Struktur von Städten (Part One). In: Bei. Z. dt, Landeskunde, Bd. 43,1969, pp. 261 - 292.

Schafer, H. : B) Same Title - Part Two. In: Bei. Z. dt., Landeskunde, Bd. 14, 1968, pp. 277 - 317.

Schmidt ,E. : Ceylon. Berlin, 1897.

Schöller, P. : Aufgabe und Probleme der Stadt Geographie. In: Erdk., Bd. V11 Heft 3, 1953, pp. 161 - 179.

Schöller, P. : Stadt und Einzugsgebiet : ein geographisches forschungsproblem und seine Bedeutung für die Kulturraumforschung.in: Studium Generale 10, 1957, pp 602 - 612.

Schöller ,P.(edit) : Zentralitätsforschung. Darmstadt, 1972.

Schweinfurth, U. : Der Sprachenstreit gefährdet Ceylon. In: Aussenpolitik, Nr .7, 1961, pp. 489 - 496.

Schweinfurth, U. : Die Teelandschaft im Hochland der Insel Ceylon als Beispiel für den Landschaftswandel In: Heidelberger Geogr. Arb., Heft 15, 1966, pp. 297 - 310.

Schweinfurth, U. : Tropical Climatology and Settlement. The Hill Station of Ceylon: Nuwara-Eliya. In: Climatological Notes, No. 30, Tsukuba, 1982, pp. 152 - 157.

Schweinfurth, U. : Landschaftswandel und Geomedizinische Folgen im Hochland der Insel Ceylon In: Erde, Jg. 113, Heft. 2, 1982, pp. 151 - 161.

Schweinfurth, U. : Landschaftsökologische Forschungen auf der Insel Ceylon, In: Erdkl. Wiss., 4.27, 1971, pp. 1 - 22.

Schweinfurth, U. : Jayewardene - eine neue Ära für Sri Lanka?, In: Aussenpolitik, 30.j.g., Nr. 4, pp. 424 - 437.

Schweinfurth, U. : Forschungen auf Ceylon II, Erdkl. Wiss., H.54, 1981, pp. 1 - 14

Schweinfurth, U. : Forschungen auf Ceylon III, Erdkl. Wiss., H.97, 1989, pp. 7 - 21.

Schweinfurth, U. : The Uva-Basin in Ceylon. Ecological Set-Up and Evaluation. In: Climatological Notes, No. 30, Tsukuba, pp. 140 - 151. (1982).

Schweinfurth, U. : Filariosen auf Ceylon: Versuch einer standörtlichen und historischen Analyse. In: Geogr. Zeitschrift, 72. Jg., Heft. 2, pp. 113 - 128. (1984).

Schweinfurth, U. : Filarial diseases in Ceylon, In: Ecol. of Diseases 1983, No. 2,4, pp. 309 - 319

Schweinfurth, U./Domrös, M. : Local Wind Phenomena in the Central Highlands of Ceylon. In: Bonner Met. Abhandg., 17, 1974, pp. 387 - 401.

Schweinfurth, U. / Marby, H. : Neue Literatur aus Ceylon über Ceylon. In: Erdkl. Wissen, Heft 54, 1981, pp. 193 - 216.

Schweinfurth, U./ Marby, H. : Die "Tea - smallholders" auf Ceylon, In: Erdkl. Wiss., H.54, 1981, pp. 117 - 141.

Selkirk, J. : Recollection of Ceylon. London, 1844.

Senevirarne, A. : Kandy: an illustrated survey of ancient monuments. Colombo, 1983.

Seneviratne, M. : Tourist- Ceylon, Colombo, 1971.

Sengupta, S. : Demarcation of the residential suburbs of Ahamadabad City. In: The Nat. Geogr. Jourl. of India, 32, 1, 199, pp. 49 - 60.

Seetharaman, S. : Accessibility, Mobility and shopping centres in Trivandrum District, Kerale. In: The Deccan Geogr. Vol. XXV11, July / Dec. 1989, NO. 12, pp. 51 7- 530.

Sievers, A. : Das singhalesische Dorf. In: Geogr. Rundschau, 10. Jg., Heft. 8, 1958, pp. 294 - 303.

Sievers, A. : Ceylon: Gesellschaft und Lebensraum in den orientalischen Tropen. Wiesbaden, 1964.

Sievers, A. : Der Tourismus in Sri Lanka. In: Erdkl. Wiss., Heft 62,1962.

Silva, C. : Ceylon under the British occupation 1795-1833. Colombo, 1953 (1), 1962 (2).

Silva, C.R.de. : The Portuguese in Ceylon 1617 - 1638. Colombo, 1972.

Silva, M / Fernando, S : The White Coir Fibre Industry in Matara District. (A Marga publication), 1982.

Silva, W.P.T. : Land Settlement and Urban Development in the Dry Zone. In: Sri Lanka Jourl. of Soc. Sc., Vol. 2, No. 1, 1979, pp: 55 - 76.

Singh, A.K. : Typology and Structural Models of Urban Centres in South Mirzapur. In: The Nat. Geogr. Jourl., Vol. 34, 1988, pp. 249 - 255.

Singh, H.H./Mishra, A.K. : Spatial characteristics and typology of towns in DunValley. In: The Nat. Geogr. Jourl. of India, Vol. 34, Pt. 3, 1988 Sept., pp. 237 - 248.

Singh, K. : Delimiting of the influence reach of competitive towns: A case study of Dehrdun - Varanasi axis, Geogr. Obs., Vol. 12, 1976, pp. 77 - 89.

Singh, S.B. : Periodic markets and rural development: A case study:In: The Nat. Geogr. Jourl. of India.

Singh, S.M. : The stability theory of rural central place development. In: The Nat. Geogr. Jourl. of India, No. 9, pp. 13 - 21.

Sjoberg, G. : The Pre-industrial City. Past & Present, New York, 1960.

Skinner, G.W. : Marketing and social structure in rural China. In:Jourl. of Asian Stud. 24, 1964, pp. 3 - 43.

Skinner, T. : Fifty Years in Ceylon, London, 1891.

Smailes, A.W. : The Indian City : Description Model. In: Geogr. Zeitschrift 57, Jg .1969, pp. 177 - 190.

Socio Economic Survey : Project Report, Matara District, Ride V11, 1986 Sept /Dec. (Agrarian Research Institute).

Soh, C.H. : A Geomedical Monograph of Republic of Korea (Medizinische Landekunde). Springer, Heidelberg, 1980.

Sommer, M. : Land Transformation Processes in Sri Lanka - A Conservationist Approach. In: Development Planning Rev. Vol. 3, Dec. 1984, No .1 & 2, pp. 15 - 34.

Structure Plan : Structure Plan of Matara Town. Vol. 1 & 2, Univ. of Moratuwa , 1980/81.

Stirrat, R.L. : Fish to Market: Traders in rural Sri Lanka, South Asian Review, Vol.7, No.3, pp. 189 - 207.

Students Admission Registers of Schools, 1984 : St. Thomas, St. Servets, Rahula, Mahamaya, Sujatha., 1984.
: Students Admission Register of Technical School, Matara, 1987/88.
: Students Admission Register of Univ. of Ruhuna, 1986 / 87.

Tenant, S.J. : Ceylon : An Account of the Island, London, 1859.

Thambyahpillai, G.S. : The Weather, Colombo, 1958.

Thunen, J.H. Von. : Der Isolierte Stadt. Hamburg, 1826, Berlin, 1875.

Thiranagamage, D./ Dias, H. : The Role of Small Towns in Rural Development: Some Lessons from the Uda Walawe Project in Sri Lanka. In: Malaysien Jourl. of Tropical Geography, Vol. 6, Dec. 1982, pp. 61 - 82.

Train Schedule : Matara Railway Station, 1987.

Ulluwishhewa, R. : Small scale fisheries, Sri Lanka (A note on some social and political factors constraining the adoption of modern technology in the Marine fishery, 1980. (A Marga Pub.).

Urban Development Authority, Matara : A Structural Analysis of Matara Town, Preliminary Report, 1981.

Urban Development Authority : Final Report, 1982.

Vagala, L.R. : Urban Land Use Planning: A conceptual and analytical frame work. (A publication of Urban Development Authority), 1983.

Ven'able Dharmakirti/ Indraratne of Mirissa : The significance of the first Buddhist Precept in relation to the fishing industry. (Marga Publication), 1980.

Verma, L.N. : Jhalrapatan - A geographical study of a market centre. In: Deccan Geogr., Vol I, 1962.

Vogel, H.J. : Die Amtskette, Munchen, 1972, p. 307.

Vorlaufer, K. : Das Netz zentraler Orte in ausgewahlten Raümen Tanzanias und die Bedeutung des zentralörtlichen Prinzips fur die Entwicklung des Landes nach den gesellschaftspolitischen Zielvorstellungen der Regierung. In: Dt. Geogr. Tag. 1971, Erlangen - Nurnberg, pp. 446 - 464.

Vorlaufer, K. : Die Funktion der Mittelstädte Afrikas in Prozess des sozialen Wandels (Das Beispiel Tansania). In: Afrika Spectrum - Urbanisierung in Afrika, (edit. Deutsches Institute für Afrika Forschung 2 / 1971, pp. 41 - 59.

Vorlaufer, K. : Der Fremdenverkehr in Sri Lanka als Faktor nationalen und regionalen Entwicklung. Frankf. Wirt. -u. Soz. Geogr. Sch. Heft 30, 1979, pp. 111 - 172.

Vorlaufer, K. : Die Fremdenverkehrswirtschaft Sri Lankas: Entwicklung, Bedeutung, Probleme. In: Geogr. Runsch. 35, Heft 12, 1983, pp. 627 - 636.

Vorlaufer, K. : Central Places and development in settlement areas of a pastoral population in east Afrika : The example of Marasbit District in Keniya. In: Appl. Geogr. & Devel. (A Biannual Collection of recent German Contribution), Vol. 31, pp. 81 - 104.

Wadia, D.N. : The Three Superposed Peneplains of Ceylon: Their Physiography and Geological Structure Rec. Dept. Mineralogy, Profess. Paper 1, 1943.

Wahrig, G. : Deutsches Worterbuch Gutersloch, 1980.

Wanamali, S. : Periodic Markets and Rural Development in India, 1981.

Weitzel, K. : Die bäuerliche Kulturlandschaft im Uva Becken: ein Beitrag zur Agrageographie der Insel Ceylon. Diss. Ph.D., Univ. Heidelberg, 1970.

Weitzel, K. : Wandlungen in der bäuerlichen Kulturlandschaft des Uva Beckens auf Ceylon, dargestellet am Beispiel der Dörfer Horatota, Ambagasduwa, Palugama. In: Erdkl. Wissen, Heft 27, 1971, pp. 103 - 165.

Wellmer, H. : Galle: Geomedical Analysis of a Tropical Town (geomedizinische Analyse einer tropischen küsten Stadt in Sri Lanka. Bei., S.As. Forschung,Heidelberg, Band 130, 1989.

Wellmer, H. : The Underground Drainage System in the Fort of Galle (Sri Lanka), In: Erdkl. Wiss., H.97, 1989, pp. 141 - 167.

Wijesuriya, G. : Architectural Development, A Report on historical preservation and conservation. Colombo, 1981. (A publication of Urban Development Authority).

Wijethunga, W.M. : Sri Lanka in Transition. Colombo, 1974.

Williams, L.C. : The Roads of Ceylon. In: Ceylon Today, 1967.

Ministry of Plan Implementation : Matara District Integrated Rural Development Project, 1981.

National Water Supply & Drainage Board, Sri Lanka : Matara Water Supply Project: Appraisal Report., 1981.

Statistics and Maps

Census of Population and Housing Statistics 1871, 1881, 1946, 1971, 1981, Dept. of Census and Statistics, Colombo.

Census of Population, Vol. 1, Part 7, Matara District, Dept. of Cen. & Sta., 1974.

Census of Population and Housing Statistics, Preliminary Release No. 1, Dept. of Cen. & Sta. 1981.

Census of Population and Housing Statistics (Population Data for Wards and Gramasewaka Divisions), Dept. of Cen. & Sat., 1981.

Census of Population and Housing Statistics, Matara District Report, Vol. 1.Part V111, Dept. of Cen. & Sta., 1981.

Basic Village Statistics - 1977 : Dept. of Cen. & Sta., 1980.

Annual Survey of Industries - 1987., Preliminary Report, 1988.

ESCAP (Economic and Social Commission for Asia and Pacific) Country Monograph Series No. 4, ESCAP, Bangkok (Thailand), 1976.

Population and You - Matara District, Vol. 1, No. 1, Population Information Centre, Matara Kachcheri, 1984.

Population and you - Matara District, Vol. 1, No. 2, 1985.

Matara District Population Plan. Ministry of Plan Implementation, Matara District, 1985.

Poshana Handa (Sound of the Nutrition), Ministry of Plan Implementation Matara District, 1985.

Statistical Hand Book of Matara District, 1981.

Statistical Pocket of the Democratic Social Republic of Sri Lanka, 1984.

Ferguson's Ceylon Directory, 1979-1981.

World Population Year 1974 : The Population of Sri Lanka, Dept. of Cen. & Sta., 1984.

Sri Lanka Telephone Directory, 1987, Mini. of Post & Telecommunication.

Statistik des Auslandes, Länderkurzbericht Sri Lanka, 1981. Statistisches Bundesamt, Wiesbaden, 1981.

Sri Lanka Economic Atlas, 1980 : Dept. of Cen. & Sta., Mini. of Plan Implementation, 1981.
Sri Lanka " One-inch-to-one-mile" Map, Matara District. Dept. of Survey, 1974.
Map of Matara Town, 8 Chains to one Inch.: Dept. of Survey, 1947 (repr. 1969)
Land Use Map - Matara and Hambantota District, 1983. Dept. Of Survey.
Town Assessment Survey Maps- Matara Town. Dept. of Survey. 1965.
The National Atlas of Sri Lanka, Survey Dept. Colombo, 1988.

Appendix

Photo 1
Brown Hill, the highest elevation of Matara;the most preferred residential area of British with natural scenic beauty and good atmospheric conditions.

Photo 2
Potential resources for the development of tourist sector, Islet Parey Duwa.

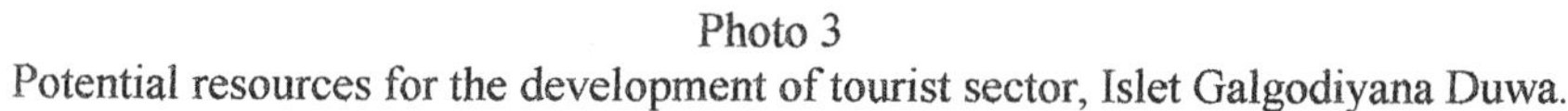

Photo 3
Potential resources for the development of tourist sector, Islet Galgodiyana Duwa.

Photo 4
Ancient port of Matara, regarded to be a prosperous port, with wealthy merchants, prior to Portuguese occupation. Lost its importancy as a harbour during the Dutch and British era but, continues to give shelter to small fishing boats.

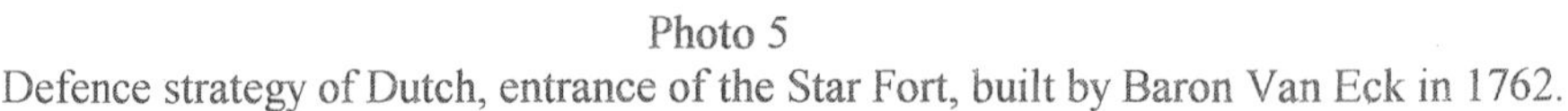

Photo 5
Defence strategy of Dutch, entrance of the Star Fort, built by Baron Van Eck in 1762.

Photo 6
Native house, belongs to temporary category, built out of mud, wood and thatched with coconut leaves. Still a commen picture in the urban land scape of Sri Lanka, inhabited by poor segment of the population.

Photo 7
Street house, the very first permanent houses in Sri Lanka, introduced by the Dutch.

Photo 8
Dutch marketing strategy, a Dutch built market, along the highway, close to port to collect the agricultural products and distribute imported goods.

Photo 9

Bungalow type house, indigenous to India, modified by Dutch and British, put up in the cultural land scape by British, inhabited by them and gradually occupied by local elites during the post colonial era.

Photo 10

Accentuation of Matara as the major commercial centre by building more storey building complexes during the post colonial era.

Photo 11

Walawwa, a house with western and indigenous architectural elements, came into existence during the British period, inhabited by local elites(bourgeois).

Photo 12

A Modern house in Fort, influenced by western style, inhabited by high income groups.

Photo 13
Jerry built houses, fishermen dwellings in Ginigasmulla. Lack basic services and inhabitants are vulnerable to health problems.

Photo 14
Combative steps towards housing problems, a housing scheme for low income groups in Walpola, with some basic services, such as; toilets, treated water and electricity. Inaugarated by the government.

Photo 15
Poor catch of fish, mainly due to the use of traditional fishing gears. Beach Seine Fishermen in Ginigasmulla.

Photo 16
Traditional fishing gears, Beach Seine Nets and Canoes in Ginigasmulla.

Photo 17

Additional source of income for the unemployed and underemployed female population, traditional method of making coir yarn ropes in Polhena.

Photo 18

Daily market at Kotuwegoda, a British introduction, provision of primary goods to urban consumer through a planned marketing system.

Photo 19
Daily market at Hunukotuwa, British origin, easily available primary good outlets to the urban consumer.

Photo 20
Periodic market at Nilwala bridge(Kotuwegoda), relatively new marketing approach, came into existence in 1975s. Provisioning mechanism for the urban centres, easily available outlets for producers to dispose of their surplus goods and a medium of primary goods to the urban consumer.

Photo 21
Broadway Road(commercial core area), the most intensively used area of C.B.D., no sign of specialization of functions, shows a combination of all kind of activities.

Photo 22
Customer orientation, fruit dealers in front of the Base Hospital, Matara.

Photo 23
Mainstreet(commercial core area), the oldest and most important road in the pre- colonial period. Lost its role as a main highway but, continues to play a major role in the commercial sphere. A high concentration of jewellery, textile and footwear shops can be found.

Photo 24
Old Tangalle Road(commercial core area), a part of the pre-colonial Mainstreet lost its role as a main highway but, continues to exist as an important commercial zone. A high concentration of hardware, ceramics and building material shops are located here.

Photo 25
Close primary goods outlets to the consumer, sub commercial centre-Hunukotuwa, located in north western part of Matara. Growth of this centre mainly attributed to the Hunukotuwa daily market.

Photo 26
Sub commercial centre-Isdeen Town, located in extreamly north western part of Matara. Annextion of Isdeen Town to Matara urban council in 1971 led to the expansion of commercial activities.

Photo 27
Sub commercial centre- Walpola, located along the Hakmana road, supply mainly short and mid-term related goods to those who are living in the northern boundary of Matara urban council area.

Photo 28
Sub commercial centre-Rahula, located at the road crossing Akuressa and Batuta road.. Its growth is mainly attributed to the closer location of the famous school Rahula and supply mainly short and mid-term goods to those who live in the north and south western part of Matara.

Photo 29
University of Ruhuna, located at eastern boundary of Matara, strengthens Matara as a education centre.

Photo 30
Base Hospital, the most important health care centre of Matara, provides specialised medical services to the entire region.

Photo 31
Institutional encroachment of public spaces, Occupation of Uyanwatta Esplanade (Dutch origin)by a Cricket stadium has reduced the organized open places for the public.

Photo 32
Land use conflicts, encroachment of Kotuwegoda Esplanade(Dutch origin), by bus terminal(institutional activities)led to further reduction of public open spaces.

Photo 33
Consciousness of environmental conditions, conversion of a dumping ground, along Kotuwegoda beach, into a recreational space.

Photo 34
A housing scheme for middle income group(police quaters) located in Meddawatta, a combative step taken by the government to slove the housing problem of the middle income groups.

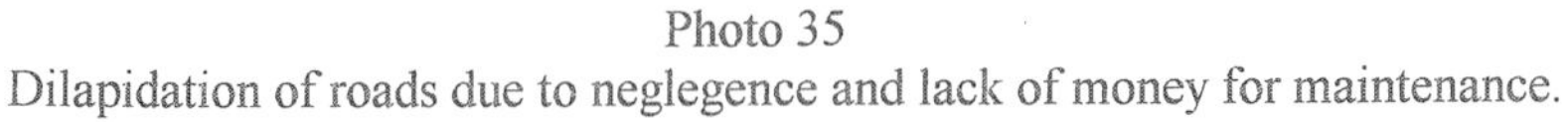

Photo 35
Dilapidation of roads due to neglegence and lack of money for maintenance.

Photo 36
Water stand posts in Fort, mainly used by low income groups, due to the non availibility of treated water connection at their homes. Indicates the limitation of accessibility for the Sri Lankan urban population to such a common basic need.

Photo 37
Surface drainage network, Nupe canal, constructed by Dutch, is subjected to stagnation and water polution due to lack of maintenance.

Photo 38
Sewerage, surface drains by the side of the roads in Fort, subject to domestic waste water stagnation, due to the slope disturbunces. These provide favourable breeding grounds for the mosquito Culex Fatigans.

Photo 39
Rahula college of Matara, one of the famous buddhist schools on the Island, which is very famous for its good examination results and better sport facilities especially for Cricket, attracts students from all over the region.

Photo 40
Rest house of Matara, Dutch origin , located in Fort. Continues to play a key role in catering services for the tourists, though experiencing a decline of business since 1966 due to increased number of hotels and restaurants.

Photo 41

Minor service centre Akuressa, located in central zone of Matara district, plays a very important role as a market place providing services to the rural consumer and producer.